# STRATEGIC THINKING IN COMPLEX PROBLEM SOLVING

# Strategic Thinking in Complex Problem Solving

*Arnaud Chevallier*

Oxford University Press is a department of the University of Oxford. It furthers
the University's objective of excellence in research, scholarship, and education
by publishing worldwide. Oxford is a registered trade mark of Oxford University
Press in the UK and certain other countries.

Published in the United States of America by Oxford University Press
198 Madison Avenue, New York, NY 10016, United States of America.

© Oxford University Press 2016

All rights reserved. No part of this publication may be reproduced, stored in
a retrieval system, or transmitted, in any form or by any means, without the
prior permission in writing of Oxford University Press, or as expressly permitted
by law, by license, or under terms agreed with the appropriate reproduction
rights organization. Inquiries concerning reproduction outside the scope of the
above should be sent to the Rights Department, Oxford University Press, at the
address above.

You must not circulate this work in any other form
and you must impose this same condition on any acquirer.

A copy of this book's Catalog-in-Publication Data is on file with the Library of Congress
ISBN 978-0-19-046390-8

*To Dad, for pushing me to be a better problem solver.
I miss you every day.*


*To Mom, for your unconditional love.*


*To Justyna, for your continuous support.*

# CONTENTS

*Acknowledgments*  ix

1. An Overview of Strategic Thinking in Complex Problem Solving  1
2. Frame the Problem  21
3. Identify Potential Root Causes  45
4. Determine the Actual Cause(s)  79
5. Identify Potential Solutions  117
6. Select a Solution  141
7. Sell the Solution—Communicate Effectively  161
8. Implement and Monitor the Solution  203
9. Dealing with Complications and Wrap Up  229

*References*  239
*Index*  279

# ACKNOWLEDGMENTS

I am deeply indebted to my dear friend, and boss, Paula Sanders, who pushed me over the years to see this project through and who has contributed immensely to its content. Thank you also for inviting me to join your team at Rice, where I have developed and tested many of the ideas in the book.

I am grateful to Tim van Gelder, Domenico Grasso, Ralph Biancalana, Jonathan Burton, Edward Kaplan, Hal Arkes, Matthew Juniper, Ken Homa, and Roberta Ness for many stimulating conversations over the years.

The book improved significantly thanks to the comments of reviewers; I am particularly thankful to Erwan Barret, Jon Bendor, François Modave, Tracy Volz, Jennifer Wilson, and Petros Tratskas.

My sister, Astrid Chevallier, provided many valuable inputs, for which I am thankful. I am also appreciative of the support from Anastasio García, Mom, Éléonore, and Thibaut.

My good friend and partner in crime in our band Kirby-sur-Seine, Frédéric Houville, showed me that music can help you be a better strategic thinker. Thank you for this, Fred! Philippe Gilbert, thank you for showing me what amazing people skills can do.

Many of my colleagues at Rice have helped me form and improve my thinking, even though they may not know it. Among them, I want to give particular thanks to David Vassar, Matt Taylor, Seiichi Matsuda, Dan Carson, Celeste Boudreaux, Penny Anderson, Galina Dubceac, Susannah Mira, Nicole Van Den Heuvel, Kate Cross, Cindy Farach-Carson, Jana Callan, Antonio Merlo, Gia Merlo, Kathy Collins, Adria Baker, Kevin Kirby, John Olson, Paul Padley, Joe Davidson, Carlos Garcia, Richard Zansitis, Bob Truscott, and Luigi Bai. I am also thankful to many of my former students, in particular to Mary Walker, David Warden, Luke Boyer, Saadiah Ahmed, Malaz Mohamad, James Hwang, and Michael Sinai.

My dear friend and *maître à penser* Pol Spanos has my gratitude for his guidance and for our many thought-provoking conversations; I look forward to many more!

My wonderful friend Mariana Téllez showed me how to think like a lawyer (in a good way) and how to be more effective in asking clarifying questions, for which I am grateful. I also wish I had even half her courage. I am also grateful to Alain Ogier aka Papou,

Beatriz Ramos, Javier Arjona, José Alfredo Galván, Marta Sylvia Del Rio, Humberto Alanís, Francisco Azcúnaga, Mario Alanís, Michael Kokkolaras, Stéphanie Page, Stuart Page, Ricardo Mosquera, María Emilia Téllez, Anthony Hubbard, Xavier Abramowitz, Nicolas Boyat, David Sandoz, Régis Clot, Jean Vincent Brisset, and Konrad Wlodarczyk.

I am much appreciative to my editors Courtney McCarroll and Abby Gross for their effectiveness and for making it such a pleasure to work with them. To Abby, I am also indebted for taking an early interest in this project and not letting it go until completion.

And, finally, thanks to you, Justyna, for being here and to William for your loyalty... and inspiration.

CHAPTER 1

# AN OVERVIEW OF STRATEGIC THINKING IN COMPLEX PROBLEM SOLVING

On a Wednesday afternoon, your cell phone rings. It's your friend John, and he is frantic: "My dog, Harry, is gone! I came home a few minutes ago and Harry's not here. I left my house at noon, and when I came back, around four, he was missing. Our house has a backyard with a doggy door in between. This is really strange, because he hasn't escaped in months—ever since we fixed the gate, he can't. I think the housekeeper is holding him hostage. I fired her this morning for poor performance. She blamed Harry, saying he sheds too much. She was really upset and threatened to get back at us. He has no collar; how are we going to find him? Also, the yard crew came today to mow the lawn. Anyway, you're the master problem solver. Help me find him!"

You and I solve countless problems every day, sometimes even without being aware of it. Harry is a real dog, whose disappearance provided me with an opportunity to describe some tools that are universally applicable through a concrete (and true!) case. This book will help you acquire techniques to become better at solving complex problems that you encounter in your personal and professional life, regardless of your occupation, level of education, age, or expertise.

In some cases, these ideas will not apply as well to your own situation, or you may feel that an alternative is better. For instance, one limitation of this technique is that it is time consuming, so it is ill-suited to Grint's *critical problems* that require decision-making under tight deadlines.[1] If that's the case, you may want to cut some corners (more in Chapter 9) or use a different route. This is perfectly fine, because this approach is meant to be a modular system of thinking, one that you can adapt to your needs.

This book shows how to structure your problem-solving process using a four-step approach: framing the problem (the *what*), diagnosing it (the *why*), finding solutions (the *how*), and implementing the solution (the *do*) (see Figure 1.1).

---

1. (Grint, 2005) [pp. 1473–1474].

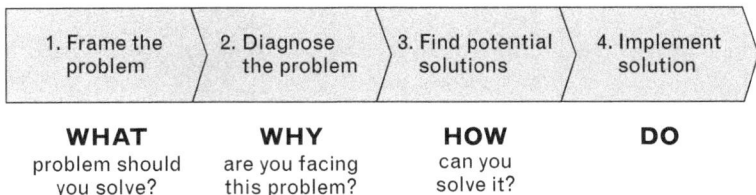

FIGURE 1.1: We use a four-step approach to solving problems.

**First, identify the problem you should solve (the *what*).** Facing a new, unfamiliar situation, we should first understand what the real problem is. This is a deceptively difficult task: We often think we have a good idea of what we need to do and quickly begin to look for solutions only to realize later on that we are solving the wrong problem, perhaps a peripheral one or just a symptom of the main problem. Chapter 2 shows how to avoid this trap by using a rigorous structuring process to identify various problem statements, compare them, and record our decision.

**Second, identify why you are having this problem (the *why*).** Knowing what the problem is, move to identify its causes. Chapter 3 explains how to identify the *diagnostic key question*—the one question, formulated with a *why* root, that encompasses all the other relevant diagnostic questions. I then show how to frame that question, and how to capture the problem in a diagnostic definition card that will guide subsequent efforts.

Next, we will do a root-cause analysis: In Chapter 4, we will diagnose the problem by first identifying *all* the possible reasons why we have the problem before focusing on the important one(s). To do that, we will build a *diagnosis issue map*: a graphical breakdown of the problem that breaks it down into its various dimensions and lays out all the possible causes exactly once. Finally, we will associate concrete hypotheses with specific parts of the map, test these hypotheses, and capture our conclusions.

**Third, identify alternative ways to solve the problem (the *how*).** Knowing what the problem is and why we have it, we move on to what people commonly think of when talking about problem solving: that is, actively looking for solutions. In Chapter 5, we will start by formulating a *solution key question*, this one formulated with a *how* root, and framing it. Next, we will construct a *solution issue map* and, mirroring the processes of Chapters 3 and 4, we will formulate hypotheses for specific branches of the map and test these hypotheses. This will take us to the decision-making stage: selecting the best solutions out of all the possible ones (Chapter 6).

**Fourth, implement the solution (the *do*).** Finally, we will implement the solution, which starts with convincing key stakeholders that our conclusions are right, so Chapter 7 provides guidelines to craft and deliver a compelling message. Then, we will discuss implementation considerations and, in particular, effectively leading teams (Chapter 8).

What, Why, How, Do. That's our process in four words.

In conclusion, Chapter 9 has some ideas for dealing with complications and offers some reflections on the overall approach.

Note that the book's primary objective is to provide a way to go through the entire problem-solving process, so it presents one tool to achieve each task and discusses that one tool in depth, rather than presenting several alternatives in less detail.[2] Most of these tools and ideas are not mine; they come from numerous academic disciplines and practitioners that provide the conceptual underpinnings for my approach. I have referenced this material as consistently as I could so that the interested reader can review its theoretical and empirical bases. A few ideas are from my own observations, gathered over 15 years of researching these concepts, applying them in managerial settings, and teaching them to students, professionals, and executives.

## 1. FINDING HARRY

Let's pretend that we just received John's phone call. Many of us would rush into action relying on instinct. This can prove ineffective, however; for example, if the housekeeper is indeed holding Harry hostage, as John thinks, there is little value in searching the neighborhood. Similarly, if Harry has escaped, calling the police to tell them that the housekeeper is keeping him hostage will not help.

**WHAT.** So finding Harry starts with understanding the problem and summarizing it in a project definition card, or *what* card, as Figure 1.2 shows. This is the *what* part of the process. You may decide that your project is finding Harry, which you want to do in a reasonable time frame, perhaps 72 hours, and that to do so, you first need to understand why he is missing.

| Project name: | Find Harry the dog | | | |
|---|---|---|---|---|
| Specific goals: (*what* you are going to do) | 1. Understand why Harry is missing (*why*) 2. Identify best way to get him back (*how*) 3. Get him back (*do*) | Out of scope: (*what* you are not going to do) | Preventing him from going missing again in the future (both the how and the implementation) | |
| Decision maker(s): | John and his wife | Other key stakeholders: | N/A | |
| Timetable: | Actions | | Needed time | Cumulative time |
| | **1. Frame the problem (define the *what*)** | | 2h | 2h |
| | **2. Diagnose the problem (find the *why*)** | | | |
| | Define the diagnostic key question and identify possible causes | | 4h | 6h |
| | Collect the diagnostic evidence, analyze, and draw conclusions | | 6h | 12h |
| | **3. Identify solutions (find the *how*)** | | | |
| | Define the solution key question and identify potential solutions | | 6h | 18h |
| | Collect evidence, analyze, and decide which solution(s) to implement | | 6h | 24h |
| | **4. Implement the chosen solution(s) (*do*)** | | 48h | 72h |
| Resources: | Money: Spend up to $150 for the *why*, $150 for the *how*, $300 for the *do* People: Up to 3 people dedicated full time | | | |
| Possible problems: | Speaking with housekeeper can backfire | Mitigation actions: | Refrain from speaking with the housekeeper until absolutely necessary | |

**FIGURE 1.2:** A project definition card—or what card—is useful to capture your plan in writing: what you propose to do by when.

---

2. For the latter, see, for instance (Polya, 1945), (VanGundy, 1988).

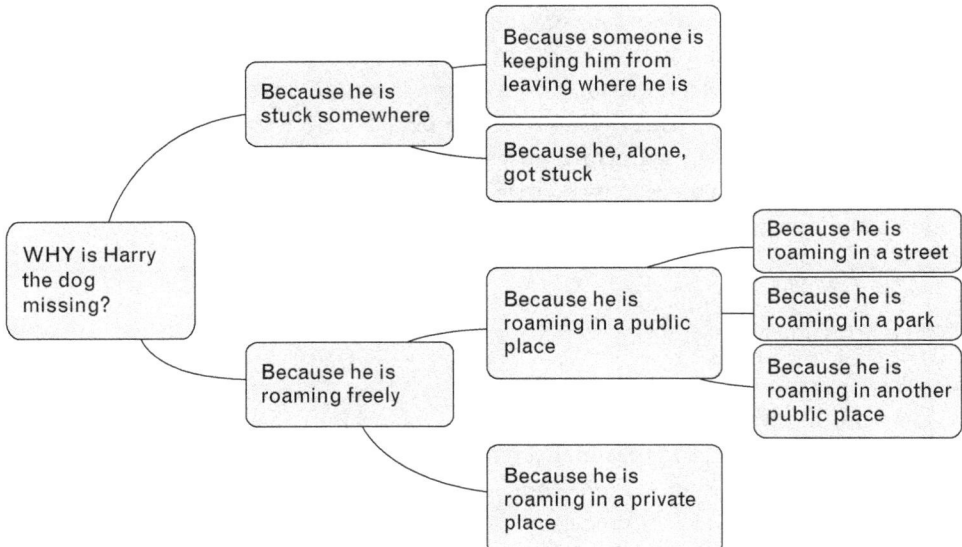

FIGURE 1.3: A diagnostic issue map helps identify and organize all the possible root causes of a problem.

**WHY.** Next, you will want to diagnose the problem. This is the *why* part of the process. Having identified a diagnostic key question—Why is Harry the dog missing?—you can look for all the possible explanations and organize them in a diagnostic issue map, as in Figure 1.3.

When I present this case to students, someone usually dismisses the possibility of Harry being held hostage as ridiculous. This is not as far fetched, however, as it might look: Statistics show that there is such a thing as dognapping, as it is called, and it is actually on the rise.[3] Others also question that someone would hold a dog hostage, but here, too, there is a precedent: In 1934, Harvard students dognapped Yale's bulldog mascot—Handsome Dan—and held him hostage on the eve of a Yale–Harvard football game.[4]

From here, you can formulate formal hypotheses, identify the evidence that you need to obtain to test them, conduct the analysis, and determine the root cause(s) of Harry's disappearance.

**HOW.** Knowing why Harry is missing, we can now identify alternative ways to get him back. This is the *how* part of the process. The procedure mirrors our diagnostic approach: We develop a solution definition card, draw an issue map (this time, a solution issue map), formulate hypotheses, identify and gather the evidence necessary to test the hypotheses, and draw conclusions.

This leads us to identify a number of possible ways to look for Harry. Because our resources are limited, we cannot implement all these solutions simultaneously; therefore, we

---

3. (Leach, 2013).

4. (Holley, 1997). One can only imagine the psychological damage to Yale students when they saw the next day their beloved Dan in the newspaper . . . happily eating a hamburger in front of John Harvard's statue.

TABLE 1.1: A Decision Tool Can Help Evaluate the Attractiveness of Competing Solutions

|  | Individual likelihood of success | Timeliness | Speed of success | Low cost | Weighted score | Ranking |
|---|---|---|---|---|---|---|
| Weight | 0.52 | 0.27 | 0.15 | 0.06 |  |  |
| $H_1$: Searching the neighborhood | 50 | 100 | 100 | 90 | 73 | 2 |
| $H_3$: Informing people likely to know about missing animals | 100 | 100 | 80 | 100 | 97 | 1 |
| $H_4$: Posting virtual announcements | 15 | 20 | 20 | 0 | 16 | 4 |
| $H_5$: Checking announcements | 0 | 0 | 0 | 100 | 6 | 5 |
| $H_6$: Enabling Harry to come back on his own | 30 | 90 | 100 | 100 | 61 | 3 |

must discard some or, at least, decide in which order we should implement them. To do so, we use a decision tool that considers the various attributes that we want to take into account in our decision and assign each of them a weight. Then, we evaluate the performance of each possible solution with respect to each attribute to develop a ranking, as Table 1.1 shows.

**DO.** Now that we have identified how we will search for Harry, the strategizing part is over, and it is time to implement our plan. The *do* part of the process starts by convincing the key decision makers and other stakeholders that we have come to the right conclusions. We then move on to agreeing on who needs to do what by when and then actually doing it. The implementation also includes monitoring the effectiveness of our approach and correcting it as needed.

The case is a real story—although I changed Harry's name, to protect his privacy—and we did find him after a few hours. This problem is relatively simple and time-constrained; therefore, it does not need the depth of analysis to which we are taking it. It provides a roadmap, however, for solving complex, ill-defined, and nonimmediate problems (CIDNI, pronounced "seed-nee"). As such, we will come back to Harry in each chapter to illustrate how the concepts apply in a concrete example.

# 2. SOLVING COMPLEX, ILL-DEFINED, AND NONIMMEDIATE PROBLEMS

A *problem* can be defined as a difference between a current state and a goal state.[5] *Problem solving*, the resolution of such a difference, is omnipresent in our lives in diverse forms, from

---

5. See, for instance (David H. Jonassen, 2000), (G. F. Smith, 1988).

executing simple tasks—say, choosing what socks to wear on a given day—to tackling complex, long-term projects, such as curing cancer. This book is about solving the latter: the complex, ill-defined, and nonimmediate problems.

*Complex* means that the problem's current and goal states, along with obstacles encountered along the way, are diverse, dynamic during their resolution, interdependent, and/or not transparent.[6] *Ill-defined* problems have unclear initial and final conditions and paths to the solution.[7] They usually do not have one "right" solution;[8] in fact, they may not have any solution at all.[9] They usually are one of a kind.[10] Finally, *nonimmediate* means that the solver has some time, at least a few days or weeks, to identify and implement a solution. At the organizational level, a CIDNI problem for a company may be to develop its marketing strategy. On a global scale, CIDNI problems include ensuring environmental sustainability, reducing extreme poverty and hunger, achieving universal primary education, and all the other United Nations' Millennium Development Goals.[11]

A fundamental characteristic of CIDNI problems is that, because they are ill-defined, their solutions are at least partly subjective. Indeed, appropriate solutions depend on your knowledge and values, and what may be the best solution for you may not be for someone else.[12] Another implication is that the problem-solving process is only roughly linear. Despite our best efforts to define the problem at the onset of the project, new information surfacing during the resolution may prompt us to modify that definition later on. In fact, such regression to a previous step may happen at any point along the resolution process.[13]

**Think about what makes your problem CIDNI.** Problems can be challenging for various reasons, and understanding these may help you choose a direction in which to look for a solution. Some problems are complex because they are computationally intensive. A chess player, for instance, cannot think of all alternatives—and all the opponent's replies—until late in the game, when the universe of possibilities is much reduced. Chess, however, is a fairly well-defined environment.

Contrast this with opening a hotel in a small village in the Caribbean and discovering that obtaining a license will require bribing local officials. The challenge here is not computational, but the problem is ill-defined in important ways: Do you still want to carry out the project if bribery is a requirement? If you want to avoid bribing officials, how can you do so successfully? And so on.

Indeed, ill definition stems in many ways when human interactions are part of the picture. Consider the case of a graduate student ready to defend her dissertation only to discover that two key members of her jury have just had a bitter argument and cannot sit in the same room for more than five minutes without fighting. How should she proceed?

---

6. (Wenke & Frensch, 2003) [p. 90], (Mason & Mitroff, 1981) [p. 5].
7. (Simon, 1974), (David H. Jonassen, 1997), (Pretz et al., 2003) [p. 4], (S. M. Smith & Ward, 2012) [p. 462], (Mason & Mitroff, 1981) [p. 30].
8. (Bardwell, 1991).
9. (David H. Jonassen, 2000).
10. (Brightman, 1978).
11. (United Nations).
12. (Hayes, 1989) [p. 280].
13. See Rittel's wicked problems (Rittel, 1972).

Or consider the case, during World War II, of the British Navy capturing an Enigma cryptography machine, which gave them deep insight into the operation of German submarines. This gave them a unique opportunity to reduce the risk of attacks to their convoys. However, they could not use this information in any way that would tip off the Germans that their naval codes had been broken; indeed, the Germans would then change the Enigma codes or introduce a new communication system. How then should the British best use this information?[14]

So, rather than thinking of CIDNI problems as one type of difficult situation, you may be better served to think about what makes your problem a CIDNI problem, given that doing so may indicate where you can search out solutions. If a problem is computationally complex, for example, exploring the support that computers and artificial intelligence can bring could be of great support. In a situation that has significant moral, emotional, or psychological components, however, such support is not likely to be of much help.

# 3. COMPLEMENTING SPECIALIZATION WITH GENERALIST SKILLS

> *It's not so much that STEM [science, technology, engineering, mathematics] graduates do not know how to solve technical problems, because, in fact, they do, but that these graduates lack the non-technical skills needed for the job.*
>
> *That's one of the points that Meghan Groome, the executive director of education and public programs at the New York Academy of Sciences, emphasized [. . .].*
>
> *"The problem is universal," Groome explained. "Students are not learning how to network, manage their time, or to work together." These skills, Groome insisted, are those that students can learn if they take the right courses.*[15]

There is widespread agreement that an ideal CIDNI problem solver (or problem-solving team) is "T-shaped," that is, both a specialist in the relevant disciplines and a generalist.[16]

Formal training programs usually focus on the discipline-specific side, the vertical bar of the "T," but they fall short on the generalist front,[17] which is problematical. For instance, a report by the National Academies notes that, because real-world problems are ill defined and knowledge intensive, they often differ considerably from the ones students solve in class.[18] This leads to some students' inability to translate what they learn on campus to practical situations,[19] what physics Nobel Prize laureate Richard Feynman called a "fragility of knowledge."[20]

---

14. See (Blair, 2000) [p. 298].

15. (Weiner, 2014).

16. (Perkins & Salomon, 1989), (Gauch, 2003) [pp. 2–3], (Grasso & Burkins, 2010) [pp. 1–10]; (Kulkarni & Simon, 1988) [p. 140], (Sanbonmatsu, Posavac, Kardes, & Mantel, 1998), (Sheppard, Macatangay, Colby, & Sullivan, 2009) [p. 175], (Katzenbach, 1993), (Savransky, 2002) [p. 18], (M. U. Smith, 1991) [pp. 10–15], (Brown & Wyatt, 2010).

17. (Theocharis & Psimopoulos, 1987), (Manathunga, Lant, & Mellick, 2006).

18. (National Research Council, 2012) [p. 76]. See also (Manathunga, Lant, & Mellick, 2007).

19. (Chi, Bassok, Lewis, Reimann, & Glaser, 1989), (David H. Jonassen, 2000). See also (National Research Council, 2014) [pp. 53–55].

20. (Feynman, 1997) [pp. 36–37].

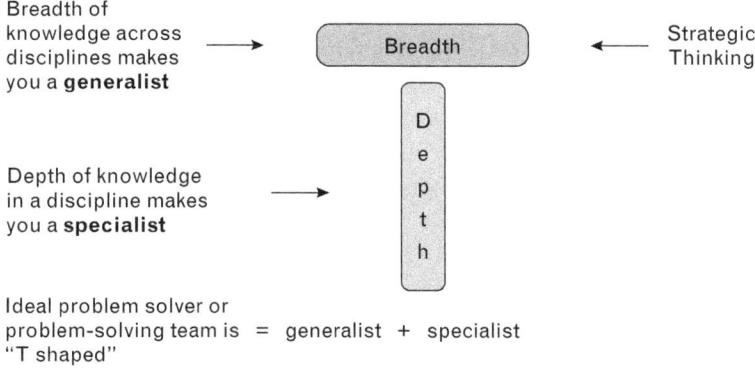

FIGURE 1.4: Effective CIDNI problem solvers are both generalists and specialists; this book helps improve generalist skills.

Another drawback of focusing solely on the vertical bar of the T is that it limits innovation as we fall prey to the "not invented here" syndrome. Yet, there is considerable value in "stealing" ideas from other disciplines. For instance, consider the use of checklists that first appeared in airplane cockpits and are now being increasingly used in operating rooms. Despite strong initial resistance by surgeons, their adoption has led to significant reductions in postsurgical complications.[21] Similarly, medical practices also are adopted by other disciplines: The rise in the 1990s of evidence-based medicine—the reliance on evidence from well-designed and conducted research to guide decision making—has helped initiate a practice of evidence-based management in the last decade.[22] In both these cases, an ability to see value in a field different than one's own was needed and paid off. Developing an ability to see past the surface features of problems to concentrate on the underlying structure, and recognizing that this may be achieved by looking at problems in other disciplines is, therefore, beneficial. As we will see in the ensuing chapters, it is also a requirement for good analogical thinking.[23]

In short, *Strategic Thinking in Complex Problem Solving* offers ways to develop that horizontal, strategic, cross-disciplinary knowledge necessary to be an effective CIDNI problem solver (see Figure 1.4).

This approach enables you to tackle any problem, even ones in which you are not a specialist, in a structured and creative way. And in today's economy, where organizations are constantly reinventing themselves, this skill makes you a very desirable asset.[24]

---

21. (Gawande, 2009).

22. (Rousseau, 2006), (Rousseau & McCarthy, 2007), (Rousseau, 2012), (Pfeffer & Sutton, 2006b), (Pfeffer & Sutton, 2006a).

23. See, for instance (Keith J. Holyoak & Koh, 1987), (National Research Council, 2011a) [pp. 136–138].

24. (National Association of Colleges and Employers, 2014) [p. 4].

# 4. FIVE KEY GUIDELINES THAT SUPPORT OUR APPROACH

Before we look in detail at the four steps of the problem-solving process, let's conclude this overview by presenting five key principles that each apply to various steps.

## 1. USE DIVERGENT AND CONVERGENT THINKING

Effective problem solving requires both divergent and convergent thinking patterns.[25] As Figure 1.5 shows, this occurs at each step of the process. Diverging, you think creatively: stretching your mind to identify new possibilities. Converging, you think critically: gathering data to analyze each possibility, compare it with others, and select the best. Whenever possible, you should defer judgment, that is, you should keep idea creation (or *ideation*[26]) separate from idea *evaluation*.[27] This is to avoid restricting your creativity.[28] We will address this again in Chapters 3 and 5.

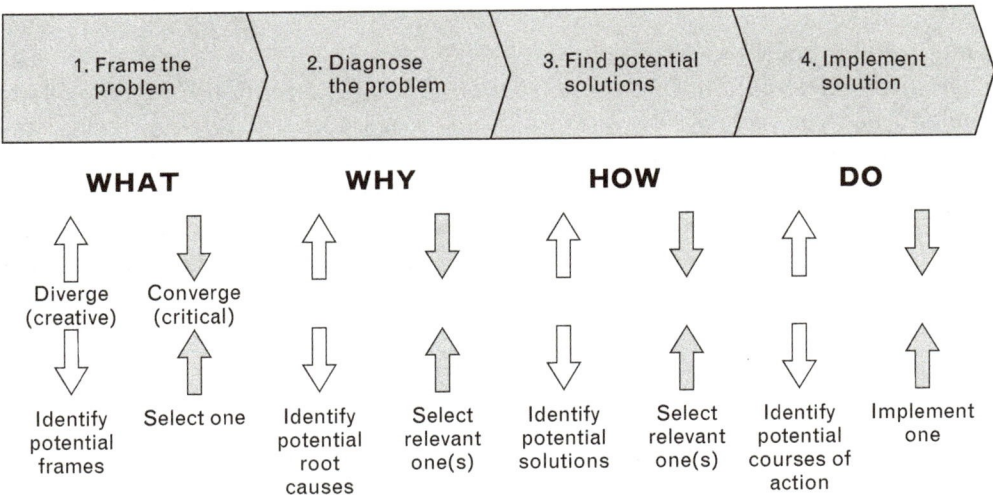

**FIGURE 1.5:** Effective complex problem solving requires alternating divergent and convergent thinking.

25. See, for instance (Basadur, Runco, & Vega, 2000), (Adams, 2001) [pp. 120–121], (Assink, 2006), (Basadur, Graen, & Scandura, 1986). For a review of divergent thinking in generating alternatives, see (Reiter-Palmon & Illies, 2004).

26. (S. M. Smith & Ward, 2012) [p. 465], (VanGundy, 1988) [p. 5], (Adams, 2001) [p. 121].

27. Although we prefer deferring judgment, an alternative approach allows applying some convergent thinking during idea production. See (Basadur, 1995) for a review.

28. See (Hammond, Keeney, & Raiffa, 2002) [p. 53].

## 2. USE ISSUE MAPS

A central tool in our methodology is the issue map, a graphical breakdown of a question that shows its various dimensions vertically and progresses into more detail horizontally. There are many types of cartographic representations of problems, including trees, diagrams, and maps. One attribute they share is that they expose the structure of the problem, thereby promoting better understanding. Graphical breakdowns of arguments, for example, have been shown to significantly improve people's critical thinking.[29] We will discuss maps extensively in Chapters 3 and 5.

Figure 1.6 shows a typical issue map. It starts with a key question on the left, in this case a solution key question, with a *how* root. It then lists and organizes solutions on the right. These solutions do not have to be desirable but, applying the principle of deferred judgment of the previous section, we refrain from evaluating them until later in the process.

Maps enable us to consider all possibilities exactly once: we do not consider a possibility more than once, and we do not leave out any. That is, maps structure the universe of answers in a set of *mutually exclusive* and *collectively exhaustive* branches (or *MECE*, pronounced "me-see").

**Mutually exclusive (ME) means "no overlaps."** Two events are mutually exclusive when the occurrence of one precludes the occurrence of the other. Organizing the answers to a question in mutually exclusive branches means that you consider each one only once, thereby not duplicating efforts. To think ME, you must think in a convergent pattern, determining whether branches are truly distinct.

So if you set yourself to answer the question, "How can I go from New York City to London?" and you reply by first dividing means of transportation between "flying" and "traveling by sea," you are organizing the possible solutions of your problem in a ME way, because you cannot be flying and traveling by sea at the same time.

**Collectively exhaustive (CE) means "no gaps."** Events are collectively exhaustive when they include all possible outcomes. So the branches of an issue map are CE when they include all the possible answers to the key question. To think CE you must think divergently,

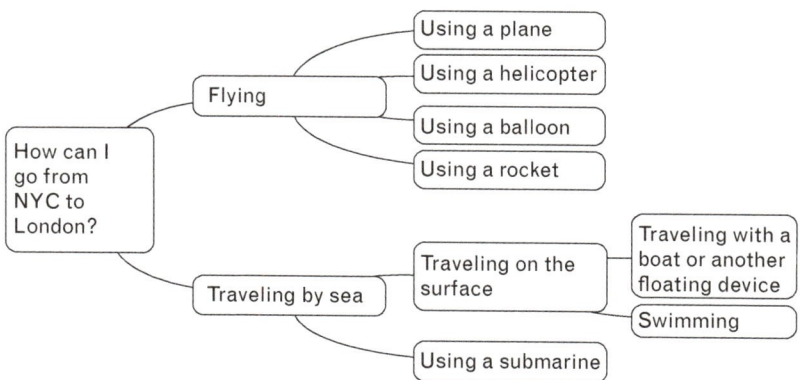

**FIGURE 1.6:** Issue maps graphically expose the structure of a question.

29. (Twardy, 2010).

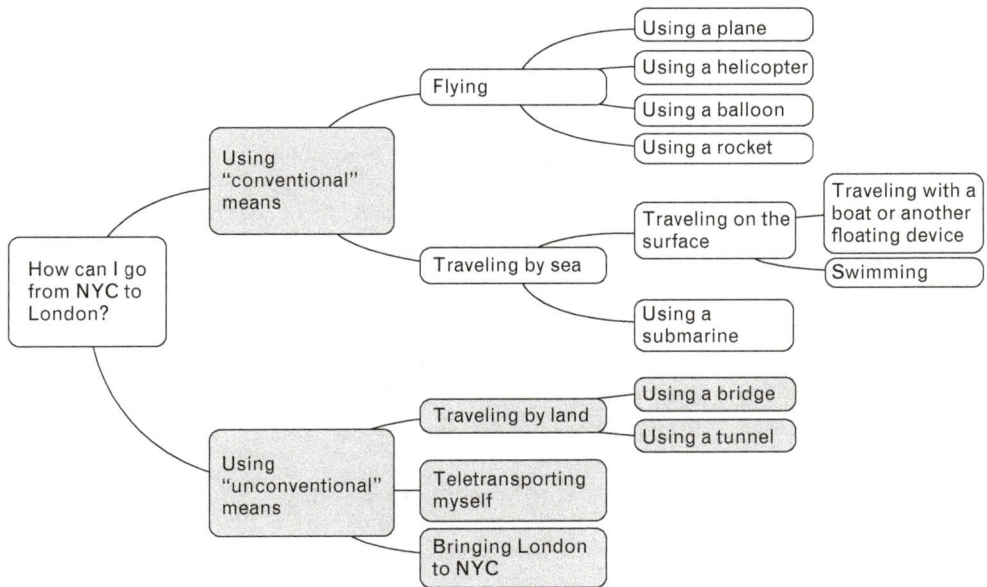

FIGURE 1.7: Part of the process is to think divergently to identify as many solutions as possible so as to leave no gaps.

asking yourself repeatedly, "*What else* could be an answer to this question?" So you must be very creative; Chapters 3 and 5 will give you ideas to do that, such as relying on analogies or existing frameworks.

When you are identifying options to go from NYC to London, CE thinking means that you are considering all possibilities. Although we initially thought that traveling by sea or air were the only possibilities, forcing ourselves to be CE results in an expanded list, as shown in Figure 1.7. The possibility of traveling by sea or air occurs quickly to people thinking about this situation, so let's stick these options into a branch that we call "conventional." Then, to be CE, we should have a "nonconventional" branch. What could this include? Well, people also travel by land. What else? Perhaps teletransport. What else? Well, maybe I should not travel to London; instead, London should travel to me. And we could go into further details there: perhaps we could have the people I was going to meet in London come to me or maybe we could create a London where I am. That sounds far-fetched. True. But, first, abiding by the principle of deferred judgment, we should not care whether it is far-fetched—not until later. And second, even if it is far-fetched, there are precedents: Las Vegas has done it with the Eiffel Tower, so why not us? Again, these new options may not be desirable. What is important is that, if we end up discarding them, we will do so because of a conscious decision, not because we forgot to consider them. We will talk more about MECE thinking in Chapters 3 and 5.

## 3. ACQUIRE THE RIGHT SKILLS

In 2001, the United Kingdom's Research Councils and the Arts and Humanities Research board released a joint statement highlighting the skills that doctoral students are expected

TABLE 1.2: Useful Skills in Research[a]

| | You should be able to ... |
|---|---|
| **Research Techniques** | Identify and solve problems<br>Think originally, independently, and critically<br>Critically assess your and others' findings<br>Document, synthesize, report, and reflect on progress<br>Apply appropriately the relevant research techniques in your field<br>Identify and access appropriate bibliographical material and other information |
| **Research Environment** | Conduct yourself appropriately (legally, ethically, responsibly, etc.)<br>Understand the context in which your research takes place<br>Understand process for funding |
| **Project Management** | Set goals and intermediate milestones<br>Prioritize activities |
| **Personal Effectiveness** | Be willing and able to acquire knowledge<br>Be creative, innovative, and original<br>Be self-reliant, work independently, and show initiative<br>Be flexible and open-minded<br>Be self-aware and identify own training needs<br>Be self-disciplined, motivated, and thorough<br>Recognize your boundaries and ask for help as needed |
| **Communication** | Write clearly with an appropriate style<br>Build coherent and compelling arguments tailored to audiences<br>Support the learning of others<br>Contribute to the public understanding of your research field |
| **Networking and Team Work** | Develop and maintain cooperative networks<br>Manage effectively relationships up, down, and sideways in your organization and elsewhere<br>Understand your contribution and impact to the success of teams (formal and informal)<br>Listen, give and receive feedback, and respond appropriately |
| **Career Management** | Partake in ongoing professional development<br>Identify key success factors for progression in your targeted professional path<br>Take ownership of your career progression: set challenging yet realistic goals and identify ways to improve your employability<br>Demonstrate insight in the transferability of your skill set to other disciplines<br>Present your profile through the use of curriculum vitae/résumés, cover letters, and interviews<br>Strike an appropriate work–life balance |

[a]After Research Councils, United Kingdom. (2001).

to develop during their research training.[30] Table 1.2 summarizes some of these skills. These are relevant to you even if you are not working on a doctorate. Indeed, solving problems requires doing research: identifying which evidence you need to gather and assessing it. We will talk about working with evidence in Chapters 4 and 6.

This book provides pathways to develop many of these skills. You may find value using this list as a roadmap for your own development.[31] Alternatively, you may elaborate your own list. But you may also face a problem before you get a chance to develop the skills; when that happens, and you should probably assume that it will, you should consider teaming up with people who have complementary skills.

**Enlist others.** Working with others may increase quality and visibility. It used to be that the works of lone geniuses were the most impactful, but this might be changing. Collaborative work has resulted in many contributions, including the discovery of DNA, the creation of the Linux operating system, and the development of the Internet.[32] Also, scientific papers with multiple authors are cited more than twice as frequently as those by single authors.[33]

**Leverage diversity.** When I teach this method in a course, it is a practical workshop. Each student brings a project that he or she is interested in and we use these as case studies. Students come from all disciplines, but they must help others and seek help from others (a large chunk of their grade depends on it) and they need to sit next to a different colleague in each session. Although this collaboration across disciplines does not come naturally to many, they quickly see its value: People with different training bring different perspectives, which helps each of them be more creative. This is in line with observations from a committee of the National Research Council: "Analysis improves when analysts with diverse perspectives and complementary expertise collaborate to work on intelligence problems."[34] We will talk extensively about the value of collaboration and diversity throughout the book.

## 4. SIMPLIFY TO REVEAL THE UNDERLYING STRUCTURE

Simplicity is central to numerous practices in many fields. In the scientific method, the parsimony principle recommends that, all other things being equal, the simplest theory that fits the facts should be preferred.[35] Copernicus used it to propose his model of motion of the earth (the heliocentric one, i.e., a daily revolution around its axis and an annual revolution around the sun) over the then-favored Ptolemaic one. Copernicus's model did not generate a better fit, but it was simpler.[36]

---

30. (Research Councils UK, 2001).
31. For other lists, see (Reeves, Denicolo, Metcalfe, & Roberts, 2012) and (Careers Research and Advisory Centre, 2010).
32. (Ness, 2012).
33. (Wuchty, Jones, & Uzzi, 2007).
34. (National Research Council, 2011a) [p. 61]. See also (National Research Council, 2014) [p. 64].
35. (Gauch, 2003) [pp. 269–270].
36. (Gauch, 2003) [p. 273].

In design, simplicity is often linked to quality and usability.[37] At Apple, Steve Jobs viewed it as the ultimate sophistication, which resulted in many Apple products *not* having the features of their competitors' and yet outselling them.[38]

Though the end product may be simple, the process to get there usually is not. Here is Steve Jobs again: "When you start looking at a problem and it seems really simple with all these simple solutions, you do not really understand the complexity of the problem. And your solutions are way too oversimplified. Then you get into the problem, and you see it's really complicated. And you come up with all these convoluted solutions . . . that's where most people stop, and the solutions tend to work for a while. But the really great person will keep on going and find . . . the key, underlying principle of the problem. And come up with a beautiful elegant solution that works."[39]

I have seen this happen multiple times. In my course, my students must reformulate their problem to make it understandable to the rest of us. This is difficult for some of them, particularly those versed in highly technical subjects, and some invariably claim that expressing their problem in simple, accessible terms is not possible. They all, however, eventually discover that it is. Moving beyond the surface features of their disciplines, they learn to focus on their problem's underlying structure, and by expressing it in simple terms, they enable others to assist them in solving it.

This challenge of simplification is worthy not just because they now have a larger and more diverse network of people to help them, but because it also forces them to clarify their understanding of their problem: having to do away with the jargon of their field, they can no longer present their problem in the terms that they have heard it expressed by specialists. They now have to answer "dumb" questions that they have been trained not to ask, which forces them to understand why (or why not!) these questions are dumb. Moving beyond surface characteristics to focus on the structure of problems is also an essential component of successful analogies,[40] so by going through this process, students learn to see similarities among disciplines.

**Transcend "that's interesting": understand the "so what?"** Gathering lots of data about a problem is not necessarily helpful; in fact, it can be counterproductive (see Table 1.3). So finding that something is interesting should not be an end point but, rather, a starting point to dig deeper. Analyze your thinking: If you find something interesting, why is it so? What is the "so what?" of your finding? Keep on assaulting your problem with critical thinking until you reach simplicity. We will talk more about this in Chapters 3, 4, and 5.

## 5. DO *NOT* FOOL YOURSELF (AND OTHERS)

In his address to the graduating class of 1974 at Caltech, Richard Feynman urged students to "not fool yourself—and you are the easiest person to fool."[41] This is in line with findings

---

37. (Karvonen, 2000).
38. (Thomke & Feinberg, 2009).
39. Cited in (Thomke & Feinberg, 2009).
40. (Keith J. Holyoak, 2012), (Keith J. Holyoak & Koh, 1987), (National Research Council, 2011b) [pp. 136–138].
41. (Feynman, 1998).

TABLE 1.3: Empirical Findings Contradict Conventional Wisdom Along the Problem-solving Process; The Book Addresses Some of These Differences[a]

| Conventional Wisdom | Empirical Findings | Mitigation Tactics |
| --- | --- | --- |
| The more information, the better. | More information is not necessarily better; in fact, it can provide unwarranted confidence and dilute the diagnosticity of other information items (Arkes & Kajdasz, 2011, p. 157). | Seek only diagnostic evidence. Ensure that sources of information are independent. See Chapters 4 and 6. |
| The more confident, the more likely we are to be correct. | Even experts may lack a strong relation between confidence and accuracy (Dawson et al., 1993; Arkes & Kajdasz, 2011, p. 147). | Seek feedback on your predictions, hold yourself accountable, and consider contrary evidence (Arkes & Kajdasz, 2011, pp. 149–150). See Chapter 4. |
| Expertise only has upsides. | Expertise comes with preconceptions that can introduce biases when considering data (Arkes & Kajdasz, 2011, p. 146) and an inability to modify old thinking (Pretz, Naples, & Sternberg, 2003, p. 15). | Use experts and novices judiciously. See Chapters 4 and 8. |
| Intuition is trustworthy. | Humans are heavily biased, so intuition is not necessarily trustworthy (Bazerman & Moore, 2008). | Decide quickly only if you are likely to pick the right answer, the cost of error is low, and swiftness brings high rewards (Kahneman, 2011, p. 79). See Chapters 3 and 5. |
| Problem solving is primarily about finding solutions. | Framing a problem and diagnosing it appropriately can be of paramount importance (Tversky & Kahneman, 1981). | Do not jump into identifying solutions before framing and diagnosing your problem appropriately. See Chapters 2 and 3. |

[a] The table is adapted from (Makridakis & Gaba, 1998) and (Arkes & Kajdasz, 2011) [pp. 143–168]. For an example of how more information can result in *worse* outcomes in a medical setting, see (Welch, 2015) [pp. 84–95].

on biases: humans are biased in many ways, often without realizing it. For instance, we have a high propensity to be overconfident;[42] to think that, had we been asked, we would have predicted an event's occurrence in advance (hindsight bias);[43] or to interpret information partially (confirmation bias).[44]

Table 1.3 summarizes some common ways in which we fool ourselves, compares those to empirical findings, and proposes remedies.

**Adopt an evidence-based approach.** In medicine, the belief that physicians' actions should be guided by evidence dates back at least 200 years.[45] And yet, many destructive

---

42. (Fischhoff, 1982) [p. 432].
43. (Arkes, Wortmann, Saville, & Harkness, 1981).
44. (Klayman & Ha, 1987), (Klayman & Ha, 1989), (Nickerson, 1998).
45. (Pfeffer & Sutton, 2006b) [p. 13].

An Overview • 15

practices remain in use; in some settings, over 30% of patients are estimated to receive care that is not consistent with scientific evidence.[46]

The modern evidence-based medicine movement advocates for integrating the best external evidence available with one's expertise and the specifics of one's situation.[47] Started in the early 1990s, it has garnered considerable attention and is credited for dramatically speeding up the process of finding effective treatments instead of relying on intuition and personal experience.[48]

Some disciplines, such as management, are now trying to emulate it,[49] while others, including the intelligence community, have been strongly advised to follow the trend.[50] This book argues that you should adopt an evidence-based approach to problem solving and we will talk about how to do this across chapters.

**Confidence-wise, brace yourself.** Steve Jobs's earlier quote illustrates how, when we approach new problems, we sometimes feel that we instantaneously understand them and know how to solve them. This is, in part, because we bring our own preconceptions. The four-step process described in this book aims at replacing these preconceptions and the unwarranted confidence they generate with warranted confidence. Although we hope that, at the end of it, you are rightfully confident in your views, getting there will probably be tumultuous.

Going through a rigorous evidence-based analysis of your preconceived ideas, you may soon feel that you become unsure of what you know and do not know, and your overall confidence will plunge before it rises. It is important to be able to welcome these doubts, because they are an integral part of Socratic wisdom, that is, of "knowing what you know and knowing what you do not know."[51]

Replacing unwarranted confidence requires you to take the risk of reducing your confidence, at least briefly. Although this may sound demoralizing, see it as progress: You may not yet know what the right paradigm is, but at least you now know that the one you trusted was wrong.

Following this approach, this book advocates that you base your practices on sound logic and solid evidence, synthesizing reliable external information with your own expertise, and integrating that approach with the judicious use of intuition. The book presents tools to help you do so.

**Respect the scientific ideal.** Cambridge's fluid dynamist Michael McIntyre defines respecting the scientific ideal as attempting to keep an open mind while deploying logical thinking, putting up with nagging uncertainty, being willing to admit ignorance, avoiding prior judgments about candidate hypotheses, and remaining skeptical about any reason to favor a theory other than the cautious application of Occam's razor (see Chapter 4). It also

---

46. (Grol, 2001), (Heyland, Dhaliwal, Day, Jain, & Drover, 2004), (Rauen, Chulay, Bridges, Vollman, & Arbour, 2008). See also (Golec, 2009), (Sheldon et al., 2004), (Straus & Jones, 2004).
47. (Sackett, Rosenberg, Gray, Haynes, & Richardson, 1996), (Straus, Glasziou, Richardson, & Haynes, 2011) [p. 1].
48. (National Research Council, 2011a) [p. 28].
49. See, for instance (Allen, Bryant, & Vardaman, 2010), (Pfeffer & Sutton, 2006b, 2007), (Rousseau, 2006), (Rousseau & McCarthy, 2007).
50. (National Research Council, 2011b) [pp. 95–97], (National Research Council, 2011a) [pp. 2–4; 88, 91, 92].
51. (Pfeffer & Sutton, 2006b) [pp. 52–53].

includes revising one's position when new evidence appears and taking a look from various viewpoints. An illustration of respecting the scientific ideal is being the skeptical juror in the movie "Twelve Angry Men," the one who insists on having one last look at the evidence in a murder trial when the other eleven already think that they know the truth.[52] These characteristics and a few more are all central to the approach described in this book.

## 5. SUMMARY: CIDNI PROBLEM SOLVING IN A NUTSHELL

Our approach to solving complex, ill-defined, and nonimmediate problems allows us to go from where we are to where we want to be, namely, to solve problems with a four-step process (What, Why, How, Do) that rests upon five key principles (see Figure 1.8).

We can visualize these key principles as a bridge with three pillars: using convergent and divergent thinking, using maps, and acquiring the right skills. In turn, these three pillars rely on two layers of foundation: simplifying and not fooling yourself.

**Do not over-design your resolution process.** Before we jump into the heart of the matter, I would like to stress one last point: the methodology described in the book assumes that you have the time and resources to conduct an in-depth analysis of all stages and that it is beneficial to do so. If this is not the case—for whatever reason, maybe because you do not have enough time to conduct a full-blown analysis or maybe because you already have trustworthy answers for, say, the diagnostic—you should cut some corners. We will discuss

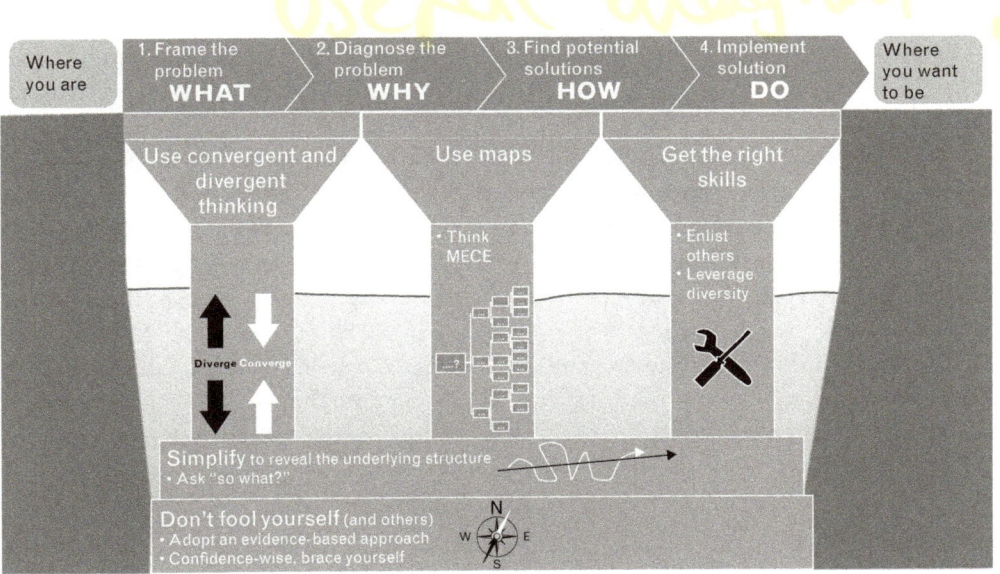

FIGURE 1.8: Five key principles support our approach to problem solving.

52. (McIntyre, 1998).

this further in Chapter 9, but you should keep this in mind as you walk your way through the resolution process.

So, if investing effort in a specific part of the resolution process seems inappropriate for your specific problem, first question this feeling, because it is easy to bypass, say, thoughtful problem framing even in situations where it is precisely what you should do. But, if after careful consideration, you think that you should fast-forward over some steps, then do so.

Having laid out a general description of our problem-solving process and an overview of each chapter, we can now move to a more detailed analysis. This starts with Chapter 2 giving some guidelines for framing the problem.

# NOTES

**Steps in solving problems.** Our approach has four steps, but this is not universal. For instance, Basadur presents a three-step process (problem finding, problem solving, solution implementation).[53] The difference here is that we have broken the problem-finding stage into two, to separate the *what* from the *why*, in an effort to bring light to the importance of these stages. Other approaches exist: Woods identified 150 published strategies used in numerous disciplines.[54]

**Treating symptoms.** Peter Senge calls treating symptoms, rather than the problem itself, "shifting the burden." This may result in having the problem recur.[55]

**The two dimensions of the T.** Being a specialist requires domain-specific or local knowledge and skills. Being a generalist relies on knowledge and skills that are transferrable across disciplines, that is, domain independent.

**From T to π.** The T-shaped metaphor can extend to π-shaped or even comb-shaped skill sets where individuals have a breadth of knowledge and expertise in more than one field.[56]

**Improve your "foxiness."** Related to the specialist/generalist differentiation is that of hedgehogs versus foxes, a dichotomy invented by philosopher Isaiah Berlin.[57] Hedgehogs are specialized, stubborn, order-seeking, and confident. Foxes are multidisciplinary, self-critical, and cautious; they accept ambiguity and contradiction as an inherent part of life. Having compared the two groups, political scientist Philip Tetlock observes that foxes are better forecasters than hedgehogs.[58]

**Strategic thinking in complex problem solving.** We define strategic thinking in complex problem solving, loosely following Beaufre: Facing a problem—that is, a gap between a current and a desired positions—it is a process that includes design, analysis, and synthesis.

53. (Basadur, 1995).
54. (Woods, 2000).
55. See (Leung & Bartunek, 2012) [pp. 170–173].
56. (National Research Council, 2014) [pp. 62–63].
57. See (National Research Council, 2011b) [pp. 155–156], (Silver, 2012) [pp. 53–73].
58. (Tetlock, 2005) [pp. 20–21].

Design to identify the key activities needed to bridge the gap, analysis to assemble and process the necessary data, and synthesis to elect a solution from various alternative courses of action. In the process, strategic thinking requires rationality, intuition, and innovation.[59] Beaufre's view: Strategic thinking "is a mental process, both abstract and rational, that combines psychological and material data. The process relies on a great capacity for analysis and synthesis; analysis is necessary to assemble the data on which to make a diagnosis, synthesis is necessary to extract the diagnosis from the data. The diagnosis amounts to a choice between alternatives."[60]

**Taxonomies of problems.** There are many types of problems and many taxonomies to describe them. Savransky defines *routine* problems as those where all critical steps are known (a *critical step* is one that is required to reach the solution).[61] *Inventive problems* are a subset of nonroutine ones where both the solution and at least one critical step are unknown. Also, a *closed* problem is one with a finite number of correct solutions.[62]

**Biases.** They abound! (See Bazerman & Moore (2008, pp. 13–41) for a review.)

**Using case studies.** Using my students' problems as cases for the class is an example of problem-based learning, which has shown superior long-term retention and skill development. (Traditional methods, in turn, are superior for short-term retention as measured by standardized exams.)[63]

---

59. See also (Graetz, 2002), (Mintzberg, 1994), (Liedtka, 1998), (Heracleous, 1998).

60. (Beaufre, 1963) [p. 23].

61. (Savransky, 2002) [p.4].

62. (Savransky, 2002) [p. 5]. For more on taxonomies of problems, see also (G. F. Smith, 1988), (M. U. Smith, 1991), (Bassok & Novick, 2012), (Kotovsky, 2003). See also (David H. Jonassen, 2000) [p. 67] for a description of well-defined and ill-defined problems. For *tame, wicked,* and *critical* problems and how they relate to managers and leaders, see (Grint, 2005) [p. 1473], (Rittel, 1972).

63. (Strobel & van Barneveld, 2009), (David H. Jonassen, 2011) [pp. 153–158].

## CHAPTER 2

# FRAME THE PROBLEM

Researchers have discovered that when we are confronted with a new problem, it is common for us to have a mistaken impression of what the actual problem is.[1] Based on my own experience, I agree. Having coached people in hundreds of cases, I have yet to find an instance where the problem's original formulation was the one that we eventually retained. So solving effectively complex, ill-defined, nonimmediate problems (CIDNI) is first about asking good questions, or defining clearly *what* you want to do. This chapter shows how to frame the problem and capture it on a problem definition card. It goes on to cover the next step in the analysis: framing the diagnosis, which we will also capture in a card.

## 1. FRAME THE PROJECT

Understanding *what* the problem is and is not, and writing it down, is important because this helps clarify your project and build a shared understanding across the team.[2] This can prove to be more difficult, however, than it might appear at first. To help you out, you may want to use a template for the problem definition card—or the *what* card—such as the one shown in Figure 2.1.[3]

To illustrate, take Harry's case. Harry has just gone missing. What is our problem? Get him back? Understand why he went missing? Ensure that he does not go missing again in the future? Something else? Many people would agree that getting him back is what matters, at least for now. Fine, but how we go about finding him depends in large part on why

---

1. (von Winterfeldt & Edwards, 1986) [p. 31], (Rozenblit & Keil, 2002). For corroboration of the importance of problem definition, see also (L. L. Thompson, 2012) [p. 186], (Markman, Wood, Linsey, Murphy, & Laux, 2009) [pp. 94–95], and (Kaplan, 2011) [pp. 39–40].

2. Note that, in our approach, we use "problem" and "project" interchangeably, same with "goals" and "objectives." Highly complex projects—say, designing and implementing a regional highway system—may call for more details in the project plan and may require us to differentiate these terms, although I have not found a consistent taxonomy. See (Eisner, 2002) [pp. 67–90] or (Kerzner, 2003) [pp. 377–448] for more.

3. For an alternative template, see (Davis, Keeling, Schreier, & Williams, 2007).

| Project name: | | | |
|---|---|---|---|
| Specific goals: (*what* you are going to do) | Your main objectives | Out of scope: (*what* you are *not* going to do) | Things that could be included in the project but that you have decided to leave out |
| Decision maker(s): | Person(s) with the formal authority to decide the direction of the project, including killing it | Other key stakeholders: | Persons who do not have formal authority but can influence the scope and outcome of the project or will be impacted by it |
| Timetable: | Actions | | Needed time | Cumulative time |
| | 1. Frame the problem (define the *what*) | | | |
| | 2. Diagnose the problem (find the *why*) | | | |
| |    Define the diagnostic key question and identify possible causes | | | |
| |    Collect the diagnostic evidence, analyze, and draw conclusions | | | |
| | 3. Identify solutions (find the *how*) | | | |
| |    Define the solution key question and identify possible solutions | | | |
| |    Collect evidence, analyze, and decide which solution(s) to implement | | | |
| | 4. Implement (*do*) | | | |
| Resources: | Resources (money, people, equipment, etc.) that you can dedicate to the project and for how long | | | |
| Possible problems: | Things that can go wrong | Mitigation actions: | Initiatives to proactively defuse the possible problems |

FIGURE 2.1: A problem definition card—or *what* card—summarizes vital information about the problem.

he went missing in the first place, so it seems logical to include this in our project. And what about preventing him from going missing again in the future? Should that be included, too?

## 1.1. ANSWERING QUESTIONS IS NOT ENOUGH; YOU MUST IDENTIFY THEM, TOO

As we discussed in the first chapter, becoming better at solving well-defined problems is not sufficient to enable you to solve ill-defined ones, because the latter requires additional skills,[4] such as framing the problem.

Just like the frame of a painting creates a clear boundary between what is part of the painting and what is not, problems must also be clearly framed. *Problem framing*, then, amounts to defining *what* problem you are proposing to solve (and including it in the *what* card of Figure 2.1). This is a critical activity because the frame you choose strongly influences your understanding of the problem, thereby conditioning your approach to solving it. For an illustration, consider Thibodeau and Broditsky's series of experiments in which they asked people for ways to reduce crime in a community. They found that the respondents' suggestions changed significantly depending on whether the metaphor used to describe crime was as a virus or as a beast. People presented with a metaphor comparing crime to a virus invading their city emphasized prevention and addressing the root causes of the problem,

---

4. See, for instance (Pretz, Naples, & Sternberg, 2003) [p. 9], (Singer, Nielsen, & Schweingruber, 2012) [p. 76], (Jonassen, 2000), (DeHaan, 2011).

22 • STRATEGIC THINKING IN COMPLEX PROBLEM SOLVING

such as eradicating poverty and improving education. On the other hand, people presented with the beast metaphor focused on remediations: increasing the size of the police force and prisons.[5]

Therefore, improving our ability to frame a problem may help us identify better solutions.[6] In some situations, when we are already familiar with the problem, this may require us to resist conditioning, our own or someone else's.

**Resist conditioning**. Consider the anecdote about the routinization of monkeys: Put five monkeys in a cage, hang a banana from the ceiling and place a ladder underneath. Soon a monkey climbs the ladder to grab the banana. As soon as he touches the ladder, spray all the *others* with cold water.

Repeat the operation when a second monkey tries to climb the ladder and, indeed, until they all learn the consequence of going after the banana. Soon, they will stop one another from climbing the ladder. Next, put the water away and replace one of the original five monkeys. The new monkey sees the banana and tries to climb the ladder. However, the other four, knowing the consequences, attack him. The new monkey has not experienced any of the water, but he has learned that he should not climb. Then, substitute another of the original monkeys with a newcomer. The new fellow sees the banana, tries to reach it but the other four—including the one that has not seen any water—beat him up, so he soon gives up. Repeat the operation until you have removed all the original monkeys. Introduce a new fellow and watch: even though none of the new monkeys have seen any water, they will all happily "explain" to the newcomer that he should not try to get the banana. Consequently, the new monkeys now all live under a banana, but none of them attempts to retrieve it. Why? As far as they are concerned, for no other reason than because it is how it has always been done around here.[7]

Conditioning is omnipresent in our lives. Consider combating the obesity crisis in North America. The traditional approach has been for physicians to stress the importance of diet and exercise. That works, but only momentarily as people easily slip back into old habits.[8] However, resisting the conditioning of focusing on these solutions may yield better results: observing that excise taxation helped reduce tobacco and alcohol consumption, public policy expert Kelly Brownell and others are proposing that we consider taxing sugared drinks.[9]

There may have been good reasons to think about a particular problem one way or another in the past, but this does not mean that these reasons are still valid. Part of the value of our methodology is to help you think about new ways to approach a problem. This requires hard work, because these new ways, by definition, will not come naturally to you. So, do not stay in your comfort zones, and certainly do not stick with the

---

5. (Thibodeau & Boroditsky, 2011). This is in line with studies by Kahneman and Tversky who obtained systematic reversals of people's preferred solutions to a problem by framing it in different ways (Tversky & Kahneman, 1981). These framing effects have been observed in many settings; see (Levin, Schneider, & Gaeth, 1998) for a review.
6. (Bardwell, 1991).
7. After (Scapens, 2006).
8. (Ness, 2012a) [p. 21].
9. (Brownell et al., 2009). See also (Institute of Medicine, 2014) [pp. 13–14].

TABLE 2.1: We Think Using One of Two Systems[a]

| System 1—Intuitive | System 2—Reflective |
|---|---|
| Unconscious, preconscious | Conscious |
| Rapid | Slow |
| Automatic | Controlled |
| Low effort | High effort |
| High capacity | Low capacity |
| Associative | Rule based |
| Intuitive | Deliberative |
| Contextualized | Abstract |

[a]After (Evans, 2012) [p. 116]. See also (Kahneman, Lovallo, & Sibony, 2011) for a friendly introduction of how the two thinking systems impact decision making.

we'll-ask-this because-this-is-what-we've-always-asked approach. To overcome habituation, epidemiologist Roberta Ness recommends that we become better observers; in particular, attend to details and question assumptions, so that we learn to see things in a different way than what we expect.[10]

In other situations, particularly when we are first exposed to a new problem, we may generate an opinion on the spot. Judicious framing in this case requires letting go of your intuition and instead switching to deeper thinking.

**Engage System 2 thinking.** A theory in psychology states that we think using one of two processes: System 1 thinking is intuitive: fast, emotional, automatic, and effortless. System 2 is reflective: slower, effortful, and more analytic (see Table 2.1).[11] Facing a problem, both our systems engage, but System 1 yields an answer faster.[12] Nobel Prize laureate Kahneman suggests that jumping to conclusions, that is, using System 1 thinking or intuition, is appropriate if one is likely to pick the right answer, the cost of an occasional error is low, and deciding quickly brings high rewards.[13] That is, System 1 is good in situations where "(1) the environment is predictable (so what happened previously is a good predictor of what will be likely to happen again); and (2) the person has had the 'opportunity to learn the regularities of the environment' through repeated exposure and feedback."[14]

When solving a CIDNI problem, it is likely that you will not meet with at least one of these conditions. Therefore, in general you should not trust your intuition but, rather, use System 2 thinking.[15]

10. (Ness, 2012b).

11. (Evans, 2012; Glöckner & Witteman, 2010; Kahneman, 2003, 2011; Kahneman & Frederick, 2002; Stanovich & West, 2000).

12. (National Research Council, 2011) [p. 123].

13. (Kahneman, 2011) [p. 79].

14. (National Research Council, 2011) [p. 122]. See also (Kahneman & Klein, 2009).

15. See (Gawande, 2009) [pp. 162–170] for a description of how successful investors attribute their success to resisting the urge to act based on System 1 thinking. Also, scuba divers are trained to pause before acting: "Stop – Breathe – Think – Act" (PADI, 2009).

## 1.2. CONSIDER VARIOUS ALTERNATIVES

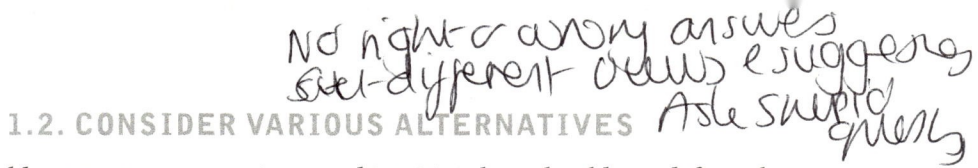

So, if you should not trust your experience and intuition, how should you define what your problem is? In short, you should generate a pool of options to choose from and gain some perspective to help you select a good one.

**Defer judgment.** To improve creativity, it is usually a good idea to decouple idea generation from idea evaluation.[16] Indeed, given that having high-quality ideas usually requires first having lots of ideas,[17] you should start by generating potential candidates without judging them.

**Enlist others.** As you consider potential candidates for your frame, enlisting the assistance of others may help increase your creativity.[18] In fact, consider enlisting people who know little about the problem and its context, because they can ask the "dumb" questions that experts have been trained not to ask. Although asking "dumb" questions may make us appear naive to experts, naivety can be an asset because it allows us to reconsider possibilities that specialists reject.[19]

If you are the reviewer for a problem, you should ask the solvers to explain why they chose one frame over another, and why they included specific aspects and rejected others. Keep probing (it's easy, keep asking *why*). Do not be fooled by their confidence: In an evidence-based setting, statements such as, "I've been in this business; I know what I'm talking about" call for deeper investigation. As Cambridge's criminologist Lawrence Sherman puts it, "evidence-based thinking asks only 'what is the evidence?' and not 'who says so?'."[20]

## 1.3. DESCRIBE THE PROJECT IN A *WHAT* CARD

The idea behind using a *what* card such as that shown in Figure 2.1 is to crystalize our understanding of the problem. This is valuable because it helps us build a shared understanding of what the project is—with both external audiences (decision maker(s) and other key stakeholders) and within our own team.[21] This will help reduce the likelihood of scope creep, the gradual expansion of an unfolding project outside of its original objectives. Also, the *what* card serves as a roadmap for future reference, which enables us to periodically step back and validate that we are on target (time-, budget-, and quality-wise).

Going back to Figure 2.1, write the name of your project at the top of the card. On the second row, specify what the project is and what it is not. In Harry's case, once we generate various candidates for our goals and discuss with our friend John, we realize that we should first identify why Harry is missing before identifying how to get him back and actually getting him back (Figure 2.2). It would be perfectly acceptable to include actions for

---

16. See, for instance (Hammond, Keeney, & Raiffa, 2002) [p. 53].
17. (L. Thompson, 2003), (Adams, 2001) [p. 121].
18. (L. Thompson, 2003).
19. See (Berger, 2010) [pp. 21–28] for how designers leverage their relative ignorance to achieve breakthrough results.
20. (Sherman, 2002) [p. 221].
21. (Eisner, 2002) [pp. 67–68].

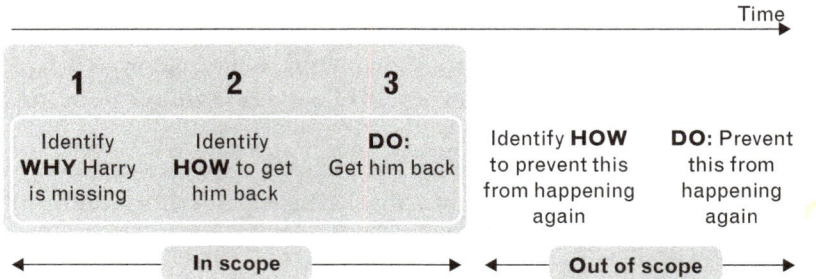

FIGURE 2.2: In Harry's case, we define the project as identifying why he is missing, identifying how to get him back, and getting him back.

preventing his disappearance from reoccurring in the future, but it may be premature to do so at this time, when such concerns are outside the scope of the project.

**Explicitly including an out-of-scope section helps remove ambiguities:** Each of us approaches a project with our own preconceptions and writing down what the project is and is not can be helpful in building shared understanding. This is critical: A 2011 report by the National Research Council found that many poorly performing teams do not validate that all members agree on the objectives and how to reach them.[22]

The next row in the *what* card is about people. *Decision makers* are people who can formally authorize, steer, or kill your project. Typically these are our bosses and/or clients. *Other key stakeholders* are people who do not have formal authority but have influence on the project or are impacted by it. Managing all key stakeholders appropriately—such as involving them in the project—may have a significant impact on the project's success. For example, if one is a hospital administrator whose project is to change the behavior of surgical staff to promote greater cleanliness in operating rooms, surgical staff would be key stakeholders. Indeed, engaging them in the effort from the beginning, so that they influence the project and feel ownership over the outcomes, may significantly improve the chances of success.[23] In Harry's case, the decision-makers are John and his wife and there are no other key stakeholders (see Figure 2.3).

Next is the timetable, showing the main phases in the process and the time we plan to devote to each. To simplify thinking through the project, the table is prepopulated with four steps (*what, why, how, do*), but you may decide to articulate your project around other milestones.

The next row lists the resources that you are ready to commit to the project. These can be money, people, equipment, and so on.

The final row lists possible problems, along with actions that you can take to mitigate them. The idea is to help you think from the very beginning about possible obstacles that could complicate your project and how you can proactively avoid them or reduce their impact. In Harry's case, for example, calling the housekeeper to confront her and find out if she is holding Harry hostage could be a way to make progress quickly, but it could also easily backfire: If she did not take him and is as unstable as John says she is, we might end

---

22. (National Research Council, 2011) [p. 177].
23. See (Ramanujam & Rousseau, 2006) [p. 823] for a discussion on the positive impact of involving people and pushing decisions down an organization's hierarchy.

| Project name: | Find Harry the dog | | |
|---|---|---|---|
| Specific goals: (*what* you are going to do) | 1. Understand why Harry is missing (*why*)<br>2. Identify best way to get him back (*how*)<br>3. Get him back (*do*) | Out of scope: (*what* you are not going to do) | Preventing him from going missing again in the future (both the how and the implementation) |
| Decision maker(s): | John and his wife | Other key stakeholders: | N/A |

| Timetable: | Actions | Needed time | Cumulative time |
|---|---|---|---|
| | **1. Frame the problem (define the *what*)** | 2h | 2h |
| | **2. Diagnose the problem (find the *why*)** | | |
| | Define the diagnostic key question and identify possible causes | 4h | 6h |
| | Collect the diagnostic evidence, analyze, and draw conclusions | 6h | 12h |
| | **3. Identify solutions (find the *how*)** | | |
| | Define the solution key question and identify potential solutions | 6h | 18h |
| | Collect evidence, analyze, and decide which solution(s) to implement | 6h | 24h |
| | **4. Implement the chosen solution(s) (*do*)** | 48h | 72h |

| Resources: | Money: Spend up to $150 for the *why*, $150 for the *how*, $300 for the *do*<br>People: Up to three people dedicated full time | | |
|---|---|---|---|
| Possible problems: | Speaking with housekeeper can backfire | Mitigation actions: | Refrain from speaking with the housekeeper until absolutely necessary |

**FIGURE 2.3**: Harry's *what* card summarizes key information for the project.

up having to divert significant resources to manage her. So we choose to avoid this liability altogether by refraining from speaking with her until later.

Framing the problem can be challenging and may require several iterations. Consider using the *what* card to guide your conversations with your project's decision maker(s) and other key stakeholders so as to converge toward a shared understanding of the project.

One final word about scope creep: Although the gradual expansion of a project outside of its original objectives is not desirable in many instances, in some situations, as your project progresses, you may discover evidence that warrants changing the scope. As long as any changes in scope are the result of conscious decisions taken while considering deadlines and resource restrictions, they are perfectly acceptable. To ensure that a shared understanding of the project remains, however, these changes should be reflected in the *what* card.

## 2. FRAMING THE DIAGNOSTIC

"There was once a village along a river. The people who lived there were very kind. These residents, according to parable, began noticing increasing numbers of drowning people caught in the river's swift current. And so they went to work devising ever more elaborate technologies to resuscitate them. So preoccupied were these heroic villagers with rescue and treatment that they never thought to look upstream to see who was pushing the victims in."[24]

---

24. (Steingraber, 2010).

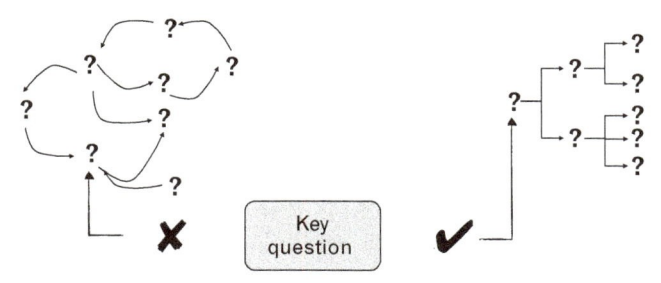

**FIGURE 2.4:** The key question encompasses all the other relevant ones.

When facing a problem, it is tempting to jump straight into "How can I fix it?" mode because doing so forces us to think about potential solutions right from the start. This gives the appearance of efficiency. As ecologist Sandra Steingraber's story illustrates, however, if you start thinking about how you can solve a problem without having understood its root cause(s), you may misdirect a great deal of effort or solve the wrong problem altogether. First, you *must* go upstream. This section explains how to do so by framing the diagnostic analysis and capturing the result in a *why* card.

## 2.1. SELECT A GOOD KEY QUESTION

Central to problem framing is identifying *the* key question you want to answer; that is, the one question from which all the other relevant ones originate (see Figure 2.4).[25] You also need to frame the key question by placing it in its environment and summarizing this information in a diagnostic definition card, or *why* card.

As we touched on in Chapter 1, diagnosing the problem requires alternating between divergent and convergent thinking. Here, divergent thinking helps us identify potential candidates for the key question; it is creative thinking or idea generation. Once we have several candidates to compare, we apply convergent thinking—critical thinking—to compare them and decide which to use.

Key questions have four characteristics: type, topic, scope, and phrasing. We will use these characteristics to improve our set of candidate key questions and help us choose the one that we should retain.

### 2.1.1. CHOOSE THE RIGHT TYPE OF KEY QUESTION

Earlier in this chapter, we started our four-step approach by identifying our overall objective for the effort: *what* we wanted to achieve. That is the *description* phase (see Figure 2.5).

Next is the *diagnosis!* A typical diagnosis question asks why we are facing this problem (e.g., Why is Harry is missing? or Why is Harry not at my friend's house?). A frequent

---

25. Concentrating on a central question is standard in the approach of some management consultants; see (Davis et al., 2007).

28 • STRATEGIC THINKING IN COMPLEX PROBLEM SOLVING

| 1. Frame the problem | 2. Diagnose the problem | 3. Find potential solutions | 4. Implement solution |

| Description phase | Diagnosis phase | Prescription phase | | Time |

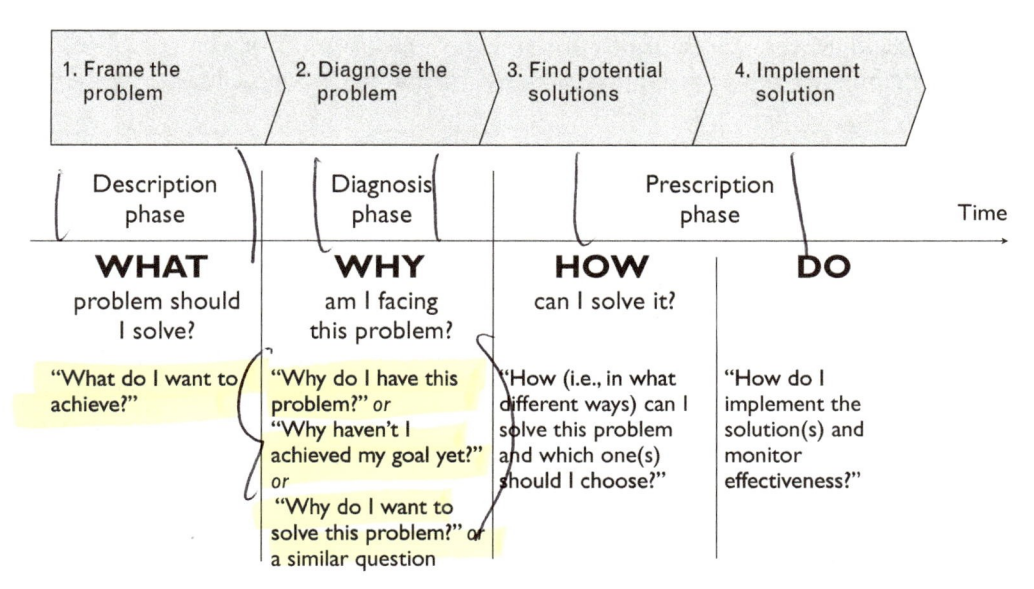

**WHAT** problem should I solve? | **WHY** am I facing this problem? | **HOW** can I solve it? | **DO**

"What do I want to achieve?" | "Why do I have this problem?" *or* "Why haven't I achieved my goal yet?" *or* "Why do I want to solve this problem?" or a similar question | "How (i.e., in what different ways) can I solve this problem and which one(s) should I choose?" | "How do I implement the solution(s) and monitor effectiveness?"

FIGURE 2.5: The key question changes as we progress toward resolving the problem.

alternative diagnosis question is why we have not achieved our overall objective yet (e.g., Why have I not found Harry yet?).

After the diagnosis comes the *prescription*: How—understood as, "in what various ways"—can we solve our problem (e.g., How can I get Harry back?)?

So, while a problem may have three major key questions (a *what*, a *why*, and a *how*), at any moment in time you are only facing one of those.

**Only ask *what*, *why*, or *how*.** Other question roots (i.e., *where*, *when*, *who*) may be useful as part of the analysis, and we will use these when we test hypotheses in Chapters 4 and 6. In my experience, however, these usually are not good roots for key questions because they can lead to confusion. Rather, using a *why* for the diagnosis phase and a *how* for the prescription phase helps structure the resolution. This is critical because, at this stage, our primary goal is to identify the correct problem, rather than one of its symptoms, or a less critical problem, and structure has been shown to improve the effectiveness of problem formulation.[26]

**Only ask *how* if you know *why*.** In our problem-solving approach, once you have identified *what* you want to do with your project, you only need to consider two kinds of key questions: *why* and *how*. *Why* analyses are diagnostics: they help uncover the root cause(s) of the problem. *How* analyses are prescriptions: they help find alternative ways to solve a problem.

Going back to Steingraber's example, fixing the symptoms (rescuing people) instead of fixing the actual cause of the problem is suboptimal. If, instead of asking, "How can we save these people?" the villagers had first asked, "Why are these people in the river?" they might have identified a better solution. Of course, in practical situations, one may have to attend to urgent matters first, and we are not suggesting that the villagers should let people drown in the river as they conduct their diagnosis. Rather, we are saying that, resources permitting, they should not bypass the diagnosis altogether.

26. (Bardwell, 1991).

Understanding your overall objective and the root cause(s) of your problem sets the foundation for a robust resolution. So, time permitting, it is usually wise to start by asking *why*.

## 2.1.2. ASK ABOUT THE RIGHT TOPIC

Once you have identified which type of question to ask, your next consideration is to make it address the right topic. This is not as obvious as it sounds.

As an illustration, consider Stockholm's struggle with traffic congestion over the 57 bridges that connect the 14 islands on which the city is built. Framing the problem on the topic of supply (by asking, for instance, "How can we increase the supply of roads?") would probably have resulted in building another bridge, a standard and expected engineering solution. Instead, when the problem arose in the early 2000s, the city framed the problem on a larger topic—that of capacity. Congestion occurs when the capacity of a system is insufficient, that is, when the supply cannot accommodate the demand. So, although it is perfectly acceptable to aim at increasing the supply, maybe decreasing the demand is also worth pursuing. On this basis, Stockholm implemented a "tax and drive" system with transponders installed in the users' cars that charged a larger amount at rush hour. Within four weeks, the system removed 100,000 vehicles at rush hours.[27] An initial trial system was put in place in 2006, which reduced travel times sufficiently for the general public to notice. This, in turn, is credited for a landslide reversal of public opinion toward supporting the measure.[28] Addressing the right topic in this case yielded a faster solution at a fraction of the cost of building a new bridge. It also came with added benefits, including reduced pollution.[29]

One important takeaway from this example is that we should strive to keep an open mind when framing our problems. If I am an engineer, for example, I should not think that a problem I am confronted with necessarily calls for an engineering solution. At times, a nonengineering solution might be more desirable.

By the way, this capacity problem—a mismatch between supply and demand—is a recurrent theme in the problems that I see and presents itself in various guises, such as ensuring that a team can accommodate the workload assigned to it (the obvious solution—hiring additional personnel—is not necessarily the best answer) or increasing a business unit's profitability. Here is another example.

Imagine that your company sells laptops and your manager asks you to think of ways to increase sales. You might brainstorm with a few colleagues and identify two general ways: make the whole market bigger—by convincing people who are not currently buying laptops to buy yours—or "steal" customers from your competitors (see Figure 2.6).

But there are other ways to increase sales; for one, you may sell more to your current customers. You also may increase the revenue of each sale. And, although revenue is good, profits—revenues minus expenses—may be even better. In fact, what you may ultimately

---

27. (Grasso & Martinelli, 2010).
28. (Eliasson, Hultkrantz, Nerhagen, & Rosqvist, 2009).
29. (Eliasson, 2009).

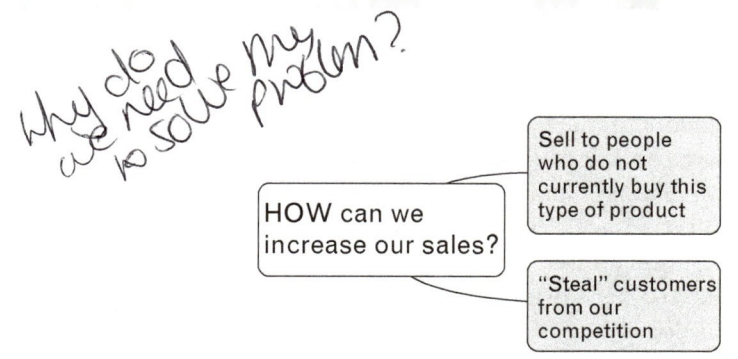

*[Handwritten note: Why do we need to solve my problem?]*

```
                          ┌─────────────────┐
                          │ Sell to people  │
                          │ who do not      │
         ┌──────────────┐ │ currently buy   │
         │ HOW can we   │─┤ this type of    │
         │ increase our │ │ product         │
         │ sales?       │ └─────────────────┘
         └──────────────┘ ┌─────────────────┐
                          │ "Steal" customers│
                          │ from our        │
                          │ competition     │
                          └─────────────────┘
```

**FIGURE 2.6:** A straightforward answer to insufficient sales is to increase the overall market size or "steal" customers from our competition.

*[Handwritten note: What are you currently after? eg. Look wholesale or increase new investment?]*

be after is sustainable return on investment (ROI). If you make the topic of your key question increasing your return on investment, your universe of possibilities grows drastically (see Figure 2.7). A focus on increasing ROI is **not** necessarily better than a focus on sales; **what matters is that you identify the right topic for your specific situation.**

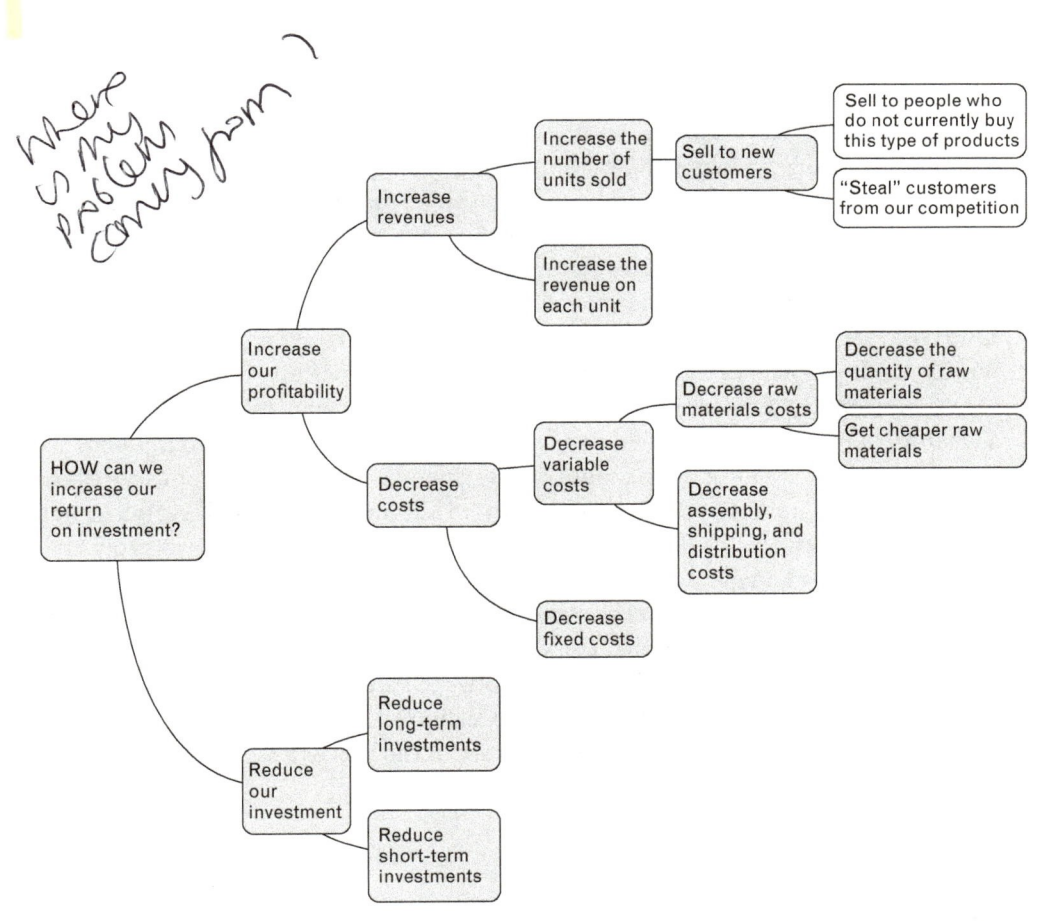

*[Handwritten note: Where is my problem coming from?]*

[Tree diagram:]
- HOW can we increase our return on investment?
  - Increase our profitability
    - Increase revenues
      - Increase the number of units sold
        - Sell to new customers
          - Sell to people who do not currently buy this type of products
          - "Steal" customers from our competition
      - Increase the revenue on each unit
    - Decrease costs
      - Decrease variable costs
        - Decrease raw materials costs
          - Decrease the quantity of raw materials
          - Get cheaper raw materials
        - Decrease assembly, shipping, and distribution costs
      - Decrease fixed costs
  - Reduce our investment
    - Reduce long-term investments
    - Reduce short-term investments

**FIGURE 2.7:** Choosing the right topic is essential because it dictates the size of the solution space for the problem.

**Question your constraints/frames.** Considering new possibilities for the topic of your key question takes time and effort. It is messy, inefficient, and unpredictable. Yet these are requirements of innovative thinking[30] and as the Stockholm example suggested, it may lead to better solutions. In fact, there is widespread agreement that reframing is beneficial.[31]

Of course, we are sometimes pressed by time or other constraints to restrict our attention to a specific topic. But in other situations, in my experience, questioning whether the initial topic of our key question is the correct one is a wise investment.

## 2.1.3. WITHIN THE TOPIC, SELECT THE RIGHT SCOPE

Related to choosing the right topic is selecting the right scope within that topic: being neither too broad nor too narrow.

Consider being asked, "How do we solve the airport's parking lot problem?" Although the question may address the right topic if the problem is related to the parking lot, it is not sufficiently precise. What is wrong with the parking lot? Is it congested? Unsafe? Dirty? Noisy? Ugly? Flooded? Too far?

**Do not make your scope too narrow**. If the key question is too broad, as in the airport parking lot example above, you may struggle to stay in touch with your problem because you will explore aspects that are only remotely connected to the central issue. But making your key question too narrow is also limiting. This can happen when we orient the question in the wrong direction or when we base it on an incorrect hypothesis. In such cases, you will overlook some ways of solving your problem or you might miss the entire point. Broadening your perspective may be beneficial. For example, Ancel Keys developed the Mediterranean diet after noticing that rates of cardiovascular diseases vary greatly depending on nations, which was noticeable only after Keys expanded his question to the international realm.[32]

One common instance of making the key question too narrow is when we guide the resolution of our problem in the question. Consider the key question: "How can we better manage our inventory to ensure that we have enough promotional materials?" Managing the inventory may or may not be the reason why we do not have enough promotional materials; until we have established that poor management is a significant root cause of our problem, we should not focus on it. Similarly, with "I do not have enough visibility; how do I persuade Marketing to dedicate one full-time employee to promoting my products?" Again, getting one FTE might not be the desirable solution to the situation. In fact, it might not even be enough! And yet we are framing our possibilities with this constraint. "Be careful what you wish for, lest it come true" comes to mind here.

In these examples, asking ourselves, "How do we ensure that we have enough promotional materials?" and "How do we increase our visibility?" might be sufficient. Whether the problem is indeed the management of the inventory or the lack of a dedicated FTE will be revealed in our analysis.

---

30. (Ness, 2012a) [p. 11].
31. (Bardwell, 1991), (Hammond et al., 2002) [p. 16, 20], (Dougherty & Heller, 1994).
32. (Ness, 2012b). On scope, see also (Heuer & Pherson, 2011) [pp. 49–51].

## 2.1.4. USE AN APPROPRIATE PHRASING

Using an appropriate phrasing for your key question means vetting every single word and, possibly, making the key question self-reliant.

**Validate every word.** In evidence-based medicine, clarity in question formulation is valuable because it helps concentrate limited resources where they are most needed and reduces communication errors.[33] Just as a minute change in the heading of an airliner right after takeoff significantly affects its position 5,000 miles later, the slightest of variations in your key question will have significant consequences on your project. That is, because a key question is the foundation of your entire problem-solving effort, each word counts.

For an illustration of how critical this is, recall Thibodeau and Boroditsky's experiment on crime resolution that we discussed earlier. They found that even a minute difference—changing *one* word in the narrative "Crime is a virus/beast ravaging the city of Addison"—resulted in people offering different solutions.[34]

An implication is that you have to use precise vocabulary, not because of pedantry but because imprecision in communication may be symptomatic of deficiencies in the underlying logic. Imagine talking to your surgeon before an intervention and hearing him make such an imprecise description of what he is going to do that it bothers even you, a nonspecialist. Surely this would push you to question whether he is trustworthy. An imprecise key question may just have the same effect.

**Consider making your key question self-reliant.** Aside from precision, you may consider making the key question self-reliant so that it is immediately understandable to someone not familiar with the problem. In this case, our key question, "Why is Harry missing?" may become, "Why is my friend's dog, Harry, missing?" "Why is my friend's dog, Harry, missing after he was left alone at home for four hours?" or something else. As is common with ill-defined problems, there is usually more than one acceptable answer.

To help formulate a good key question, you may want to start by generating five or more candidates. Then use the four filters above (type, topic, scope, and phrasing) to compare them and understand the implications of using one versus another. You may then want to combine them, stealing elements from some to build an optimal one. Be sure to seek feedback from others to challenge your preconceptions.

## 2.1.5. WHAT ABOUT HARRY?

The first row of Table 2.2 shows several ideas for a diagnostic key question in Harry's case. These initial candidates do not have to be perfect. Instead, generate many candidates, approaching the problem from different perspectives. To help you do so, you may want to ask others to pitch in their ideas.

Next, run each candidate through the four filters. The template of Table 2.2 allows you to capture the surviving ideas after each filter as well as the thought process that led you to

---

33. (Straus, Glasziou, Richardson, & Haynes, 2011) [p. 21].
34. (Thibodeau & Boroditsky, 2011).

TABLE 2.2: In Harry's Case, Using the Filters Helps Us Identify a Key Question and Documents Our Thinking Process

**Objective** (what do I want to achieve?): **Find Harry the dog**

**Initial, unfiltered candidates for the key question:**
Why is Harry not at my friend's house?
How can I get Harry back?
Why is Harry missing?
Why can't we find Harry?
Why was Harry able to leave my friend's house?

| Filter | Reasoning | Filtered candidates for key question |
|---|---|---|
| **Type filter:** | Because we do not know yet why Harry is missing, it is premature to think of ways to get him back. | Why is Harry not at my friend's house? <br> ~~How can I get Harry back?~~ <br> Why is Harry missing? <br> Why can't we find Harry? <br> Why was Harry able to leave my friend's house? |
| **Topic filter:** | I am primarily interested in Harry being missing, as opposed to how he left the house. | Why is Harry not at my friend's house? <br> Why is Harry missing? <br> Why can't we find Harry? <br> ~~Why was Harry able to leave my friend's house?~~ |
| **Scope filter:** | There are reasons why we cannot find Harry besides his disappearances (e.g., we are incompetent), but we decide that they are not worth pursuing at this time. | Why is Harry not at my friend's house? <br> Why is Harry missing? <br> ~~Why cannot we find Harry?~~ |
| **Phrasing filter:** | The two remaining formulations seem equivalent, so we go with the more concise. Further, we think that specifying that Harry is a dog will help enlist others efficiently. | ~~Why is Harry not at my friend's house?~~ <br> **Why is Harry [the dog] missing?** |

each updated candidate pool. This may help you clarify your thinking and it can be useful later in the process if you need to explain your approach.

To compare candidates, think of their implications—their *so what?* Looking at the problem from one particular perspective may make some of its characteristics more apparent. For instance, concentrating on how Harry left the house ("Why was Harry able to leave my friend's house?") versus where he is now ("Why is Harry not at my friend's house?") can help you map out in more precision the events that resulted in his disappearance. If you decide, however, that what really matters is where he is now, such an approach may not result in the best question.

Note that, as you compare options, it is perfectly acceptable to steal elements from some options in order to improve others.

Once you are confident that you have found an appropriate type, topic, and scope, you should improve the form of your question. Does your question ask precisely what it ought to ask? Could it say the same thing with fewer words? Is it sufficiently self-reliant? Once this is done, you are ready to integrate the question into an introductory flow.

## 2.2. USE AN INTRODUCTORY FLOW

The key question is a central element in framing your diagnostic, but it is only one of several components. It fits into an introductory flow consisting of a situation and a complication, and it is completed by a description of the context of the problem. The following sections describe these elements.

### 2.2.1. DEFINING *YOUR* UNIVERSE WITH THE SITUATION

One way to look at introductions is to think about them as being stories with three components: a situation, a complication, and a key question.[35] As such, an introduction is analogous in many ways to a scene of exposition in theatrical pieces and movies where the audience learns the information necessary for them to understand the story—past events, key people and relationships, circumstances, and so forth.[36]

The situation sets the stage by presenting the part of the universe in which you are interested; it aims at generating a "yes, I know/understand all this, so why are you telling it to me?" reaction in your audience. It does so by presenting only the information that is necessary, sufficient, positive, and uncontroversial.

**Include only the necessary and sufficient information.** Distractions reduce our working memory—our ability to acquire and retain information in short-term memory—so unnecessary complexity hinders problem solving.[37] As such, it is advisable to include in the situation only the information that is necessary to understand the setting and to leave out peripheral elements.

This "less is more" approach can be difficult because it is tempting to include lots of information and let our audience decide what is really important. Many presentations I have seen start with an overcrowded "background" slide in which the writers' thinking seems to be: "I cannot quite explain why I think this is important, but I'll put it anyway, and if they do not see value in it, they can just ignore it." Or, "I know this is not relevant, but this is usually how we talk about this subject so I'll put it out there." The issue with these approaches is that recognizing the real problem out of a mass of information is a difficult task, one that usually requires careful thinking and various iterations. Therefore, it is unreasonable to assume that our audience can do it on the go.

So it is *you*, the problem solver, who should do this thinking, including only the elements that you have identified as critical. It may be that your audience will disagree with you, but you will have set the stage for a constructive debate that may take your analysis to a higher level than you could have reached by yourself.

In practice, this means that you should be able to *justify* the presence of every word in your introductory flow; in particular:

---

35. (Minto, 2009) [pp. 37–62].
36. See (Mackendrick, 2004) [pp. 22–26].
37. See, for instance (Shaw, 1958) and Chapter 3.

**Do not include data simply because you think your readers might find it useful or interesting.** You must do this work yourself: Why is it important that your readers know about this? To help you do this, do not accept, "That's interesting" as a justification. If you think something is interesting, understand and articulate why you think it is.

**Do not include data by habit**, simply because this is how someone else introduced the problem to you. Do not just assume that they have thought critically through the information that they have presented to you. Blindly following them may just be perpetuating a mistake long after it should have been caught (think about the monkeys).

**Do not include events in chronological order**, or in the order you learned them, simply for that reason. Usually, presenting data in chronological order is not the most effective way, as we will discuss further in Chapter 7.

The important matter should stem out because of the absence of irrelevant information, not because of repeated mentions. Remember, our approach is about simplifying the solution process; in engineering terms, this means making the signal apparent by filtering out the noise.

**Include only positive information.** At this stage, all is well in the universe; you are merely defining which part of the universe you want to talk about. In screenwriter Robert McKee's words, "A story begins with life being in balance, things are good, and daily activities occur more or less according to the way that our people of interest want them to occur."[38]

**Include only uncontroversial/undisputed information.** One of the proverbial stories I heard as a management consultant was that of a colleague who had worked on a project over three months. He had conducted the analysis, assembled an attractive presentation, and convened the executives of his client firm to present them with his report. As he showed them his first slide—the situation—the chief financial officer (CFO) interrupted: "Actually, this is not what is happening. Rather what is happening is . . ." In the best-case scenario, the CFO was wrong and all that was lost was some momentum in the presentation. But the alternative is much gloomier: If the consultant's understanding of the situation was wrong, then the entire basic premise of his work is incorrect! Including only uncontroversial information—information that you have vetted with knowledgeable stakeholders—helps you validate that you are building on a solid foundation and starting from a point of shared understanding and agreement. As Cambridge mathematician Michael Thompson puts it, get your first equation right because "research is not like an undergraduate examination question where you might get 8/10 for a good try, despite that little slip at the beginning! You have to get 10/10 every time."[39]

**Be concise.** The situation portion of the introduction does not have to be long. In fact, in my experience, good ones seldom are. Even my students who feel that their situation is too complex to be presented in one paragraph eventually manage to do so. They also usually find the end product to be more effective than their original blurb.[40]

In Harry's case, the situation could be as simple as explaining that my friend has a dog that he sometimes leaves home alone (see Table 2.3, Alternative 1).

Another approach is to be more inclusive, as the second alternative in Table 2.3 shows, mentioning that the dog has not escaped for a while and that today was particular. Both

---

38. (McKee & Fryer, 2003).
39. (J. M. T. Thompson, 2013).
40. See (Gershon & Page, 2001) for an example of how a short, memorable story can be more effective than a list of bullet points.

TABLE 2.3: Two Alternatives for a Situation Statement in Harry's Case—One Focusing on Conciseness, the Other on Precision

|  | Situation |
|---|---|
| **Alternative 1:** | Sometimes, my friend leaves his dog Harry alone at his house. |
| **Alternative 2:** | Sometimes, my friend leaves his dog Harry alone at his house. Harry used to escape but has not escaped recently. This morning, my friend fired his housekeeper because of poor performance, which she blamed on Harry's shedding. She was extremely upset and threatening. |

alternatives are concise and comply with the other prescriptions discussed above; therefore, both are acceptable. My preference is for the first because it is shorter, and, unlike the second alternative, it does not put forth any particular explanation.

## 2.2.2. INTRODUCE THE NEED FOR CHANGE WITH THE COMPLICATION

The *complication* upsets the original situation and thereby leads to the key question.[41] This is where the problem emerges. All was reasonably well in our part of the universe but, with the complication, something is not.

Finding a good complication can be challenging, so you may find it useful to write down various possibilities and compare them, as we did with the key question. When you compare them, you gain a better understanding: some of them might be part of others, for instance, or they might be consequences of others.

In the end, you must have only one complication. It may have several components, but they should all support the same central point. So work out how the various elements relate to one another, select the correct complication, and be specific; for instance, feel free to include numerical data to support your point. Refrain from solving the problem, however, because this is not yet the time to do so. Table 2.4 shows a complication for Harry's case.

TABLE 2.4: The Complication Builds on the Situation to Lead to the Key Question

| **Situation:** | Sometimes, my friend leaves his dog Harry alone at his house. |
|---|---|
| **Complication:** | Today, when my friend came home after being absent for four hours, Harry was missing. |
| **Diagnostic key question:** | Why is Harry the dog missing? |

---

41. See (McKee, 1997) [p. 189]. In screenwriting, the complication is called the *inciting event* (McKee & Fryer, 2003), (Burke, 2014) [p. 295].

Frame the Problem • 37

TABLE 2.5: **The Complication May Be Supported by Several Points (Bullets) but These Must Come Under a Unique Argument**

| | |
|---|---|
| **Situation:** | PR, Inc. is a boutique graphic design company. |
| | Traditionally, it has provided design services for movie posters, brochures, and corporate logos. |
| | Last year, it started a new service: photographic portraits of artists in their environment. |
| **Complication:** | Over the last six months, PR's revenues have not grown as rapidly as planned: |
| | • Its traditional services acquired seven new clients instead of the ten planned. |
| | • Its portrait services acquired three new clients instead of the five planned. |
| **Diagnostic Key Question:** | Why have PR's revenues over the last six months not grown as rapidly as planned? |

Table 2.5 shows another example of a situation–complication–key-question sequence in a management setting. Here, the complication (the revenue growth being slower than planned) is supported by two points (the revenue growth is not as quick as planned in traditional services and in portrait services).

Upon reading the situation and complication group, there is only one logical third step: the key question, which should be the conclusion of your introductory funnel. Figure 2.8 shows how the situation–complication–key-question sequence focuses attention on a specific problem in a specific part of the universe. Your job is to make this focusing as simple and effective as possible. This usually can be achieved concisely not just in the situation but in the entire introductory flow.[42]

### 2.2.3. FINE TUNE YOUR INTRODUCTORY FLOW

As you put together your situation, complication, and key question, you may find that they do not fit perfectly together.

**Use the rabbit rule and the holding hands rule.** Tim van Gelder at the University of Melbourne, Charles Twardy at George Mason University, and their colleagues have looked at how argument mapping can improve critical thinking. One of their tools is the *rabbit rule*: "To pull a rabbit out of a hat, there must be a rabbit in the hat to begin with."[43] That is, every element of the key question must have appeared in the situation and/or the complication.

---

42. For an illustration, see the minimalist manner in which La Fontaine sets up his fable *Les deux coqs* in two succinct verses: *Deux coqs vivaient en paix : une poule survint,/Et voilà la guerre allumée.* ("Two cocks in peace were living, when/A war was kindled by a hen.") (de La Fontaine, 1882).

43. (Twardy, 2010), (Rider & Thomason, 2010) [p. 115].

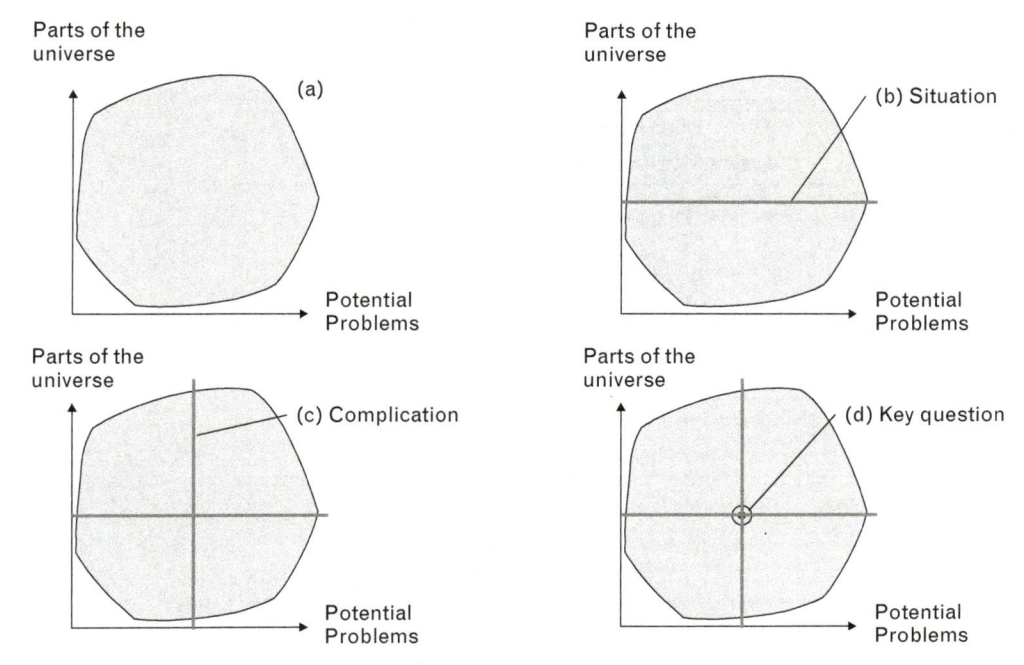

**FIGURE 2.8:** The introductory flow is a funnel: In two intermediary steps (the situation [b] and the complication [c]) it takes the audience from all possible problems (a) to the key question (d).

Similarly, every meaningful term in any one part of the introductory flow (the situation, the complication, or the key question) must appear at least once in another part of the flow—that's the *holding hands rule*.[44] Both these rules help prevent "dangling" terms, that is, information that is not needed in the flow.[45]

Consider the introductory flow for Harry's case in Figure 2.9 (a).

We complied with the rabbit rule, so no new elements appear in the key question. We did not entirely follow the holding hands rule, however, because some elements of the situation and the complication were left unused. To comply with both rules, the key question requires some rewording, as Figure 2.9 (b) shows. Twardy notes that complying fully with both rules can make arguments significantly wordier, so he recommends that one initially practice full compliance before deciding if a shorter version is better.[46] I have found that approach useful with my students, and we will resort to using shortcuts in further sections.

**Keep it simple.** In the words of 17th-century French writer Nicolas "That which is well thought-out is expressed clearly, and the words to say it come easily." Einstein agrees: "If you cannot explain it simply, you do not understand it well enough." So if you cannot express your thoughts clearly, your thinking needs some work, and clarifying your communication might be just what you need. Aim at making your introductory flow

---

44. (Twardy, 2010), (Rider & Thomason, 2010) [p. 115].
45. (Austhink, 2006).
46. (Twardy, 2010).

Frame the Problem • 39

(a)

| Situation: | My friend has a dog—Harry—and lives in a house. Sometimes, he leaves Harry alone at the house. |
| Complication: | Today, when my friend came home after being absent for 4 hours, Harry was missing. |
| Diagnostic key question: | Why is Harry the dog missing? |

Realizing that we do not comply fully with the holding hands rule (HH)...

HH ✗

(b)

| Situation: | Sometimes, my friend leaves his dog Harry alone at his house. |
| Complication: | Today, my friend left Harry alone for 4 hours. When he came home, Harry was missing. |
| Diagnostic key question: | Why is my friend's dog Harry missing from his house where he was left alone for 4 hours? |

... we edit the introductory flow

HH ✓

FIGURE 2.9: Ensure that the introductory flow complies with the rabbit and holding hands rules.

understandable by a novice when he or she reads it for the first time. This will help on two counts. First, it will help avoid those cases where a lack of clarity results in people misunderstanding the issue altogether.[47] And second, in my experience, the investment necessary to clarify a problem statement is low in comparison with the value added by gaining additional insight. Indeed, many of my students must reformulate the introductory flow to their technical problems so that nonexperts in the class, including me, can understand them. They are often reluctant to do so at first, but they usually realize and confess that they originally did not understand their problems sufficiently well. By having to express the problem in simple terms, they cannot just repeat what they had heard or read but, instead, have to develop a deeper understanding. So, to help clarify your problem statement, give it to a novice to read out loud. Observe whether she or he can go through it and understand it the first time out. If a novice has to re-read a part of it, chances are it is not as simple as it should be, so improvement is needed. (Consider asking the novice to help you improve the statement.)

**Ensure that the key question is the logical destination of the {situation + complication} sequence.** Reading a good introductory flow, the key question can be such a natural destination for the {situation + complication} sequence that it may seem almost superfluous. But this apparent triviality is the result of targeted efforts and reaching it is indeed significant progress. As one of my mathematics professors used to say, "This problem is trivial, the difficulty is to see that it is trivial."

The checklist in Figure 2.10 summarizes the rules we discussed for introductory flows. Validate that your introductory flow complies with these rules before moving forward.

---

47. (MacDonald & Picard, 2009). See also (J. M. T. Thompson, 2013).

A good introduction ...
- ... has the right elements
  - Has a good situation (S)
    - Has all the necessary information to identify the part of the universe we are interested in
    - Has only the necessary information
    - Has only information that is positive and undisputed/uncontroversial
  - Has a good complication (C)
    - Has a unique problem in that part of the universe (potentially illustrated by one or several of its symptoms/consequences)
  - Has a good key question (KQ)
    - Is of the right type (based on the right root: why or how)
    - Is on an appropriate topic
    - Has an appropriate scope (neither too broad nor too narrow)
    - Has an appropriate phrasing (understandable without anything else)
- ... and the elements work well together
  - The flow complies with the rabbit rule (i.e., nothing new appears in the KQ)
  - The flow complies with the holding-hands rule (i.e., if something appears in the S or C, it is in the KQ, too)
  - The flow is understandable by a novice after one read
    - No gaps, no overlaps
    - Appropriate order
    - No jargon

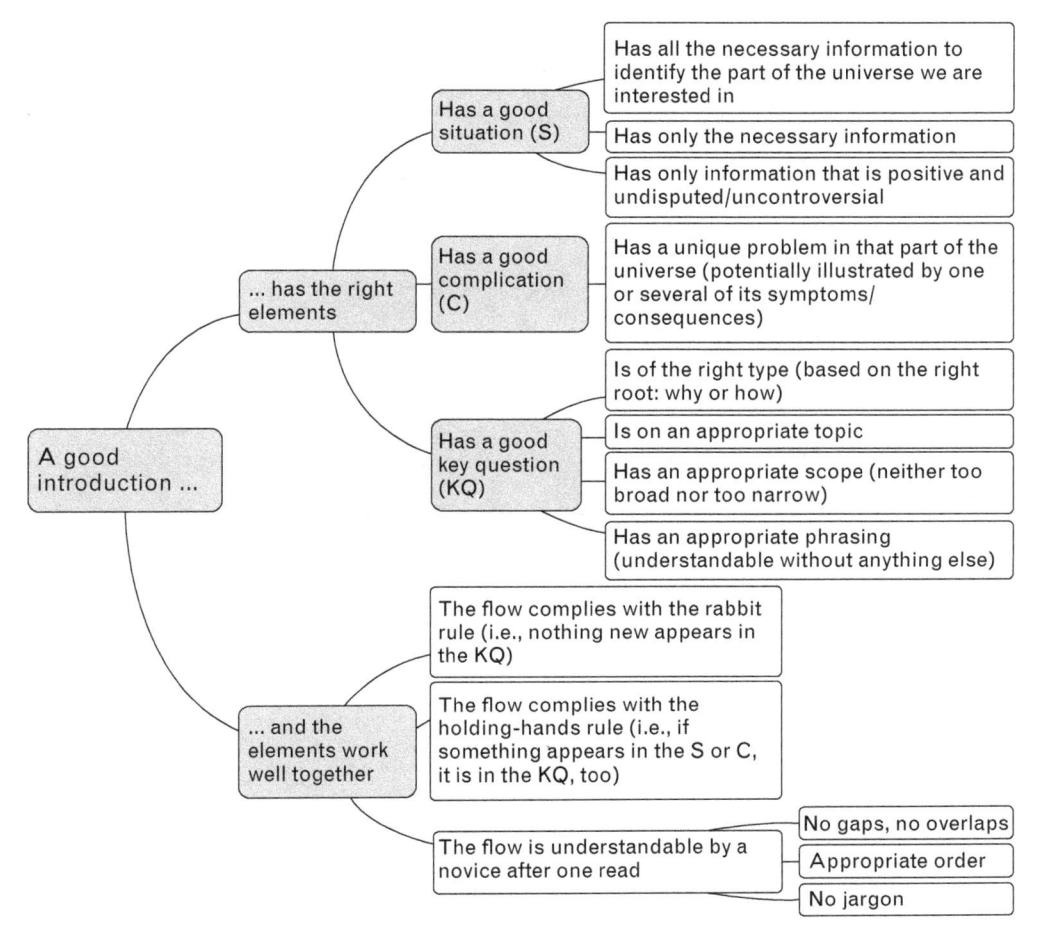

**FIGURE 2.10:** A good introduction has the right elements and these work well together.

## 2.3. SUMMARIZE YOUR DIAGNOSTIC FRAME IN A *WHY* CARD

Mirroring how we captured the scope of our project in a *what* card, summarize the diagnostic problem in a diagnostic definition card, or *why* card, as Figure 2.11 shows. You should periodically refer back to the *why* card during your diagnosis to ensure that you are staying on target or that, if the goal changes, it is the result of a conscious decision.

The top half of the card is the introductory flow: the situation, complication, and key question. The bottom half summarizes the context of the problem, first listing decision makers and key stakeholders. Then come the goals and logistics for your diagnosis: How much time will you invest in that part of the project? How much of your resources will you dedicate to it? What will be the deliverables or end products? The last section lists the voluntarily left-out answers, that is, actions we could take but decide not to take. For instance, in Harry's case, it would be perfectly acceptable to doubt John's statement that Harry is not at home. But we also can choose to believe this statement without checking it, and we would

| | |
|---|---|
| Situation: | The information that is necessary and sufficient to specify which part of the universe you are considering. *Only* the necessary information. This information should be positive (i.e., there is no problem at this stage) and undisputed (i.e., people reasonably familiar with the setting agree with it) |
| Complication: | The one problem in that part of the universe; that is, the unique need for change (potentially illustrated by one or several of its symptoms/consequences) |
| Diagnostic key question: | *The* one diagnostic question that you want to answer. It<br>1. Is phrased as "**why**...?"<br>2. Addresses an appropriate topic<br>3. Has an appropriate scope<br>4. Has an appropriate phrasing |
| Decision makers: | The person(s) who have the formal authority to direct your project/authorize your recommendation |
| Other stakeholders: | The person(s) who do not have formal authority but who can influence the project |
| Goals and logistics: | Budget, deadlines, types of documents, quantitative objectives, etc. |
| Voluntarily left-out answers (things that we could do but decide not to): | The actions under your control that you choose not to take |

FIGURE 2.11: A *why* card captures the frame of the diagnostic problem.

then include a mention in the *why* card to that effect; for instance, "Consider that John is mistaken or lying when saying that Harry is not at the house" (see Figure 2.12). In general, as in the previous example, it is useful to phrase all these voluntarily left-out answers as actions *you* conceivably could take.

As you finalize your *why* card, remember three important guidelines.

**Do not diagnose the problem yet.** This is only the diagnostic *definition* card, not the actual diagnosis. You will have your entire analysis to solve your problem, so refrain from putting on the card what you think might be the cause of the problem. In CIDNI problem solving, thinking before acting pays off.[48] An analogy is to imagine driving to a new location without having charted your path first (and without a GPS locator): You may be lucky and get on the right road the first time, but chances are that looking at the map first (developing a good *why* card), while delaying your departure, will ultimately result in time savings. Also, anyone who has ever embarked on a slightly wrong road knows how difficult it is to make a U-turn and go back to the previous intersection.[49] Intellectually, it is just easier to keep going and find a remedial trajectory, even when knowing full well that going back would be more efficient.

**Remove distractions.** Thinking is hard work and chances are you will look for excuses to avoid it. So remove all the noise in your *why* card: use correct grammar, precise vocabulary, and so forth.

---

48. (Smith, 1988).
49. This is called the *sunk-cost fallacy* (Arkes & Ayton, 1999; Arkes & Blumer, 1985).

| | |
|---|---|
| Situation: | Sometimes, my friend John leaves his dog Harry alone at his house |
| Complication: | Today, when John came home after being absent for 4 hours, Harry was missing |
| Diagnostic key question: | **Why** is Harry the dog missing [from my friend's house where he was left unattended for 4 hours]? |
| Decision makers: | My friend and his wife |
| Other stakeholders: | N/A |
| Goals and logistics: | Spend up to $150 on the diagnosis, design diagnostic analysis within 6 hours, conduct diagnostic analysis within 12 hours |
| Voluntarily left-out answers (things that we could do but decide not to): | Call the housekeeper to accuse her of holding Harry hostage without first making sure<br>Consider irrational explanations such as alien abduction<br>Consider that John is mistaken or lying when saying that Harry isn't at the house |

**FIGURE 2.12:** A *why* card for Harry's case.

**Do not get discouraged.** Writing a good *why* card might look simple, but it is not. It is hard and stressful, so do not panic if you encounter trouble, that is normal. Just keep at it, giving it your best for some time. Because the *why* card defines what you will do for the next few days or weeks, resist settling for mediocrity.

Once all team members agree that the *why* card is good, run through the introduction checklist one last time (see Figure 2.10). Is something bothering you? Even if you cannot yet identify what it is, this is a good indicator that you should probe further.

But if you are happy with your *why* card, and if you have captured it electronically, copy your key question and paste it onto a white page, because you are about to grow your diagnostic issue map from it.

## 3. WHAT ABOUT HARRY?

Figure 2.12 shows a *why* card for Harry. As shown, we have opted for a shorter version of the key question.

Having framed our problem—and captured it in a *what* card—and identified our diagnostic key question and captured it and other relevant information in a *why* card, we can now proceed to uncovering the root causes of the problem. Chapter 3 explains how to leverage a graphical tool, *issue maps*, to look for potential root causes and organize them so as to consider all of them exactly once.

# NOTES

**Key characteristics of projects.** Project manager Davidson Frame notes that projects are directed to achieve specific results; are finite in time with a beginning and an end; require coordinating interrelated activities; and are all unique to some degree.[50]

**Introductions in storytelling.** Director Alexander Mackendrick's analysis of classic stories provides a parallel to the situation–complication–key question approach to introductions. The situation includes the place and time period, the protagonist, and the action of the protagonist ("once upon a time . . .," "there lived a . . .," "who . . .," respectively). The complication is the obstacle ("but . . ."). Then comes the key question, the "point of attack" when the action starts.[51]

**Wicked problems.** Another name for ill-defined problems is wicked.[52] See Conklin (2005) for further description and ideas to solve those.

**Even smart monkeys get conditioned.** In the mid-1990s, Robert Cousins, a physicist at the University of California, Los Angeles, asked why every physicist was not a Bayesian (see Chapter 4). His conclusion: "The most superficial answer [. . .] is that people have generally been taught classical methods rather than Bayesian methods."[53] Decision theorists von Winterfeldt and Edwards agree.[54] (However, Stanford statistician Efron looked at the question 10 years earlier and had a different viewpoint.[55])

**The importance of framing.** For instance, see Tversky and Kahneman (1981) for how framing influences decisions and Posner's Bird–and–Trains problem discussed in Bassok and Novick (2012, p. 415) for how clever framing can significantly simplify a problem.

**System 1 versus System 2 thinking.** Barbara Spellman's introduction (National Research Council, 2011, pp. 123–125) is easily readable and Kahneman's Nobel lecture (Kahneman, 2002) offers a more detailed summary. See also Moulton, Regehr, Lingard, Merritt, and MacRae (2010) for factors that may influence transitioning from System 1 to System 2.

**Business as usual.** The legal system of some countries, including the United States and England, is based on stare decisis: the expectation that a court will decide issues in accordance with how they have been decided in the past.[56]

**Linearity of the problem-solving process.** The resolution process may be thought of as roughly linear, except for instances where new evidence warrants a revision of previous conclusions.

**Working memory.** More on how it relates to problem solving in Chapter 3.

---

50. (Frame, 2003) [pp. 2–6].
51. (Mackendrick, 2004) [pp. 78–79].
52. (Rittel, 1972), (Bardwell, 1991).
53. (Cousins, 1995).
54. (von Winterfeldt & Edwards, 1986) [pp. 161–162].
55. (Efron, 1986).
56. (Schauer, 2009) [p. 37].

CHAPTER 3

# IDENTIFY POTENTIAL ROOT CAUSES

Remember Sandra Steingraber's villagers of Chapter 2 who were so busy saving drowning people that they never thought to ask why they were caught in the river in the first place? Having framed our diagnosis, we need to uncover the problem's root causes or risk being in the same position as the villagers: working hard and achieving some success but not achieving as much as we could.

To uncover the problem's root causes, we will use a diagnostic issue map: a graphical analysis of our diagnosis question that we will build using a three-step approach. First, we will map the problem space by identifying all the possible root causes that could explain our diagnosis key question, classifying them, and developing a set of formal hypotheses. Second, we will prioritize how we want to test these hypotheses, possibly by doing a preliminary assessment of the relative probabilities of these hypotheses to focus first on the most probable ones—what physicians call establishing a differential diagnosis. Third, we will design the analysis plan for each relevant hypothesis, conduct the analysis, and draw conclusions. Chapter 4 explains how to carry out these last two steps. For now, let's look at how to build issue maps.

## 1. ISSUE MAPS: DIAGNOSTIC MAPS AND SOLUTION MAPS

An issue map is a graphical analysis of a problem; it starts with the key question on the left and explores the problem's structure by laying out its various dimensions vertically and becoming more detailed horizontally (see Figure 3.1). Such structuring aims at enhancing the clarity, thoroughness and coherence of the analysis.[1] It also provides a reference point to visualize how each piece fits in the overall picture of the problem.[2]

---

1. (Brownlow & Watson, 1987). This approach is an example of a divide and conquer approach; see (Schum, 1994) [pp. 138–139].
2. (Prime Minister's Strategy Unit, 2004) [p. 91].

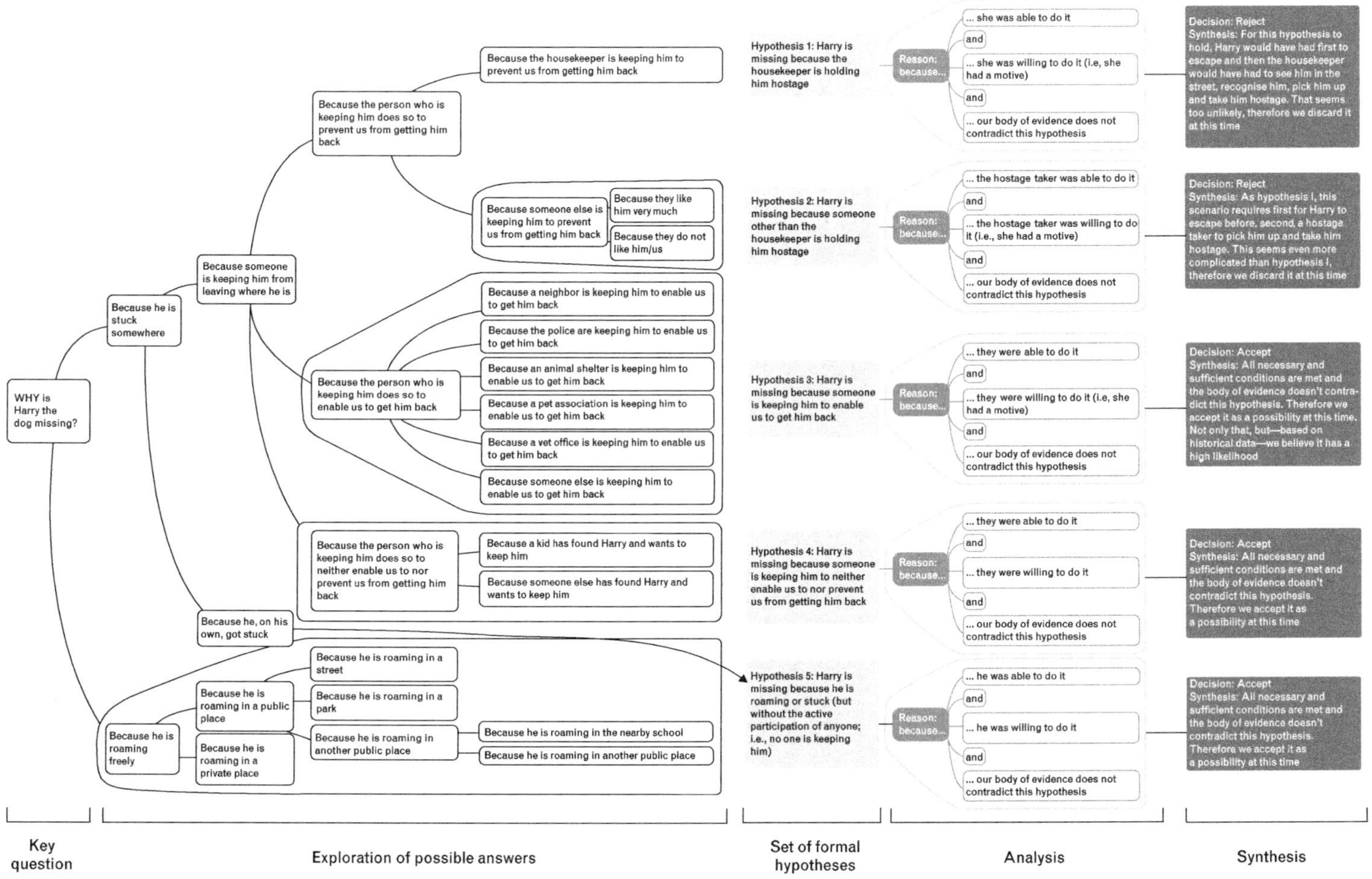

**FIGURE 3.1:** An issue map starts with the key question on the left and explores all of its possible answers. Then, it lists a set of formal hypotheses. For each hypothesis, it captures the analysis and the conclusion.

The map then summarizes these possible answers in a set of formal hypotheses to be tested before spelling out the analysis needed for the tests and capturing the evidence. Finally, the map includes the conclusion for each hypothesis.

In that respect, issue maps share properties with a number of cartographic approaches to analyze problems, such as *fault trees*,[3] *logic trees*,[4] *decision trees*,[5] *issue trees*,[6] *value trees/value hierarchies*,[7] *objective hierarchies*,[8] *probability trees*,[9] *Ishikawa* (or *cause-and-effect* or *fishbone*) *diagrams*,[10] *why–why* and *how–how diagrams*,[11] *influence diagrams*,[12] *issue diagrams*,[13] *evidence maps*,[14] *mind maps*,[15] *concept maps*,[16] *dialogue maps*,[17] *argument maps*,[18] *Wigmore charts*,[19] and *Bayesian networks*.[20]

Issue maps can help you be more complete in your logic by first making you think in a divergent pattern and then making you converge onto the most important elements. That is, you first broaden your perspective by consider various options instead of directly focusing on one, which is necessary to minimize the impact of a number of interrelated issues including:

- *Fixation*, that is, being unable to search away from a given direction;[21]
- *Premature closure*, that is, reaching a conclusion without considering all alternatives;[22]
- *Anchoring*, that is, considering options in the light of the first information received—either given in the problem or formed subjectively;[23]

---

3. (Dube-Rioux & Russo, 1988; Eisenführ et al., 2010; Fischhoff, Slovic, & Lichtenstein, 1978; Lee, Grosh, Tillman, & Lie, 1985; J. Edward Russo & Kolzow, 1994; Vesely, Goldberg, Roberts, & Haasl, 1981; von Winterfeldt & Edwards, 2007).

4. (Bommer & Scherbaum, 2008).

5. (Eisenführ et al., 2010; Kazancioglu, Platts, & Caldwell, 2005; Mingers, 1989; Quinlan, 1986, 1987), (von Winterfeldt & Edwards, 1986) [pp. 63–89].

6. (Wojick, 1975).

7. (Keeney, 1992), (Goodwin & Wright, 2009) [p. 35] (Brownlow & Watson, 1987; von Winterfeldt & Edwards, 1986).

8. (Eisenführ et al., 2010), (Keeney, 1992).

9. (Goodwin & Wright, 2009) [p. 103].

10. (Breyfogle III, 2003; Hackman & Wageman, 1995; Ishikawa, 1982).

11. (Cavallucci, Lutz, & Kucharavy, 2002; Higgins, 1994).

12. (Goodwin & Wright, 2009; Howard, 1989) (Eisenführ et al., 2010) [pp. 39–43], (Howard & Matheson, 2005).

13. (Ohmae, 1982).

14. (Mitchell, 2003).

15. (Buzan, 1976; Davies, 2010).

16. (Brinkmann, 2003; Novak, 1990; Novak & Cañas, 2006).

17. (Conklin, 2005).

18. (Gelder, 2005; Heuer & Pherson, 2011; Reed, Walton, & Macagno, 2007; Twardy, 2010; Van Gelder, 2001, 2003, 2005).

19. (T. Anderson, Schum, & Twining, 2005) [pp. 123–144], (Schum, 1994) [pp. 160–169].

20. (Hepler, Dawid, & Leucari, 2007), (Fenton, Neil, & Lagnado, 2012), (Vlek, Prakken, Renooij, & Verheij, 2013).

21. (Duncker & Lees, 1945; Jansson & Smith, 1991; Pretz, Naples, & Sternberg, 2003; Smith & Blankenship, 1991; Smith & Ward, 2012; Smith, Ward, & Schumacher, 1993; van Steenburgh, Fleck, Beeman, & Kounios, 2012; Weisberg & Alba, 1981), (Smith & Ward, 2012) [p. 467], (Pretz et al., 2003) [p. 19], (Linsey et al., 2010).

22. (Estrada, Isen, & Young, 1997; Keinan, 1987).

23. (Elstein & Schwarz, 2002; John S Hammond, Keeney, & Raiffa, 1998; Kahneman, 2011), (Hora, 2007) [pp. 142–143].

- Overconfidence, both *attitudinal overconfidence*, such as, "I know all I need to know," and *cognitive overconfidence*, such as not knowing what you do not know;[24] and
- *Confirmation bias*, that is, generating and interpreting evidence to favor one's own beliefs,[25] which is notoriously difficult to overcome.[26]

Also, by exposing a problem's underlying structure, maps may help you acquire a better representation of the problem, which is particularly useful for solving poorly understood problems.[27] This is especially relevant when diverse groups of people, each with their own incomplete view of the problem, are brought together to solve a problem. A map may help them understand how the pieces fit together.[28]

Another attribute of maps is that—by making explicit the structure of your analysis for each hypothesis, as argument maps do—they help improve your thinking.[29]

Finally, by grouping information in clusters[30] and serving as a problem's central information repository where all items of evidence are linked to the relevant hypotheses,[31] maps may help improve working memory—one's capacity to keep information in short-term

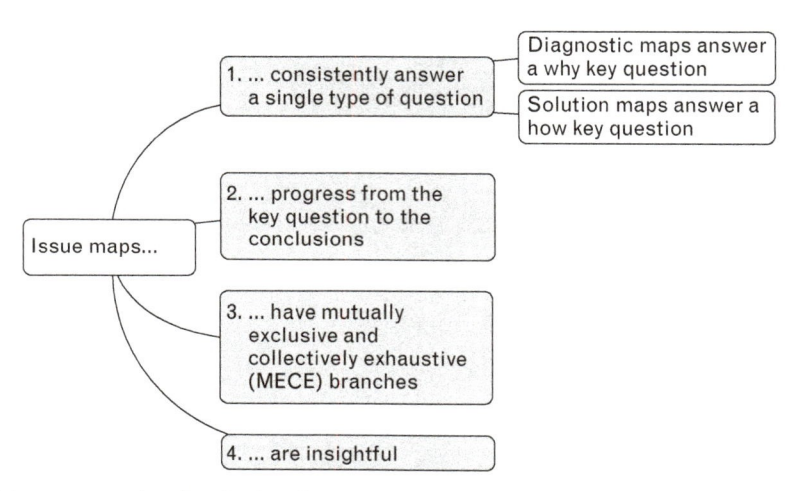

**FIGURE 3.2:** Issue maps obey four basic rules.

---

24. (Berner & Graber, 2008; Fischhoff, 1982; Klayman, Soll, González-Vallejo, & Barlas, 1999; McKenzie, 1997; Taleb, 2007; Yates, Lee, & Shinotsuka, 1996), see also (Hora, 2007) [p. 144].
25. (Chamberlin, 1965; Dunbar & Klahr, 2012a; Ness, 2012; Platt, 1964) (Ditto & Lopez, 1992; Dunbar & Klahr, 2012b; Macpherson & Stanovich, 2007; Nickerson, 1998).
26. (Dunbar & Klahr, 2012b; Elstein, 2009; Macpherson & Stanovich, 2007). This list is not exhaustive; see (Croskerry, 2002; Tversky & Kahneman, 1974) for more on bias and heuristics shortfalls.
27. (Blessing & Ross, 1996; Buckingham Shum et al., 1997; Cox, Irby, & Bowen, 2006; Kulpa, 1994).
28. (Brownlow & Watson, 1987).
29. (Rider & Thomason, 2010; Twardy, 2010).
30. (Bettman, Johnson, & Payne, 1991).
31. (Larkin & Simon, 1987).

memory and manipulate it despite distractions.[32] This is valuable because limits in our working memory constrain our ability to solve complex problems.[33]

In a complete analysis, one builds two issue maps: first, a diagnostic map to identify the potential root causes of the problem, and, second, a solution map to identify potential solutions. Both types obey the same four basic rules, shown in Figure 3.2. Let's look at those.

## 2. MAPS CONSISTENTLY ANSWER THE KEY QUESTION

The first rule of issue maps is that they consistently answer the key question. As we have seen in the previous chapter, we only need to consider two types of key questions: diagnostic and solution ones. So, if our key question is diagnostic, our entire map will answer *why* questions.

Ensuring that a map consistently addresses only one type of question sounds trivial, but it is easy to lose one's focus when dealing with complex problems. To avoid confusion, populate maps with complete hypothetical answers to the key question in the form of self-contained affirmations rather than titles. Indeed, if an element is a title, the reader has to guess how to interpret it, which can cause confusion.

To illustrate, consider Figure 3.3 (a). Breaking down, "Why is our profitability so low?" into the titles "revenues" and "costs" is not sufficient, because it requires guesswork on the reader's part. What about revenues? Are they concentrated on too few clients, too low, too dependent on economic cycles? In contrast, Figure 3.3 (b) shows how using complete ideas removes ambiguities.

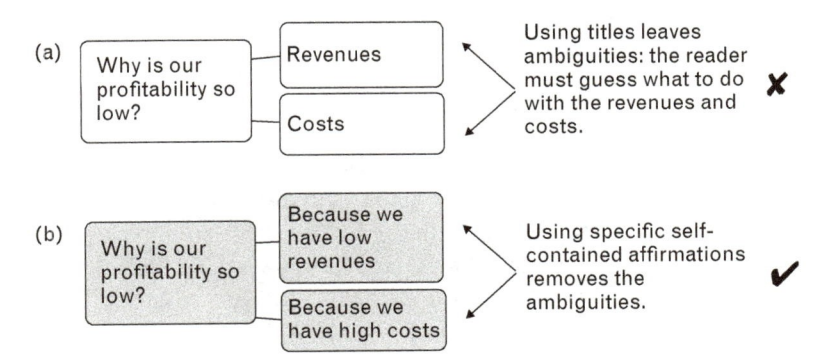

**FIGURE 3.3:** The elements of an issue map are complete hypothetical answers to the key question—in the form of self-contained affirmations—to leave no ambiguities.

---

32. (Baddeley, 2003; Green & Dunbar, 2012).
33. (Baddeley, 1992; Dufresne, Gerace, Hardiman, & Mestre, 1992; Dunbar & Klahr, 2012b; Halford, Baker, McCredden, & Bain, 2005; Miller, 1956), (Brownlow & Watson, 1987), (Olson, 1996) [p. 10]. See also (Simon, 1996) [pp. 66–67].

It might seem obvious that, when talking about increasing profitability, we are talking about increasing revenues and decreasing costs, but, in the context of complex problems, perceived obviousness is dangerous for at least three reasons:

- First, because what is obvious to you might not be so to someone else;
- Second, because what is obvious today might not be so in the future as you uncover new evidence in your analysis and your thinking evolves; and
- Third, because accepting things as obvious undermines creativity. At times, innovative thinking requires that we unlearn obsolete mental models. That is, we replace old logic with something radically new.[34] If, however, you implicitly expect yourself and the project team to question assumptions in some instances and to understand "obvious" elements in others—and to know when to do one or the other—you are undermining this creative process.

In mathematician J. E. Littlewood's words, "two trivialities omitted can add up to an *impasse*." Applied mathematician Michael McIntyre notes that masters of writing know how much omission they can get away with but notes that, for the rest of us, it is wiser to play it safe.[35] The idea then is to make things unambiguous so that, if anything appears ambiguous, it stands out and can be questioned.

In addition, formulating the elements of your map as ideas requires constructing phrases with action verbs. Making those actions parallel can help sharpen your thinking by eliminating potential gaps, as we will discuss more extensively in Chapter 5.

So, the first rule of a diagnostic map is to consistently answer a *why* key question. Next, let's look at how it progresses.

## 3. MAPS PROGRESS FROM THE KEY QUESTION TO THE CONCLUSIONS

Going back to Figure 3.2, the second rule of issue maps is to progress from the key question to your conclusions. This starts with exposing the structure of the question by identifying its various dimensions. The map begins with the key question and breaks it down into its parts. Then it breaks these parts into smaller parts, revealing the details of the problem as the map progresses to the right (see Figure 3.4).

Starting with a *why* question, a diagnosis map displays hypotheses: Harry is missing because he is stuck somewhere or because he is roaming freely. These can be further refined into sub-cases: he may be stuck as the result of someone keeping him or because he, Figures 3.4, 3.5, 3.6, 3.10, 3.29, got stuck. If someone is keeping him, it may be to prevent us from getting him back, to enable us to get him back, or neither. Other elements in the map can be broken down similarly. The idea is to explore the problem space by uncovering

---

34. (Assink, 2006; Baker & Sinkula, 2002).
35. (McIntyre, 1997).

```
                                              ┌─────────────────────┐
                                              │ Because the person who is │
                                              │ keeping him does so to    │
                                              │ prevent us from getting him│
                                              │ back                      │
                          ┌──────────────────┐ ├─────────────────────┤
                          │ Because someone is│ │ Because the person who is │
                          │ keeping him from  │─│ keeping him does so to    │
         ┌─────────────┐  │ leaving where he is│ │ enable us to get him back │
         │ Because he is│──┤                  │ ├─────────────────────┤
         │ stuck        │  └──────────────────┘ │ Because the person who is │
         │ somewhere    │                       │ keeping him does so to    │
┌────────┤              │                       │ neither enable us to nor  │
│ WHY is │              │                       │ prevent us from getting   │
│ Harry  │              │  ┌──────────────────┐ │ him back                  │
│ the dog│              │──│ Because he, on his│ └─────────────────────┘
│ missing│              │  │ own, got stuck    │
│   ?    │              │  └──────────────────┘
└────────┤              │                       ┌─────────────────────┐
         │              │                       │ Because he is roaming│
         │ Because he is│   ┌─────────────────┐ │ in a street          │
         │ roaming      │───│ Because he is   │ ├─────────────────────┤
         │ freely       │   │ roaming in a    │─│ Because he is roaming│
         │              │   │ public place    │ │ in a park            │
         └─────────────┘    └─────────────────┘ ├─────────────────────┤
                            │                   │ Because he is roaming│
                            │                   │ in another public place│
                            │                   └─────────────────────┘
                            │ ┌─────────────────┐
                            └─│ Because he is   │
                              │ roaming in a    │
                              │ private place   │
                              └─────────────────┘
```

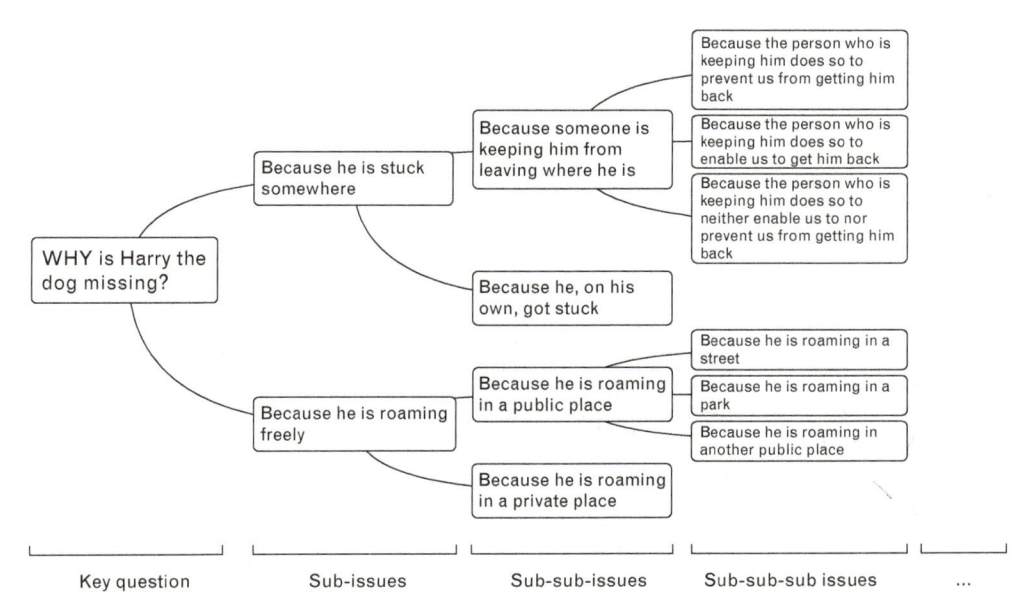

| Key question | Sub-issues | Sub-sub-issues | Sub-sub-sub issues | ... |

**FIGURE 3.4:** Issue maps break the key question into increasingly detailed parts, thereby revealing the structure of the question.

all the possible root causes of the key question and creating a framework where they can be systematically and thoroughly analyzed.[36]

**First, make explicit the structure of your key question.** Breaking down elements continues until the description of each potential cause is sufficiently explicit. This will probably result in a map with many elements. For instance, Figure 3.5 shows how, for even a rather simple problem, the map expands extensively. Once you have achieved that level of sufficient explicitness (the next section discusses how to recognize when that happens), stop developing your map and switch to convergent thinking to develop a set of hypotheses.

**Second, lay out your hypothesis set.** When the structure is sufficiently explicit, associate a hypothesis with each element or group of elements in your map. You can associate a hypothesis with a terminal element, (i.e., one without any child, that is, without any elements to its right), with an internal element, or with a combination, as Figure 3.6 shows.

Maps commonly contain dozens of terminal elements. Although one could analyze each independently, it is usually not desirable to do so. Instead, organize elements in judicious groups and assign a formal hypothesis to each group (more on this in Chapter 5).

Technically, all the elements of the map to the right of the key question are hypotheses. But what we mean by a "set of formal hypotheses" is a group of two to ten precise summary statements, each of which is testable and affirms: "This part of the map is a significant cause of the key question."

Formal hypotheses are useful to improve our thinking because they help overcome memory limitations and help narrow the size of the problem space.[37]

---

36. This process corresponds to Schum's *mutation of hypotheses* (Schum, 1994) [pp. 192–194].
37. (Joseph & Patel, 1990).

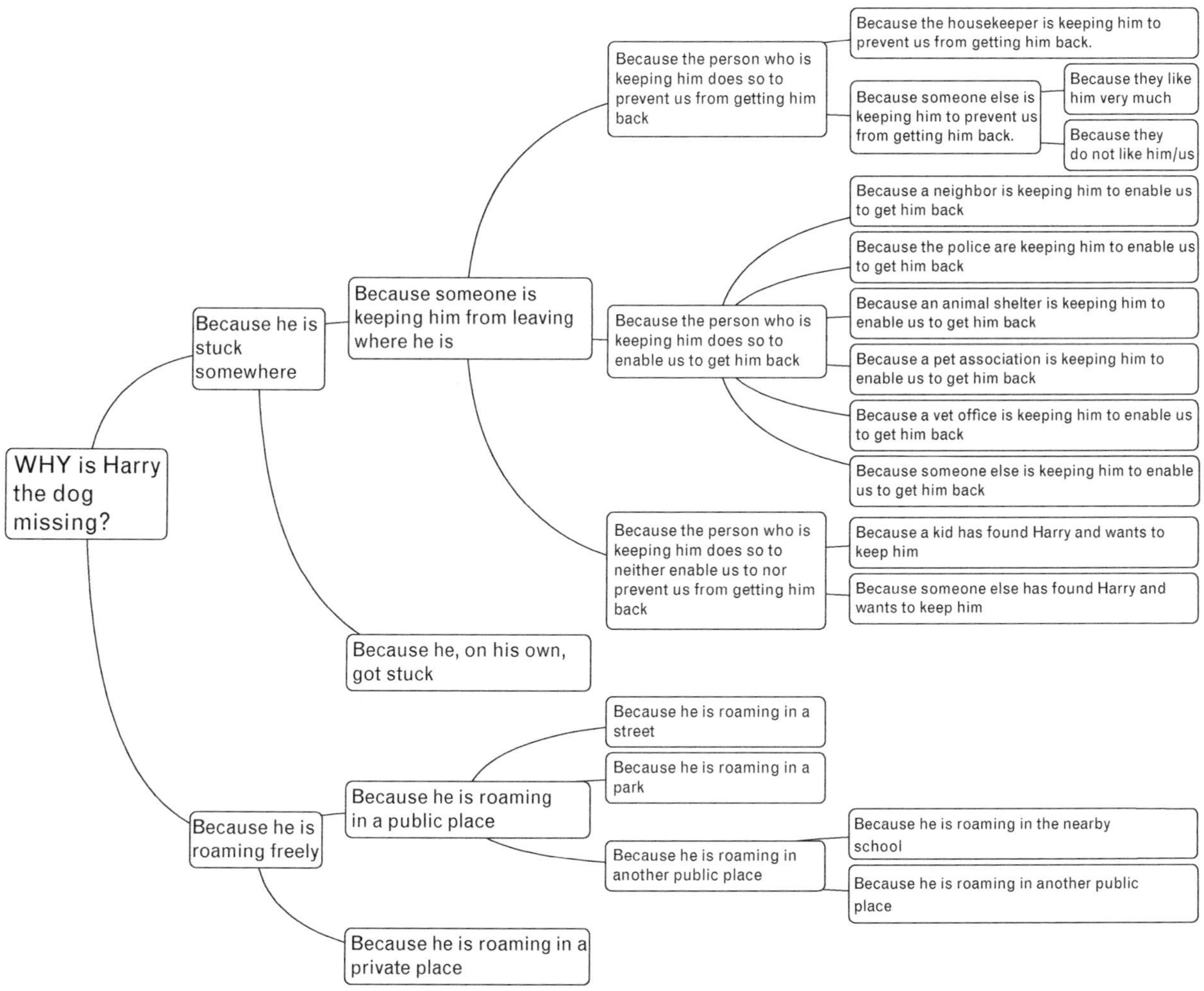

**FIGURE 3.5:** Keep drilling into the problem by identifying new layers of structure.

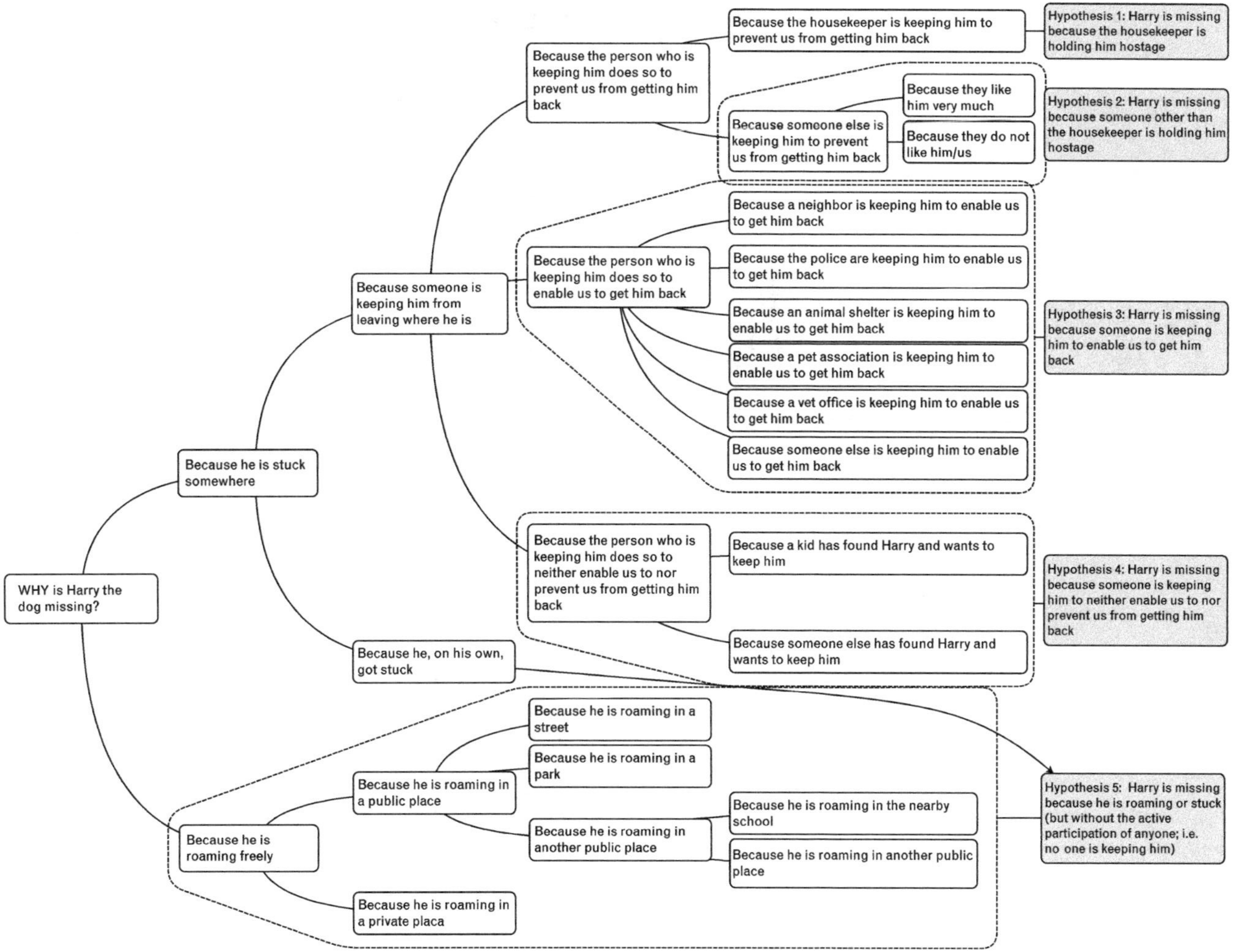

FIGURE 3.6: Associate each element in the map to a formal hypothesis.

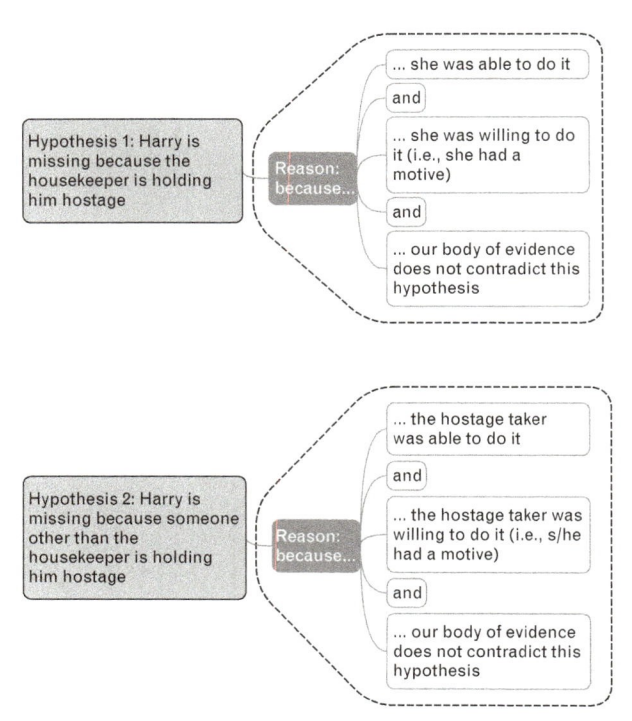

**FIGURE 3.7:** For each hypothesis, identify the required analysis.

It is important that every element in the map be associated with exactly one hypothesis—either directly or through its children. That way, your set of hypotheses covers your entire problem: This is important because, if you have correctly identified all the possible answers to your key question, you now *know* that the solution is in one (or more) of these hypotheses.

**Third, explain how you will test each hypothesis.** The next step is to identify the analysis that you need to conduct to test each hypothesis (see Figure 3.7).

To illustrate, let's go to our case study. Harry is missing, and, as Figure 3.7 shows, we suspect that the housekeeper may be keeping him hostage. How should we test this? We propose to identify a set of necessary and sufficient conditions. Specifically, Was she able to do it? Was she willing to do it (i.e., has she got a motive?)? and Is our body of evidence consistent with this hypothesis? An affirmative answer to all three questions would significantly raise the probability that this hypothesis is correct. Similarly, if there is strong evidence against any of these conditions, there is a high probability that she did not do it.

Someone might disagree with this analysis: perhaps other conditions besides these three should be included. Or perhaps we should not think in terms of necessary and sufficient conditions; indeed, many case law issues, for instance, are not decided by necessary and sufficient conditions.[38] For instance, a detective might look for means (the ability to commit the crime), motive (the reason to commit the crime), and opportunity (the chance

---

38. (Hafner, 1987).

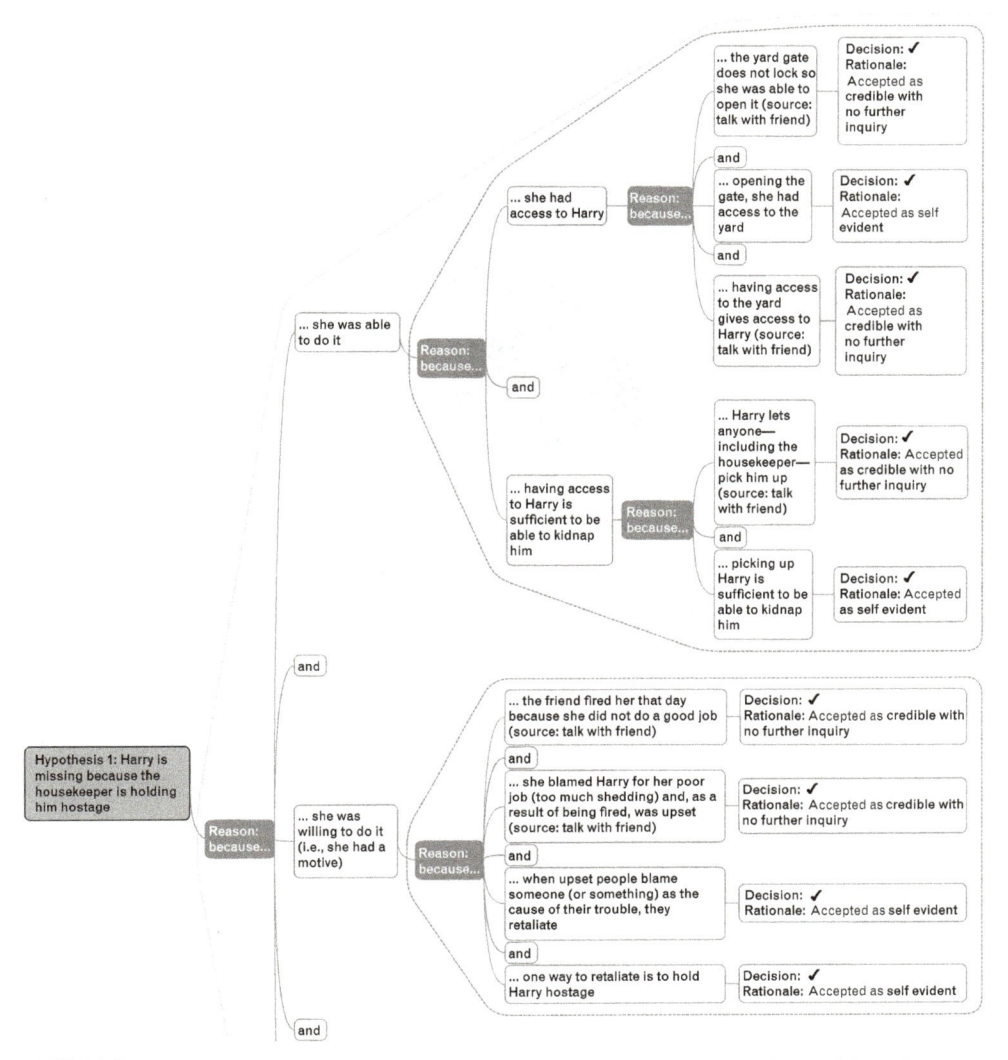

**FIGURE 3.8:** Issue maps are also useful to capture the analysis and synthesis for each hypothesis.

to commit the crime). These are worthy objections, and the project team should have these conversations and decide whether this is the right approach. The point is, however, that by explicitly showing the proposed analysis, the map helps provoke these conversations and enrich them.

**Fourth, prioritize the analysis and conduct it.** Our approach so far has been to include all possible answers to the key question, irrespective of their likelihood. Having laid out this analysis plan, you should now decide which hypotheses to test first. While you prioritize, call upon your intuition to decide with which hypothesis to start your analysis. As you conduct it, capture both your logic and the evidence in the map. Figure 3.8 shows how a map is useful to record the information that will help you decide whether to accept or reject

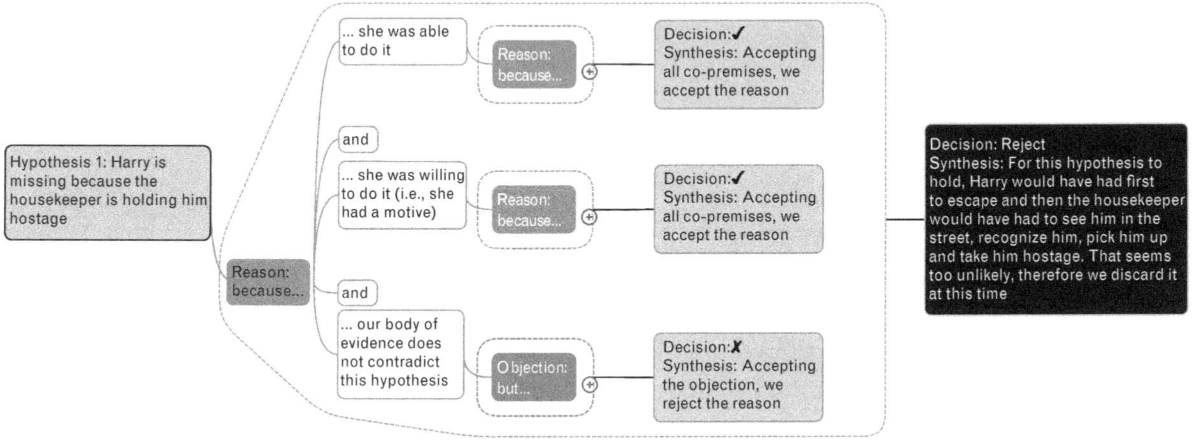

**FIGURE 3.9:** The last step in an issue map is to conclude on each hypothesis.

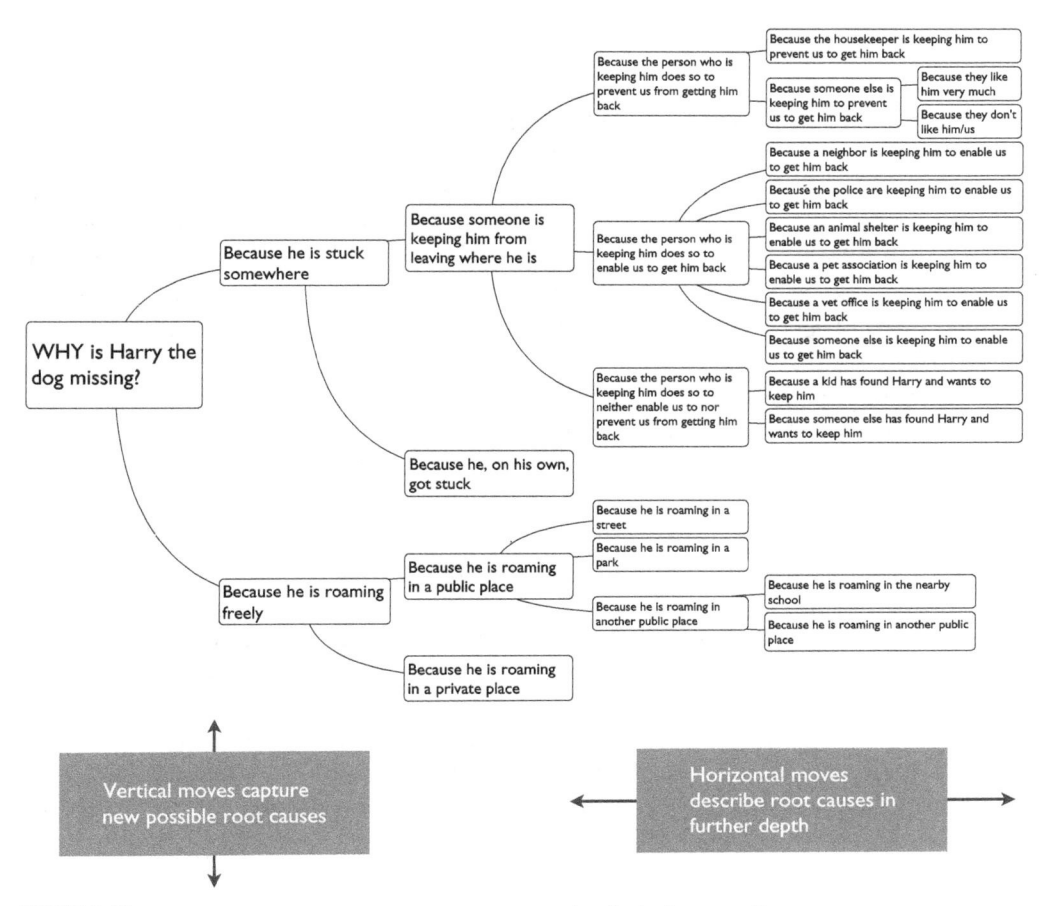

**FIGURE 3.10:** Maps use both dimensions to map out completely the key question.

each hypothesis.[39] That is, your diagnostic map becomes the road map of your analysis. It will also be a central repository where, at a glance, you can view what you have done and what is missing. As such, your map will evolve during your analysis: far from sticking rigidly to your original understanding of the problem, your map should reflect your latest thinking, showing which ideas you have discarded, which you are still pursuing and, possibly, which you are favoring. Therefore, as you uncover evidence, do not hesitate to cross out some of its branches, highlight existing ones, and develop new ones.

**Fifth, draw your conclusions.** Once you have gathered evidence and decided which hypotheses are valid, conclude on the root causes of your problem and capture these conclusions in your map (see Figure 3.9). Chapter 4 will discuss these processes in detail.

Summarizing, the first two rules of issue maps govern their general purpose and mechanics. As Figure 3.10 shows, vertically, maps consider alternative answers to the key question and horizontally they investigate the nature of these answers in further depth.

The last two rules are about how to structure maps.

---

39. Technically, especially in a statistical sense, you do not accept a hypothesis but, rather, fail to reject it. See Chapter 4.

Identify Potential Root Causes • 57

# 4. MAPS HAVE A MECE STRUCTURE

The third rule of maps helps us be complete and efficient in our analysis by considering every potential answer exactly once, having neither involuntary overlaps nor gaps in our analysis.

Having no overlaps means that a map's branches are mutually exclusive (ME): If you consider a potential answer to the key question in one branch, do not consider it in another.

Figure 3.11 illustrates the ME concept. Imagine that you are driving and getting to an intersection. You can go straight or turn left, but you cannot do both at the same time: choosing one course of action precludes you from choosing the other; therefore, the actions are mutually exclusive.

Having no gaps means that the branches of a map, taken as a whole, are collectively exhaustive (CE); that is, they account for all potential answers at least once. So, if you are getting to that crossroad, you might continue straight in your lane, change lanes, turn left, make a U-turn, or stop (see Figure 3.12).

Figure 3.13 illustrates how these two properties combine. In the resulting mutually exclusive and collectively exhaustive (MECE) structure, you have considered all possible elements exactly once.

**The structure of maps is MECE.** Note that the MECEness of issue maps applies only to their structure, not to the answers themselves. This is an important distinction, so let's look at it in further detail.

Mutual exclusivity implies a preclusion: Including an answer to your key question in a branch of your map precludes you from including it in another branch. This preclusion for the structure of the map is good because it prevents redundancies, which helps you be efficient. If you consider an idea once, there is no need to consider it again.

**The answers themselves, however, are not necessarily MECE.** This preclusion requirement does not necessarily apply to the answers themselves. For instance, a company might not be profitable because it has low revenues *and* high costs, as Figure 3.14 shows. Having one problem—low revenues—does not preclude the company from also having the

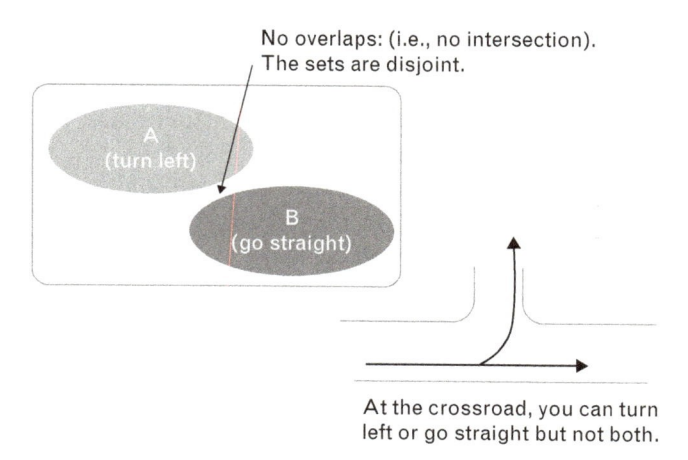

**FIGURE 3.11:** "Mutually exclusive" means that there are no overlaps in the structure of a map. If an element is in one branch, it cannot be in another.

No gaps: you have considered all options.

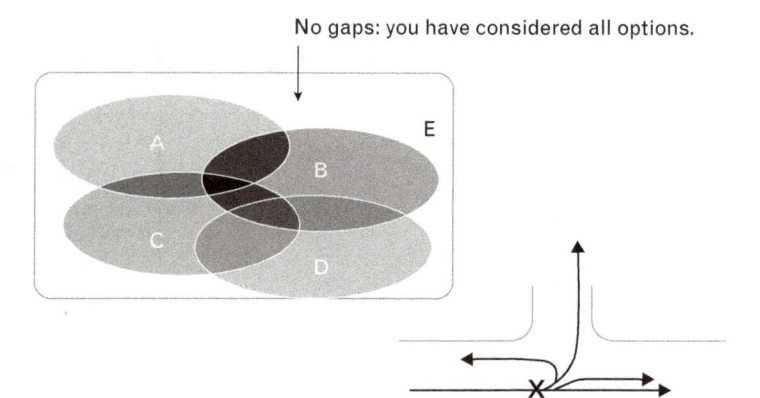

At the crossroad, you can drive straight, change lanes, turn left, make a U-turn, or stop.

**FIGURE 3.12:** "Collectively exhaustive" means that there are no gaps: you have considered all potential answers at least once.

other—high costs. (In medicine, this simultaneous presence of independent conditions is called *comorbidity*.)

The takeaway is that the answers in the map are not MECE, they are independent and collectively exhaustive, or ICE. Here, *independent* means distinct: An element of the map does not require the help of another to answer the key question. (This is analogous to the independence of claims in critical thinking, which is different from independence in probability theory where the occurrence or nonoccurrence of one event does not affect the occurrence or nonoccurrence of another.)[40]

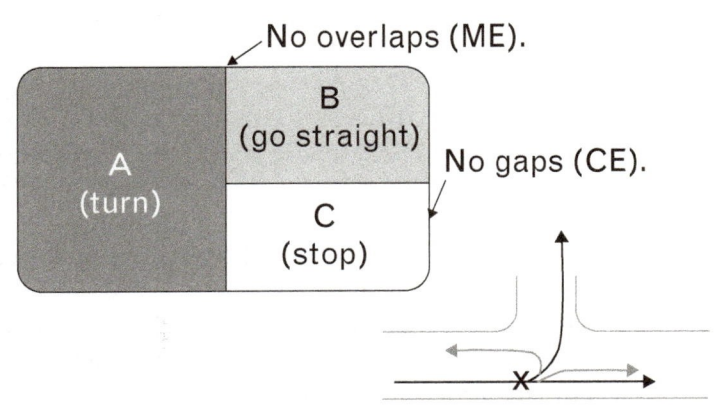

No overlaps (ME).
No gaps (CE).

A (turn)
B (go straight)
C (stop)

At the crossroad, you can A. turn (including taking the left road, changing lanes or making a U-turn), B. go straight. or C. stop. This is a MECE structure for your actions.

**FIGURE 3.13:** (A) turning; (B) going straight; or (C) stopping is a MECE structure for describing what you can do at the crossroad.

---

40. (Twardy, 2010). For more on probabilistic independence, see (Schum, 1994) [pp. 150–151].

Identify Potential Root Causes • 59

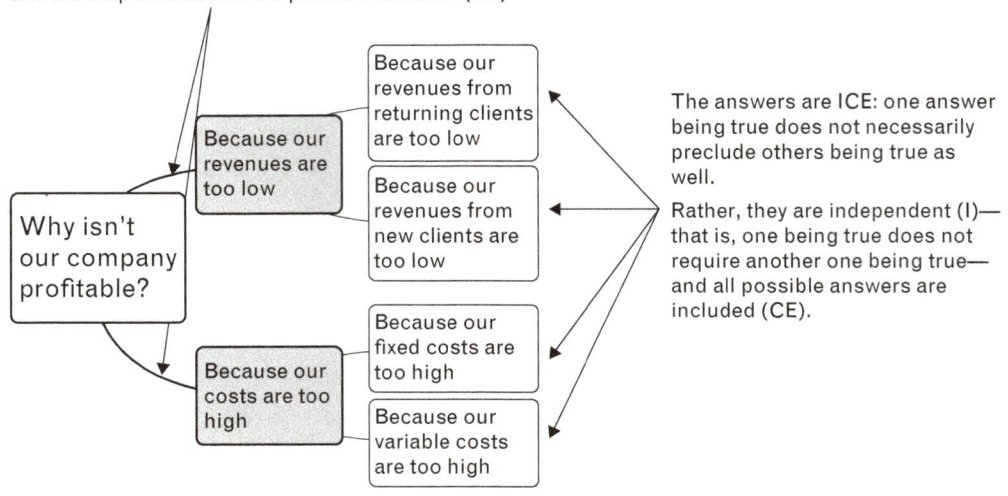

**FIGURE 3.14:** Although the structure of the map is MECE, the answers themselves are ICE.

In the profitability example, Figure 3.15, (a) shows how one can force both the structure and the answers to be MECE. Here, the first level has three branches: one situation where only revenues are too low, one where only costs are too high, and, to achieve collective exhaustiveness, a third situation where both happen concurrently. By adding an exclusionary criterion (the word "only") in the first two branches and an inclusionary criterion ("both") in the third, we ensure that the answers are not just independent but truly mutually exclusive.[41]

But forcing answers to be MECE comes at a price. First, the map is less user-friendly in that some readers may have to think longer to understand the breakdown structure. Second, it raises a significant challenge when thinking about the next level of the map: How will you break down that third branch? Furthermore, it is unclear whether the resulting map is more insightful than the one in Figure 3.15 (b) with ICE answers (more on insight in the next section). Therefore, forcing the answers to be MECE has little value in this case. This seems to be generalizable: It usually pays off to focus on making the structure MECE and not worry whether the answers themselves are MECE or ICE.

Having established the importance of MECEness in maps, let's talk about how to make your structures more MECE.

**Generate potential answers before the structure.** When dealing with an unfamiliar subject, it may be easier to first generate potential answers—trying to be collectively exhaustive—before structuring them in a map (being mutually exclusive), rather than the reverse. That is, first apply creative thinking and then critical thinking.

**Defer criticism.** This is idea generation, not idea evaluation (that will come when testing hypotheses, in the next chapter). Thinking creatively requires suspending judgment.[42]

---

41. See (First, 2005).
42. (De Bono, 1970).

60 • STRATEGIC THINKING IN COMPLEX PROBLEM SOLVING

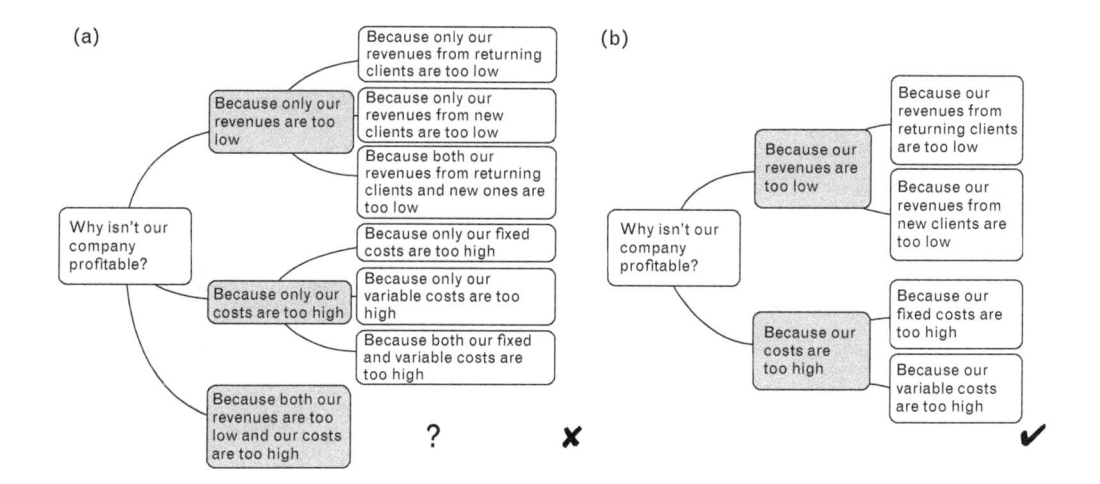

**MECE structure with MECE answers**

One can find such a structure, but it complicates the map...

**MECE structure with ICE answers**

...instead, it is usually desirable to use a MECE structure and accept that the answers might only be ICE.

**FIGURE 3.15:** One could have a MECE structure with MECE answers, but this is not necessarily desirable.

Paraphrasing creativity theorist Tim Hurson, the creative thinking process is generative, producing something out of nothing, but its product is fragile: The ideas generated are not ready to sustain serious criticism.[43] Therefore, you need to let your ideas gather some strength, so do not be too quick in deciding that they do not belong in your map; judging new ideas too early restricts innovation (see Figure 3.16 for an illustration).[44] Instead, strive to be nonjudgmental, at least until your idea has gathered some strength and stands a chance to resist a critical-thinking analysis; and make sure to capture everything that occurs to you.[45]

Psychologist Edward De Bono points out that some potential answers will be obviously inappropriate.[46] But the point of delaying judgment in these cases is to extract as much usefulness out of these ideas as possible before discarding them. For instance, can they be modified so that they can become appropriate? Or can they lead you to understand your problem better? Or can they lead you to realize that your current perspective is wrong? Observing that in the early 20th century, the idea of sinking battleships by having planes drop bombs on them was ridiculed by experts including the U.S. Secretary of War, University of Pennsylvania's Paul Schoemaker points out that smart people frequently make wrong assumptions about the future with great certainty.[47] So entertaining even "dumb" ideas for some time may not be a waste of time after all.

43. (Hurson, 2007).
44. (Adams, 2001).
45. (Maier, 1963) [pp. 125–126], (John S. Hammond, Keeney, & Raiffa, 2002) [p. 53].
46. (De Bono, 1970).
47. (Schoemaker, 1995).

Identify Potential Root Causes • 61

"Nice, but we'll need an environmental-impact study, a warranty, recall bulletins, recycling facilities, and twenty-four-hour customer support."

FIGURE 3.16: At first, withhold judgment of ideas and consider every logically valid one.
Reproduced with permission from Tom Cheney/The New Yorker Collection/The Cartoon Bank.

Steven Sample, an engineer and the former president of the University of Southern California, calls this process free thinking: "The key to thinking free is first to allow your mind to contemplate really outrageous ideas, and only subsequently apply the constraints of practicality, practicability, legality, cost, time, and ethics. Thinking free is an unnatural act; not one person in a thousand can do it without enormous effort."[48]

So, withhold judgment: do not give any consideration to whether an idea is too unlikely to be a cause for your problem. If it is a logically valid answer to your key question—no matter how far-fetched—and it is not in the "voluntarily left-out answers" section of your *why* card, include it in your map.

**Be more CE by balancing satisficing and optimizing.** *Satisficing* combines "satisfying" and "sufficing." The term was coined by economics Nobel Prize laureate Herbert Simon in the 1950s; it is defined as, when looking for answers to a problem, accepting an available option as soon as you find one that meets a minimal threshold.[49] Satisficing is especially appealing when there are many alternatives to choose from and the lack of a known structure in the problem makes it difficult to evaluate alternatives.[50]

At the other end of the spectrum, *optimizing* means looking for the best possible answer. No matter how good the answers you find along the way, you keep looking for a better one.

In regards to culinary tastes, a pure satisficer will always go to the same restaurant and order the same dish (see Figure 3.17). After all, if he likes it, why take a chance on something

---

48. (Sample & Bennis, 2002). See also (Berger, 2010) [pp. 61–66] for how designers break free of conventional patterns.
49. (Simon, 1972).
50. (Simon, 1990).

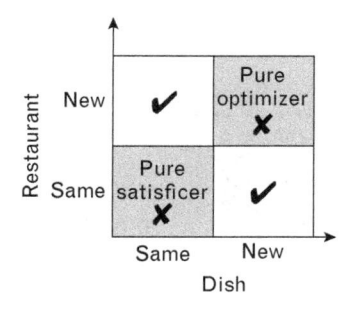

**FIGURE 3.17:** A pure satisficer always sticks to a known, acceptable solution whereas a pure optimizer never stops looking for a better one. Neither of these approaches is ideal when solving complex problems.

else? Conversely, a pure optimizer will always try a new restaurant and a new dish because, no matter what she has tried before, surely there is something better out there.

The pure satisficer has found an answer that is good enough and sticks with it. So he throws away innovation and there is no room for progress. On the other hand, the pure optimizer throws away practical considerations, such as deadlines. In fact, real-world optimization is impossible.[51] So neither extreme is ideal; instead, you should adopt a balanced approach. You may do so by trying the chocolate soufflé in numerous restaurants or sticking to one place and trying every dish on the menu. Either way, consider using several sittings to do so.

**First, strive to optimize.** Decision scientist Baruch Fischhoff and his collaborators showed that people presented with pruned fault trees did not realize how much was left out and, as a result, overestimated the exhaustiveness of the tree. So you must make your diagnostic map as exhaustive as possible.[52]

Paraphrasing American psychologist Osborn—the man who popularized brainstorming—before having a good idea, you need to have lots of ideas, and it is okay to have bad ones.[53] Celebrated chemist Linus Pauling agrees; as he put it, "The way to get good ideas is to get lots of ideas and throw the bad ones away."[54] For an illustration, consider Edison's famous experiments of passing electricity through hundreds of materials during several years before selecting carbon filaments.[55]

So your quest for answers should start with optimization. This is the divergent thinking part where you are looking for innovative ways to answer your key question. Actively looking for new answers, even absurd ones, will get you out of your comfort zone and force you to explore new ways.[56]

---

51. See (Simon, 1996) [pp. 28–29].
52. (Fischhoff et al., 1978), see also (Hora, 2007) [p. 143].
53. (Osborn, 1953).
54. See also (Bo T. Christensen & Schunn, 2009) [pp. 48–49].
55. (Ness, 2012). Exploring various options supports effective group decisions; see (Nixon & Littlepage, 1992) for empirical evidence and a discussion.
56. (Adams, 2001).

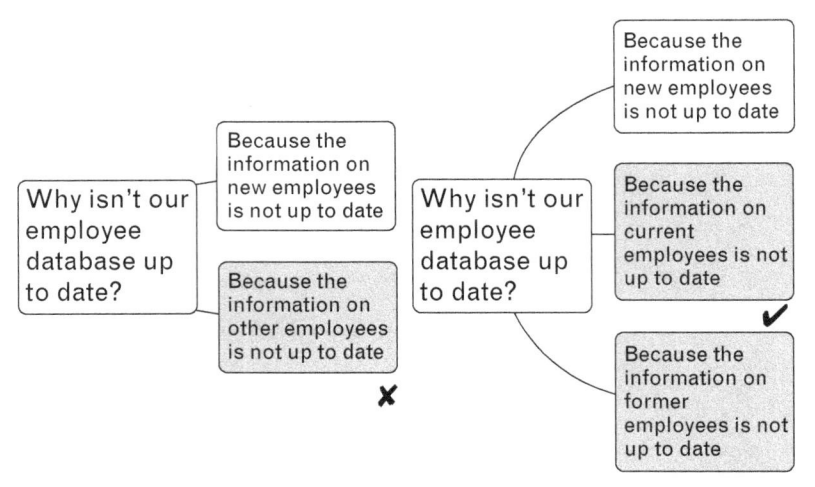

**FIGURE 3.18:** Spell out all the elements in your map.

Do not stick with the usual suspects for answers: go look for the irrational ones, the dumb ideas, the suggestions that will make people laugh at you.[57] At this stage, the plausibility of an answer is irrelevant. Rather, you are interested in mapping the universe of possibilities; that is, being as collectively exhaustive as possible. (Chapter 5 has more ideas to help you do that.)

You can use your map to help you improve your divergent thinking. For instance, do not settle for a branch that says "other." Instead, make a conscious effort to name the elements of that branch (see Figure 3.18). This is especially true for the early nodes of the map, because each of those impact a large part of the map.

Let's apply this to the example of an information technology company that wants to understand why it is not more profitable. Figure 3.19 shows how a standard breakdown of profitability between revenues (top branch) and costs (bottom) can be initially used. Revenues may then be broken down by types of products (maintaining licenses vs. maintenance services). And we can drill deeper; for instance, the reason why our volume of sales is too low might be because some of our clients switch to competitors or because they stay with us but do not contract maintenance.

Those clients who switch might do so because our offering is inferior to our competitors' or because it is competitive but clients still think it is inferior. If it is inferior, it might be because our price, our product, our promotion, and/or our place (the "4Ps" of the marketing mix, see further in this chapter) are not right.

And, indeed, you should break these down even further: our price can be wrong because it is too high or because it feels too high; perhaps because we do not price our goods in the right way, such as asking clients to pay cash when they want to pay on a monthly basis or asking for a monthly payment that is too high for too short a time. By now, we are at the seventh level of detail and the map can go on for several more.

---

57. Designers are encouraged to leverage ignorance to be creative; see (Berger, 2010) [pp. 24–28]. See also (Thompson, 2011) [pp. 205–206] for the value of exposing teams to unusual or even incorrect options.

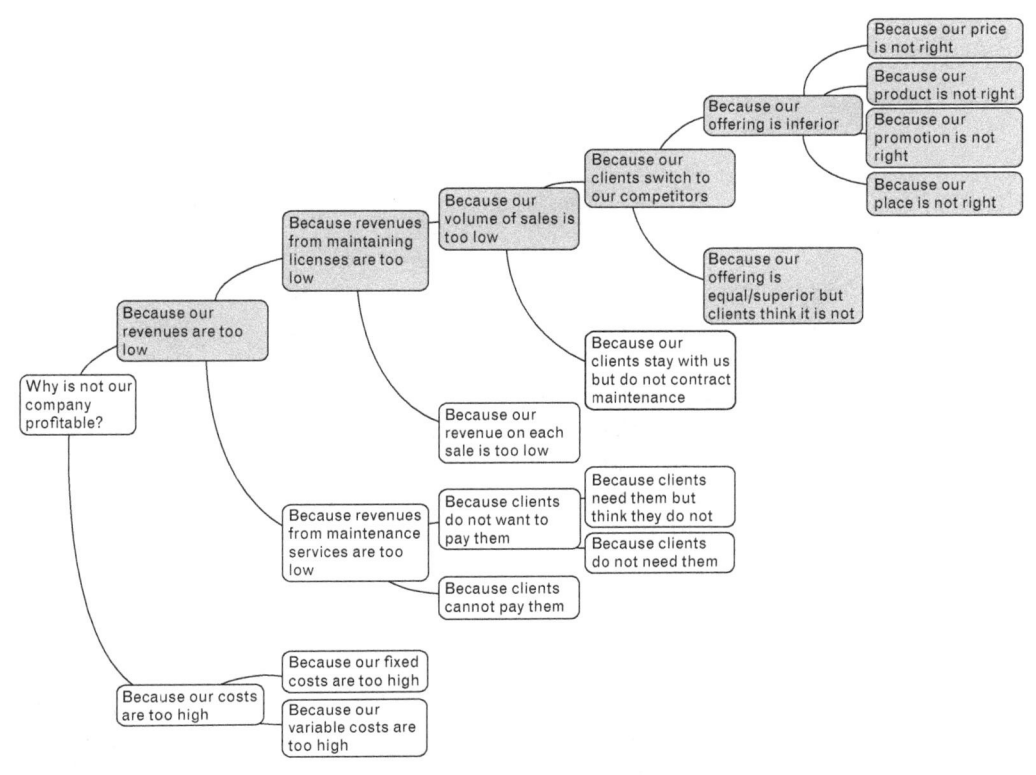

**FIGURE 3.19:** Your diagnostic map can support your divergent thinking by showing branches that are less developed than others.

When seeing this for the first time, some are skeptical, arguing that maps make the problem-solving process more complicated. Furthermore, creating a map is time consuming, and it seems easier to just "go with your gut."

But the complexity is in the problem, whether one maps it out or not. Just as a geographic map helps us navigate a new territory, an issue map helps clarify an unfamiliar problem, making the complexity explicit by helping you identify all the relevant elements and placing them in the analysis. A map also clarifies which analysis is necessary, helping to devise a systematic plan to test hypotheses.

It is true that creating a map requires a time investment, sometimes several days. This might not be worthwhile for a simpler problem or one in which you have extensive expertise. For CIDNI problems, however, especially ones where a misdiagnosis is costly, going through this process may be a better approach than going with a gut-feeling answer and being wrong.

**Decide when to stop.** If you were to take the instructions to be collectively exhaustive literally, you would become stuck in looking for additional causes indefinitely. This is not desirable.

Indeed, information has economics, with costs and benefits of obtaining additional information. As we will discuss in Chapter 4, more information is not always better. For instance, looking for additional information has an opportunity cost: While you are doing it, you are not doing other things that may be more beneficial for solving your

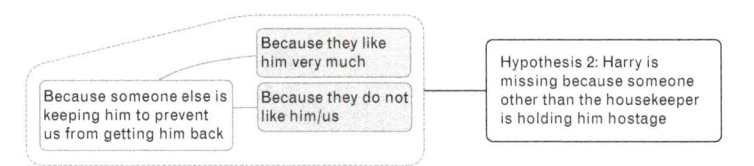

**FIGURE 3.20:** Stop drilling when expanding further does not bring additional practical value.

problem. Or, if more information is expensive to obtain—in time and/or money—but will only have a small payoff, its costs exceed its benefits and you may be better off not pursuing it.

So you will need to decide when to stop expanding your issue map and move on to formulating your hypothesis set. There is no hard-set rule to know when that moment has come because it is highly case-dependent, but here are some indicators.

If you are on a deadline, you can set up a maximum time for your analysis. But beware: Time pressure does not promote creativity and, in general, is linked to decreased performance, so avoid being pressured by the clock if you can.[58]

Alternatively, you can set a goal for a total number of ideas. This is also risky because you might sacrifice quality just to reach your goal. If you are using this approach, consider picking a high number and be prepared to decide which ideas actually count as new contributions.

Yet another way is to set a goal based on the levels of breakdowns. The five whys root-cause analysis, for instance, is widely used by quality engineers and managers. It states that one should drill into the key question through at least five layers.[59]

This is also risky, because if your goal is too low, you might not push yourself enough and, if it is too high, you might include some artificial levels of breakdown just to reach it.

Perhaps the best approach is to think in terms of the added value of each node.[60] To decide, use two questions: ask yourself, "What else?" and "In what specific ways?"

"What else can be the cause of the problem?" helps you develop the map vertically, ensuring that you have considered all of its variables or dimensions.[61]

"In what specific ways is this contributing to the original problem?" helps you develop the map horizontally: It helps you identify all potential states of each variable. You know you can safely stop expanding your map once answering this question does not provide any additional practical insight.

Figure 3.20 shows how we have reached this stage in Harry's case. We ventured that someone might be keeping Harry to prevent us from recovering him either because they like him very much or because they dislike him/us. In what specific ways do they like him so much? Maybe Harry is cute. Maybe he is friendly, funny, or his hair color matches the finder's sofa color. Although valid, we feel—and this is just that, a judgment call—that these considerations do not bring additional practical insight to explaining why Harry is missing,

---

58. (Elstein, 2009; Parnes, 1961; Reiter-Palmon & Illies, 2004; Shalley, Zhou, & Oldham, 2004).

59. See, for instance (Andersen & Fagerhaug, 2006; Arnheiter & Maleyeff, 2005; Collins & Porras, 1996).

60. This criterion is somewhat similar to Browne's difference threshold (Browne & Pitts, 2004; Browne, Pitts, & Wetherbe, 2007).

61. (Barrier, Li, & Jensen, 2003).

so we decide to stop expanding that branch. As with many other rules in solving CIDNI problems, it is *your* decision whether to keep expanding your map.

So far, we have seen how maps consistently answer the key question, progress from the key question to the conclusions, and have a MECE structure. The fourth and final rule of issue maps is to develop them in a way that helps clarify the problem; in one word, they should be insightful.

## 5. MAPS ARE INSIGHTFUL

Any key question can be broken down in more than one way, each complying with the first three rules. But you must pick only one of these breakdowns; ideally, you would use the most insightful one.

The first three rules are absolute: either your map complies with them or not. Your map and the rule are the only two things you need to consider. On the other hand, insightfulness is relative: you need to compare alternatives before deciding whether your map complies.

Here, being insightful amounts to adding value. To illustrate, imagine that you are walking down the street and come across a stopped car. The driver rolls down his window and asks, "Where am I?" You reply, "In a car." Of course, you could have replied, "At the intersection of ____ and ____ roads." Both answers are factually true, but the value they add differs. In the overwhelming majority of cases, the second answer brings the most value, which makes the first so absurd that it might become funny.

But the first answer is funny only because we assume that the driver is lost and asking for directions. Instead, assume that he was just involved in an accident, lost consciousness, and is only now coming back to his senses; would the first answer not be the insightful one, then? In fact, in that case the second becomes so irrelevant that it might become the funny one.[62]

This is the relativity aspect of insightfulness: To assess how insightful an answer is, you must compare the value it adds with that of its alternatives. So let's talk about how we incorporate that notion to create insightful maps.

**First, generate alternatives for the first node of your map.** The process starts by identifying at least two alternative variables to investigate your key question.

As an illustration, consider having to classify the numbers on a casino roulette wheel, shown in Figure 3.21.

Alternative 1 might be number based—with its states being "evens" and "odds." Alternative 2 might be color based—with its states being "black," "red," and "green." Those are the standard ways, but there are others. Alternative 3 could be another number-based one—with states being "from 0 to 10," "from 11 to 27," and "from 28 to 36." And so on. All these alternatives are MECE structures, so they are all candidates.

---

62. Schum's counterfactual assertions are related to our concept of insightfulness: He points out that, in any situation, there is a background of conditions, any of which can be brought up. The key is to bring up the appropriate one(s) to stand against that background (Schum, 1994) [pp. 149–150].

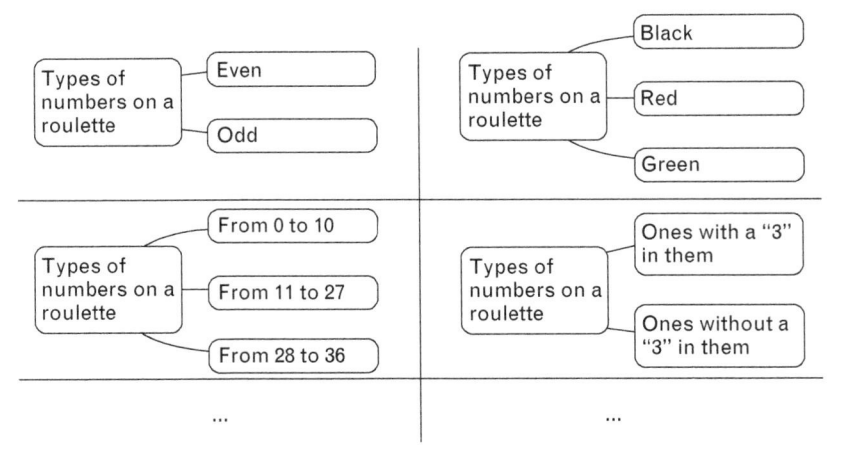

**FIGURE 3.21:** There are always alternative structures to build an issue map; consider at least two of these alternatives and pick the most insightful one.

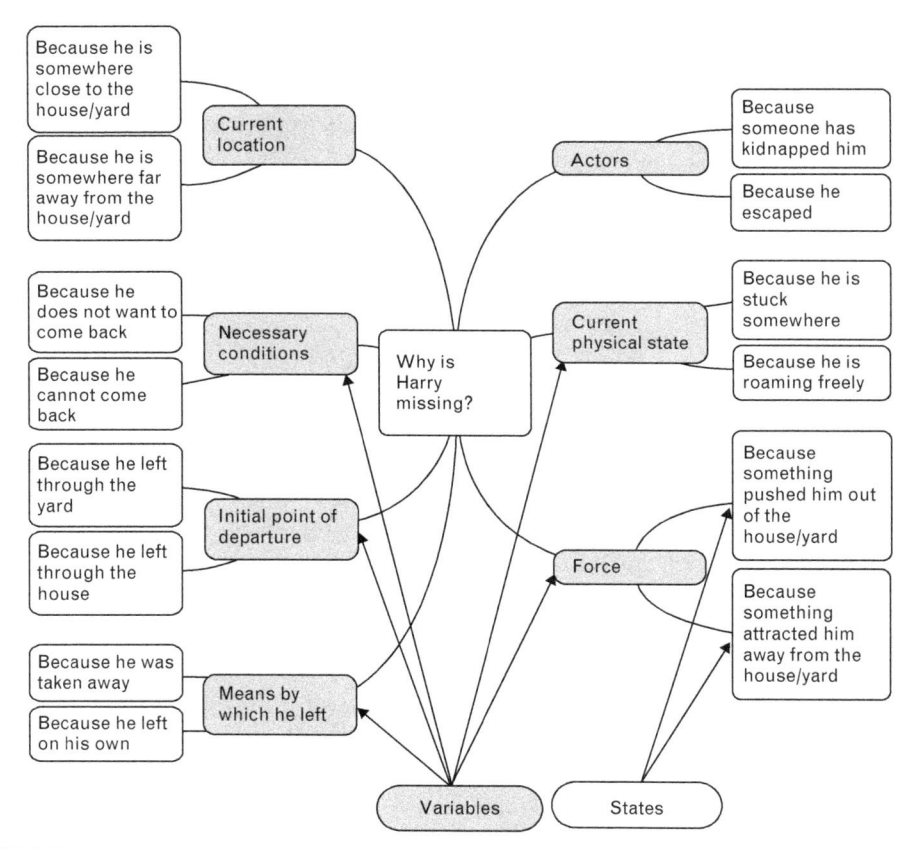

**FIGURE 3.22:** To generate alternative breakdowns, consider all the variables that you could use to describe the key question.

TABLE 3.1: Compare Variables to Identify Their Respective Insightfulness

| Variable | Implications | Decision |
|---|---|---|
| **Actors:** | Helps identify whether we should involve the police; therefore, it helps select the means to find Harry. However, it focuses on the cause of disappearance, not on Harry's current situation, which is not very solution oriented (maybe someone has kidnapped him and then released him). | ✗ |
| **Current physical state:** | Helps select the means to find Harry and focuses on Harry's current situation. | ✓ |
| **Force:** | Focuses primarily on the cause of disappearance, not on Harry's current situation. | ✗ |
| **Current location:** | Helps select the means to find Harry and focuses on Harry's current situation. | ✓ |
| **Necessary conditions:** | Focuses on Harry, not on what we can do to bring him back. | ~ |
| **Initial point of departure:** | Focuses on the disappearance, not on Harry's current situation. | ✗ |
| **Means by which he left:** | Focuses on the disappearance, not on Harry's current situation. | ✗ |

Generating alternative breakdowns can be challenging because it can be hard to look past the one or two obvious structures (what psychologists call fixation, as we have seen earlier in this chapter). Your job is to look for possible alternatives—that is, the variables—on which you can develop a breakdown. In the roulette example, we found two: colors and numbers, with various number-based variables. To help you do this, you may have various members of the team work independently.[63] Figure 3.22 shows that for Harry's case we found several more possible structures.

So the process starts with identifying these variables. Next, think of all the states that these variables can take.[64] Because each of your variables maps the entire key question, you must choose only one, otherwise there would be redundancies in your map.

**Next, assess the insightfulness of each alternative by understanding its "so what?"** The insightfulness of an alternative depends on its context. In the roulette example, you would not choose a number-based framework to describe a roulette to a child who cannot count. Similarly, it would be a poor choice to use a color-based classification if your interlocutor is color blind.

Pitch alternatives against one another to uncover the benefits and drawbacks of each. Analyze their respective "so what?" for your diagnosis. To help you do so, consider using a formal template, such as that in Table 3.1, for the case study. This also has the benefit of capturing your thinking for future reference.

---

63. (Prime Minister's Strategy Unit, 2004) [p. 91].
64. These states are called *values* in Artificial Intelligence parlance; see (Quinlan, 1986).

Comparing these variables helps us identify how we should decide among them. First, it becomes apparent that some variables focus on Harry's disappearance while others highlight his current state. From a practical perspective, we realize that how he came to be missing is only important if it relates to how we can find him. Therefore, we would prefer a structure focusing on his current state, which will be more solution oriented. Second, some structures seem to help us select means of retrieval but others do not. Finally, some breakdowns put us—versus someone else—in the driver's seat ("What can *I* do to find him?"). This is a recurrent theme in our approach: you should phrase your problem as much as possible in terms of what *you* can do to solve it. Even if you need the help of others, you should be thinking about how you can influence them to help you.

Passing our various variables through these filters leaves us with two possibilities—current physical state and current location. We are unable to rank their relative insightfulness further, so we conclude that either one of them is a good initial variable for the map and, having to select one, we choose the first.

**Having selected the most insightful alternative, discard the others and start developing your map.** Going through the comparative exercise described above is especially worthwhile for the initial node. As you move to deeper nodes, choosing a specific variable over another has lower impact because each only impacts an increasingly smaller part of the problem. So you might decide that you do not need to be as cautious and you advance more quickly.

Next, we list the variable's states in a MECE way: Harry is missing because either he is stuck somewhere or he is roaming freely. Then write a MECE list of their respective states. Continue until you have achieved your desired level of explicitness.

# 6. IDEAS TO START YOUR MAP

Let's look at a few ideas to help you get started drawing issue maps.

**Work in a setting that is right for you.** We all have different work habits. One's thinking and productivity varies with the time of the day, the availability of interactions with other team members, the length of a work session, the level of distractions, the amount of caffeine ingested, whether one has seen a comedy recently, and a plethora of other factors.[65] The more problems you solve, the more self aware you become. Notice how you work in various settings and use this information to create an environment that is right for you.

**Use analogies to approach unfamiliar problems.** You do not have to start each new map from scratch; instead, think of leveraging previous efforts whenever possible. Analogical thinking is a type of reasoning that relies on comparing situations to understand patterns of relational roles in a familiar situation, the *source,* and apply them to an unfamiliar one, the *target.*[66]

---

65. See, for instance (Isen, Daubman, & Nowicki, 1987; Martins & Terblanche, 2003; Oldham & Cummings, 1996; Shalley, 1995; Shalley et al., 2004; Spellman & Schnall, 2009). For an example, see (Gick & Holyoak, 1980).
66. (Keith J. Holyoak, 2012). Note: In this book, I do not distinguish between analogies and metaphors.

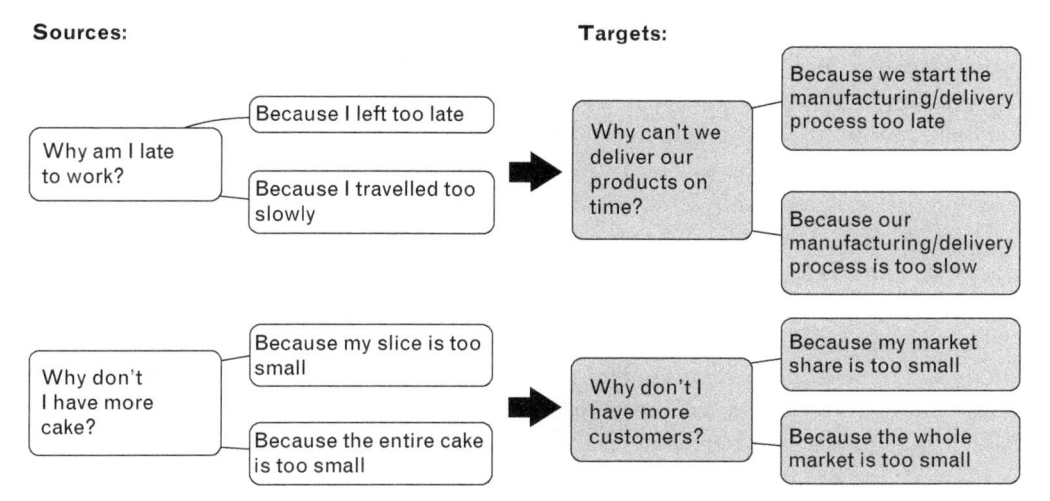

**FIGURE 3.23:** Using analogies can help you shed light on unfamiliar problems.

Assume that you are facing a logistics problem—say, you are to diagnose why your company does not deliver its products on time—but you know little about logistics. By equating the problem to one that you are more familiar with—for instance, getting to work late—you can gain some insight into your unfamiliar problem (see Figure 3.23).

Similarly, imagine that you want to understand why you do not have more customers for one of your products but you do not know much about business administration. By equating the number of customers to something that you know about, say, cake, you are in the business of understanding why you do not have more cake, a situation that anyone with siblings knows rather well. Maybe *your* slice/number of customers is too small, perhaps because your siblings/competitors are forcing it to be. Or, maybe *the entire* cake/market is too small, that is, there are not enough people currently buying this type of product, either yours or your competitors'.

A critical component of a good analogy is for the structure and its content to be a good model of the target.[67] This may require you to let go of surface features to focus on the underlying structure of the problems,[68] looking at the relations between objects as opposed to the attributes of objects.[69] With this requirement in mind, you can find analogies anywhere, from cases that are structurally close to your problem—say, studying the flow of traffic by studying fluid dynamics—to distant ones, such as equating the clustering of ions on graphene in a battery charging under high current to that of people crowding into a subway car at rush hour. Distant analogies, in particular, may promote creativity.[70]

---

67. (Gavetti & Rivkin, 2005; Keith J. Holyoak, 2012).
68. (Keith J. Holyoak & Koh, 1987), (National Research Council, 2011) [pp. 136–138].
69. (Gentner, 1983).
70. (Bo T. Christensen & Schunn, 2007; Smith & Ward, 2012) (Keith J. Holyoak, 2012) [p. 240]. (This is contested; see (Enkel & Gassmann, 2010) for a discussion.)

Keep in mind, however, that two aspects of using analogies can be dangerous. First, an analogy can be constraining, limiting one into looking at a problem from just one perspective when several may be available.[71] For instance, epidemiologist Roberta Ness observes that our conditioning to thinking of cancer as an enemy limits us in how we manage it and that also thinking of cancer as a neighbor might open additional avenues such as, in some cases, proper containment.[72]

Also, because analogical inference is an inductive process, it is uncertain.[73] So, although the process may be useful, check periodically to ensure that you are drawing correct inferences.

**Recycle discarded variables.** Having selected one variable for your map's first node, you should keep the others because they may help you build deeper nodes in your map. For instance in Harry's case, in the "because he is stuck somewhere" branch, you may decide that it is insightful to look into whether an actor is involved in keeping Harry stuck. As such, the efforts you have deployed to think of alternatives for the first node are not wasted.

**Consider using existing frameworks.** Drawing an issue map is hard work, which sometimes can be eased considerably when you use an existing framework. Figure 3.24, Figure 3.25, Figure 3.26, and Figure 3.27 are examples of a few common frameworks from various disciplines. These frameworks provide a potential structure on which to base part

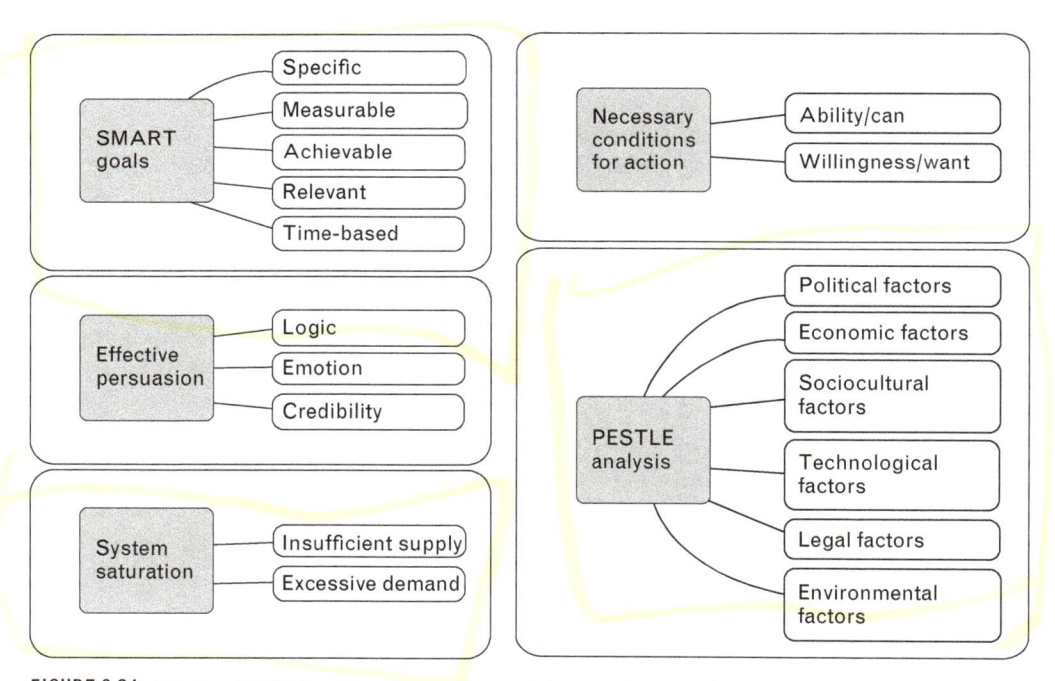

**FIGURE 3.24:** Existing MECE frameworks can be useful to create a new issue map.

71. This is called functional fixedness. See, for instance (Bo T. Christensen & Schunn, 2009) [pp. 50–54].
72. (Ness, 2012) [pp. 38–39].
73. (Keith J. Holyoak, 2012). See also (De Bono, 1970; Dunbar & Klahr, 2012b; Gentner, 1983; Gentner & Toupin, 1986; Gick & Holyoak, 1980; Keith J. Holyoak & Thagard, 1989, 1997; Ribaux & Margot, 1999; Spellman & Holyoak, 1996).

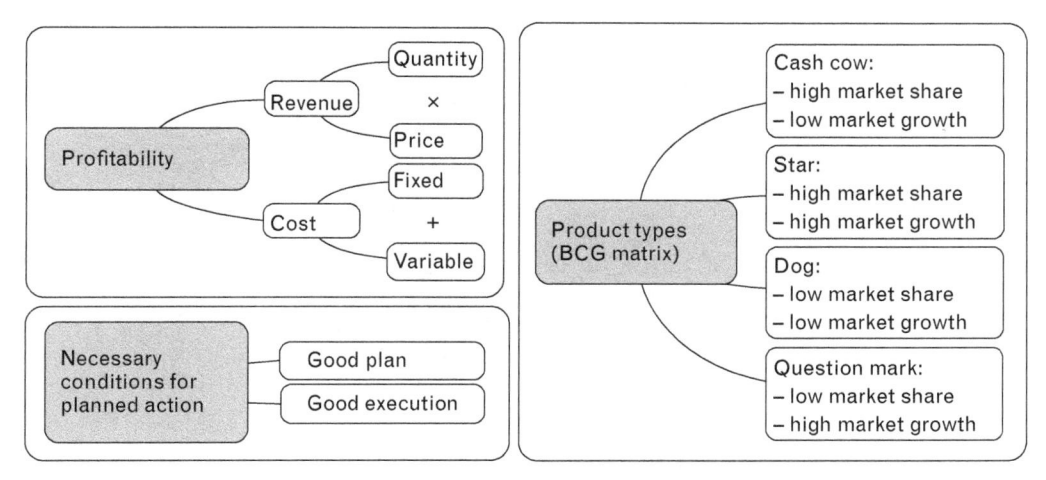

**FIGURE 3.25:** Existing MECE frameworks can be useful to create a new issue map (continued).

of your issue map. These can be a good starting point, as long as you remain cautious. In particular, do not assume that their MECEness is foolproof.

To illustrate, consider the marketing mix of Figure 3.26. First introduced in the 1960s, the concept says that when marketing a product, one should adopt a holistic approach, looking at 4Ps: the product itself, as well as its price, place, and promotion.[74]

Although it is still the go-to approach for many marketers the world over, this structure is not fully MECE. For instance, Van Waterschoot and Van den Bulte note that "the sales promotion subcategory of promotion overlaps to a large extent with the advertising and personal selling subcategories."[75]

Problems may arise on the collective exhaustiveness side, too. For instance, the Gricean maxims shown in Figure 3.26 are principles to facilitate cooperation, and they can be a good basis to develop an issue map related to communication. But it is unclear if the set is CE. Some argue, for instance, that a fifth principle—be polite—is relevant.[76]

Therefore, although an existing framework might provide a shortcut, you should see these structures as starting points that may need to be adapted, rather than trustworthy correct answers. In the end, you still have to ensure that whichever structure you adopt is MECE and insightful for your specific problem.

**Consider structuring your map following a MECE process.** Some diagnostic maps may benefit from thinking in terms of a process with various steps. In a setting where a problem occurs because at least one of a process's parts does not function properly, all you have to do is recreate the process as a succession of MECE steps and test each step to identify the defective one(s). For instance, suppose that you want to understand why parts that your plant orders from a provider do not get to you on time (see Figure 3.28). You may do so by

---

74. See, for instance (Grönroos, 1997).
75. (Van Waterschoot & Van den Bulte, 1992).
76. (Pfister, 2010).

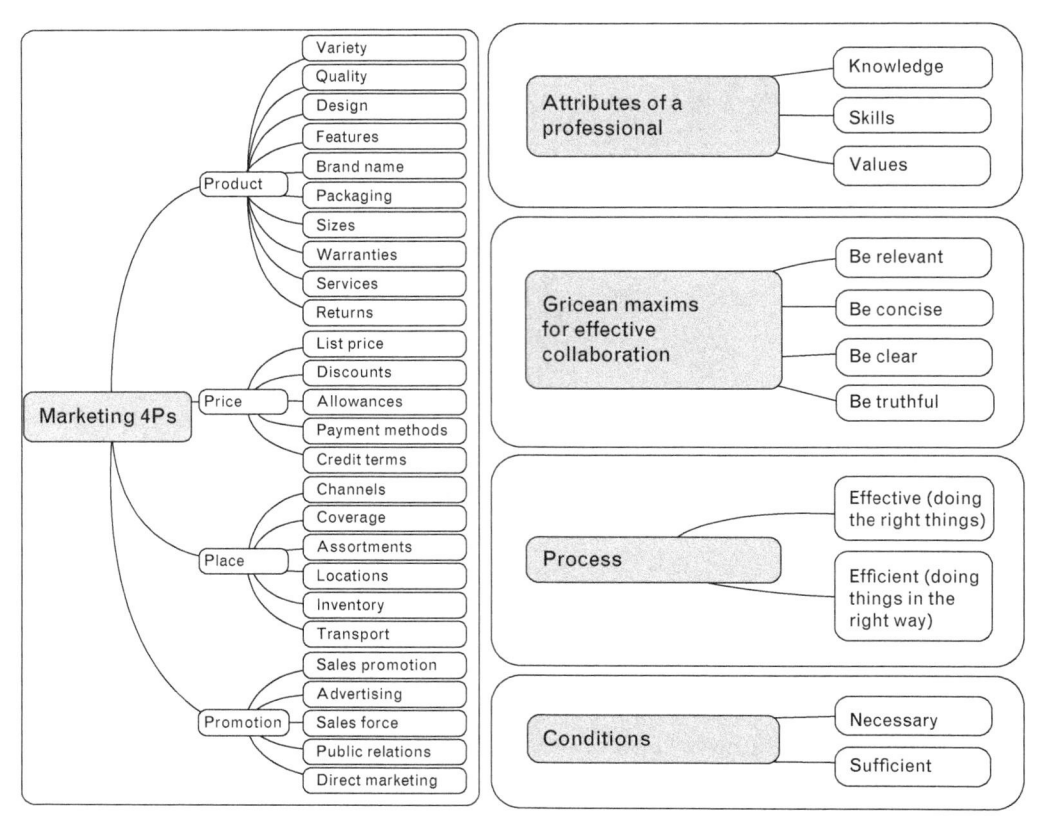

**FIGURE 3.26:** Existing MECE frameworks can be useful to create a new issue map (continued).

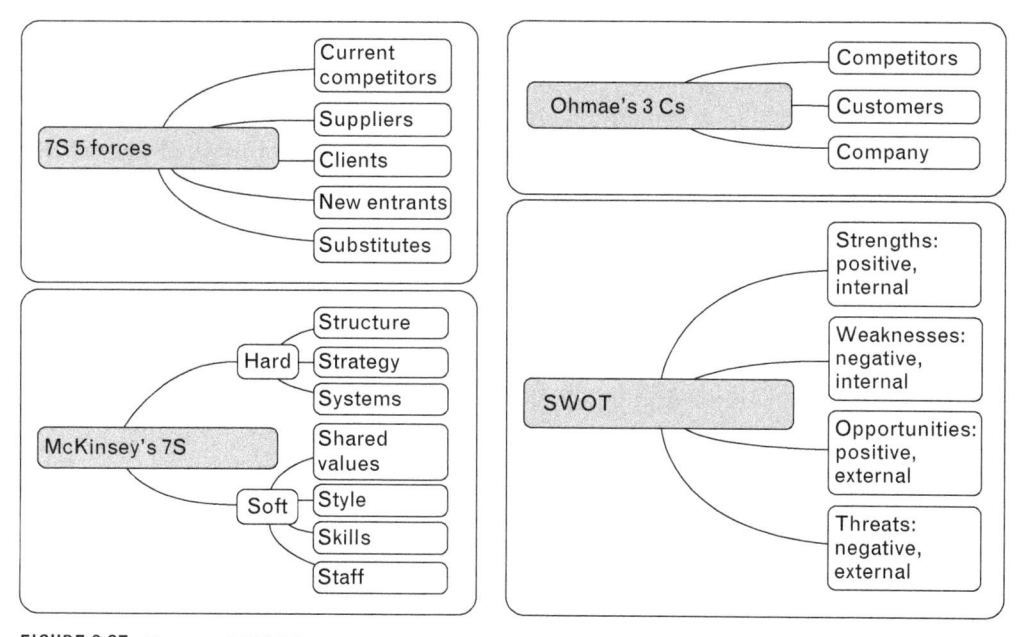

**FIGURE 3.27:** Existing MECE frameworks can be useful to create a new issue map (continued).

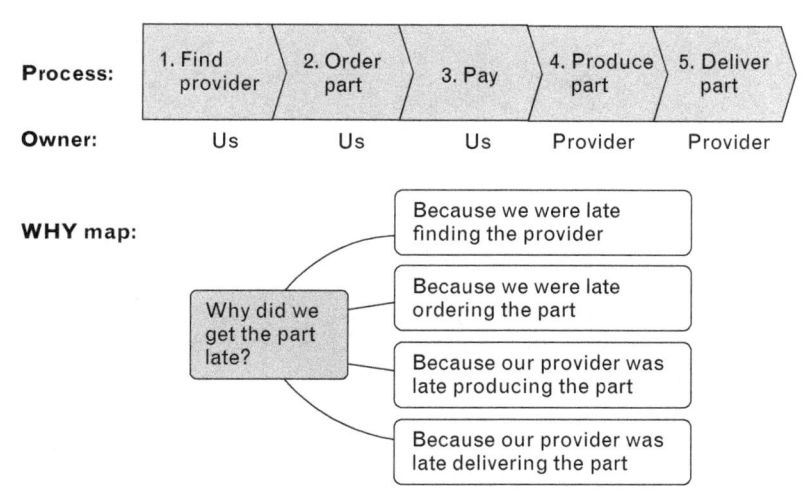

**Process:** 1. Find provider → 2. Order part → 3. Pay → 4. Produce part → 5. Deliver part

**Owner:** Us — Us — Us — Provider — Provider

**WHY map:**

Why did we get the part late?
- Because we were late finding the provider
- Because we were late ordering the part
- Because our provider was late producing the part
- Because our provider was late delivering the part

**FIGURE 3.28:** A MECE process can be a good basis to structure your diagnostic map.

first mapping out the process as a succession of steps. These can now be a candidate for the basic structure of your diagnostic map.

An existing framework or process might be helpful to start a map, but you still need to decide if it is insightful for your specific problem. So, do not assume an existing framework or process to be automatically better than one you develop. Instead, treat it as one potential option and assess its insightfulness for your specific problem by comparing it with alternatives.

# 7. WHAT ABOUT HARRY?

Figure 3.29 shows the diagnostic map for our case study. Having decided that the most insightful initial variable is to consider Harry's current physical state, we continue developing the map. Some branches stop quickly (for instance, "because he, Figure 3.29, got stuck") because we feel they reach explicitness right away. Other branches progress further.

When considering that someone might be keeping Harry from leaving where he is, thinking of those doing so to prevent us from recovering him and of those doing so to enable us to recover him is not enough. To be collectively exhaustive, the options in that breakdown also need to include the case of someone keeping him with neither intention. Continuing the breakdown of that branch, we have a specific idea in mind: that of a kid who would have picked up Harry and liked him so much that he decided to keep him without even thinking about the consequences for us. Surely there are other people who might do the same, but we cannot think of one in particular and feel that spelling them out does not bring value to the map, so we lump them together in a "someone else" branch. This is equivalent to using "others," which as we discussed earlier is to be avoided but is acceptable, especially if it is deep in a map, where its impact is limited. The final map of Figure 3.29 completely breaks down our key question, or at least we think it does. And this is a major achievement because,

Identify Potential Root Causes

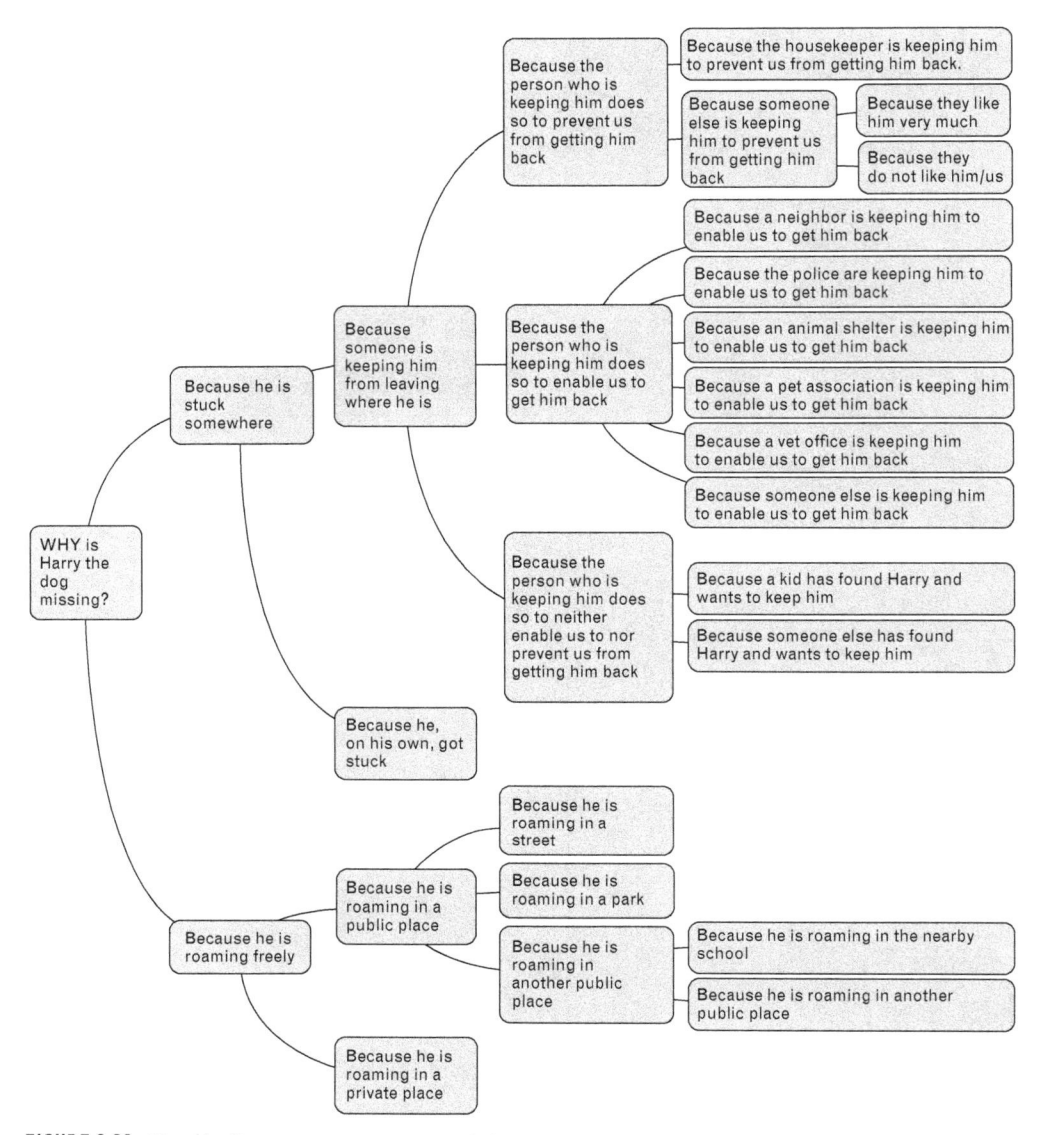

**FIGURE 3.29:** Harry's diagnostic map starts with his current physical state and develops to various levels of detail, depending on the branch.

if we have worked well, the reason why Harry is missing—whatever it may be—is in it; we have now fully identified the solution space.

Chapter 5 provides further ideas for building good maps. You might want to look at it now, but you already know enough to develop solid maps.

It is easy to feel overwhelmed the first few times that you build an issue map, so try to keep things simple. Focus on following the four rules as best you can and resist your initial urge to satisfice. But do not focus too much on making it perfect. If you have worked reasonably well, you will now have identified all the potential causes of your problem. Next, you will need to determine which of those is the actual cause. That is the object of Chapter 4.

# NOTES

**Issue maps.** Many strategy consultants are trained to map complex problems and call the product one of several names (e.g., issue tree, logic tree, or hypothesis tree). Unfortunately, there is little available material on how to develop them. Consultants have been using trees for a while—Ohmae[77] mentioned them in the 1980s—but the technique of using a graphic to connect a question with potential answers has been around since at least the Second World War.[78] In my experience, most consultants only worry about one rule—MECEness—while developing trees. It seems, however, that asking students to also use the other three rules helps them create consistently better trees/maps. I started calling these structures maps after conversations with Tim van Gelder, partly as an effort to help people stop referring to them as decision trees, which they are not, and partly to differentiate them from some issue trees from strategy consultancies that connect a key question to related questions as opposed to potential answers.[79]

**Graphical tools related to problem solving and strategic thinking.** See also Ainsworth, Prain, and Tytler (2011, Buckingham Shum, MacLean, Bellotti, and Hammond (1997), Clark (2010), Conklin (2005), Diffenbach (1982), Dwyer, Hogan, and Stewart (2010), Eden (1992), Eden (2004), Eisenführ, Weber, and Langer (2010), Eppler (2006), Fiol and Huff (1992), Kaplan and Norton (2000), Ohmae (1982), Okada, Shum, and Sherborne (2010), Rooney and Heuvel (2004), Shachter (1986), and Shum (2003).

**Refraining from using "others."** Smith and Ward note that divergent thinking is like naming the members of a category. Both tasks require retrieval of information from memory and imagination.[80]

**Linking hypotheses and data.** In forensic science, reducing *linkage blindness*—the inability to recognize a connection between things—has been shown to bring valuable insight.[81]

**Using multiple hypotheses.** See Platt and Chamberlin for friendly and compelling cases on why you should work with several hypotheses.[82]

**Confirmation bias.** Nickerson makes a strong argument that one has to work very hard to not fall prey.[83]

**Mapping out the analysis.** van Gelder and Twardy make strong cases for the use of graphical methods to improve critical thinking. van Gelder & Monk also has a friendly online tutorial.[84]

---

77. (Ohmae, 1982).
78. See Duncker's 1945 radiation problem (Duncker & Lees, 1945), also explained in (Bassok & Novick, 2012) [p. 414].
79. See (Wiebes, Baaij, Keibek, & Witteveen, 2007) [pp. 41–50] for an example.
80. (Smith & Ward, 2012) [p.465].
81. (Ribaux & Margot, 1999).
82. (Platt, 1964), (Chamberlin, 1965). Alternatively, see (Tweney, Doherty, & Mynatt, 1981) [pp. 83–85] for a summary.
83. (Nickerson, 1998).
84. (van Gelder, 2003), (Twardy, 2010), (van Gelder & Monk, 2016).

**MECE versus ICE.** Management consultants use "MECE" extensively, possibly after Minto helped popularize it.[85] They also, however, routinely misuse the "ME" part. Differentiating mutual exclusivity from independence is not pedantry: If potential solutions are not truly mutually exclusive, then one should consider combining them. Sometimes, a problem gets resolved by combining several partial (and independent) solutions. An illustration of this is the long-tail concept. For instance, selling a multitude of books that each appeal to a small audience may amount to sizable revenue.[86] Thanks to Matthew Juniper at Cambridge for an enlightening e-mail exchange on the subject.

**The case against MEness.** Striving for mutual exclusiveness helps avoid redundancies, which helps us be more efficient. In some cases, however, redundancies are desirable. For instance, redundancies in airplanes' flight control systems help pilots retain some control of the plane even when primary systems fail.[87] Similarly, power grids are designed so that the failure of one key component (or, in more robust designs, more components) does not result in a blackout.[88] Likewise, shipping companies such as FedEx orbit empty cargo aircraft at night, which can be diverted quickly to locations where demand suddenly surpasses capacity.[89] The takeaway is that there are some situations where *not* being ME is better than being ME.

**Insightfulness and frames of reference.** Our concept of insightfulness relates to Spellman's recommendation for intelligence analysts: "In analysis it is essential to get the "compared to what" correct.[90]

**Ideas to fix overconfidence.** See (J. Edward Russo & Schoemaker, 1992; Arkes, Christensen, Lai, & Blumer, 1987).

**Improving critical thinking skills.** We can all use help. A study comparing the problem-solving skills of 30 PhD scientists and 15 conservative ministers found no significant differences between the two groups, concluding that in "summary, the present findings raise serious questions about the presumed superiority of at least some scientists' reasoning and problem-solving skills."[91]

---

85. (Minto, 2009).

86. See (C. Anderson, 2004), (Brynjolfsson, Hu, & Smith, 2006), (Brynjolfsson, Hu, & Simester, 2011).

87. See (Orasanu, 2010) [pp. 158–159].

88. (Pinar, Meza, Donde, & Lesieutre, 2010).

89. (Leonhardt, 2005).

90. (National Research Council, 2011) [p. 136]. See also (Schum, 1994) [pp. 126–130] for a discussion on the value and the drawbacks of redundancies.

91. (Mahoney & DeMonbreun, 1977).

CHAPTER 4

# DETERMINE THE ACTUAL CAUSE(S)

You have drawn your diagnostic map, thereby identifying all of the problem's potential root causes. Next, you will lump these causes into judicious groups, each summarized in a formal hypothesis, decide the order in which you want to test these hypotheses, conduct the testing, and draw your conclusions.

## 1. DEVELOP AN INSIGHTFUL SET OF HYPOTHESES

Having exposed the structure of your key question in the diagnosis map, you have come a long way. Indeed, you are now facing a well-defined problem: whatever the answer to your question is, if you have done your job well, it is already in your map.[1] Now it is "only" a matter of finding it.

Because a map usually contains many elements, it is usually not practical to analyze each individually. Instead, it is better to lump them into judicious groups, each under a formal hypothesis. A hypothesis is a proposition, a potential answer to your key question, which may or may not be true. In a diagnostic map, a hypothesis says, "this part of the map is a significant cause of my problem."

---

[1]. This is analogous to how using scenarios can help simplify a complex planning task by capturing the environment in a limited number of possible states (Schoemaker, 1995).

## 1.1. SUMMARIZE YOUR MAP IN A SET OF HYPOTHESES

Focus your efforts on the important parts of your problem, and you will have a higher return on investment. Here are some ideas for doing so.

**Link all elements in the map to exactly one hypothesis.** In Anderson et al.'s words, "hypotheses are like nets; only he who casts will catch,"[2] so you must associate each element in your map with a hypothesis. Furthermore, associating an element to more than one hypothesis generates unnecessary duplication of effort. So, to be both effective and efficient, associate every element in your map with exactly one hypothesis.

**Keep the number of hypotheses under control.** Although you need to associate all elements with exactly one hypothesis, you do not need to have an individual hypothesis for each element. Figure 4.1 shows how you can lump some elements in a group and write a hypothesis for the entire group. This will clarify your map by reducing the visual and cognitive clutter.

A hypothesis set should have at least two hypotheses to reduce the chance of confirmation bias that comes with considering a single hypothesis.[3] The set should also be practical, so you should not have too many hypotheses. Limitations in our working memory make it risky to have to consider more than seven elements.[4] However, because maps allow us to write down these elements, thereby expanding our working memory, you may be able to stretch that upper limit a little bit. From experience, aiming at no more than 10 or 15 hypotheses usually is advisable and, in fact, limiting yourself to a smaller set (say, two to five hypotheses) may be beneficial.

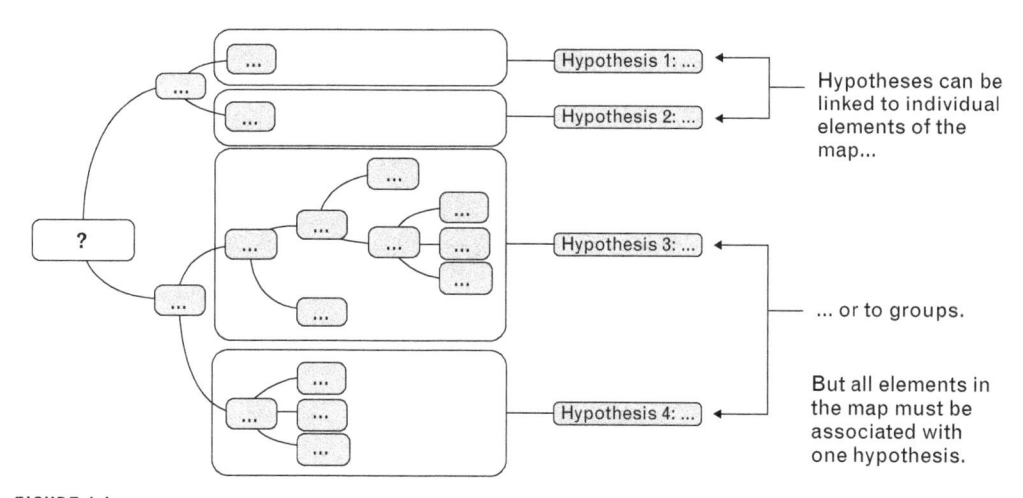

FIGURE 4.1: Each element in your map must be associated with exactly one hypothesis.

---

2. (Anderson, Schum, & Twining, 2005).
3. (Chamberlin, 1965), (Platt, 1964).
4. (Miller, 1956); see also (Cowan, 2000).

## 1.2. CONCENTRATE ON WHAT YOU THINK MATTERS

Use broader hypotheses for the parts of the map that you think are least likely. That way, if you can find sufficient evidence opposing that hypothesis you can rule out large parts of your diagnosis map. Here is an analogy to understand this approach and an application in Harry's case.

When designing a mechanical part, an engineer must ensure that it will resist the stresses to which it will be subjected. A popular way to test this is to use finite element analysis (FEA): a computerized model of the part that allows the engineer to numerically simulate its reaction to physical constraints.

Just as an issue map breaks down a complex question into its components, a finite element model breaks down a mechanical part into small elements that form a mesh. Then the engineer applies a (numerical) load on the mesh to see how each element reacts. The sum of the elements' reactions is the reaction of the entire part.

The smaller the elements, the more precise the analysis, so a fine mesh is valuable. But a fine mesh comes at a price because one must have more elements to cover the same geometry and, therefore, one needs more computational power to run the simulation.

Stresses usually are not equal everywhere on a mechanical part. For instance, if one applies force to a part that has a hole in it, stresses concentrate around the hole. Similarly, a cantilever beam (a beam that is anchored at one end and free at the other—think of a diving board) subject to gravity will generate unequal stresses: greater closer to the anchored edge as Figure 4.2 shows.

We already know that the stresses are unequal so the basic approaches of using either a fine mesh everywhere or a coarse mesh everywhere are not ideal. Instead, it is better to use a mesh whose element sizes are tailored to the situation. That is, you can optimize your FEA by making your mesh finer where you think the problems are more likely to occur. This requires an initial investment because you need to think about where you want to concentrate your analysis as opposed to meshing everything uniformly but, in some instances, this investment is worth it.

You can apply this same technique when deciding how to assign hypotheses in your issue map. Typical maps have at least 30 elements, and usually far more. You can treat each element as an individual hypothesis—that is, use a fine FEA mesh everywhere—but this is problematical for three reasons. First, it is time consuming to analyze. Second, it is probably not necessary: If you have been collectively exhaustively building your map, you already have listed all theories, including downright unlikely ones. These do not deserve as much attention as likely ones, at least not initially. And third, this method may generate confusion: giving every element the same weight makes it difficult to identify the important ones.

So only use finer hypotheses to test the parts of your map that are the most important. And, according to the Pareto principle, there *will* be parts of your map that are most important. The *Pareto principle* (also called the 80/20 rule) is a heuristics, or rule of thumb, which states that in any cause-and-effect events, a few causes—say, 20%—account for the most effect—say, 80%. Italian economist Vilfredo Pareto postulated the rule at the turn of the 20th century to describe wealth distribution after he observed that 20% of the people

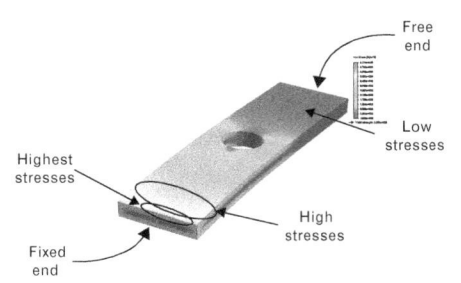

1. A beam anchored to a wall is subjected to a vertical force, which results in unequal stresses. An engineer can analyze it numerically using one of various finite element models:

2. A *coarse mesh* has low computational requirements but yields imprecise results everywhere.

3. A *fine mesh* yields precise results everywhere but has high computational requirements.

4. An *optimized mesh* yields precise results only where they matter, thereby keeping computational requirements reasonable. The price to pay for this is effort in planning (to identify where to focus).

**FIGURE 4.2:** A mesh made of elements of various sizes helps optimize the value of a FEA model, focusing efforts where they are most needed. This approach also can be used with issue maps.

owned 80% of the land in Italy. Allow for a few percentage point changes and the distribution holds true for many types of events across disciplines.[5]

Let's illustrate this using Harry's case. We identified that one possible explanation for him being missing is that he is being held hostage. We suspect that the housekeeper might be holding him hostage, so we think that she deserves her own hypothesis, as Figure 4.3 shows. But we do not really suspect anyone else to be keeping him hostage. Therefore, although some 7 billion people other than the housekeeper potentially might hold him hostage, and each could theoretically have his or her own hypothesis, we choose to lump all those unlikely suspects in one hypothesis and map the "Harry is being held hostage" eventuality with just two hypotheses: $H_1$. The housekeeper is holding him hostage or $H_2$. Someone other than the housekeeper is holding him hostage. If, during our analysis, we encounter evidence supporting that Harry is being held hostage by someone other than the housekeeper, we can always revisit that decision and breakdown $H_2$ into various groups.

To represent the entire map in our set of hypotheses, we also need to consider the case where people have found Harry and are holding on to him to help us find him (hypothesis 3);

---

5. See, for instance (Juran, 1975), (Brynjolfsson, Hu, & Simester, 2011).

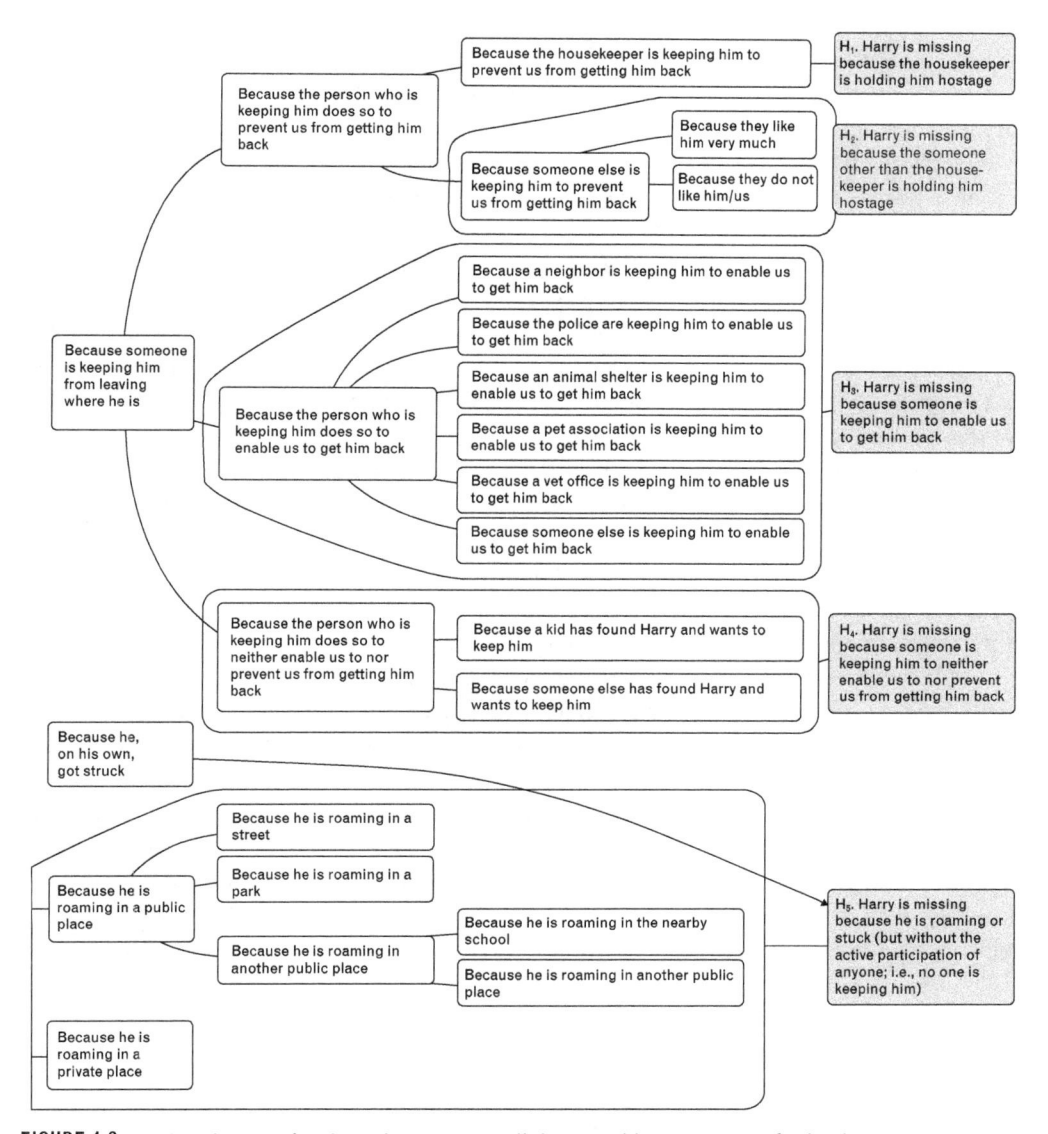

**FIGURE 4.3:** In Harry's case, five hypotheses cover all the possible root causes for his being missing.

the case where someone is holding on to Harry with no interest in either preventing us from recovering him or helping us do so (hypothesis 4); and the case where Harry is roaming or stuck but without anyone else's active participation (hypothesis 5).[6] That is, these five hypotheses cover the entire universe of root causes.

---

6. In Harry's case, note that the hypotheses are not just independent but truly mutually exclusive: one being true *excludes* others being true. So, if we have done a proper job of mapping our problem, the answer is in one—and only one—of those.

Determine Actual Causes • 83

## 1.3. PHRASE HYPOTHESES WELL

Good hypotheses are testable, unequivocal, and related to the key question. In addition, whenever useful, consider making them comparative.

**Make your hypotheses testable.** A hypothesis should be phrased so that it is falsifiable (i.e., it is possible to demonstrate that it is wrong) and supportable (i.e., it is possible to demonstrate that it can be supported). In Platt's words, "There is no point making hypotheses that are not falsifiable because they do not say anything. It must be possible for an empirical scientific system to be refuted by experience."[7] Citing philosopher Karl Popper and the American Association for the Advancement of Science, Gauch notes: "To be useful, a hypothesis should suggest what evidence would support it and what evidence would refute it. A hypothesis that cannot in principle be put to the test of evidence may be interesting, but it is not scientifically useful."[8]

One way to approach hypotheses is to think of them as fair bets: you want to give your hypothesis the opportunity to be proven wrong as well as the opportunity to be vindicated.[9]

**Make your hypotheses unequivocal.** Using unequivocal hypotheses helps clarify what is needed to test them. Figure 4.4 shows an example of unequivocal hypotheses: They are clear, unambiguous, and it is reasonable to expect that everyone will get the same meaning out of reading them. To make your hypotheses unequivocal, be as explicit as possible and include numerical data whenever possible. For instance, instead of, "a non-negligible part of our costs are due to delays from our manufacturing division that could be avoided," favor, "15% of our costs are due to delays from our manufacturing division that could be avoided."

**Relate hypotheses to the key question.** "The housekeeper is holding Harry hostage" is shorter than "Harry is missing because the housekeeper is holding him hostage." So, all other things being equal, it is preferable. But not all other things are equal: The second statement relates the hypothesis to the key question, which brings additional clarity and helps you relate each bit of analysis back to your overall objective. In general, it is good to

$H_1$: Harry is missing because the housekeeper is holding him hostage

$H_2$: Harry is missing because someone other than the housekeeper is holding him hostage

**FIGURE 4.4:** Ensure that your hypotheses are testable and unequivocal and that they directly address your key question.

7. (Platt, 1964).
8. (Gauch, 2003) [p. 98].
9. (Mitchell & Jolley, 2009) [pp. 70–71].

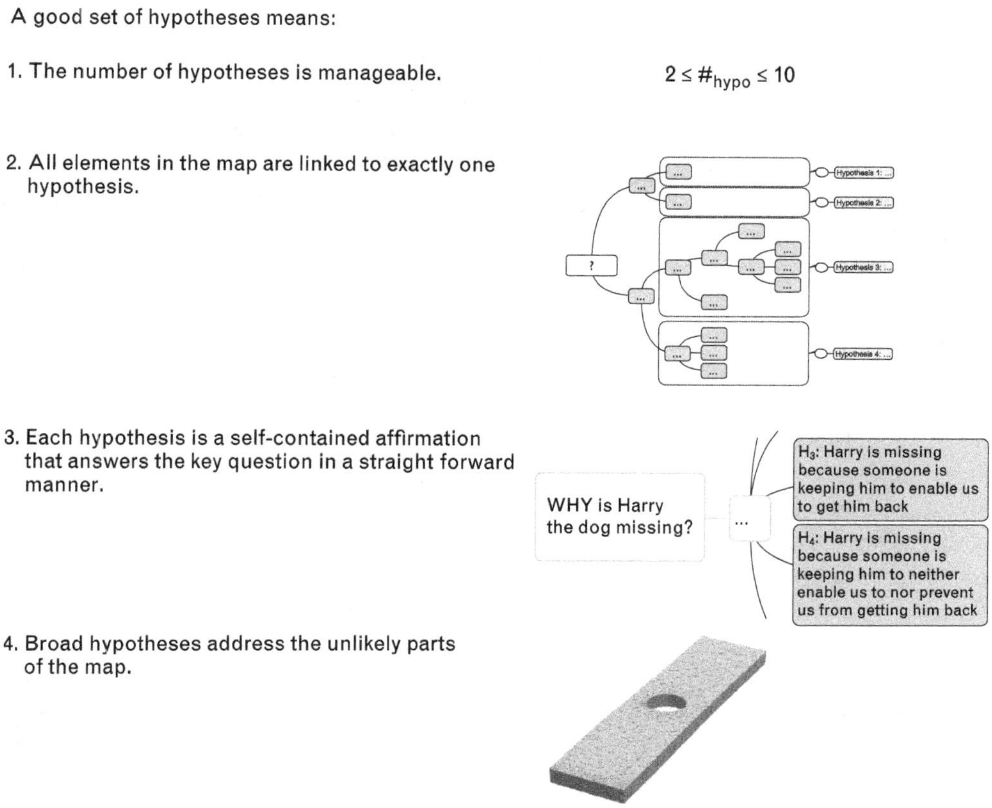

A good set of hypotheses means:

1. The number of hypotheses is manageable.    $2 \leq \#_{hypo} \leq 10$

2. All elements in the map are linked to exactly one hypothesis.

3. Each hypothesis is a self-contained affirmation that answers the key question in a straight forward manner.

4. Broad hypotheses address the unlikely parts of the map.

FIGURE 4.5: Ensure that you have a good set of hypotheses.

formulate your hypotheses as full declarative sentences that include the key question; for example, "Harry is missing because the housekeeper is holding him hostage."[10]

**Consider using comparative hypotheses when possible.** You might consider using comparative hypotheses—that is, phrasing hypotheses in a way that you pitch them against one another. An example would be, "The housekeeper keeping Harry hostage is the most likely explanation as to why he is missing." These comparative hypotheses might be particularly useful in cases where it is possible to quantitatively estimate the probabilities of the various scenarios.

Figure 4.5 summarizes the main attributes of a good set of hypotheses.

# 2. PRIORITIZE THE TESTING OF HYPOTHESES

Once you have formulated your hypotheses, you must decide the order in which to test them. Although you could take your hypotheses in the somewhat arbitrary order that they

---

10. One way to think about diagnostic hypotheses is to see them as scenarios, that is, coherent presentations of the sequence of events. See (Vlek, Prakken, Renooij, & Verheij, 2013).

Determine Actual Causes • 85

appear in your issue map, it might be useful to prioritize them in a more reasoned fashion. Absent tangible information about your specific situation, prioritizing the analysis is one particular activity in the problem-solving process that explicitly calls for intuition.

There are various ways to prioritize hypotheses. One common way is to start with the most plausible one(s),[11] which is similar to Sutton's law in medicine to "go where the money is."[12]

Anderson and Schum recommend that you take into account not only the hypotheses' plausibility but also their seriousness and easiness to check.[13] Yet another way is to test first those hypotheses that will have a large impact on your resolution strategy: If we can rule out that Harry is held hostage, then we know that requesting the police to investigate the housekeeper is not appropriate.

**(Temporarily) discard hypotheses that are too unlikely.** In our quest for collective exhaustiveness, we have considered all logically possible answers to our question, irrespective of their plausibility. Now is the time to decide if some are too far-fetched. If some are, it is appropriate to make a judgment call and discard them without further analysis. It is also important, however, to keep them in mind in case our analysis of other hypotheses leads us to reject all of those. In that case, we would need to go back to the discarded hypotheses and test them. In the words of Sherlock Holmes: "When you have eliminated the impossible, whatever remains, *however improbable*, must be the truth."[14]

Here are a couple of additional ideas if you still cannot decide how to start.

**Consider going wide before going deep.** If you have insufficient insight into the problem to judge the hypotheses' properties, you may want to progress iteratively in more detail. That is, before you jump into a full-blown analysis of any one hypothesis, do a preliminary test of various ones to see if you can gain any insight.

**Enlist others.** If you have a team of people, you might want to ask for help in establishing the priority list, given that teams can be wiser than individuals. Surowiecki proposes that four requirements must be met to form a wise crowd: diversity of opinion, independence, decentralization, and aggregation.[15]

*Diversity of opinion* means that individuals should have private information about the problem, even if it is partial; what matters above all is that they think differently.[16]

*Independence* is about ensuring that participants' opinions are not anchored by others'. If you put your team in a room and ask them which hypothesis they think is the most likely, whatever answer comes first is likely to influence all the following ones.[17] Instead, capture team members' opinions individually and, perhaps, anonymously.

*Decentralization* allows people to specialize and use local knowledge.

Finally, *aggregation* means that you have a mechanism to collect and integrate the answers.

---

11. (Klahr, Fay, & Dunbar, 1993) [p. 114].
12. (Macpherson & Stanovich, 2007) [p. 178].
13. (Anderson & Schum, 2005) [pp. 49–50].
14. (Hill, 1965).
15. (Surowiecki, 2005).
16. (Page, 2008).
17. (Tversky & Kahneman, 1974).

In Harry's case, our first hypothesis is related to a criminal act: the housekeeper is holding him hostage. Because finding a kidnapped dog is a lot different from finding an escaped one, and because our friend John is convinced that the housekeeper is keeping Harry, we decide to first analyze this hypothesis.

# 3. ANALYZE

Having stated your hypotheses and prioritized their analysis, you are ready to test them. Criminal justice professors Ronald Clarke and John Eck advise that you should distance yourself from your hypotheses: "You should (1) clearly state your hypotheses, (2) not be wedded to them, and (3) use data to objectively test them. Expect all hypotheses to be altered or discarded once relevant data have been examined because no hypothesis is completely right. For this reason it is often best to test multiple conflicting hypotheses."[18]

When a datum or an item of information is associated to a hypothesis, it becomes evidence;[19] in the words of Dunbar and Klahr, hypothesis testing is then "the process of evaluating a proposition by collecting evidence regarding its truth."[20]

Gauch's Presuppositions–Evidence–Logic (PEL) model is useful to think about how information and logic come together in arguments. *Presuppositions* are necessary beliefs for any of the hypotheses to be true, but they are nondifferential regarding the credibilities of the individual hypotheses. *Evidence* is data that is differential regarding the credibility of one hypothesis over others. *Logic* combines presuppositions and evidence with valid reasoning to reach a conclusion. Gauch notes that "every scientific conclusion, if fully disclosed, involves three kinds of premises, regarding presuppositions, evidence, and logic."[21]

In broad strokes, your analysis should integrate the steps from the evidence-based medicine approach: formulate a clear question to test your hypothesis; identify the evidence needed and the ways to gather it, including searching the literature, designing experiments, etc.; critically appraise the evidence; and integrate your findings into the bigger picture.[22]

## 3.1. USE DEDUCTION, INDUCTION, AND ABDUCTION

When working with hypotheses, we use deductive, inductive and abductive logic.

**Deduction** applies a universal rule to a particular case to derive specific conclusions. A classic example of deductive logic is: All men are mortal. Socrates is a man. Therefore,

---

18. (Clarke & Eck, 2005).
19. (D. Schum, Tecuci, Boicu, & Marcu, 2009).
20. (K. N. Dunbar & Klahr, 2012) [p. 705].
21. (Gauch, 2003) [pp. 124–131, 269]. In the rest of the book, I am lumping presuppositions and evidence under the term evidence.
22. See (Rosenberg & Donald, 1995) for more on evidence-based medicine.

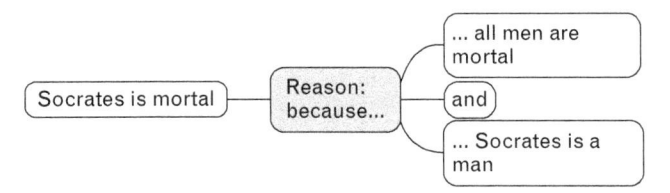

**FIGURE 4.6:** Deductive inference applies a general rule to a particular case.

Socrates is mortal. (See Figure 4.6 for a representation using argument mapping conventions; more on that later in this chapter.)

If the premises of a deductive inference are true, so is its conclusion.[23] There is, however, a price to pay for this certainty. Deduction cannot bring us more information than we already know; it only makes it more explicit.[24] Note also that deduction relies on universal rules, which—outside of mathematics and logic—are extremely rare. For instance, in Figure 4.7 (a), the universal rule is that "all dogs have four legs" but, because of accidents or genetic defects, some dogs have fewer. Despite this limitation, deductive logic is useful in generating new hypotheses; for example, we owe to it the discovery of the planet Neptune.[25]

*Induction* relies on particular cases to generate a general rule that is likely true. Because the sun has risen every day for a few billion years, it seems safe to assume that it will rise tomorrow. The price we pay for accessing this new knowledge is the possibility of error: unlike deductive inferences, inductive inferences based on true premises are not guaranteed to be true; rather, they are probabilistic in nature. If the sun explodes later on today, it will not be rising tomorrow. Induction is useful to evaluate the likelihood of a hypothesis based on the available evidence.[26]

An example of an incorrect induction is that of philosopher-trader Nassim Taleb's turkey before Thanksgiving, or the example of Russell's chicken (the birds differ but the example is the same). Observing that the farmer feeds it every day, this American turkey concludes that the farmer is its friend and comes to expect that he will continue to feed it ad infinitum. Unfortunately, it is proven wrong on a fateful Thanksgiving morning.[27] One way to sidestep this limitation of induction is to use triangulation: instead of relying on only one source of information, one should find alternate and independent ways to assess whether one's conclusion is correct. For instance, our turkey might have looked for old turkeys on the farm, to see if there were such as thing as an old turkey.

*Abduction*—also known as inference to the best explanation (IBE)—is the formulation of a hypothesis as a result of observing a surprising event,[28] or being in a situation of having "evidence in search of hypotheses."[29] We use abduction when we conclude that the theory

---

23. (D. A. Schum, 1994) [p. 23].
24. (George & Bruce, 2008) [p. 174].
25. (Reichenbach, 1973) [pp. 100–103].
26. (Tecuci, Schum, Boicu, Marcu, & Russell, 2011).
27. (Taleb, 2007) [pp. 40–42].
28. (Gabbay & Woods, 2006; Kakas, Kowalski, & Toni, 1992; Pople, 1973).
29. (Tecuci et al., 2011).

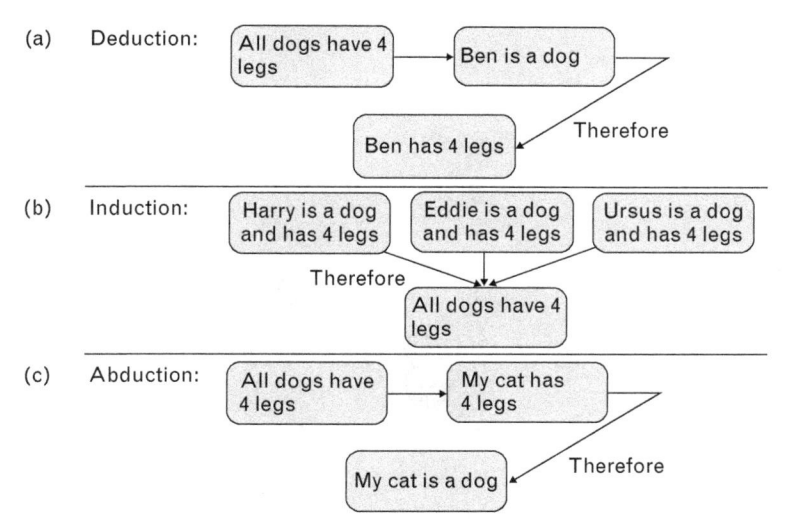

(a) Deduction:
- All dogs have 4 legs
- Ben is a dog
- Therefore Ben has 4 legs

(b) Induction:
- Harry is a dog and has 4 legs
- Eddie is a dog and has 4 legs
- Ursus is a dog and has 4 legs
- Therefore All dogs have 4 legs

(c) Abduction:
- All dogs have 4 legs
- My cat has 4 legs
- Therefore My cat is a dog

**FIGURE 4.7:** Deduction, abduction, and induction combine elements in different ways to go from premises to conclusions.

of evolution best explains species variations or that the fact that Napoléon existed best explains the historical records about him.[30] Philosopher Charles Peirce, who coined the term abduction, saw it as the only form of reasoning to discover something new.[31]

We already have used abduction extensively in developing our diagnosis map when observing that Harry was missing (evidence) and generating potential reasons why (hypothesis 1: the housekeeper is holding him hostage; hypothesis 2: someone else is holding him hostage, etc.).

A major weakness of abduction is that, as is the case with induction, it is probabilistic: it identifies *possible* truths that still may not be correct.[32] Figure 4.7 (c) shows such an example. Losing sight of the probabilistic nature of abduction can be problematic because evidence usually is compatible with several hypotheses, and it is possible, and indeed not unusual, to reach the wrong conclusion.

**Use both forward- and backward-driven reasoning strategies.** Using hypotheses to guide one's analysis is known as the hypothetico-deductive approach or backward-driven reasoning. Some have criticized this approach, pointing out its limitations.[33] Although issue maps are organized and naturally flow from the hypotheses to the data, this does not mean that they constrain one's thinking in such a unidirectional flow. If new data appears that is not consistent with any of the hypotheses listed, one should modify one's set of hypotheses to incorporate that new information. Therefore, using an issue map is not equivalent to limiting oneself to using a hypothetico-deductive approach. Rather, an effective analysis combines backward-driven and forward/data-driven reasonings (see Figure 4.8).[34]

---

30. (Pardo & Allen, 2008).
31. (Van Andel, 1994).
32. (K. N. Dunbar & Klahr, 2012) [p. 707].
33. See, for instance (Patel, Arocha, & Zhang, 2012).
34. (Kell & Oliver, 2004). See also (D. A. Schum, 1994) [pp. 139–140].

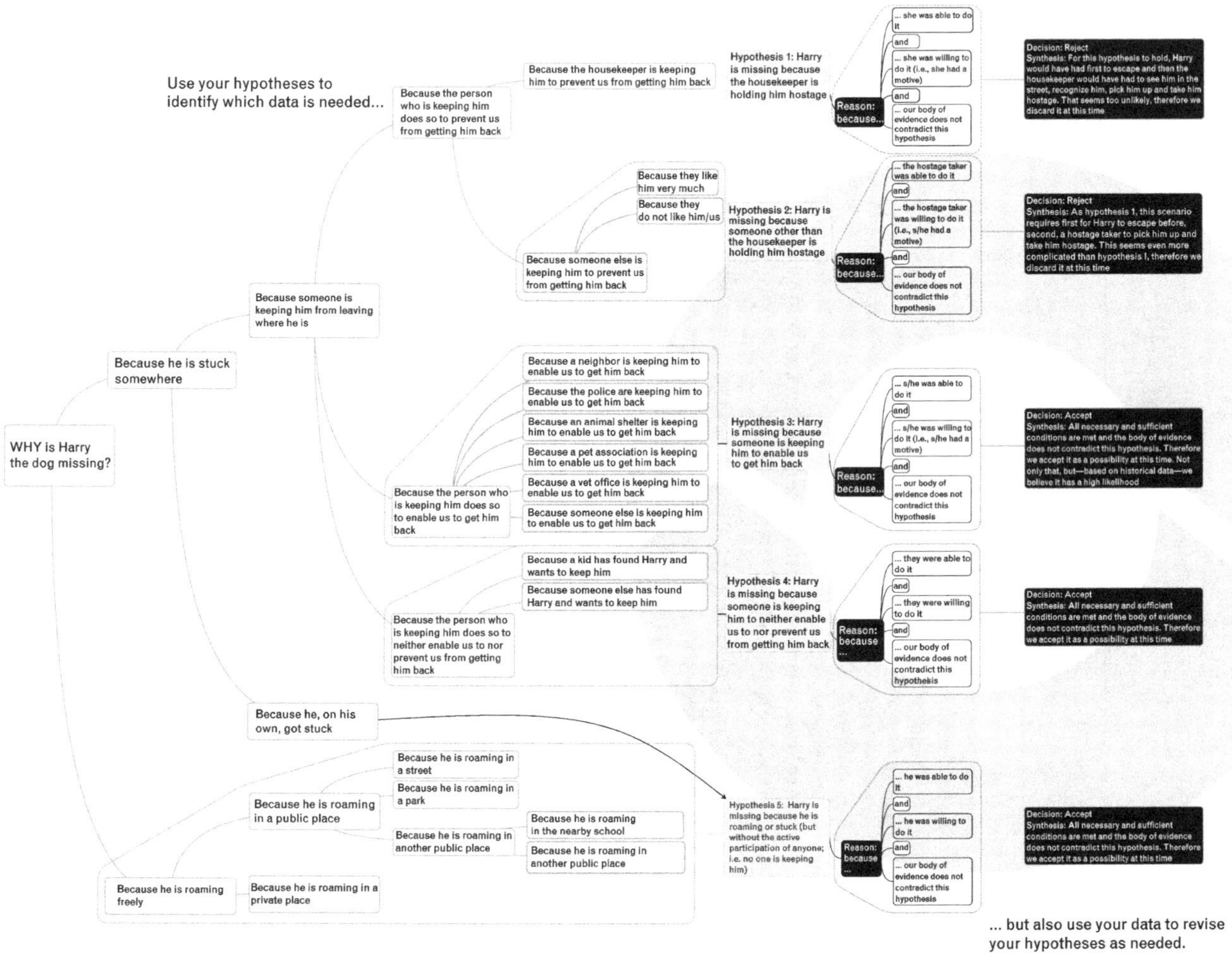

FIGURE 4.8: An ideal search will include both going from the hypotheses to the data and from the data to the hypotheses.

Therefore your analysis will include three situations:[35]

- One in which you go from observing a piece of evidence to relating it to a hypothesis; that is, "what hypothesis would explain these observations?" This is evidence in search of a hypothesis. It requires abductive thinking,
- One in which you go from a having hypothesis to identifying which evidence is needed to test it; that is, "assuming that the hypothesis is true, what other things should be observable?" This is a hypothesis in search of evidence. It requires deductive thinking, and
- One in which you must evaluate the likelihood of a hypothesis based on the available evidence; that is, "what is the likelihood of the hypothesis based on the available evidence?" This is an evidential test of a hypothesis, which requires inductive thinking.

One implication is that, as you conduct your analysis, you should also record the data that you accidentally uncover and relate it to the appropriate hypotheses, or generate new ones if needed.

## 3.2. IDENTIFY THE ANALYSIS NEEDED FOR EACH HYPOTHESIS

To test your hypotheses, you should endeavor to stay clear of common diagnosis problems—misdiagnoses, pseudodiagnoses, and overdiagnoses. To help you do so, identify the data and variables that can help you rule out competing hypotheses. Mapping out your hypotheses might be useful.

**Avoid diagnosis problems: pseudodiagnosing, overdiagnosing, and misdiagnosing.** *Pseudodiagnosing* is the tendency to seek diagnostically worthless information and alter one's conclusion based on that information.[36] *Misdiagnosing* is reaching the wrong diagnosis. This may be because of problems with evidence; for instance, if it is incomplete or inaccurate. But misdiagnoses also may stem from problems with logic. In particular, a piece of evidence is usually compatible with more than one hypothesis. A farmer may be feeding his turkeys because he really likes them or because he really likes eating them (or because he sells them, etc.). Jumping to the first conclusion is unfortunate but, as Taleb exposes, all too frequent as we extrapolate past events to predict future ones when we should not do so.[37]

*Overdiagnosing* is the diagnosis of a condition that will not cause any harm, such as the diagnosis of a cancer that will not cause symptoms or death during the patient's lifetime.[38] This is different from misdiagnosing: here, the disease is real but treating it is not necessary and may, in fact, cause harm.

---

35. (Tecuci et al., 2011), (Tecuci, Schum, Marcu, & Boicu, 2014).
36. (Doherty, Mynatt, Tweney, & Schiavo, 1979).
37. (Taleb, 2007) [p. 41].
38. (Welch, 2015) [p. 69–77]. See also (Gawande, 2015), (R. B. Ness, 2012a) [p. 38].

When it comes to data, more is not necessarily better, because gathering lots of peripheral data is time consuming, may mask important data, and may lead you to acquire unwarranted confidence.[39] Also, lots of noncritical information may hide important but weak signals,[40] or significantly decrease the impact of diagnostic information—a phenomenon called *dilution effect*.[41] So, it is not necessarily enough to gather information about the subject; in general, you will want to think carefully about what specific information you should be gathering.[42]

Putting it another way, if, as American zoologist Marston Bates said, research is the process of going up alleys to see whether they are blind,[43] it stands to reason that one should want to sharpen one's vision (i.e., select the right data) to identify as quickly as possible after stepping into an alley whether it is blind.

Academic physician Gilbert Welch has some advice for identifying whether a proposed analysis should be carried out. He recommends that patients ask their doctors two questions if they suspect they are being excessively tested: "What are we looking for?" and "If we find what we are looking for, what will we do differently?" If the data sought will not change the course of action, then we should not seek it.[44]

Also note that the absence of suspected evidence can be as informative as the presence of unsuspected evidence: In the novel *Silver Blaze*, Sherlock Holmes infers that the dog guarding the stable probably was familiar with the person who took the horse because the dog did *not* bark.[45] In Schum's words, "there seem to be three possibilities [to explain missing evidence]: (1) The evidence does not exist, (2) you looked in the wrong place, or (3) someone is concealing it."[46]

**Focus on variables that rule out competing hypotheses.** Ideally, your analysis should aim at uncovering evidence that allows you to rule out competing hypotheses.[47] Indeed, such a method of exploration with a high systematic power is possibly why distinguished scientists like Pasteur were able to move to a new field every two or three years and make breakthrough discoveries, when specialists—who were much more knowledgeable about these fields than he was—were hardly moving.[48]

To keep track of the analysis needed, the evidence gathered, and one's standing on a set of competing hypotheses some in the Intelligence Community use an approach called the Analysis of Competing Hypotheses (ACH).[49] ACH consists of capturing in a matrix all competing hypotheses, each in a column, and all existing items of evidence in rows. The analyst then writes down if each item of evidence is consistent, inconsistent, or has an ambiguous relationship with each hypothesis.

---

39. See (Oskamp, 1965), (Son & Kornell, 2010). See also (Bastardi & Shafir, 1998).
40. (Pope & Josang, 2005), (Oliver, Bjoertomt, Greenwood, & Rothwell, 2008).
41. (Nisbett, Zukier, & Lemley, 1981), (Arkes & Kajdasz, 2011) [p. 157].
42. (Beyth-Marom & Fischhoff, 1983; Tweney, Doherty, & Kleiter, 2010).
43. (Mitchell & Jolley, 2009) [p. 72].
44. (Welch, 2015) [pp. 114–115].
45. (Anderson et al., 2005) [p.74].
46. (D. A. Schum, 1994) [p. 33].
47. (Zimmerman, 2000) [p. 111], (Klahr et al., 1993) [p.114].
48. (Platt, 1964).
49. (Heuer, 1999; Heuer & Pherson, 2011), (George & Bruce, 2008) [p. 185].

TABLE 4.1: Hypotheses Maps are Made of Claims, Reasons, Objections, and Rebuttals

| Element | Description | Example |
|---|---|---|
| Claim: | An idea that someone says is true, phrased as a full declarative sentence. | Hypotheses, reasons, objections, and rebuttals are all types of claims. |
| Reason: | A set of claims that work together to provide evidence that another claim is true; in effect, to *support* that other claim. | The hostage taker was willing to take Harry hostage (i.e., he/she had a motive) **Reason: because ...** ... taking Harry hostage is a way for the hostage taker to make money **and** ... the hostage taker wants to make money |
| Objection: | A set of claims that work together to provide evidence that another claim is false; in effect, to *oppose* that other claim. | Taking Harry hostage is a way for the hostage taker to make money **Objection: but ...** ... Harry doesn't have any monetary value **and** ... Harry must have a monetary value for the hostage taker to make money |
| Rebuttal: | An objection to an objection. | ... Harry must have a monetary value for the hostage taker to make money **Rebuttal: however ...** ... the hostage taker will use my friend's affection for Harry to extort a ransom **and** ... my friend's affection for Harry enables the hostage taker to make money despite Harry having no monetary value |

Although some influential thinkers in that community have strongly advocated for ACH,[50] others point out that there is little evidence supporting its effectiveness.[51]

An alternative to ACH is argument/hypothesis mapping, a graphical representation of how hypotheses and items of evidence relate that shares many characteristics with issue mapping. Using argument mapping has been shown to improve students' critical thinking skills,[52] so we will briefly introduce it here.

**Use argument/hypothesis mapping.** As issue maps, argument maps are two-dimensional representations of a position under analysis. The map starts with the position on the left, lays out claims that support or oppose it in the middle and finishes on the right with unsupported claims that are accepted with no further inquiry (or accepted as self evident).[53] Table 4.1 introduces the four types of elements in an argument map: claims, reasons, objections, and rebuttals and Figure 4.9 shows how they interrelate in an argument.

Twardy reports that the most common error with argument mapping is to confuse multipremise reasons with independent ones.[54] An independent reason supports a claim without needing additional support, whereas a multipremise reason must have all of its premises true to be valid. Figure 4.10 shows such an example of incorrect mapping: "She was willing to do it," by itself, does not yield that the housekeeper is holding Harry hostage. Instead, *all* three premises ("she was willing to do it," "she was able to do it," and "our body of evidence does not refute this hypothesis") must be true for the claim to be supported.

Because all three conditions must be *simultaneously* true for us to accept the hypothesis, they should be considered as a single multipremise reason, as Figure 4.11 illustrates. One way to help formalize that a reason is a multipremise one is to add "and" between the various premises: that is, for the argument to hold, the housekeeper must have been *willing* to hold Harry hostage *and* must have been *able* to hold him hostage *and* our body of evidence

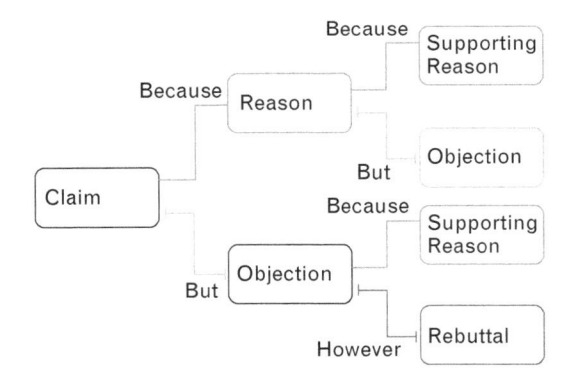

**FIGURE 4.9:** Hypothesis maps have four types of elements: claims, reasons, objections, and rebuttals.

50. (Heuer, 1999) [pp. 95–109], (Heuer & Pherson, 2011) [pp. 160–169].
51. (National Research Council, 2010) [p. 19].
52. (Twardy, 2010). Alternative graphical tools to marshal evidence and relate it to hypotheses also include Wigmore charts and (object-oriented) Bayesian networks; see (Hepler, Dawid, & Leucari, 2007).
53. (Twardy, 2010).
54. (Twardy, 2010).

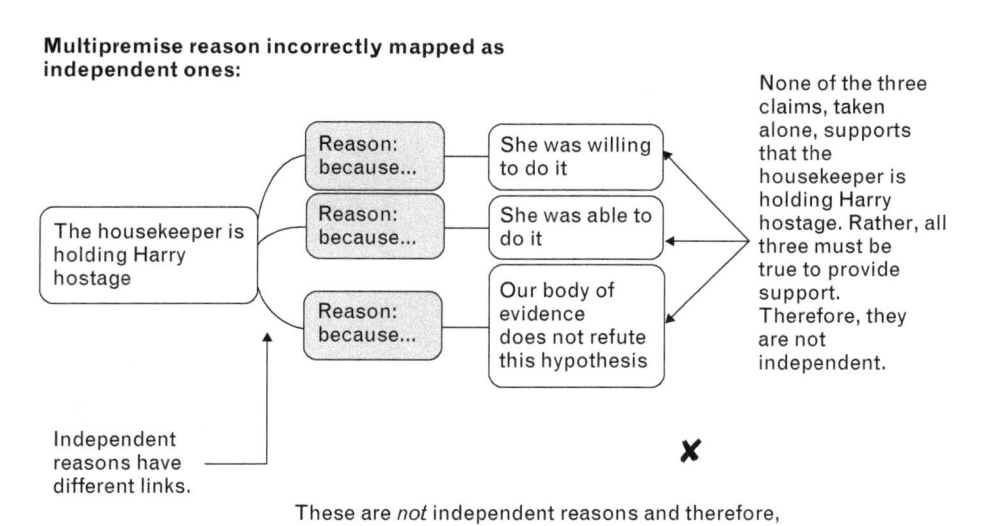

**Multipremise reason incorrectly mapped as independent ones:**

```
                    ┌─────────────┐    ┌──────────────┐
                    │ Reason:     │───▶│ She was willing│◀──┐
                    │ because...  │    │ to do it     │    │
                    └─────────────┘    └──────────────┘    │
┌──────────────┐    ┌─────────────┐    ┌──────────────┐    │
│ The housekeeper is│ Reason:     │───▶│ She was able to│◀─┤
│ holding Harry │   │ because...  │    │ do it        │    │
│ hostage      │    └─────────────┘    └──────────────┘    │
└──────────────┘    ┌─────────────┐    ┌──────────────┐    │
        ▲           │ Reason:     │───▶│ Our body of  │◀──┘
        │           │ because...  │    │ evidence     │
        │           └─────────────┘    │ does not refute│
        │                              │ this hypothesis│
        │                              └──────────────┘
Independent
reasons have
different links.
```

None of the three claims, taken alone, supports that the housekeeper is holding Harry hostage. Rather, all three must be true to provide support. Therefore, they are not independent.

✗

These are *not* independent reasons and therefore, should not be mapped as they are above.

FIGURE 4.10: Premises that need others to support a claim are not independent.

does not refute this hypothesis. Also, to further differentiate multipremise reasons from independent ones, note how in this graphical convention all the premises of a multipremise reason stem from a single "reason" box (Figure 4.11), whereas independent reasons stem from different "reason" boxes (Figure 4.10).

In contrast, independent reasons do not need one another to support an argument; as such, you can link them with "and/or," as Figure 4.12 shows.[55] Even if one of these is rejected, the claim is supported by the remaining one(s).

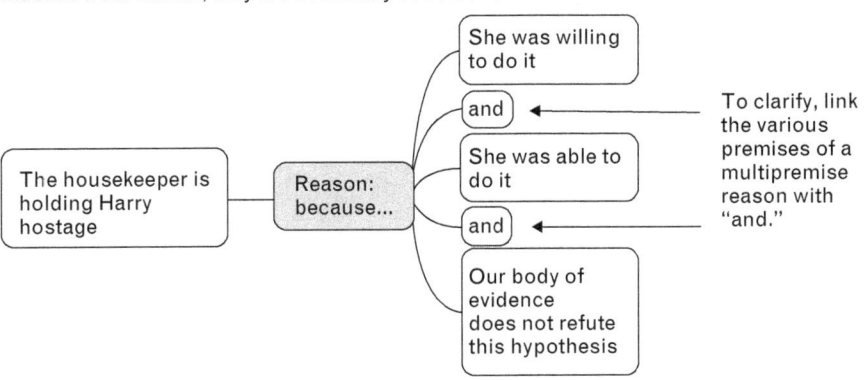

**Multipremise reason:**

To support an argument, **all** the premises of a multipremise reason must be true. That is, they are necessary conditions.

```
                                    ┌──────────────┐
                                   ┌│ She was willing│
                                   ││ to do it     │
                                   │└──────────────┘
                                   │   ┌─────┐
                                   │   │ and │◀────
                                   │   └─────┘
┌──────────────┐   ┌──────────┐    │┌──────────────┐
│ The housekeeper is│ Reason:  │───┼│ She was able to│
│ holding Harry │   │ because...│   ││ do it        │
│ hostage      │   └──────────┘    │└──────────────┘
└──────────────┘                   │   ┌─────┐
                                   │   │ and │◀────
                                   │   └─────┘
                                   │┌──────────────┐
                                   └│ Our body of  │
                                    │ evidence     │
                                    │ does not refute│
                                    │ this hypothesis│
                                    └──────────────┘
```

To clarify, link the various premises of a multipremise reason with "and."

FIGURE 4.11: Multipremise reasons belong together.

---

55. See also Schum's concept of *convergent evidence* (D. A. Schum, 1994) [pp. 401–409].

Determine Actual Causes • 95

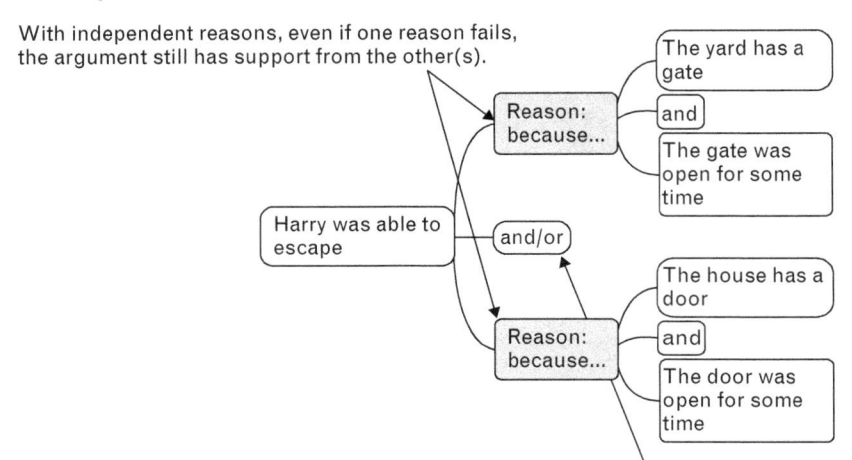

**Independent reasons:**

With independent reasons, even if one reason fails, the argument still has support from the other(s).

```
Harry was able to escape
    ├── and/or ──► Reason: because...
    │                 ├── The yard has a gate
    │                 ├── and
    │                 └── The gate was open for some time
    └──────────────► Reason: because...
                      ├── The house has a door
                      ├── and
                      └── The door was open for some time
```

To clarify that the reasons are independent, make them stem from different reason boxes and link those with "and/or."

FIGURE 4.12: Independent reasons do not need the help of other elements.

In Figure 4.12, the two reasons that we propose to explain how Harry could escape is that he could have done so through the yard or through the house. Even if one of these reasons fails, the argument still has support from the other.

All simple arguments have at least two co-premises. Making your thinking explicit means identifying those and mapping them. This can be useful to identify weaknesses. For instance, consider mapping the classic inductive argument that all swans are white because all swans we know are white (Figure 4.13).[56]

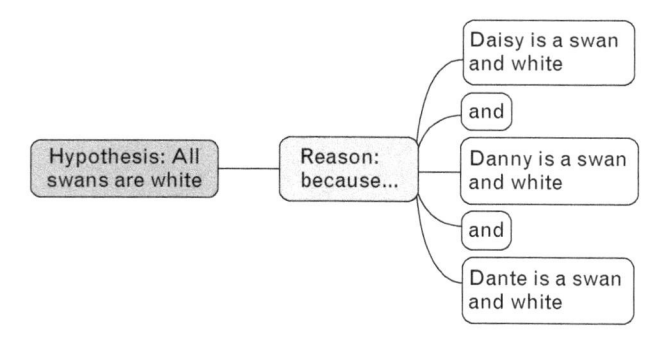

```
Hypothesis: All swans are white ──► Reason: because...
                                       ├── Daisy is a swan and white
                                       ├── and
                                       ├── Danny is a swan and white
                                       ├── and
                                       └── Dante is a swan and white
```

FIGURE 4.13: Using a map may help you realize that just listing the cases of occurrences to support a conclusion does not expose your entire argument.

---

56. See (King, 2010).

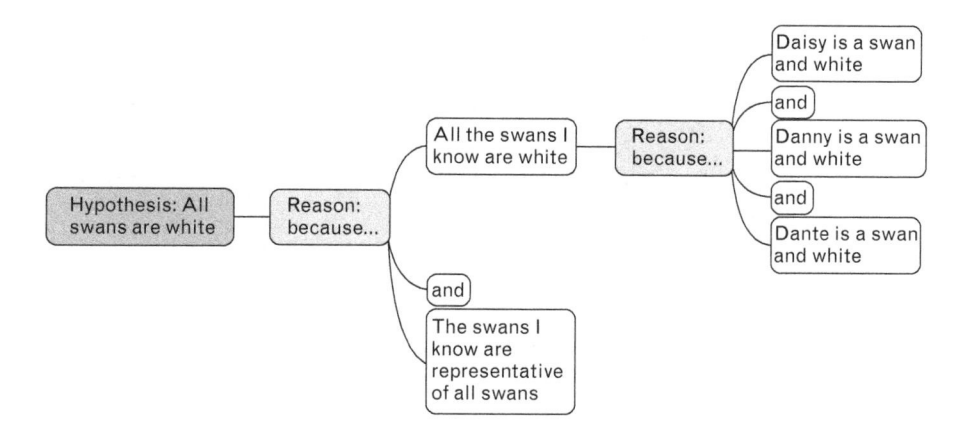

**FIGURE 4.14:** Completing the induction in a map format might help identify where the weakness in your thinking is.

Putting the argument in a map format may help you realize that just listing cases captures only part of your reasoning. Completing the argument also requires assuming that the swans you know are representative of all swans (Figure 4.14).

This is key, because it is the second part of the argument—the one that usually remains implicit—that is the weak part of this induction.

### 3.3. WORK WITH EVIDENCE

> *"Before taking the country to war, this Administration owed it to the American people to give them a 100 percent accurate picture of the threat we faced. Unfortunately, our Committee has concluded that the Administration made significant claims that were not supported by the intelligence," Rockefeller said. "In making the case for war, the Administration repeatedly presented intelligence as fact when in reality it was unsubstantiated, contradicted, or even non-existent. As a result, the American people were led to believe that the threat from Iraq was much greater than actually existed."*[57]

When working with evidence, you should consider its properties—relevance, credibility, and inferential force—and seek both supporting and opposing information. You also should identify an appropriate standard of proof. Five major characteristics describe how evidence—taken individually or as a body—relates to hypotheses:[58]

- Evidence is *incomplete*, in that we never have watertight support of a hypothesis and there is always room for doubt and uncertainty,[59]

---

57. (U.S. Senate Select Committee on Intelligence, 2008).
58. (Tecuci et al., 2014), (Tecuci et al., 2011).
59. (Prakken, 2014), see also (von Winterfeldt & Edwards, 1986) [p. 171].

Determine Actual Causes • 97

- Evidence is frequently *inconclusive*, in that a single piece of evidence usually is compatible with more than one hypothesis,
- Evidence is frequently *ambiguous*, that is, it is unclear what the evidence is actually telling,
- A body of evidence frequently has some level of *dissonance*, with items supporting some hypotheses and others opposing them, and
- The sources from which the evidence originates are not perfectly credible; rather there are gradations of *believability* or *credibility*.

**Evaluate relevance, credibility, and inferential force.** An item of evidence has three principal characteristics: relevance, credibility, and inferential force or weight.[60]

A *relevant* item of evidence is one that makes a hypothesis more or less probable.[61] Using a hypothesis map helps you evaluate the relevance of each item of evidence to each hypothesis: items should be linked on the map to all hypotheses (there often is more than one) to which they are relevant.

The *credibility* of an item of evidence measures how much it should be believed. Unless an item of evidence is perfectly credible, you should not assume that having evidence that an event occurred means that the event *did* actually occur.[62] Indeed, a neighbor saying that he saw Harry alone in front of the house does not mean that Harry was alone in front of the house. Maybe the neighbor was mistaken—perhaps he saw another dog—or maybe he is lying to us.

To evaluate the credibility of evidence, Anderson et al. recommend differentiating *tangible* evidence—which includes documents, objects, and measurements—from *testimonial* evidence. Table 4.2 summarizes some of the key credibility attributes of evidence.

In a map, you assess the credibility of an item of evidence by questioning it and its supporting claims until you reach a basic level where you accept unsupported claims. Figure 4.15 shows how we reached that level in Harry's case, hearing the friend's assertion that the yard gate does not lock, we could choose to go check it for ourselves. Instead, we decide to accept it as credible with no further inquiry.

The third characteristic of evidence is its *inferential* (or *probative*) *force*, which is a measure of how strong the evidence is in supporting or opposing the claim under investigation.[63]

Establishing the relevance, credibility, and inferential force requires both creative and critical reasoning.[64]

---

60. See, for instance (Anderson et al., 2005; D. A. Schum, 2009), (Boicu, Tecuci, & Schum, 2008).
61. (Anderson et al., 2005) [p. 62].
62. (Anderson et al., 2005) [pp. 64–66].
63. (Anderson et al., 2005) [p. 71].
64. (Boicu et al., 2008).

TABLE 4.2: Credibility Attributes of Evidence[a]

| Type of Evidence | Credibility Attributes |
|---|---|
| Tangible evidence | **Authenticity**—is the item of evidence what it purports to be? Deliberate deceptions or mistakes affect authenticity. |
| | **Accuracy/sensitivity**—if a sensing device was used to obtain the evidence, did it provide the degree of resolution needed? |
| | **Reliability**—is the process of generating the item of evidence repeatable, dependable, or consistent? |
| Testimonial evidence | **Basis for assertion**—how did the witness acquire the data? Is the witness appropriately qualified to comment? |
| | **Veracity**—is the witness being truthful and sincere? Are there no conflicts of interest? |
| | **Objectivity**—is the witness's belief based on evidence rather than on expectations or desires? Is the belief free from any significant dispute among relevant experts? |
| | **Observational sensitivity**—did the witness have adequate sensors (vision, hearing, touch, smell, and taste) under the circumstances (e.g., alcohol consumption, poorly lit scene)? |

[a]Integrating elements of (Anderson et al., 2005) [pp. 64–67], (Twardy, 2010). See also (D. A. Schum, 2009) [p. 213] for a list of grounds for testimonial credibility impeachment and (D. A. Schum & Morris, 2007) for questions that can help to analyze how much credence we should give to specific testimonial evidence.

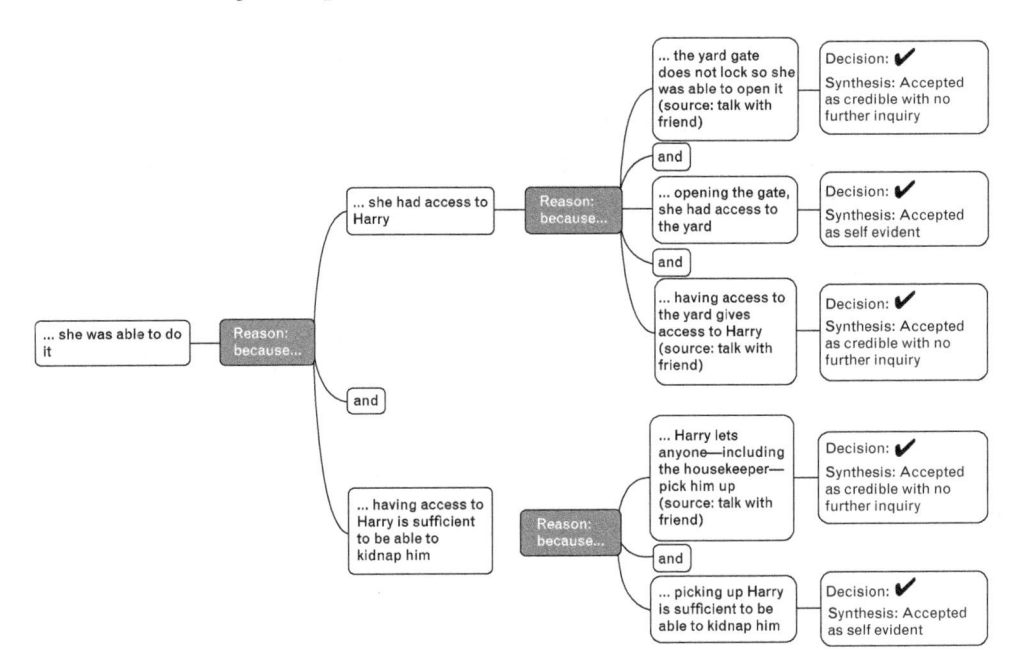

FIGURE 4.15: Test the credibility of evidence until you reach a level where you feel comfortable leaving the claim unsupported.

TABLE 4.3: You Can Express the Relationship between a Hypothesis and Evidence in Various Ways

| Supporting Favoring Confirming Confirmatory | ... evidence ... | is consistent with substantiates supports corroborates confirms validates asserts (verifies) (proves) | ... your hypothesis, leading you to, potentially ... | think it more probable. fail to reject it. consider it valid. provisionally accept it. (accept it). |
|---|---|---|---|---|
| Then, your hypothesis ... | is consistent complies coheres | ... with the evidence. | | |
| Opposing Contrary Countering Negative Refuting Disfavoring Disconfirming Disconfirmatory Incompatible Inconsistent | ... evidence ... | opposes undermines rebuts refutes contradicts challenges counters falsifies disconfirms | ... your hypothesis, leading you to, potentially, ... | think it more improbable. reject it. |
| Then, your hypothesis ... | is inconsistent | ... with the evidence. | | |

**Seek both supporting and opposing evidence.** Assuming that an item of evidence is relevant to a hypothesis, it is going to help support it or oppose it. (See Table 4.3 for ways to express the relationship between a hypothesis and evidence.[65])

There is widespread agreement that, when testing hypotheses, people tend to resort to using a positive test strategy—trying to find evidence compatible with the hypothesis, which Klayman and Ha called +Htests—rather than −Htests, or looking for incompatible evidence.[66] Klayman and Ha note that this default mode has advantages because it rules out false positives, which is usually desirable when one has to "live with one's mistakes."[67] Also, in some cases, this approach might be the only one that can lead to a correct conclusion. They also warn, however, that this approach can be inappropriate in other settings because it might lead to the wrong conclusion. This has been shown by cognitive psychologist Wason through an experiment that has come to be known as the Wason 2–4–6 task.[68]

65. The terms in parentheses should not be used or, if they are, they should be used with extreme care because, technically, there is no such thing as verifying or accepting a hypothesis. See discussion below for more.

66. (Klayman & Ha, 1987, 1989; Mahoney & DeMonbreun, 1977; Snyder & Swann, 1978; Wason, 1960) (K. N. Dunbar & Klahr, 2012) [p. 705].

67. (Klayman & Ha, 1987).

68. (Wason, 1960). For a discussion, see (Michael E Gorman & Gorman, 1984).

The 2–4–6 task consists of asking subjects to guess a rule that the experimenter has in mind that applies to sets of three numbers. The experimenter then gives the subjects the three numbers 2–4–6, telling them that the sequence complies with the rule, and asks them to write down sets of three numbers with reasons for their choice. Then, the experimenter tells the subjects whether their sequences conform to the rule, and if not, invites them to try again. Once they are confident that they have guessed the rule, the subjects announce it.

Only six of the original 29 subjects gave the correct rule at their first announcement. Subjects tended to form hypotheses that were too specific. They also tended to only propose sequences that were consistent with their hypotheses. For instance, if a subject supposed that numbers were increasing by two, they would propose confirmatory sequences—4–6–8 or 10–12–14—as opposed to using a disconfirmatory approach, proposing, say, 2–3–4 or 7–54–5. By the way, the rule was "ascending numbers."

The scientific approach to hypothesis testing, following Francis Bacon's (and, later, Karl Popper's) idea, is to look for falsifying evidence.[69] This makes sense because countless verifications can be countered by a single falsification, which is why, technically, one does not accept a hypothesis, at best, one only accepts it provisionally.[70] In other words, there are only conclusive falsifications, no conclusive verifications[71] or, in Taleb's words, "You know what is wrong with a lot more confidence than you know what is right."[72] So Platt and others recommend that, when identifying evidence, one should keep in mind the information needed to refute one's hypothesis.[73] According to this view, one should vigorously attack each hypothesis, and only then select—favoring the hypothesis that best resisted the attacks. This is called *induction by elimination*.[74]

The problem is that our natural tendency to seek confirmation of our hypotheses gets in the way of seeking disconfirmation. This is true even with trained scientists who perform no better than nonscientists, including ministers.[75]

Luckily, there are ways to continue to seek disconfirmation: Cowley and Byrne observe that people readily seek falsification of someone else's hypothesis[76] and that experts are better than novices at seeking falsification.[77] So, in your project, perhaps you can "outsource" the design of the testing of your hypotheses to an otherwise-noninvolved colleague with the specific instruction that the tests should aim at disconfirmation. Similarly, you might seek the help of subject matter experts in the design of the tests.

Seeking disconfirmation has other issues as well, among them that the falsification itself may be erroneous.[78] Indeed, just as we should not discard the fact that the earth's

---

69. (Popper, 2002). See also (D. A. Schum, 1994) [p. 28].
70. In this book, however, we use "accept" instead of "fail to reject" as an attempt to improve clarity.
71. (Klayman & Ha, 1987) [p. 214]. See also (Oreskes, Shrader-Frechette, & Belitz, 1994), (McIntyre, 1998).
72. (Taleb, 2007).
73. (Platt, 1964).
74. (Anderson et al., 2005) [p. 257].
75. (Mahoney & DeMonbreun, 1977).
76. (Cowley & Byrne, 2005).
77. (Cowley & Byrne, 2004).
78. (Tweney, Doherty, & Mynatt, 1981) [pp. 81–82].

gravitational field has an average magnitude of 9.81 m/s² the moment a student's test finds otherwise,[79] it is advisable to question the value of each item of evidence, especially in complex problems where conflicting evidence is common. To that end, keeping a healthy dose of skepticism when facing new evidence by implicitly asking "Must I believe this?" can be useful.[80]

Various factors—including whether feedback is available, whether the resolution is carried out by a single individual or a group, whether confirmation is sought before disconfirmation—seem to influence the effectiveness of a confirmatory versus a disconfirmatory approach.[81]

So, having identified that both supporting and opposing evidence may have benefits, a prudent general approach seems to look for both types. Tweney et al. suggest starting by looking for confirmatory evidence so as to generate good hypotheses before looking for disconfirmatory evidence.[82] You should then characterize the value of each hypothesis in terms of how much it agrees with the overall body of evidence.[83] In Thagard's words, "An explanatory hypothesis is accepted if it coheres better overall than its competitors."[84] Having done so, capture your conclusion in your issue map.

Note that you might gather evidence as a result of actively looking for it or happening upon it. Although we try to structure our approach and concentrate on the information that we need, at times we accidentally uncover unexpected information. The key is to recognize when such information is valuable—as the next section explains—and ensure that you consider it. As an illustration, in Harry's case, we went to talk to a neighbor to see if he knew where Harry was. He did not, but he did volunteer a critical item of evidence: He had seen Harry alone in front of the house. This item is critical because of its diagnosticity: The chances of it appearing are significantly different depending on the hypothesis.[85] Indeed, if we believe our neighbor that Harry was alone in front of the house, his being held hostage implies that he somehow got to the street, where he was first alone and then taken hostage ($H_1$ or $H_2$) as opposed to his having escaped ($H_3$, $H_4$, or $H_5$).

## 3.4. EMBRACE—AND FACILITATE—SERENDIPITY

Although we may fool ourselves into thinking that human progress is the result of concerted strategies and careful executions, history tells another story, namely, that chance is

---

79. (National Research Council, 2011b) [p. 132].

80. See (E. Dawson, Gilovich, & Regan, 2002).

81. (Michael E. Gorman, Gorman, Latta, & Cunningham, 1984), (Mynatt, Doherty, & Tweney, 1978), (Tweney et al., 1980).

82. (Tweney et al., 1980) [pp. 110–111].

83. See (Mynatt et al., 1978) [p. 405]. Looking for both supporting and opposing evidence shares some characteristics with an adversarial process—such as the Anglo-American judicial system. The system consists of having adversarial parties present their evidence, analyzing this evidence through cross-examination, and deciding on what the truth is (or as close an approximation as can be) (Schauer, 2009) [p. 208]. See also (D. Schum et al., 2009), (D. A. Schum, 1994) [pp. 55–58].

84. (P. Thagard, 1989).

85. (Zlotnick, 1972).

of paramount importance. *Serendipity*—the appreciation of the chance encounter of something valuable while looking for something else—accounts for a sizable chunk of discoveries in all disciplines. Indeed, the discoveries of pulsars, X-rays, coffee, gravity, radioactivity, Post-it notes, painting styles, penicillin, America, Pluto—the list goes on—are all credited to happy accidents.[86]

Note that serendipity requires not just stumbling upon an unexpected result but also recognizing its value. For instance, take Alexander Fleming's discovery of penicillin: mold growing on his petri dishes had killed the bacteria that he was studying. Others had experienced this problem before, but Fleming was the first to recognize the opportunity and capitalize on it.[87] So it is essential to synthesize these chance encounters into insight—what some call being sagacious[88]—which is an example of a correct abduction.

Van Andel identified 17 serendipity patterns, including using analogies (Laënnec inventing the stethoscope after observing kids scratching pins on one end of a piece of wood and listening to the effect on the other end) or capitalizing on apparent errors (the 3M Company inventing the removable Post-it note after discovering that seemingly bad glue opened the door to a "temporarily permanent" adhesive).[89]

Serendipity, then, requires understanding the "so what?" of one's observation and being willing to brand as victories those events that might not seem victorious. It, therefore, requires a particular state of mind, perhaps best summarized by Picasso's *"Je ne cherche pas, je trouve."*[90]

# 4. DECIDE

Having conducted your analysis, you should now decide which of your hypothesis/ses explain(s) why your problem exists in the first place. To help you do so, let's talk about biases, Bayesian inference, and Occam's razor.

### 4.4. AVOID BIASES

Tversky and Kahneman in the 1970s proposed that people use heuristics—mental tactics—to cope with the complexities of estimating probabilities. Although these heuristics can be useful, they also can lead to systematic biases.[91]

When testing hypotheses, one needs to guard against various biases. One of those is *belief preservation,* the tendency we have to favor evidence that supports our point of view

---

86. (Kell & Oliver, 2004; R. B. Ness, 2012b; Van Andel, 1994), (Fine & Deegan, 1996; Vale, Delfino, & Vale, 2005), (Cannon, 1940).
87. (R. Ness, 2013).
88. (André, Teevan, & Dumais, 2009).
89. (Van Andel, 1994).
90. (Van Andel, 1994). Equally appropriate is Pasteur's *"Dans les champs de l'observation le hazard ne favorise que les esprits préparés"* which translates to "0," see (Cannon, 1940).
91. (Tversky & Kahneman, 1974), (Tversky & Kahneman, 1973).

over evidence that opposes it.[92] [V]an Gelder describes how belief preservation manifests itself: We look for evidence that supports our beliefs and disregard or do not look for evidence that opposes them. We give more credit to evidence that supports our beliefs; and we continue in our beliefs despite overwhelming contrary evidence.[93]

As we have seen in the previous section, hypothesis testing requires a willingness to attempt to falsify hypotheses.[94] Correcting belief preservation requires you to actively monitor if you are at risk for it and take mitigating action such as looking for contrary evidence, giving such evidence extra credit, and nurturing the ability to change your mind and admit that you are wrong.

Done properly, this approach has a ludic component to it. Davis notes that "if investigators test multiple hypotheses prevailing in their field with disconfirmatory tests rather than simply defend their own views, science becomes more a game than a war."[95] Recognizing one's errors is also inherently educational; Bazerman and Moore point out that "we learn the most about how we accomplish our goals not by observing successes, but by taking account of failures."[96]

Working with several hypotheses helps us acquire this flexibility: by explicitly listing all hypotheses, you already know that you are wrong on some. Therefore, instead of having to deal with whether you are wrong, the issue becomes identifying where you are wrong, which might be a little more ego friendly.

To minimize confirmation bias, it helps to analyze all aspects of hypotheses, not just the ones that might result in the outcome you are hoping for, and document all. You may want to do this in your issue map using check marks and crosses to record which arguments you accept as valid and which you reject (as we have done earlier in Figure 4.15).

## 4.5. USE BAYESIAN INFERENCE

"When the facts change, I change my opinion. What do you do, sir?"

—John Maynard Keynes

Bayesian inference can help you reduce biases by providing a framework to update your beliefs as you uncover new evidence.[97] Specifically, it allows you to revise your original estimate of how likely a hypothesis is (called your *prior probability* or *prior*) in light of a new item of evidence to get a *posterior probability* or *posterior* of the hypothesis: The posterior equals your prior times the conditional probability of the evidence given the hypothesis divided by the probability of the evidence. In mathematical form, assuming that

---

92. (Lord, Ross, & Lepper, 1979).
93. (Tim van Gelder, 2005).
94. (Wason, 1960).
95. (Davis, 2006).
96. (Bazerman & Moore, 2008) [p. 179].
97. (Tenenbaum, Kemp, Griffiths, & Goodman, 2011).

$n$ hypotheses may be true, the posterior probability of hypothesis $h_i$ after collecting item of evidence $d$ is:

$$P(h_i|d) = P(h_i)\frac{P(d|h_i)}{P(d)}$$

$$P(h_i|d) = P(h_i)\frac{P(d|h_i)}{\sum_{i=1}^{n} P(d|h_i)P(h_i)}$$

Equation 1: Bayes' theorem.

Bayesian inference can be a powerful tool in a solver's toolkit because people usually do not integrate new information into their judgment as much as they should.[98] So let's introduce it with a simple case and discuss some of its benefits and limitations when applied to practical cases.

**Understand the basics of Bayesian inference.** Imagine a dark urn in front of you with four balls in it. You cannot see the color of the balls but know that two hypotheses are equally likely:[99]

$h_{blue}$: The urn contains three blue balls and one white
$h_{white}$: The urn contains three white balls and one blue

Your task is to evaluate whether $h_{blue}$ is true with no more than 1 chance in 1,000 of being wrong. To do so, you are allowed to pick one ball at a time, note its color, update your thinking, and replace it in the urn without looking at the other balls. How should you do this?

One way to proceed is to use Bayes's theorem. Adapted to this case, it reads:

$$P(h_{blue}|d) = P(h_{blue})\frac{P(d|h_{blue})}{P(d|h_{blue})P(h_{blue}) + P(d|h_{white})P(h_{white})}$$

Equation 2: Bayes's theorem applied to the urn problem.

Now we need to replace each of these terms with their quantities. Assume that your first draw gets you a white ball (i.e., $d$ = *drawn a white ball*).

We know that the hypotheses are equally likely, therefore, the priors are equal: $P(h_{blue}) = P(h_{white}) = 0.5$.

---

98. See, for instance (Phillips & Edwards, 1966).
99. This example is adapted from (Gauch, 2003) [pp. 226–232].

Determine Actual Causes • 105

Because in $h_{blue}$ only one of the four balls is white, then $P(d|h_{blue}) = P(\text{drawing a white ball}|h_{blue}) = 0.25$ (read "the probability of drawing a white ball given $h_{blue}$") and, conversely, $P(d|h_{white}) = 0.75$.

Therefore,

$$P(h_{blue}|white) = 0.5 \frac{0.25}{0.25 \cdot 0.5 + 0.75 \cdot 0.5} = 0.25$$

Assume that, on your second pick, you draw a blue ball. The posterior probability of your first test becomes the prior for this one and you can compute the updated posterior:

$$P(h_{blue}|blue) = 0.25 \frac{0.75}{0.75 \cdot 0.25 + 0.25 \cdot 0.75} = 0.5$$

Repeating the experiment, you get something that looks like Table 4.4.

**Understand the benefits and limitations of Bayesian inference.** In this example, relying on *Bayesian inference helps avoid unnecessary experiments*. Consider solving the problem above with an intuitive approach in lieu of a Bayesian one by, say, asking a group of experts to conclude on the correct hypothesis with a 99.9% level of confidence considering that, out of 15 draws, four yielded a white ball and 11 yielded a blue one. It is reasonable to think that convincing such a group would take more than 15 experiments. Yet, we have achieved the required level of confidence with just 15 draws, so there is no need for further draws. Here, generating new data is inexpensive so the downside of overcollection is minimal. But that

TABLE 4.4: Evolution of the Probability of Having Three Blue Balls in the Urn as Experiments Proceed

|  | Observation | $P(d|h_{blue})$ | $P(h_{blue})$ | $P(d|h_{white})$ | $P(h_{white})$ | $P(h_{blue}|d)$ |
|---|---|---|---|---|---|---|
| Experiment 1 | White | 0.250 | 0.500 | 0.750 | 0.500 | 0.250 |
| 2 | Blue | 0.750 | 0.250 | 0.250 | 0.750 | 0.500 |
| 3 | White | 0.250 | 0.500 | 0.750 | 0.500 | 0.250 |
| 4 | Blue | 0.750 | 0.250 | 0.250 | 0.750 | 0.500 |
| 5 | Blue | 0.750 | 0.500 | 0.250 | 0.500 | 0.750 |
| 6 | Blue | 0.750 | 0.750 | 0.250 | 0.250 | 0.900 |
| 7 | Blue | 0.750 | 0.900 | 0.250 | 0.100 | 0.964 |
| 8 | Blue | 0.750 | 0.964 | 0.250 | 0.036 | 0.988 |
| 9 | Blue | 0.750 | 0.988 | 0.250 | 0.012 | 0.996 |
| 10 | White | 0.250 | 0.996 | 0.750 | 0.004 | 0.988 |
| 11 | Blue | 0.750 | 0.988 | 0.250 | 0.012 | 0.996 |
| 12 | White | 0.250 | 0.996 | 0.750 | 0.004 | 0.988 |
| 13 | Blue | 0.750 | 0.988 | 0.250 | 0.012 | 0.996 |
| 14 | Blue | 0.750 | 0.9959 | 0.250 | 0.004 | 0.9986 |
| 15 | Blue | 0.750 | 0.9986 | 0.250 | 0.001 | 0.9995 |

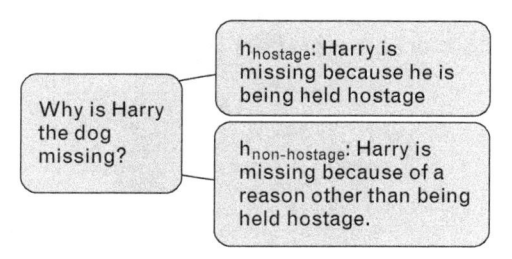

**FIGURE 4.16:** You can formulate Harry's case considering only two hypotheses.

is not the case in many real-life situations; in those, you would want to know the minimum data necessary to help you reach a given level of confidence.

*Bayesian inference requires quantifying judgment.* Quantifying judgment is not too complicated when dealing with a laboratory case such as picking balls out of an urn. It becomes more complicated, however, when dealing with problems where information is limited. To illustrate, let's go back to Harry. Suppose that you want to identify whether he is being held hostage, because that will dictate whether you should call the police, and you think that this should be your foremost consideration. You might then consider two hypotheses, as Figure 4.16 shows, and you may want to test $h_{hostage}$, the hypothesis that Harry is being held hostage against $h_{non\text{-}hostage}$, the hypothesis that he is missing for whatever other reason. Applied to this situation, Bayes's theorem becomes:

$$P(h_{hostage}|d) = P(h_{hostage}) \frac{P(d|h_{hostage})}{P(d|h_{hostage})P(h_{hostage}) + P(d|h_{non\text{-}hostage})P(h_{non\text{-}hostage})},$$

where you now need to identify numerical values for all quantities on the right-hand-side of the equation.

Based on prior information—such as your past experience, what you have heard from neighbors, what you have read in the local press or in peer-reviewed journals—you might decide that cases of pets held hostage are much rarer than those of pets missing for other reasons, leading you to set your priors as $P(h_{hostage}) = 0.1$ and $P(h_{non\text{-}hostage}) = 0.9$. (Or you might decide that these priors are inappropriate and should be 0.01 vs. 0.99 or 0.5 vs. 0.5; this illustrates how incomplete data introduces subjectivity and may produce disagreements.[100])

Next, consider a first datum of information that you think should be accounted for: $d_1$: Harry went missing on the very day that your friend fired his housekeeper, a seemingly unstable and upset person who blamed the dog for losing her job and threatened retaliation. This comes in the context of Harry having not gone missing for months. Highly emotional, your friend insists that this just *cannot* be a coincidence. You might decide that $P(d_1|h_{hostage}) = 0.9$ and $P(d_1|h_{non\text{-}hostage}) = 0.1$. Applying Bayes's theorem yields a first posterior for $h_{hostage}$: $P(h_{hostage}|d_1) = 0.5$.

---

100. How to set priors in a Bayesian approach is a source of controversy; see (D. A. Schum, 1994) [pp. 49–51] for a discussion. See also (Prakken, 2014), (Puga, Krzywinski, & Altman, 2015), (Cousins, 1995), and (Gustafson, Edwards, Phillips, & Slack, 1969) for related considerations.

TABLE 4.5: Evolution of the Probability of Harry Being Held Hostage Considering New Evidence

| | Observation | $P(d\|h_{hostage})$ | $P(h_{hostage})$ | $P(d\|h_{non\text{-}hostage})$ | $P(h_{non\text{-}hostage})$ | $P(h_{hostage}\|d)$ |
|---|---|---|---|---|---|---|
| $d_1$ | Disappears on day housekeeper is fired | 0.90 | 0.10 | 0.10 | 0.90 | 0.50 |
| $d_2$ | Seen alone | 0.05 | 0.50 | 0.95 | 0.50 | 0.05 |

Next, consider as $d_2$ the fact that a neighbor saw Harry, alone, in front of the house. You might reason that it is highly unlikely that Harry first somehow got out of the house/yard (so that he could be seen alone) and that someone then took him hostage. Indeed, once he was out of the house, it seems much more likely that he just kept on going as opposed to being spotted and picked up by someone who was willing and able to take him hostage. So you might decide that $P(d_2|h_{hostage}) = 0.05$ and $P(d_2|h_{non\text{-}hostage}) = 0.95$. The new posterior is now $P(h_{hostage}|d_2) = 0.05$ (see Table 4.5).

Reviewing the other items of information, you might decide that their diagnosticity is poor, that is, $P(d_i|h_{hostage}) \simeq P(d_i|h_{non\text{-}hostage})$. Therefore, their inclusion in the analysis would not provide additional insight and, so, you leave them out.

Based on the evidence considered, the probability that Harry was taken hostage (by the housekeeper or anyone else) is 5% while the probability that he is missing for another reason is 95%. You might decide that this is a sufficiently conclusive diagnostic: you can reasonably assume that he is not held hostage and that you should look for him accordingly.

As noted above, a major difficulty resides in assigning priors and likelihood for real-life cases. Zoltnick observes that supporters of the intuitive approach point out that people are likely to disagree on what those should be but also observes that these disagreements exist whether one quantifies them or not,[101] just as we do not all have the same understanding of what "very likely" or "very unlikely" mean. Unequivocal values for these concepts are desirable.[102] Some fields—such as weather forecasting—assign numerical values to their predictions and the National Research Council, for one, is exhorting the Intelligence Community to transition to similarly explicit scales.[103]

For its part, the Bayesian approach has been shown to be more desirable than the intuitive approach in studying intelligence problems, at least in some settings.[104] Fisk proposes a Bayesian approach for assembling and updating the opinions of several people—shown in Table 4.6—that can be readily adapted to other settings. Imagine that you are interested in having five analysts quantify the probability that a war between two countries will occur within four weeks of today (day $t$):

---

101. (Zlotnick, 1972). Fenton et al. make a similar point (Fenton, Neil, & Lagnado, 2012) [p.9].

102. (Kent, 1964).

103. (National Research Council, 2011b) [pp. 84–85]. Note that this difficulty often can be considerably reduced by considering ranges of probabilities, rather than single values, see (Fenton et al., 2012) [pp. 7–8], (Fenton & Neil, 2010).

104. (Fisk, 1972).

TABLE 4.6: A Process for a Bayesian Approach in Evaluating the Probability of War within Four Weeks[a]

| Step | Task |
|---|---|
| 1 | On day $t$, ask the five analysts to estimate the prior; i.e., the probability $p(h_{war})$ that war will occur within four weeks. |
| 2 | On day $t + 7$, ask each analyst to list all the events that occurred within the previous week that influenced their opinion. |
| 3 | From these separate lists, generate a master list of events that contains all the elements that the analysts mentioned ensuring that they are approximately independent from one another. |
| 4 | Ask each analyst to estimate the probability that each of these events actually happened. |
| 5 | Ask each analyst to estimate $p(d_i \mid h_{war})$ and $p(d_i \mid h_{non-war})$ for each event $d_i$ on the master list. |
| 6 | Use Bayes' theorem to calculate the posterior probabilities of each analyst. |
| 7 | On day $t + 14$, repeat steps 2–6 using the posteriors that you have just calculated as the priors of that new iteration. |
| 8 | On day $t + 21$ (or on whichever day(s) that you want to re-evaluate the probability), repeat step 7. |

[a] After Fisk, C. E. (1972). The Sino-Soviet border dispute: A comparison of the conventional and Bayesian methods for intelligence warning. *Studies in Intelligence, 16*(2), 53–62.

## 4.6. USE OCCAM'S RAZOR

The parsimony principle, also known as Occam's razor (or Ockham's razor) may be summarized in a simple maxim: all other things being equal, favor the simplest hypothesis that explains your observations.[105]

Occam's razor may be seen as part of a broader set of properties aimed at favoring the better hypothesis. But "better" can be hard to define. Pardo and Allen suggest that "[a]n explanation is, other things being equal, better to the extent that it is consistent, simpler, explains more and different types of facts (consilience), better accords with background beliefs (coherence), is less ad hoc, and so on."[106]

Occam's razor is a central component of the scientific method and has led to countless major breakthroughs.[107] And yet, although it is a good guide, Occam's razor is not a universal rule, so you should not follow it blindly. For instance, Galileo applied it incorrectly to postulate that all undisturbed motion was circular.[108] And to use a more modern-day example, most of the time, when the warning light monitoring your car engine's oil level is unlit, it means that there is sufficient oil. Applying Occam's razor in this case leads you to conclude that the reason the light is unlit is because you have enough oil; trusting that the light functions properly saves you from manually checking your oil level. But, it may also happen that the light malfunctions and fails to light up despite a low level of oil. In this case,

---

105. See, for instance (Blumer, Ehrenfeucht, Haussler, & Warmuth, 1987), (Gauch, 2003) [p. 269].

106. (Pardo & Allen, 2008) [p. 230]. Thagard defines best as satisfying consilience, simplicity, and analogy (P. R. Thagard, 1978) [p. 89].

107. (Gauch, 2003) [p. 269], (McIntyre, 1998).

108. (Gauch, 2003) [p. 274].

trusting Occam's razor might cost you your engine. Here, as in many other places in the resolution process, there is no hard rule to apply except that of following your best judgment.

## 4.7. DRAW CONCLUSIONS

Summarizing the key concepts of this chapter, and following the precepts of Platt and others,[109] you should refrain as much as possible from having a favorite explanation. Instead, you should state the potential answers to your key question as hypotheses and treat them as such along your analysis. An implication is that you should not feel discouraged if your analysis shoots down your favorite hypotheses but, rather, embrace this as progress towards solving your problem.

> "I have not failed 700 times. I have not failed once. I have succeeded in proving that those 700 ways will not work. When I have eliminated the ways that will not work, I will find the way that will work."
>
> —Thomas Edison

As you uncover new items of evidence, continuously integrate them into your map, relating them to hypotheses. Then step back and periodically ask yourself whether your diagnostic is sufficiently precise or whether you need additional information. If the latter, identify which additional information is needed. This stepping back process is critical because failure to do so may induce you to continue to diagnose when you are ready to move on into finding solutions. For instance, the scientific community has long been characterized by policymakers and the media as divided and disagreeing on climate change. Yet, when historian of science Oreskes stepped back and analyzed 928 papers published in referred journals, she found that this representation was incorrect; there was an overwhelming consensus in the scientific community that anthropogenic climate change is real.[110] If you identify that you have a sufficiently good diagnostic of your problem, capture your conclusions and then move on to finding solutions.

# 5. WHAT ABOUT HARRY?

Starting with our set of hypotheses, we decide to interview key people to understand better what happened that afternoon. Table 4.7 shows the information that we gathered.

Examining this information, we uncover a discrepancy: Given that Harry barks loudly whenever the lawn crew comes to the house and given that the crew came between 1 and 2 p.m., but did not see Harry, he had to be missing before 1 p.m. This is inconsistent with him still being in front of the house at 2:20 p.m. for the neighbor to see him there. (Indeed,

---

109. (Platt, 1964), (Chamberlin, 1965).
110. (Oreskes, 2004).

TABLE 4.7: Gathering Information about Harry's Disappearance

| Action | Information |
|---|---|
| Talk with friend: | Friend was away from noon to 4 p.m. |
| | Harry can go between house and yard |
| | Harry has not escaped in months, since friend fixed the gate |
| | Harry has no collar |
| | The backyard gate was closed when friend came back |
| | There are no holes in or under the fence |
| | The backyard gate does not lock |
| | Harry cannot jump over the fence or gate |
| | Friend fired housekeeper that morning because of poor performance |
| | Housekeeper was upset and blamed Harry for shedding. Threatened retaliation |
| | Harry escapes whenever possible, follows scents, and ends up lost |
| | Whenever the lawn crew is there, Harry barks loudly enough for the crew to hear |
| Talk with neighbor: | Saw a police car in front of the house at 2:20 p.m. |
| | Saw Harry out on the street by himself at ~2:20 p.m. |
| Talk with lawn crew supervisor: | Crew came today between 1 and 2 p.m. |
| | Crew knows Harry but did not see him today |

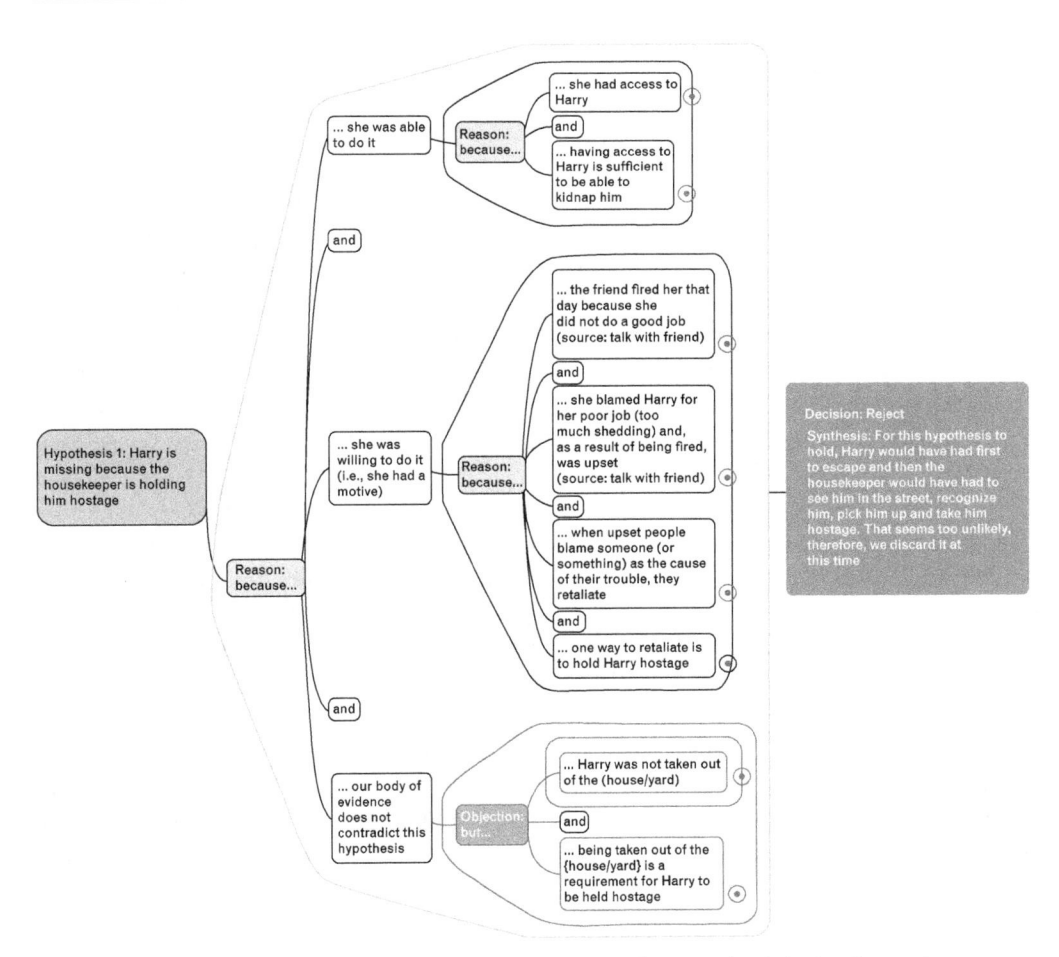

FIGURE 4.17: We capture the evidence, our thought process, and our synthesis in the diagnosis maps.

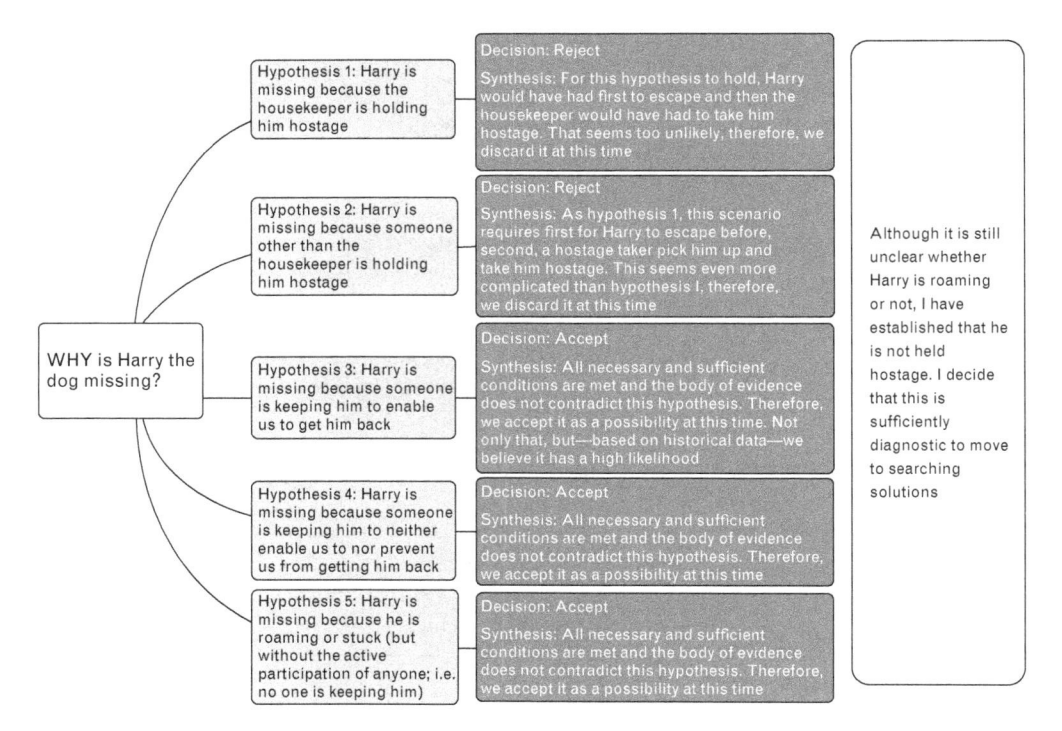

**FIGURE 4.18:** Periodically review your diagnostic to decide whether it is sufficiently conclusive. If it is, no need to push it further, instead move on to finding solutions.

given that Harry follows scents, it is unlikely that he would stay in front of the house for over one hour.) So either the lawn crew manager is mistaken or lying or the neighbor is mistaken or lying. We decide that it is more likely for the lawn crew manager to be mistaken or lying, and we accept that the neighbor's sighting of Harry is convincing evidence that he was indeed in front of the house alone around 2:20 p.m.

So now, any hypothesis where Harry is held hostage must assume that Harry first got out of the house, was seen sufficiently far from anyone for the neighbor to think that he was alone, and then been taken hostage. This seems far more complicated than the alternative: Harry escaped.

Therefore, applying Occam's razor, we conclude that Harry must have escaped, and we capture the evidence, our thought process, and our synthesis in the map (see Figure 4.17).

Although we do not know which of the remaining three hypotheses is the correct one (see Figure 4.18), we can conclude that we should search for Harry as we would for a lost dog, not one that is held hostage. As such, there is no point involving the police in our search or accusing the housekeeper. We decide that this is a sufficient level of diagnosticity and move to finding a solution to get him back.

The process we will follow to find a solution has some similarities with our diagnostic approach: We will develop an overriding key question, capture it and its context in a card, use an issue map to identify and classify all possible answers, and analyze those possible answers before drawing conclusions. Chapter 5 explains how to do the first three of these activities.

# NOTES

**Finite element analysis**: Thanks to Javier Arjona for guidance in optimizing the FE mesh of the beam.

**Pareto principle:** The 80/20 is indicative but distributions can be much more concentrated. For instance, 1% of patients in Camden, New Jersey, accounted for over 30% of the city's medical costs.[111] Similarly, 16 composers produced 50% of the classical music currently recorded and performed.[112] Also, out of the 30,000 tech startups that emerge every year in Silicon Valley, venture capitalist Mike Maples estimates that only 10 will end up representing 97% of the total value of them and one will amount to as much value as all the others combined.[113]

**Going wide before going deep:** This is analogous to "breadth-first search" in artificial intelligence.[114]

**Data and evidence:** (Mislevy, 1994) cites Schum in differentiating data from evidence: "A datum becomes evidence in some analytic problem when its *relevance* to one or more hypotheses being considered is established. . . . Evidence is relevant on some hypothesis [conjecture] if it either increases or decreases the likeliness of the hypothesis. Without hypotheses, the relevance of no datum could be established."

**Data, information, useful knowledge, and wisdom.** There is a hierarchy among data, information, knowledge, and wisdom. Think of a team of codebreakers, such as the British who monitored German encoded radio traffic during World War II:[115]

- *Data* is the enciphered radio traffic. It is the product of *observation*;
- *Information* is what the data means when deciphered; it is data that is processed to be useful;
- *Useful knowledge* is what that information tells us about the enemy's intentions; it is the application of data and information; and
- *Wisdom* refers to using that knowledge to decide what to do.

**Limitations of ACH:** See van Gelder's summary of issues about the approach.[116]

**Maps and more maps:** Argument mapping can be traced as far back as Toulmin (1958) and Wigmore (1913).[117] To my knowledge, Tim van Gelder coined the term *hypothesis mapping*.

**Grading the credibility of evidence:** Not all evidence should have the same credibility. Even experts are known to, at times, have poor inferences and confide in them too

---

111. (Gawande, 2011).
112. (Pfeffer & Sutton, 2006) [p. 87].
113. (Lemann, 2015).
114. (Russell, Norvig, Canny, Malik, & Edwards, 1995) [p. 74].
115. See (Ringle, 1990), (Rowley, 2007).
116. (T. van Gelder, 2008). See also (National Research Council, 2010) [pp. 18–21].
117. (Rowe & Reed, 2010).

much.[118] The medical community, for instance, grades the results of randomized, controlled trials higher than expert opinion.[119] Clinicians have attempted to grade the value of evidence based on as objective factors as possible.[120]

**On belief preservation**, see also (Bazerman & Moore, 2008) [pp. 29–30], "people naturally tend to seek information that confirms their expectations and hypotheses, even when disconfirming or falsifying information is more useful."

**More on confirmation bias.** "People tend to discredit or reinterpret information counter to a hypothesis they hold."[121] This works in concert with *motivated reasoning*: using different standards of evidence to evaluate propositions they wish were true as opposed to those they wish were false; that is, when evaluating an agreeable proposition, people tend to ask, "*Can* I believe this?" whereas when evaluating a threatening proposition, we tend to ask, "*Must* I believe this?"[122] Strong commitment to a hypothesis may reinforce confirmation bias.[123] See (K. N. Dunbar & Klahr, 2012) [pp. 750–751] for ways to overcome confirmation bias.

**Elasticity in asymmetrical skepticism:** Ask et al. corroborated that subjects evaluated the reliability of contradicting evidence lower than that of supporting evidence.[124] They also noted that the asymmetry depended on the type of evidence: The reliability of witness evidence, for instance, varied widely depending on whether it supported a subject's preconception or opposed it; that asymmetry was not as pronounced for DNA evidence, for instance.

**Dealing with situation where no amount of opposing evidence seems to be enough.** When involving someone who has a strongly held position on a situation, Neustadt and May offer to ask Alexander's question: What new data would bring you to change your position?[125] This forces people to state up front what would constitute highly diagnostic opposing evidence, thereby reducing the chance of it being distorted or dismissed if it does surface.

**Establishing a causal relationship:** In epidemiology, the Hill criteria—named after Sir Bradford Hill—can help identify whether a relation of cause and effect exists between two entities. The criteria are: 1. Strength, 2. Consistency, 3. Specificity, 4. Temporality, 5. Biological gradient, 6. Plausibility, 7. Coherence, 8. Experiment, and 9. Analogy.[126]

---

118. (National Research Council, 2011a) [p. 34], (Arkes & Kajdasz, 2011) [p. 147], (Spellman, 2011) [p. 118], (N. V. Dawson et al., 1993).

119. (Giluk & Rynes-Weller, 2012) [p. 150], (Philips et al.), (Barends, ten Have, & Huisman, 2012) [pp. 35–36], (Shekelle, Woolf, Eccles, & Grimshaw, 1999).

120. (Thompson et al., 2012) [p. 818], (Schunemann et al., 2006) [p. 612].

121. (Klayman & Ha, 1987) [p. 211]. See also [p. 117] of (Koriat, Lichtenstein, & Fischhoff, 1980) and (Edwards & Smith, 1996).

122. (E. Dawson et al., 2002). Thagard makes a similar observation calling the first mechanism a *default pathway* and the second a *reflective pathway* (P. Thagard, 2005). See also (Nickerson, 1998) [p. 187].

123. (Church, 1991).

124. (Ask, Rebelius, & Granhag, 2008).

125. See (Neustadt & May, 1986) [pp. 152–156] and (Fischhoff & Chauvin, 2011) [p. 165].

126. (Hill, 1965).

**Idiographic versus nomothetic hypotheses:** An idiographic hypothesis applies to a particular case whereas a nomothetic one applies to a class of cases.[127] Maxfield and Babbie note that "criteria for assessing an idiographic explanation are: (1) how credible and believable it is and (2) whether rival hypotheses were seriously considered and found wanting."[128]

**Gathering evidence:** Hoffman et al. have reviewed various ways to elicit knowledge from experts.[129]

**Relevance of evidence:** Federal Rule of Evidence FRE 401 stipulates that "Evidence is relevant if: (a) it has any tendency to make a fact more or less probable than it would be without the evidence; and (b) the fact is of consequence in determining the action."[130]

**Usefulness of contradictory evidence:** Koriat et al.: "People who are interested in properly assessing how much they know should work harder in recruiting and weighing evidence. However, that extra effort is likely to be of little avail unless it is directed toward recruiting contradicting reasons."[131] Also, Arkes and Kajdasz note that having to generate a contrary reason significantly improves the match between one's confidence and accuracy.[132]

**Looking for consistent evidence is not necessarily bad.** A hypothesis (or story) needs to have sufficient support to be considered.[133] Doing so while keeping an open mind may lead you to formulate other, correct hypotheses.[134]

**Embracing untestable hypotheses:** Dunbar observes that, in some cases, untestable hypotheses are required: "Charles Darwin could never have written the *Origin of Species* had he believed that untestable hypotheses were anathema, or forbidden. Even today, much of the Darwinian theory remains essentially untestable. We accept Darwinism not on the basis of logic, but because an overwhelming number of observations can be most satisfactorily 'explained' by that theory."[135]

**Influence of feedback on search strategy:** Gorman et al. recommend aiming at disconfirming when feedback is unavailable; when it is, combine both.[136]

**Data-driven and hypothesis-driven reasoning strategies:** Patel et al. report that physicians with ample experience in a clinical setting use forward/data-driven reasoning while resorting to backward/hypothesis-driven reasoning when dealing with unfamiliar cases, pointing out that, in the latter, the physicians lack the knowledge necessary to recognize patterns.[137]

**Serendipity and carefully designed research:** the two are not mutually exclusive. Van Andel remarks that "they complement and even reinforce each other. In practice

---

127. (Maxfield & Babbie, 2012) [p. 55].

128. (Maxfield & Babbie, 2012) [p. 58].

129. (Hoffman, Shadbolt, Burton, & Klein, 1995).

130. (Cornell University Law School).

131. (Koriat et al., 1980).

132. (Arkes & Kajdasz, 2011) [p. 150].

133. (Bex & Verheij, 2012).

134. (National Research Council, 2011b) [p. 129].

135. (M. Dunbar, 1980).

136. (Michael E. Gorman et al., 1984).

137. (Patel et al., 2012).

it is not by design *or* by serendipity, but rather by design *and* by serendipity, and/or vice versa."[138]

**Diagnosticity of evidence:** Anderson et al. note that the likelihood ratio of an item of evidence—the factor that, multiplied by a hypothesis's prior yields its posterior—integrates both the credibility and relevance ingredients of the evidence.[139]

---

138. (Van Andel, 1994).
139. (Anderson et al., 2005).

CHAPTER 5

# IDENTIFY POTENTIAL SOLUTIONS

Having identified the root cause(s) of our problem, we can now identify potential solutions. The process mimics what we have done in the diagnostic: first write a solution definition card before developing an issue map. The map shows alternative ways to answer the key question, introduces a formal set of solution hypotheses, helps structure the analysis of these hypotheses and capture their results, and paves the way to deciding which one(s) we will implement (Chapter 6).

## 1. WRITE A SOLUTION DEFINITION CARD

As in the diagnostic phase, it is essential to focus on solving the right problem and to build a shared understanding across the project team. To do so, it helps to write a solution definition card or *how* card; see Figure 5.1.

Your *how* card does not have to be very different from your *why* card. In fact, your situation and complication may only change slightly. The one major difference between a *how* and a *why* card is the key question. To form it, decide whether you want to integrate results of the diagnostic in your key question. Figure 5.2 shows that, in Harry's case, we have integrated them, pointing out that no one is preventing us from recovering him. But asking, "How can we get Harry the dog back?" would be equally acceptable. Integrating the results of the diagnostic reduces the size of the solution space: We are not looking for all the ways to get a missing dog back, only the ways corresponding to non-hostage situations.

| | |
|---:|---|
| Situation: | The information that is necessary and sufficient to specify which part of the universe you are considering. *Only* the necessary information. This information should be positive (i.e., there is no problem at this stage) and undisputed (i.e., people reasonably familiar with the setting agree with it) |
| Complication: | The one problem in that part of the universe; that is, the unique need for change (potentially illustrated by one or several of its symptoms/consequences) |
| Solution key question: | *The* one solution question that you want to answer. It<br>1. Is phrased as "**how**... ?"<br>2. Addresses an appropriate topic<br>3. Has an appropriate scope<br>4. Has an appropriate phrasing |
| Decision makers: | The person(s) who have formal authority to direct your project/authorize your recommendation |
| Other stakeholders: | The person(s) who do not have formal authority but who can influence the project |
| Goals and logistics: | Budget, deadlines, type of documents, quantitative objectives, etc. |
| Voluntarily left-out answers: (things that we could do but decide not to): | The actions under your control that you choose not to take |

FIGURE 5.1: Describe your solution problem in a *how* card.

| | |
|---:|---|
| Situation: | My friend John has a dog—Harry—who went missing a few hours ago |
| Complication: | Although we initially suspected Harry might have been kidnapped, we now believe that no one is preventing us from recovering him |
| Solution key question: | **How** can we get Harry the dog back, knowing that no one is preventing us from recovering him? |
| Decision makers: | John and his wife |
| Other stakeholders: | John's neighbors and other people whom we enlisted to partake in the search |
| Goals and logistics: | Identify all possible solutions within 4 hours;<br>Pick and implement subset within 12 hours;<br>Bring Harry back within 24 hours |
| Voluntarily left-out answers: | Ask neighbors to invest significant time in helping us locate Harry |

FIGURE 5.2: In Harry's case, we choose to include our conclusion of the diagnostic in our *how* card.

## 2. DEVELOP A SOLUTION MAP

Although it is tempting to jump to the first solution that comes to mind, there is value in considering alternatives. To illustrate, consider the following example[1]: The guests of a hotel complain about having to wait too long for elevators. To address this, the manager consults an engineer, who recommends installing another elevator. Unimpressed by the price tag of the solution, the manager seeks a second opinion, that of a psychologist, who recommends giving the guests something to do while they wait for the elevator; for example, by installing mirrors or televisions or providing magazines. Upon implementing the psychologist's recommendation, the complaints stop. Verberne notes that the ability to think in divergent patterns is what prevents us from jumping to the obvious—and usually most expensive—solution.[2]

Applied to finding solutions for our problem, this refusal to satisfice right away means that before settling on whatever potential solution occurs to us, we should first consider at least several, as Figure 5.3 shows.

Does it sound like too much work for a limited payoff? Well, decision theorist Hammond and his colleagues disagree, pointing out that first, you can never choose an alternative that you have not considered and, second, irrespective of how many alternatives you have identified, your choice can only be as good as the best of those. "Thus," they conclude, "the payoff from seeking good, new, creative alternatives can be extremely high."[3]

If this sounds familiar, it is because this process of refusing to close too early on an obvious solution is similar to the one that we have used for formulating our diagnosis (see Chapters 2 and 3). The good news is that solution maps use the same four major rules as

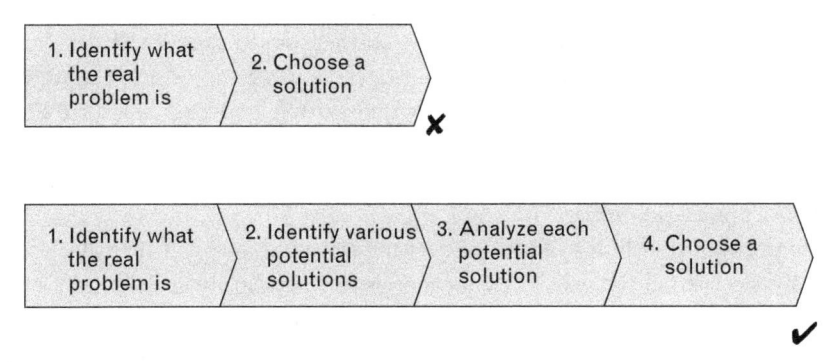

**FIGURE 5.3:** Solution finding should start with the conscious decision to first generate options before reviewing them and selecting one, as opposed to selecting whichever option happens to come to mind naturally.

---

1. From (Verberne, 1997).

2. Three decades earlier, Rusell Ackoff also reported a similar problem in an office building and solved it in the same way; see (Mason & Mitroff, 1981) [p. 25].

3. (John S. Hammond, Keeney, & Raiffa, 2002) [p. 45].

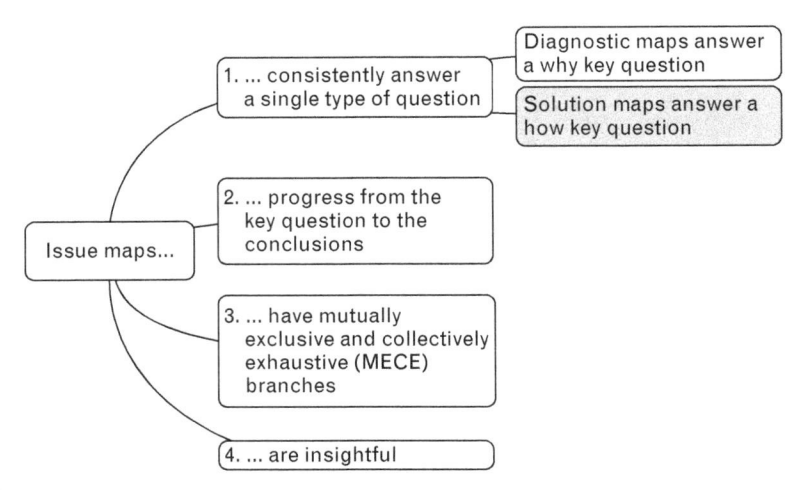

FIGURE 5.4: Solution maps use the same four major rules as diagnostic ones.

diagnostic ones (see Figure 5.4), so we can build on what we discussed earlier and use our issue maps as a way to engage our System 2 thinking. This chapter also introduces other ideas that can help the development of both types of maps.

## 2.1. LOOK FOR ALTERNATIVES, NOT PROCESSES

There are two ways to answer a *how* question. The first is to describe a process: a sequence of steps to answer the question in one particular manner. The second is to describe various alternatives or channels, each of which could potentially answer the question.

Use solution maps for the latter, to lay out alternatives to solve a problem, not to describe the sequence of steps to answer the key question in a specific way (see Figure 5.5). This may be challenging: In my experience, people tend to be more comfortable describing processes than identifying alternatives. So chances are that sticking to identifying alternatives will take a conscious effort.

**Validate the independence of branches.** One way to help you ensure that you are staying away from describing processes in your map is to periodically ensure that branches are independent. Because solution maps spell out alternatives, each branch of the map must be independent from the others; that is, any one branch does not *need* the help of another to answer the question. In particular, you never have a time relation between any two, that is, you never *have to* follow one branch before following another. That means that the elements in your map all are potential answers to your key question. In Figure 5.5 (b), "using a rocket" or "swimming," for instance, both independently answer "How can I go from NYC to London?" These solutions do not need any other elements to answer the question. The same is not true of "buy a ticket," for instance, in Figure 5.5 (a).

**Ignore desirability and feasibility for now.** At this stage, we are not interested in the desirability and feasibility of elements. As long as an element is a potential logical answer to the key question (and it is not part of the voluntarily-left-out-answers section of your

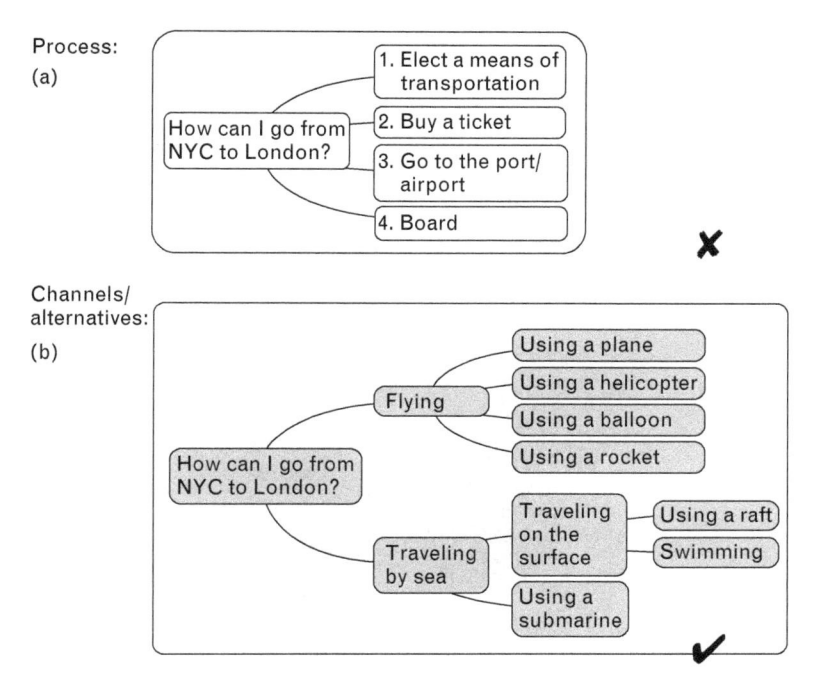

**FIGURE 5.5:** Use solution maps to identify alternatives, not to spell out a sequential process.

*how* card), it should be in your map. Negotiation expert Roger Fisher and his colleagues observe that this requires concerted effort, noting that "inventing options does not come naturally."[4]

## 2.2. PROGRESS FROM THE KEY QUESTION TO THE CONCLUSIONS

As with diagnostic maps, you should start your solutions map with the key question, identify various possible answers, summarize those in a set of formal hypotheses, test these hypotheses, and record your conclusions.

**Make branches diverge.** As decision trees, until they reach the set of hypotheses, issue maps only have *burst nodes* (also called *splitting paths*); that is, each element has at least two children. If you get to a situation as that of Figure 5.6 where you want to break several issues in the same way, you will still need to develop one distinct branch for each issue.

This is because, once they diverge, elements are distinct and may evolve in different ways. Part of the value of maps is to expose these differences.

To avoid repeating large groups of elements it may be useful to put a recurring branch into a box, give that box a number, and refer to that number in other parts of the map that use the same structure (see Figure 5.6 [b]).

---

4. (Fisher, Ury, & Patton, 1991) [p. 57].

Identify Potential Solutions • 121

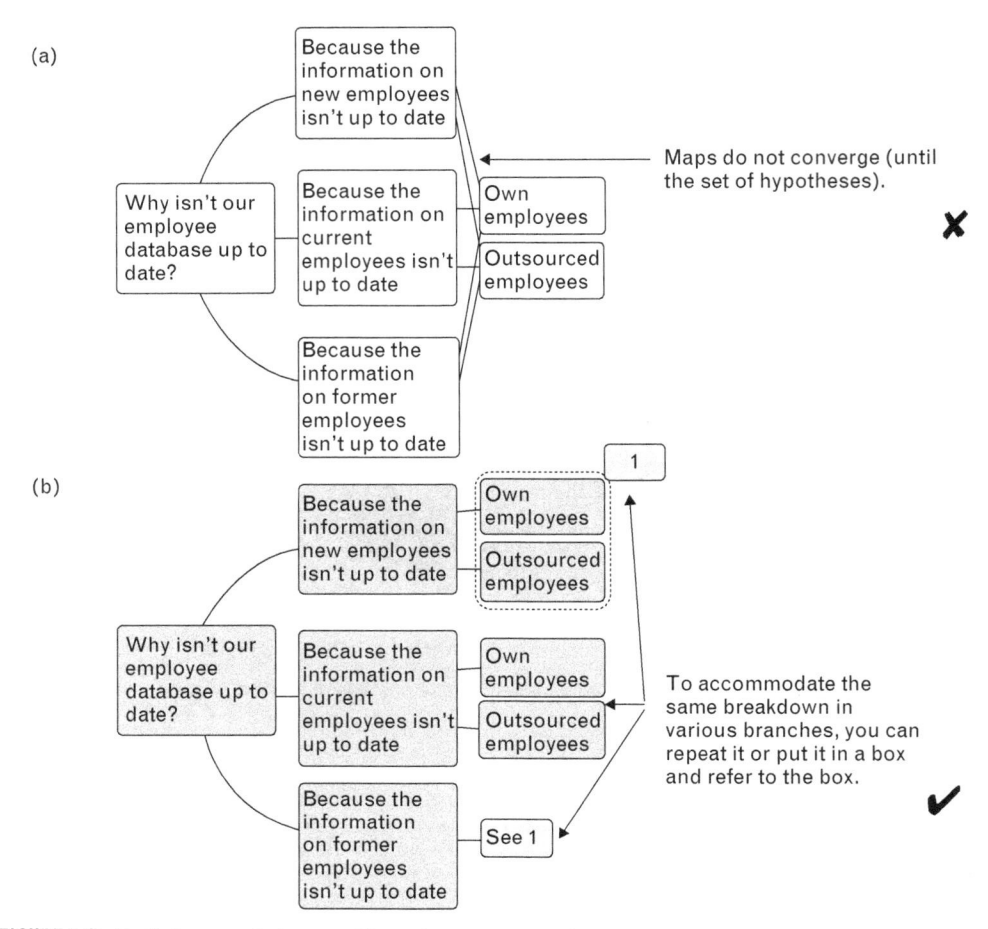

FIGURE 5.6: Until they reach the set of hypotheses, maps only have burst nodes, that is, they always expand when moving to the right. To avoid repeating large branches, you can label them and refer to the label.

**Eliminate instances where a node has a single child.** When an element only has one child, you are having one of two problems: either you are not being collectively exhaustive—that is, you have forgotten other possibilities—or the group {element + child} is redundant. Either way, modify the group: in the first instance by adding the missing children and in the second by modifying the element, the child, or both.

**Further control the number of children: too many is impractical, but two is not necessarily ideal either.** Perhaps the simplest way to break down elements is to separate them into two children. But maps based on such dichotomous branchings take longer to reach a given level of detail than maps that have nodes with more children. So the price of simplicity is a bigger map, which can make it difficult to focus on important parts. Therefore, do not automatically settle for a binary approach. On the other hand, when an element has more than, say, five children, it can become complicated to test the MECEness of the group. You should balance these considerations when deciding how to break down a specific node; based on experience, systems that have two to five nodes are usually the most appropriate.

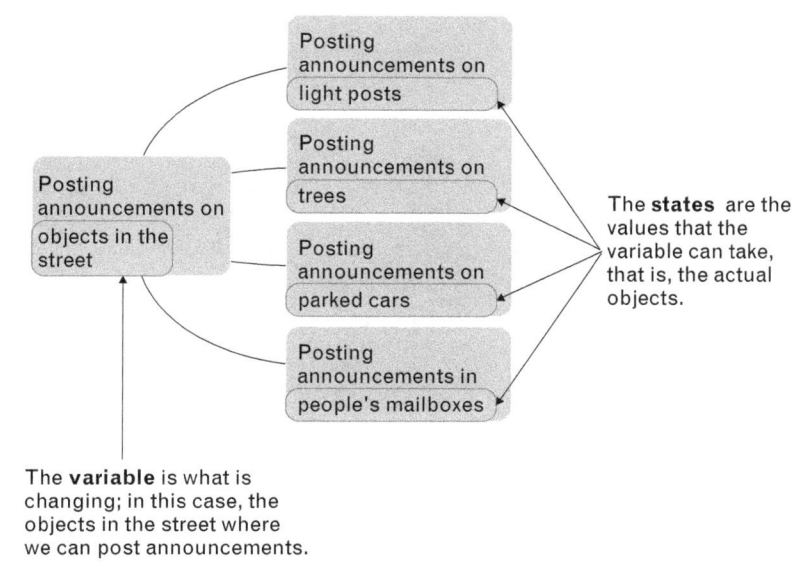

FIGURE 5.7: To help ensure that nodes add value, identify the variable that is changing in each node.

**Identify the value of each node.** Each node should add clear value, otherwise you are just adding structure for structure's sake, and soon your map will be immense but not necessarily useful. To help you add value with each node, make a conscious effort to name the variable that is changing in that node (see Figure 5.7). The children are then the various states that the variable can take.

**Do not force branches to have the same depth if not needed.** Some branches of your map will be sufficiently explicit after only a couple of steps. Others may require a dozen steps or perhaps more. These differences are fine. Do not feel obliged to use the same number of steps in all branches just for consistency. Instead, make sure that each branch develops in an insightful manner to sufficient explicitness (see next point).

**Stop drilling when the map is sufficiently explicit.** The considerations given to stopping your map that we introduced in Chapter 3 are also valid for solution maps: You should develop your map while doing so creates an explicitness that adds value but not develop it further. Consider searching for Harry (see Figure 5.8). Starting from our house, we could be searching in four directions.

Is there value in specifying those directions? Well, experts say that dogs tend to travel into the oncoming wind so, indeed, highlighting this as a good direction seems to make sense, because it would give us a concrete direction in which to start our search. As for whether we should specify the other three directions, it really is a judgment call, but if you cannot find a good-enough reason, you should decide that this element is sufficiently explicit as it is and move on.

In general, higher explicitness is better. Apart from helping you organize your thinking in a MECE and insightful way, much of the value of issue maps comes from identifying concrete, precise answers. In the early stages of a map, most of what you do is organizing. But the right side of a map is where you get to work on the second value generator: identifying specific solutions. Do not satisfice here and stop your thinking at a level where answers

Identify Potential Solutions • 123

If further refining the idea is likely to bring value, then it is worth doing so. In this case, pointing out the one direction where the dog is likely to have traveled makes sense.

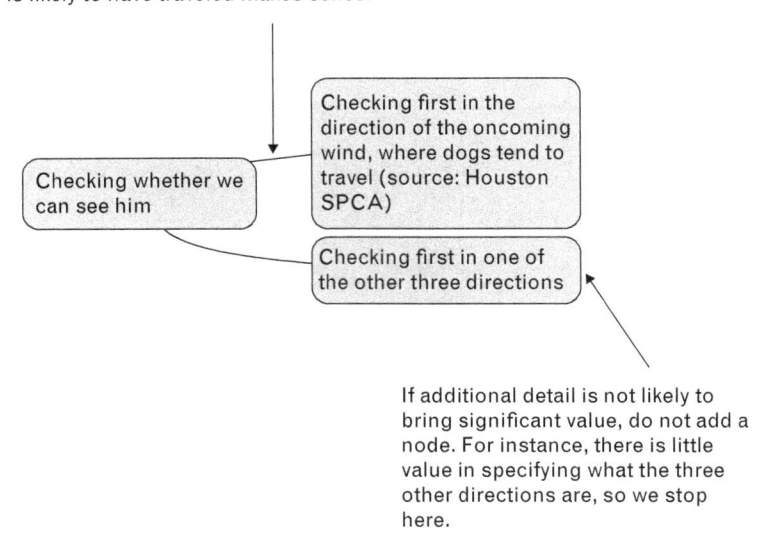

- Checking whether we can see him
  - Checking first in the direction of the oncoming wind, where dogs tend to travel (source: Houston SPCA)
  - Checking first in one of the other three directions

If additional detail is not likely to bring significant value, do not add a node. For instance, there is little value in specifying what the three other directions are, so we stop here.

**FIGURE 5.8:** To identify whether adding a node is warranted, first reflect on the value of adding it.

remain generic or vague. Instead, force yourself to go deeper in detail than you think is necessary, because even if you will not apply most of the ideas you generate, they can trigger additional useful ideas.

### 2.3. BE MORE MECE

Ensuring that your map is a MECE classification of all potential answers to the key question has as much value in solution maps as in diagnostic maps. This implies that you should include *all* potential answers to the key question that are logically valid, irrespective of their desirability, feasibility, or any other property. Chapter 3 presented some basic ideas to help you think in MECE ways. Here are a few more suggestions.

**Be more MECE by following the holding hands rule.** The holding hands rule that we discussed for introductions (see Chapter 2) also applies to issue maps; that is, the contents in the element and its children should not appear in only one box.[5] In Figure 5.9, we ensure holding hands compliance by varying nothing but the type of action that Harry can take to come back.

**Be more ME by differentiating causes from consequences.** A list of items cannot be MECE if the items are not of the same kind. A corollary is that the items in a list cannot be the causes—or the consequences—of items in the same list.

---

5. See (Rider & Thomason, 2010) [p. 115].

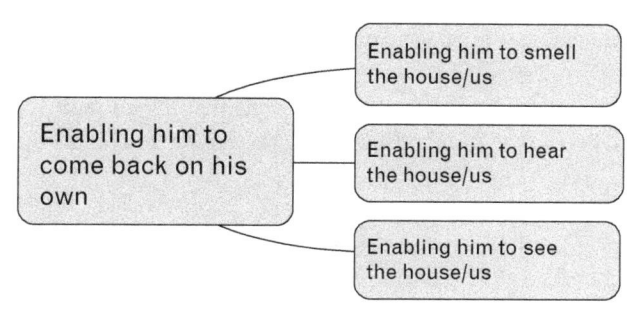

FIGURE 5.9: An element and its children should hold hands.

**Be more CE by choosing the right idea-generation macro activity.** Many of us are not good at divergent thinking. We limit our own creativity by falling into one of several obstructive patterns, either self-limiting—relying on what we know, replicating past experiences, feeling uncomfortable with uncertainty—or letting ourselves be influenced by others, that is, groupthinking. So we need help to overcome our natural limitations. One way is to set up specific idea-generation dynamics. Brainstorming, brainwriting, and using the Delphi method are three popular techniques that provide increasingly more privacy to contributors.[6]

**Brainstorm.** Group brainstorming consists of having various people share ideas to solve a problem: put several people in a room, ask them to think out loud about a subject, and capture the results.

To brainstorm effectively, you need a few participants, say, four to six; a moderator; a quiet and comfortable place; and 30 minutes or so.[7] You also need to ensure that everyone abides by four rules:[8]

- Forbid criticism. Do *not* worry about whether an idea might or might not work—brainstorming is about idea generation, not idea evaluation;
- Encourage strange/"dumb"/wild ideas. Participants should not feel constrained in any way;
- Shoot for quantity of ideas, not quality; and
- Encourage the use of one idea to generate others (cognitive stimulation, i.e., build on ideas).

Brainstorming is widely popular; it is used in many organizations, including the design and innovation consultancy IDEO, a firm famous for having developed many innovative products, including the first Apple mouse.[9] Its popularity is explicable by the fact that, in some settings, group brainstorming can be as productive as, or even more productive than individuals working independently.[10] There is considerable empirical evidence, however, that

---

6. See also (Prime Minister's Strategy Unit, 2004) [pp. 107–111], (Linsey et al., 2011) for additional ideas.
7. (Geschka, Schaude, & Schlicksupp, 1976).
8. (Osborn, 1953) [pp. 297–308].
9. On IDEO, see (T. Brown, 2008), (Kelley, 2001) [pp. 53–66].
10. (Oxley, Dzindolet, & Paulus, 1996), (Kavadias & Sommer, 2009).

group brainstorming usually underperforms compared to the same number of people brainstorming individually, both in the quantity and quality of ideas generated.[11] The remainder of this section discusses the issues associated with brainstorming and ways to overcome them.

Northwestern University's Leigh Thompson points out four major problems that limit the effectiveness of brainstorming:[12]

- *Social loafing* is a tendency for people who are part of a group to not work as hard as they would individually. Loafing is accentuated when people feel that their contributions will not be discernible from those of others;[13]
- *Conforming* is adapting one's ideas for fear of negative evaluations, which drives contributions toward conservativeness and similarity;[14]
- *Production blocking* is losing one's train of thought as a result of having to listen to others' ideas;[15] and
- *Downward norm setting* is having the performance of group members converge toward that of the least-performing individuals in the group.

Despite these limitations, group brainstorming remains widely used, and researchers and practitioners have proposed ways to ward off its problems. Tom Kelley, a partner at IDEO, proposes some ideas to improve the effectiveness of brainstorming: start with an open-ended question but a clear definition of the problem, number the ideas to motivate the participants (e.g., shoot for 100 ideas per hour), and use Post-its or other props to show progress and facilitate your future categorizing.[16]

Try to assemble a team with functional diversity, given that more heterogeneous teams are likely to be more creative.[17] Ancona and Caldwell found that teams with more heterogeneous members spoke to more people outside the team, in various departments of organizations, which was related with higher ratings for innovation by management.[18] They also found value in tenure diversity.

Ex-CIA analyst Morgan Jones stresses the importance of receptivity: There is no point in having your team create many ideas if they are going to shoot them down right there and then.[19] So you must avoid critiques, both negative *and* positive. As a moderator, do not offer encouragements when you hear ideas; for example, "This is good" or "I like that," might motivate one contributor but may demotivate all those whom you did not praise when they

---

11. See, for instance (B. Mullen, Johnson, & Salas, 1991), (Diehl & Stroebe, 1987), (Vroom, Grant, & Cotton, 1969), (Paulus, Larey, & Ortega, 1995).

12. (L. Thompson, 2003); see also (L. L. Thompson, 2011) [pp. 212–215].

13. (Bettenhausen, 1991).

14. (Kohn & Smith, 2011).

15. (Diehl & Stroebe, 1987).

16. (Kelley, 2001) [pp. 56–58].

17. (Kavadias & Sommer, 2009), (L. Thompson, 2003), (Hong & Page, 2001). See also (National Research Council, 2014) [p. 64].

18. (Ancona & Caldwell, 1992).

19. (Jones, 1998) [pp. 72–79].

spoke. When someone contributes an idea, repeat it as you write it down, just write it down, or ask for clarification if needed.

Do not spend too much time on any single idea: describe only their broad strokes and leave the peripheral details for later. The goal is to produce many ideas in a short time to raise the probability that a creative (defined as novel and useful) one will be among them.[20] You will always have time in other sessions to drill into each idea.

Oxley et al. found that a highly trained facilitator can enable a brainstorming group to outperform individual brainstorming. They suggested that this may be due to the experience of the facilitators, the extent of their training recognizing ideas and keeping the group focused on generating ideas, and/or their focus on reintroducing ideas that were not fully discussed.[21]

You might want to jumpstart the session with a warm-up, such as asking the group to name 10 types of trees. Another way to start the session is to have participants speak one word at a time: Have people pair up (or not), start with "once upon a time" and use a loose subject (e.g., I moved to London). This requires participants to let go of their own idea and build on those of others.[22]

Because brainstorming has been found to underperform in many situations, Diehl and Stroebe suggest that "it might be more effective to ask subjects first to develop their ideas in individual sessions and next have these ideas discussed and evaluated in a group session. The task of the group would then consist of evaluating, rather than producing, ideas."[23] Thompson agrees, pointing out that individuals are better than groups at divergent thinking, but groups are better at convergent thinking.[24] Perhaps one way to move in that direction is to use brainwriting instead of brainstorming.

**Brainwrite.** Brainwriting is similar to brainstorming in that one gathers a few people in a room, defines a common problem for the group, and asks every member to contribute ideas to solve it. Brainwriting reduces the interactions between team members, however, by having them think individually, write down their ideas silently, and only then share their ideas with others.

Start by giving each team member a piece of paper and a limited time to come up with several ideas, say three ideas in five minutes. At the end of the allocated time ask everyone to give their pieces of paper to the person sitting to their right and ask everyone to consider the ideas of their colleague as a trigger for developing their own ideas. Repeat as needed.

Apply the brainstorming rules in brainwriting: capture everything that is potentially a logically correct answer to the problem, without considering its practicality, and encourage people to think of unique ideas. When you share results, do not judge positively or negatively. Frequently remind the group that you are aiming for quantity, not quality.

Compared with brainstorming, brainwriting reduces the impact of production blocking because people do not have to wait their turn to capture ideas. It also may reduce the impact of anchoring, because people are not set to look at the problem under someone else's

---

20. (Geschka et al., 1976) [p. 49].
21. (Oxley et al., 1996) [p. 644].
22. See also the "inventing proverbs" exercise in improvisation (Madson, 2005) [pp. 32–33].
23. (Diehl & Stroebe, 1987) [p.508].
24. (L. Thompson, 2003).

perspective,[25] and of conformity—writing is more anonymous than speaking.[26] A third advantage of this approach is that it may be more effective when engaging larger groups and it is time-effective as everyone works simultaneously.

There is empirical evidence that, at least in some settings, brainwriting results in greater productivity than individual production.[27]

Brainwriting shares some of brainstorming's advantages as it allows participants to build on others' ideas rather quickly. But it also shares some of brainstorming's drawbacks, because contributions are not fully anonymous and some participants still may feel intimidated. If this is a concern, using the Delphi method may be advantageous.

**Use the Delphi method.** The Delphi method offers more privacy still: Participants never meet face to face; instead they write down individually their proposed solutions for the problem as well as their rationales. The facilitator then sends these responses to all participants as well as any data that has been requested.[28] Next, the participants revise their solutions, taking into account the views of their colleagues. The process continues iteratively until convergence or until there is no further progress.

This method works best when engaging five to twenty participants with heterogenous expertise.[29] Keeping the participants anonymous helps reduce the convergence of points of view toward that of the most renowned expert in the group. The technique is also useful when participants are in different physical locations or are so conflictual with one another that going through a meeting is impractical.[30] A limitation of the method is the time it takes to process the answers, especially with a large group.

Idea-generation dynamics in a group setting trade the privacy of participants for the ability to build on other members' ideas quickly. Identify which characteristic is more important to you in your particular situation and select the optimal technique. Note that the methods are not necessarily mutually exclusive; in fact, alternating solitary and group sessions may be desirable.[31]

**Be more CE by choosing the right idea-generation micro activity.** Within brainstorming (group or nominal), brainwriting, and the Delphi method, one can improve idea generation by applying any one of several approaches.

**Use analogies.** As we have discussed in Chapter 3, using a familiar problem can be a powerful way to explore ways to solve an unfamiliar one. Psychologists Smith and Ward point out that the most useful analogies typically are the ones where similarities are in the concepts of the situations rather than their superficial characteristics.[32]

---

25. (John S. Hammond, Keeney, & Raiffa, 1998).

26. (Heslin, 2009), (L. Thompson, 2003) [p.104]. See also (L. L. Thompson, 2011) [pp. 205–206] for the superiority of having team members working independently on divergent thinking tasks.

27. (Paulus & Yang, 2000) [p.84].

28. (Dalkey & Helmer, 1963).

29. (Rowe & Wright, 2001).

30. (L. Thompson, 2003) [p.104].

31. (V. R. Brown & Paulus, 2002).

32. (Smith & Ward, 2012) [p.469].

Sometimes, using analogies can equate to "stealing" ideas from other settings. This can be challenging to do, in part because of the *not-invented-here* syndrome, a tendency to reject ideas from outsiders.[33] "Problem solving in medicine is not the same as in military" or so the thinking goes. Of course, there are obvious differences and these differences call for specialized training. But there are also common denominators. Indeed, problem solving in medicine *can* be the same as in the military. Such an instance is Duncker's radiation problem: Imagine having to treat the tumor in the stomach of a patient without destroying neighboring healthy tissue. Any rays of sufficient intensity would destroy both types of tissue. Dunker identified various alternative solutions—send rays through the esophagus, use chemical injections to desensitize the healthy tissues, expose the tumor with an operation, etc.—and organized them in a search-tree representation (which is the earliest ancestor of issue maps that I have seen). He then selected one of these solutions: From various points around the patient, simultaneously project rays of low intensity that all converge at the tumor to amount to a ray of sufficient intensity to destroy the tumor.[34] When confronted with this problem, subjects who first read a military analogy (attacking a fortress in a countryside protected by minefields that let small groups of men through but not an entire army) are significantly better at finding the solution,[35] thereby supporting the idea that keeping an open mind is valuable.

This borrowing from other fields is helped by the advent of open innovation, a paradigm shift where entities invite both internal and external ideas to solve their problems. Open innovation is facilitated by websites such as InnoCentive, a crowdsourcing company that links organizations with problems to people who win cash prizes for solving them. Other efforts include initiatives to push people to look beyond the boundaries of their disciplines, such as the Pumps & Pipes symposium that aims at fostering the exchange of ideas among the National Aeronautics and Space Administration (NASA), the medical industry, and energy companies.[36]

**Challenge assumptions.** How do you fit four elephants in a car? Two in the front, two in the back. Psychologist Edward de Bono contends that challenging assumptions is a critical component of lateral thinking.[37] Hammond et al. agree: Before you accept constraints, separate the *real* constraints from the *assumed* ones (which represent a mental state of mind rather than reality).[38]

Grab a piece of paper, a pen, and a stopwatch. You have three minutes to think about everything you can do using a bottle. We are going for quantity: the highest number wins. Ready? Go.

If you are like most of my students, you probably came up with 10 to 25 answers. You have thought about the obvious (fluid container, circle-drawing guide) and the somewhat less obvious (flower pot, weapon, hammer, magnifier, art object). But have you taken your thinking sufficiently far? Can you feed yourself with a bottle (yes, if it is made of, say,

---

33. (Katz & Allen, 1982).
34. (Duncker & Lees, 1945), (Bassok & Novick, 2012) [p. 414].
35. (Gick & Holyoak, 1980).
36. (Orlando, 2015).
37. (De Bono, 1970) [p.105].
38. (John S. Hammond et al., 2002) [p. 49].

chocolate), can you make a boat with a bottle (absolutely, if it is big enough), can you use it as clothes (yes, if you break down its plastic into pellets, these can be used as textile)? In fact, you can make furniture out of a bottle, you can make it a deity, you can make it a currency, you can make it an underwater breathing apparatus, you can even fly (if it is large and light enough, just fill it with helium or hot air).

So, if there are so many things we can do with a bottle, why can I only come up with 25 answers? Nobody specified the bottle's dimensions and material. *I* placed these restrictions onto myself. To challenge an assumption, identify it, pretend that it does not exist, and create alternatives that appear from its absence. If the alternatives are sufficiently attractive, you might decide that it is worth your while to remove the constraint.[39]

**Do not limit yourself to eliminating the problem.** An important instance of challenging assumptions is to consider not only solutions that eliminate the problem but also those that can manage its consequences. Indeed, sometimes management may be more desirable. For instance, in a clinical study of patients with a partial obstruction of coronary arteries—a heart disease called angina—surgical intervention was performed on some patients. This means either surgery or removal of the obstruction through balloon angioplasty. These mechanical interventions are examples of fixing the problem by eliminating it. The other group of patients was treated by clinical intervention or "medical management," which consisted of taking medication to lower cholesterol and blood pressure levels. Both approaches have similar likelihood of heart attack or death. But, given that a mechanical intervention comes with the risk of heart attack, stroke, and death during the operation, academic physician Gilbert Welch observes that the medical management of the condition might be more desirable than its elimination, at least as an initial response.[40]

Management solutions require stretching our comfort zone because they usually imply coexisting peacefully with the problem. This is what would happen in switching our approach to treating cancer from waging a war against it to thinking about it as a neighbor (good fences make good neighbors).[41] And this is probably why we are quick at dismissing such solutions. Management solutions, however, can be perfectly acceptable ones and, when elimination solutions are comparatively expensive or risky, might even be the more preferable ones.

**Think about the opposite.** Let's go back to our bottle. There are many more things you can do than what you probably originally thought. In fact, you can do so many things that you might want to think about the inverse. So, here is a similar exercise: you have three minutes to think about all the things that you *cannot* do using a bottle. Start now.

How many did you find? There cannot be much more than a handful, because now you know how to relax the constraints that you originally placed on your thinking process. And that is the point of this exercise: sometimes, to identify how to do something, it can be helpful to try and think about how you cannot do it.

A related approach is to use the worst ideas. Imagine you have a group of people looking to solve a problem. The approach, as presented by Stanford's Tina Seelig, goes like this: break out the group into teams. Ask each team to think of the best and the worst idea

---

39. (John S. Hammond et al., 2002) [p. 49].
40. (Welch, 2015) [pp. 28–34].
41. (R. B. Ness, 2012) [pp. 38–39], see Chapter 3; see also (Welch, 2015) [pp. 58–61].

(i.e., not efficient or not effective) to solve the problem and capture each idea on a piece of paper labeled best and worst. Collect the answers, shred all the papers labeled "best," and redistribute the "worst" ones while ensuring that each team receives an idea generated by another team. Ask each team to turn the bad idea into a great one. Seelig reports that most teams quickly realize how to make brilliant ideas out of lemons.[42]

**Dissect the problem.** Consider the Birds-and-Trains problem:[43] "Two train stations are 50 miles apart. At 2 PM one Saturday afternoon two trains start toward each other, one from each station. Just as the trains pull out of the stations, a bird springs into the air in front of the first train and flies ahead to the front of the second train. When the bird reaches the second train, it turns back and flies toward the first train. The bird continues to do this until the trains meet. If both trains travel at the rate of 25 miles per hour and the bird flies at 100 miles per hour, how many miles will the bird have flown before the trains meet?"

Focusing on the flight path of the bird results in a difficult problem for most people. A much simpler alternative is to dissect the problem, finding out first how long it takes the trains to meet (one hour, the time to cover 50 miles at twice 25 mph) and how far the bird will fly during that time (100 miles).

**Differentiate innovation from Innovation.** In the 1990s when one wanted to store information away from one's computer hard drive, one used a CD-ROM. Coming from a world of floppy disks and, before those, punch cards, these were convenient. Until, of course, the advent of DVDs which offered a way to store more information on a device of the same size. What would be the next step? More information still on a disk-size device? As much information on a smaller disk? No, rather, a new device: a USB flash drive.[44]

This illustrates the difference between "better, faster, cheaper" (or incremental/evolutionary/small "i") innovations and "brand new world" or breakthrough/revolutionary/big "I" innovations.[45]

Incremental thinking leads to small improvements. That gets you from the CD-ROM to the DVD. Breakthrough thinking leads to radical changes, it revolutionizes the existing: it gets you from the cassette to the CD to the MP3. Incremental and breakthrough thinking are not compatible in the sense that no matter how many improvements you make to your DVD, these do not add up to a flash drive. As a result, it is frequent for experts to only be able to give you incremental answers, because they are already conditioned to stay within conventional mental sets.[46] So if you are looking for breakthrough answers, use novices—or experts in *other* fields.

One type of thinking is not consistently better than the other. For instance, incremental thinking requires less effort and/or different—or even fewer—skills, so it might be useful for quick fixes. It may also be the right way to proceed when the consequences of failure are high.

---

42. (Seelig, 2009) [pp. 37–38].
43. (Posner, 1973).
44. And USB flash drives also have fallen victim to relentless innovation with the advent of cloud storage, see (Kaur, Kumar, & Singh, 2014).
45. See, for instance (R. Ness, 2013) [pp. 4–5].
46. (Finke, Ward, & Smith, 1992) [p. 33].

The point is that you should explore both types of answers. For instance, you could separate a work session into two parts and ask your team to first think about incremental solutions before asking them to think about breakthrough ones.

**Debate.** Although criticism is strictly forbidden in brainstorming, Nemeth et al. have found that encouraging groups to debate and criticize results in *more* creativity.[47] Debating and deferring criticism are not mutually exclusive. You can organize sessions so that ample free thinking comes first, followed by organized debates. Further, debates do not have to be about whether or not to consider an idea; they may also be about how to make an idea stronger.

**Evaluate your creativity.** You can characterize the ideas you generate in terms of four metrics: *quantity,* the number of ideas you generate; *quality,* the feasibility of an idea and how close it is to the original specifications; *novelty,* how unusual or unexpected an idea is compared with others; and *variety,* the number of different categories of ideas generated.[48] By assessing the performance of your ideas along these four dimensions, you may identify weak spots and focus on those.

**Give your subconscious time to work.** Identifying creative alternatives is hard work. You might find that you work better in shorter, frequent sessions rather than one or two long ones. Realize that breaking the task into various sessions also works for you between sessions, as your subconscious has time to work.[49] Stepping back has worked for many illustrious thinkers across time, including mathematician Henri Poincaré who found that spending a few days at the seaside to think about anything but his problem helped him see a solution.[50]

## 2.4. BE MORE INSIGHTFUL

**Reframe your thinking.** Sometimes, the direct way is not the best one. Consider the old Arabic tale: A farmer dies, leaving his 17 camels to be split between his three sons. He wants the eldest to have half the camels, the second to have a third, and the youngest to have a ninth.

But 17 is not dividable in whole numbers by 2, 3, or 9, so the sons are confused. Not knowing what to do, they seek help from an elder. The elder is as lost as the three brothers, but he offers them his own camel, in case it can be of some help. That camel is old and none of the sons wants it, but they agree nonetheless.

So now they have 18 camels; the eldest son can have his half (9), the second his third (6), the youngest his ninth (2), and since 9 + 6 + 2 only sums to 17, the wise man can have his old camel back. Problem solved.[51]

---

47. (Nemeth, Personnaz, Personnaz, & Goncalo, 2004).

48. (Shah, Smith, & Vargas-Hernandez, 2003).

49. (John S. Hammond et al., 2002) [pp. 52–53]. See also (VanGundy, 1988) [pp. 71–210], (Smith & Ward, 2012) [p. 469], (Clapham, 2003), (Snyder, Mitchell, Ellwood, Yates, & Pallier, 2004).

50. (Poincaré, 1908) wrote: "Disgusted with my lack of success, I went to spend some days at the sea-side and thought of quite different things. One day, walking along the cliff, the idea came to me, always with the same characteristics of brevity, suddenness, and immediate certainty [. . .]." Translation by (Gray, 2013) [p. 220].

51. See also (L. L. Thompson, 2012) [pp. 186–187] for a negotiation impasse that was resolved by involving a third party.

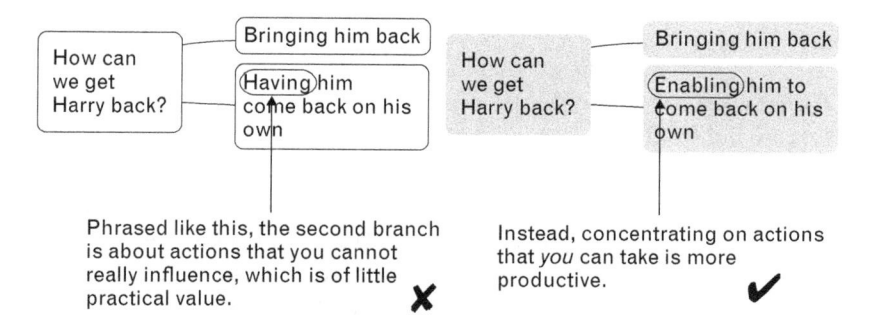

**FIGURE 5.10:** Concentrate on what you can do to solve the problem.

Being stuck looking at the problem from only one direction (e.g., how to divide 17 in whole numbers?)—the *fixation* phenomenon introduced in Chapter 3—we may fail to see that a solution exists. So if you cannot find a solution given how you originally framed your problem, you should step back and consider it from a different angle. To help you reframe your thinking, the story offers a couple of clues:

*Enlist a wise advisor.* Stepping back from a situation is hard work, especially if you have been at it for a long time or if you are emotionally connected. Get external help. Also, get "dumb" help: novices.

*Use a catalyst.* In chemistry, a catalyst is a substance that initiates or accelerates a reaction without itself being affected. Getting an old camel that no one wants cannot possibly solve our deadlock until it actually does . . . and the camel goes back to his owner.

**Formulate all elements as actions that *you* can take.** Your map helps you identify alternative ways to solve your problem, but you should phrase its elements as actions that *you* can take. Even in situations where you are not in control (e.g., Figure 5.10), you should still think in terms of what *you* can do to influence the person in control.

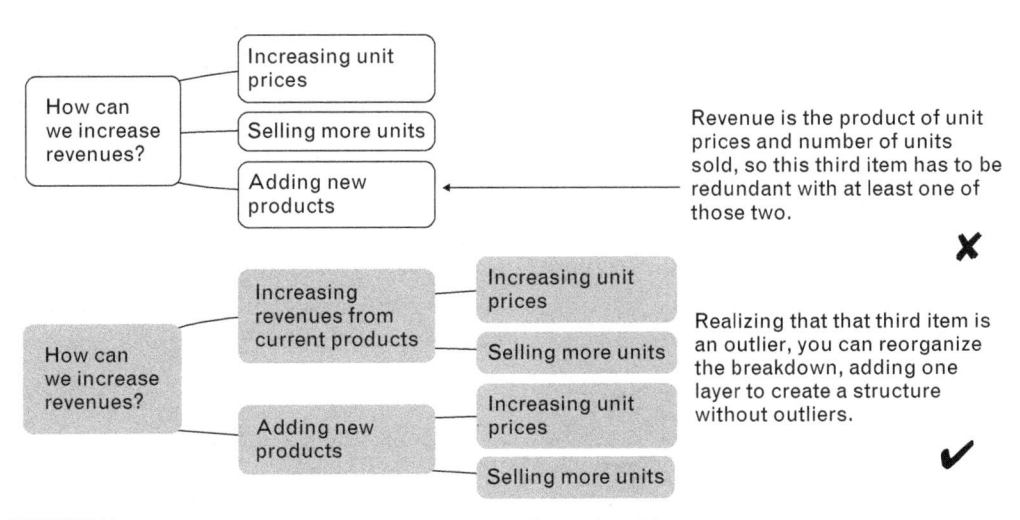

**FIGURE 5.11:** Chasing outliers can help you acquire additional insight.

Identify Potential Solutions • 133

**Chase outliers.** If all but one of the children in a node belong to a single category, take a moment to understand the mechanics fully, as you might acquire additional insight. Consider the example of Figure 5.11. Increasing unit prices, selling more units, and adding new products are indeed three ways to increase revenues.

But further inspecting the list reveals that the three elements are not similar: the first two directly influence revenues (as revenues equal price times volume) but the last does not. So you might realize that the latter segments the products between new ones and, one can only guess, current ones. Restructuring the elements to make this structure apparent helps you investigate the value of adding new products: would that help prices and/or volumes?

**Introduce one variable per node.** To reduce the risk of introducing gaps in your logic, it is usually advisable to introduce only one variable per node. Although this may make your map bigger, it simplifies reviewing the logic and ensuring that no gaps have appeared.

## 2.5. ELIMINATE DISTRACTIONS

Because drawing an issue map requires both creative and analytical thinking, it is strenuous. So chances are that your mind will try to lure you away into doing anything but developing the map. One way to help you focus on the analysis is to eliminate distractions: close your e-mail, do not answer the phone, use the Internet only to fish for specific items of information, do not worry about the format of your arguments, etc.

You may further reduce distractions through higher clarity, which can be enhanced by standardizing elements, for instance, by repeating similar elements in various branches instead of unnecessarily varying them. Although this will arguably make a map somewhat boring, clarity should take precedence over flamboyance.[52] You will also benefit from using parallelism.

**Be parallel.** Making elements parallel in your issue maps allows you to simplify them, thereby reducing the cognitive load needed to check whether the logic is sound.

In Figure 5.12 (a), when looking at ways to improve our clients' experience, we divide the experience into two MECE components: up to the sale and after the sale. Then we propose to improve the shopping experience, that is, everything up to the sale, which is fine. The problem arises when we propose to only follow up after the sale, because following up is not all that we can possibly do to improve the post-sale experience (for instance, we could offer a discount for a second purchase), so our map is not CE. Changing our argument to a parallel one—improving the shopping experience *and* improving the post-sale experience—helps us realize that there is a gap in our logic.[53]

Parallelism in construction, or grammar, is also useful: by using a consistent phrase construction in all elements of a map, you reduce distractions and make it easier to check your logic. In Figure 5.12 (b), we branch off into three sub-issues. Although all three are

---

52. Physicist Michael McIntyre thinks that variation in writing is overrated. He argues that "lucid, informative writing uses more repetition, and less variation, than the reader might think" (McIntyre, 1997).

53. Indeed, parallelism of arguments is a necessary condition for MECEness, so if a category has elements that are not parallel, you know that you need to modify it.

(a) **Ensure parallelism in action:**

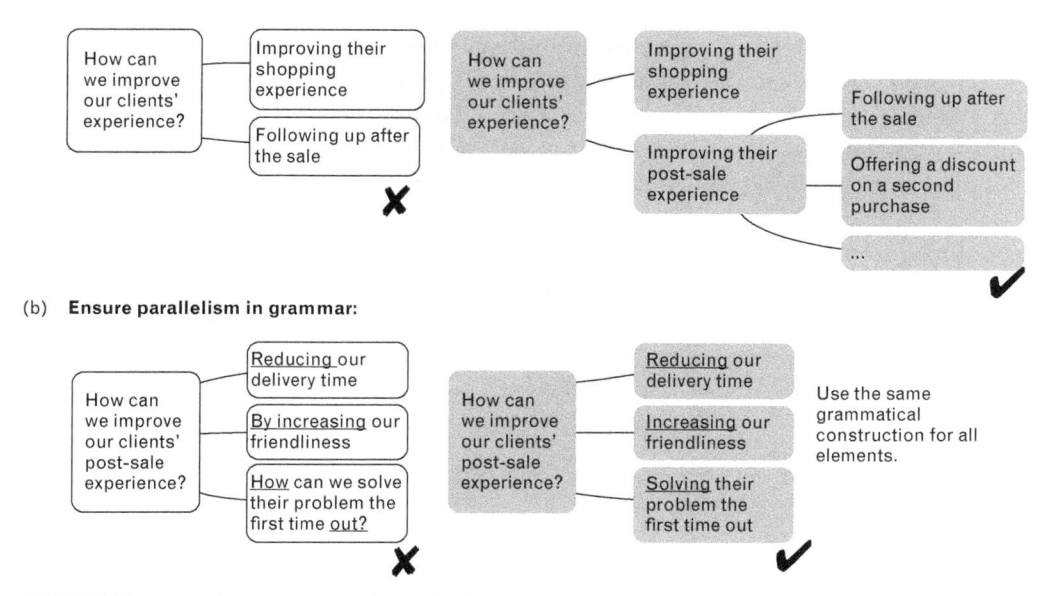

FIGURE 5.12: Parallelism applies both to how the ideas are formulated and what they actually are.

(b) **Ensure parallelism in grammar:**

acceptable, using all three in a given map makes it more difficult to validate the map. Instead, you should use the same grammatical construction in all elements.

## 2.6. ASSEMBLE A GOOD TEAM

In general, diverse teams have been shown to be more performant, in the long run, than homogeneous ones.[54] To leverage diversity better, Hammond et al. recommend that you start by identifying alternative solutions on your own, so as to not be too constrained by what is commonly accepted in the discipline.[55] Only then, should you enlist others to help.

**Include people with heterogeneous knowledge.** There is no consensus on the impact of diversity on a team's performance,[56] but some studies have found that diversity positively influences a group's performance.[57] People with heterogeneous backgrounds filter information in different ways, which helps information and knowledge to emerge.[58]

Hong and Page found that teams of people randomly selected from a diverse pool of intelligent agents outperform teams of best-performing agents. This is because, as the

---

54. (McLeod et al., 1996) [p. 257], (Hoffman & Maier, 1961) [p. 407], (Watson, Kumar, & Michaelsen, 1993).
55. (John S. Hammond et al., 2002) [p. 50].
56. See (Kozlowski & Bell, 2003) [p. 13] for a review.
57. (Jehn et al., 1999), (Hoffman & Maier, 1961).
58. (National Research Council, 2011a) [p. 64]. See also (Jeppesen & Lakhani, 2010).

population of agents to choose from becomes larger, the very-best-performing agents have to grow more similar, squeezing out diversity.[59] Although both diversity and ability are important, under certain conditions, diversity trumps ability.[60]

**Ensure that you can overcome the price of diversity.** Although team diversity may result in better performance, this comes at a price. Homogeneous groups, for instance, are initially more effective than heterogeneous ones[61] and, for it to have a net positive effect on group performance, diversity requires careful management,[62] such as using more negotiation and conflict-resolution skills than when managing homogeneous teams.[63] The added value brought by diversity is also conditional: Page points out that diversity needs to be relevant to the task ("if a loved one requires open-heart surgery, we do not want a collection of butchers, bakers, and candlestick makers carving open the chest cavity") and that the team members must be able to get along.[64]

## 2.7. LINK ALL ELEMENTS TO A FORMAL HYPOTHESIS

As with a diagnostic map, once your solution map is sufficiently explicit, you need to specify hypotheses, the analysis that you need to do to test these, the evidence that you will consider, and your conclusions.

Overall, developing solution maps is similar to developing diagnostic ones: All elements must be linked to a hypothesis; otherwise, you will have "holes" in your analysis. Also, you do not have to write an individual hypothesis for each element: you can group elements judiciously. When you do, make sure that you concentrate your energy on the branches that you think offer the best solutions.

At this point we are finished with the bulk of our divergent thinking. Next, we will need to test our hypotheses to find the best solution(s). Before we see how to do that, let's go back to Harry.

## 2.8. WHAT ABOUT HARRY?

Figure 5.13 shows that, in Harry's case, we identified six major ways to get him back.

We further analyzed each of those, identifying concrete ways to achieve them, specifying which direction we would start our search in or which websites we would check for announcements. Of note is the last branch: Even though it depends entirely on Harry, it is

---

59. (Hong & Page, 2004).
60. (Page, 2007) [pages xxvi, xxix, and 10].
61. (Watson et al., 1993).
62. (Williams & O'Reilly, 1998)
63. (Ancona & Caldwell, 1992)
64. (Page, 2007) [p. 5 and xxix]. See also (Mannix & Neale, 2005) [p. 32] for a review and (Eesley, Hsu, & Roberts, 2014) for a discussion of settings in which diversity may not be beneficial.

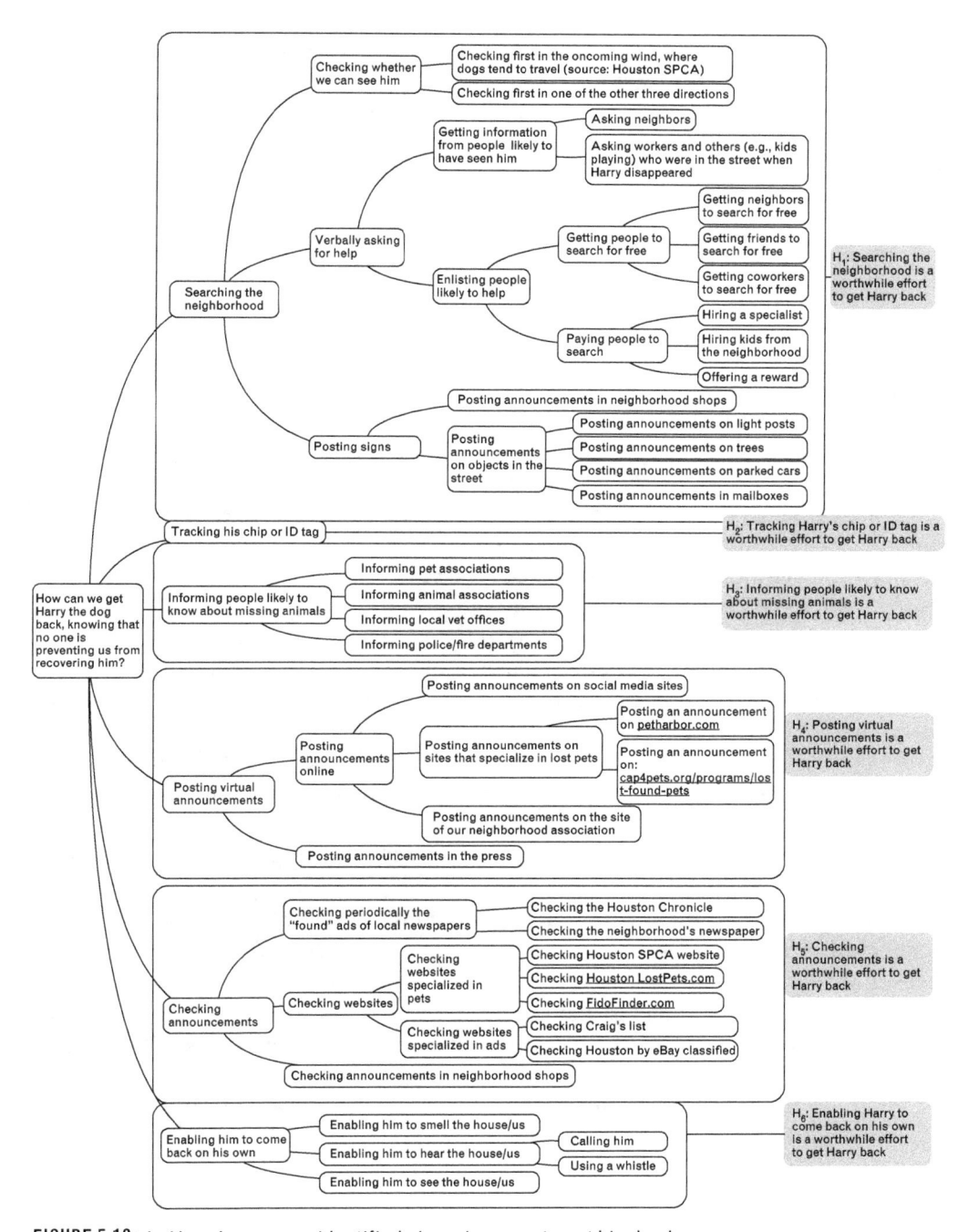

FIGURE 5.13: In Harry's case, we identified six major ways to get him back.

formulated as actions that *we* can take—how can we enable him to come? We then developed a set of formal hypotheses following the principles of Chapter 4.

This chapter showed how to map out the solution space for our problem: as in Chapter 3, if we have worked well, all the possible ways in which we can solve our problem are explicitly laid out in our *how* map. Next, we need to select the one(s) we want to pursue. Chapter 6 explains how to do so.

# NOTES

**Value of decoupling solution generation and evaluation.** See our discussion on System 1 versus System 2 thinking in Chapter 3.

**Include all answers in your map.** Include all ideas in your map, even implausible ones, because they can prime other ideas.[65] Also, Nemeth has shown that exposing people to a wrong answer helps improve their creativity (see [Lehrer, 2012]: "Even when alternative views are clearly wrong, being exposed to them still expands our creative potential.")

**Convergence and divergence of maps.** In decision-tree parlance, maps have only burst nodes (splitting paths), no sink nodes (converging paths).

**More on groupthink.** Groupthink is a tendency of people who are part of highly cohesive groups to become more interested in unanimity than appraising alternatives.[66]

**Functional diversity and team performance.** Higher functional diversity has not always been found to be associated with higher performance.[67]

**Analogical problem solving.** For an in-depth treatment, see (Holyoak, 2012).

**Measuring creativity.** Psychologist J. P. Guilford proposed to measure creativity along three dimensions: fluency (confronted with a problem, *how many* different ideas can the respondent think of), flexibility (*how many different types* of ideas), and originality (*how unique* are the ideas).[68]

**Training for creativity works.** Training can improve creativity, especially programs focusing on developing cognitive skills and involving skill application.[69]

**Brainstorming.** The term was coined by Alex Osborn, a U.S. advertising executive, to describe how to use "the brain to storm a creative problem—and doing so in commando fashion, with each stormer attacking the same objective."[70] In Spanish, it is called an "idea rain" (*lluvia de ideas*)—perhaps a better image.

**What is brainstorming/brainwriting?** There are various versions of brainstorming and brainwriting.[71]

---

65. See (Nemeth et al., 2004) [p. 368] citing a paper by Dugosh, Paulus, Roland, and Yang (2000).
66. (Ginnett, 2010) [p. 92]. See (Turner & Pratkanis, 1998) and (L. L. Thompson, 2011) [pp.157–165].
67. For a review, see (Mathieu, Maynard, Rapp, & Gilson, 2008) [p. 438].
68. See Thompson for further description (L. Thompson, 2003).
69. (Scott, Leritz, & Mumford, 2004). See also Basadur et al. (Basadur, Graen, & Scandura, 1986).
70. (Osborn, 1948).
71. See (VanGundy, 1988) [p.73–74] for a typology.

**Love the bottle (or the brick).** Identifying as many uses as possible for an object—usually, a construction brick—is known as the Unusual Uses test or the Alternative Uses test.[72]

**More on Delphi.** See also (Goodman, 1987), (National Research Council, 2011b) [p. 187][73]

**Interactions in group problem-solving.** Although Vroom et al. found that interactions among members of the solving team during the generation phase were dysfunctional, they also found that interactions during the evaluation phase were beneficial.[74]

**Value of diversity.** Although diversity is reported to add significant value under some settings[75,76] it comes at a cost. Diverse groups may be more subject to conflict[77] or take longer to generate results of comparable or superior quality to homogeneous groups.[78] It may be useful to consider the impact of these limitations in deciding how diverse a team should be.

**Leveraging diversity by changing tasks.** Page remarks that diversity works best on *disjunctive* tasks—those where the success of any individual results in the group's success—rather than on *conjunctive* tasks, where everyone's success is critical.[79] If possible, transform conjunctive tasks into disjunctive ones. InnoCentive's engagement of thousands of individuals on their clients' problems is an example of how to do this.

**Is brainstorming really underperforming?** Sutton and Hargadon point out how critics of brainstorming use its comparatively lower number of ideas generated by unit of time as evidence of its ineffectiveness.[80] But this is a measure of efficiency, not effectiveness. Sutton and Hargadon point to other types of value that brainstorming brings, including supporting the organizational memory, diversifying the skill set of participants, promoting a wisdom-based attitude (i.e., acting with knowledge while constantly reassessing one's belief), using competition to acquire status, impressing clients, and providing income for the firm.

**Transcending brainstorming.** Van de Ven & Delbecq found that both brainwriting and Delphi are more effective than traditional brainstorming.[81]

**Some connectivity helps.** Analyzing the performance of Broadway shows, Uzzi and Spiro found that the best teams were part of a "small world network," where people have an intermediate level of social intimacy (they called it a "bliss point"): sufficiently connected but not so much that they start acting alike.[82]

---

72. (Guilford, 1956).
73. (P. M. Mullen, 2003).
74. (Vroom et al., 1969).
75. (Page, 2007), (Hargadon & Sutton, 1997), (Loewenstein, 2012) [p. 762].
76. (National Research Council, 2011a) [p. 27].
77. (Jehn, Northcraft, & Neale, 1999).
78. (McLeod, Lobel, & Cox, 1996).
79. (Page, 2007).
80. (Sutton & Hargadon, 1996).
81. (Van de Ven & Delbecq, 1974).
82. (Uzzi & Spiro, 2005), (Lehrer, 2012).

CHAPTER 6

# SELECT A SOLUTION

Developing a solution map has helped you identify the alternatives available to answer your key question. Next, you need to select the one(s) that you should implement.

We, as people, are notoriously good at fooling ourselves into thinking that we are good intuitive decision makers, but, in reality, we are influenced by all sorts of factors, some of which have nothing to do with the decision under consideration. For instance, the weather impacts university admissions (clouds make nerds look better)![1] So adopting a structured decision-making approach for dealing with complex problems is advisable.

There is considerable literature on decision analysis, a discipline defined by Decision Sciences professor Ralph Keeney as, "a formalization of common sense for decision problems which are too complex for informal use of common sense."[2] We will only brush the surface of decision analysis by presenting one method.[3]

Our approach to selecting a solution has two steps: First, we will screen the hypotheses that we obtained in Chapter 5 to remove the unsuitable alternatives. Then, we will compare the remaining solutions to identify which we should implement.

## 1. REMOVE UNSUITABLE ALTERNATIVES

Our solution map led us to a set of hypotheses, each a form of the statement, "following this course of action is a worthwhile effort to solve our problem." Now we need to decide which one(s) to pursue. Up to now, we have not considered the desirability or feasibility of these hypotheses, focusing instead on fostering creativity by considering all courses of action that are logically valid answers to the key question. So, identifying which solution(s) to pursue starts with eliminating those that are not suitable.

One way to do this is to pass them through a screen to identify whether the solutions meet all necessary and sufficient conditions. Perhaps the simplest such screen is that of

---

1. (Simonsohn, 2007). For another example, see (Ariely & Loewenstein, 2006).

2. (Ralph L Keeney, 1982) [p. 806].

3. For more on the subject, see (Goodwin & Wright, 2009) [pp. 13–30], (Ralph L Keeney, 1992), (Eisenführ, Weber, & Langer, 2010), (Luce & Raiffa, 1957), or (von Winterfeldt & Edwards, 1986).

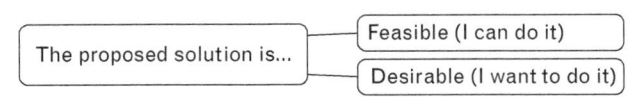

**FIGURE 6.1:** A screen can help you validate that the option you are considering meets all your necessary criteria.

Figure 6.1, where we assess whether the alternative under consideration is feasible and desirable.

Alternative screens are available. That of Figure 6.2 borrows concepts from various sources, including Gauch's full-disclosure model, which advocates spelling out all aspects of

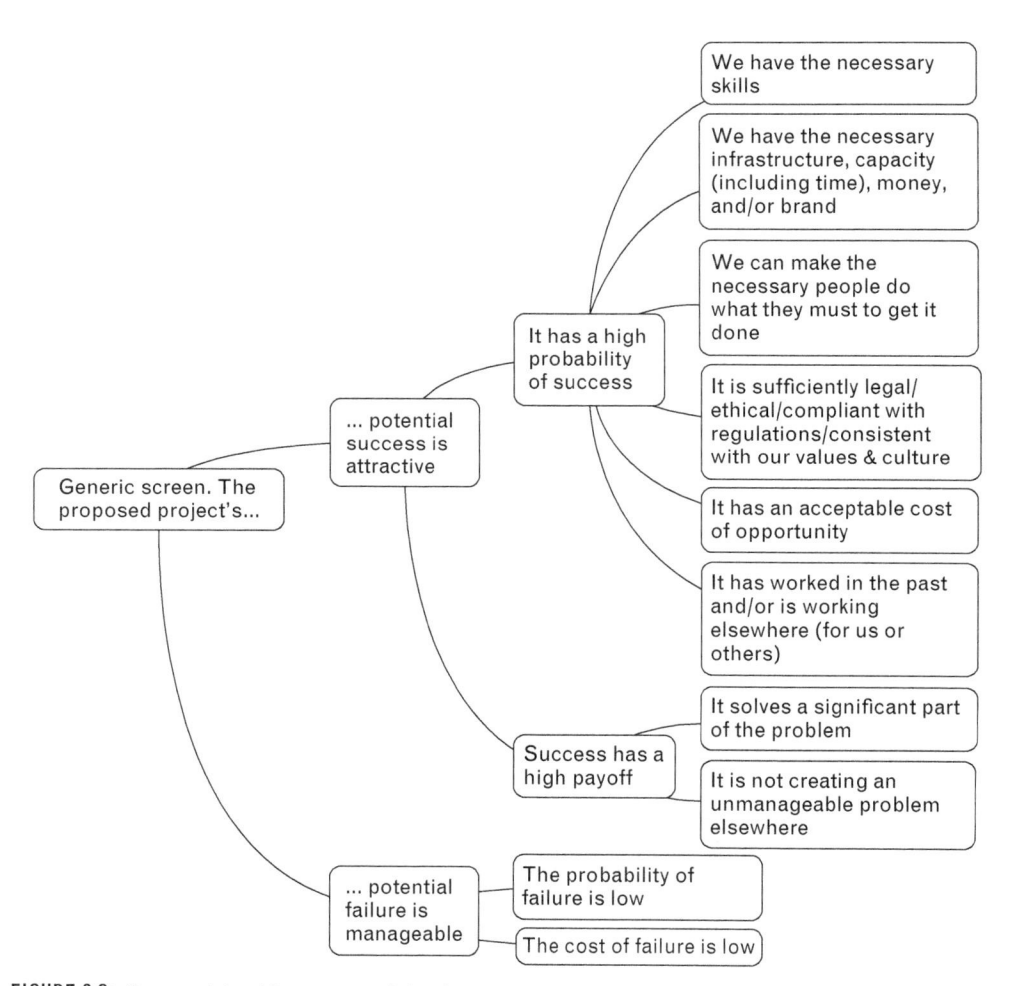

**FIGURE 6.2:** Screens/checklists are useful to further understand possible courses of action.

142 • STRATEGIC THINKING IN COMPLEX PROBLEM SOLVING

one's reasoning,[4] along with the management concept that one should consider the return on investment of projects in deciding whether to authorize them.[5]

Screens may be more specialized. For instance, faced with the decision of whether to authorize a project, you may use van Gelder's (see Figure 6.3).[6] An alternative is to use Rice's David Leebron's SAILS screen,[7] which validates that a project is Strategic, Accountable, Impactful, Leveraged, and Sustainable.

As an alternative to using an existing screen, you may prefer to develop your own. But, irrespective of your personal preference, keep in mind that using a screen is advisable, because it facilitates comparing solutions on a set of similar measures, thereby enabling a more equitable comparison of options.[8] So, for a specific project, you should identify one screen and use that for all of your hypotheses.

**van Gelder's screen. The proposed project is...**
- Strategically sound
- Financially sound
- Operationally sound
- Prudentially sound (i.e., acceptable from a risk perspective)
- Ethically sound
- Legally sound

**Leebron's SAILS. The proposed project is...**
- Strategic
- Accountable
- Impactful
- Leveraged
- Sustainable

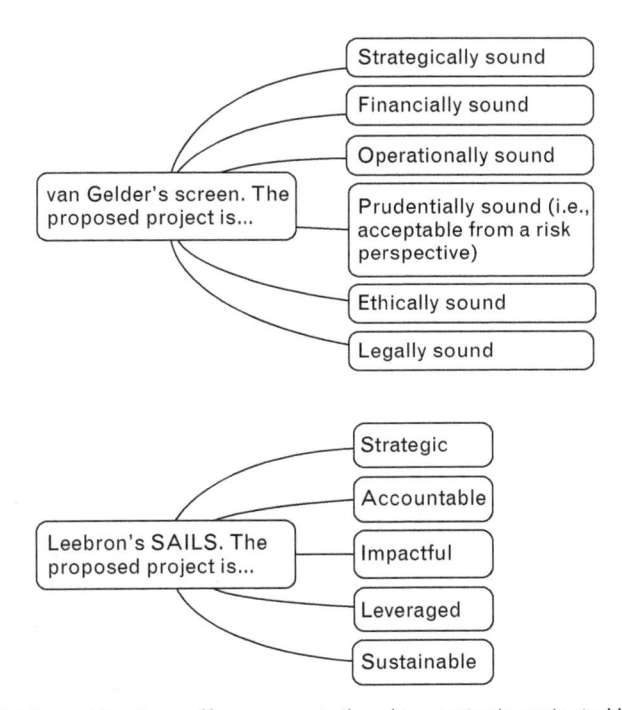

FIGURE 6.3: [V]an Gelder and Leebron offer screens tailored to strategic projects. Van Gelder's screen is from: van Gelder, Elements of a major business decision

---

4. (Gauch, 2003) [p. 128].
5. There are alternatives to using ROI for project evaluation; see (Archer & Ghasemzadeh, 1999) for a discussion.
6. (van Gelder, 2010).
7. (Leebron, 2015).
8. (Archer & Ghasemzadeh, 1999).

As you run a hypothesis through a screen, you might reject it quickly. For instance, considering Hypothesis 2—locating Harry's chip or ID tag is a worthwhile effort to get him back—and realizing that Harry does not have either, leads us to abandon $H_2$ without having to go through the entire battery of questions (see Figure 6.4).

### 1.1. LOOK FOR EVIDENCE

Evaluating whether a proposed method is a suitable solution requires gathering evidence. But for many of us not used to doing so, using quality evidence can be harder than it appears. In particular, Stanford's Pfeffer and Sutton identified six substitutes that business managers use instead of the best evidence:[9]

- **Obsolete knowledge**, that is, relying on old data that does not incorporate more recent advances;
- **Personal experience**—because information acquired personally is more vivid than other information, we sometimes disregard the biases of our own experience and prefer it to research;[10]
- **Specialist skills**, that is, defaulting to the particular approach with which we have the most experience;
- **Hype**, namely, doing something because everyone else does it or because gurus recommend to do so (based on weak evidence);[11]
- **Dogma/belief**, that is, letting ourselves being influenced by ideology; and
- **Inappropriate benchmarking**, that is, imitation of top performers when it is not warranted.[12]

Others come to mind—for instance, reliance on data from a mistaken or purposefully misleading source. You, therefore, should be careful in selecting the evidence that you use to test your hypotheses. This can be challenging because chances are that some of your sources of information have a vested interest in being partial—such as pharmaceutical vendors in medicine[13] and consultants, gurus, and business schools in management[14] to name just two—or may be suffering from biases.[15]

To help you use evidence, carefully analyze the logic behind each item of evidence to uncover incorrect cause-and-effect reasoning.[16] Ask and encourage others to ask questions and adopt an inquisitive relationship with evidence. Learn to look for empirical evidence

---

9. (Pfeffer & Sutton, 2006a) [p. 5].
10. (Denrell, 2003); see also, the *ease of recall bias* and the *retrievability bias* (Bazerman & Moore, 2008) [pp. 18–21].
11. (Rousseau, 2006) [p. 257].
12. (Pfeffer & Sutton, 2006b) [pp. 6–8].
13. (Pfeffer & Sutton, 2006a).
14. (Abrahamson, 1996).
15. (Tversky & Kahneman, 1974).
16. (Pfeffer & Sutton, 2006a).

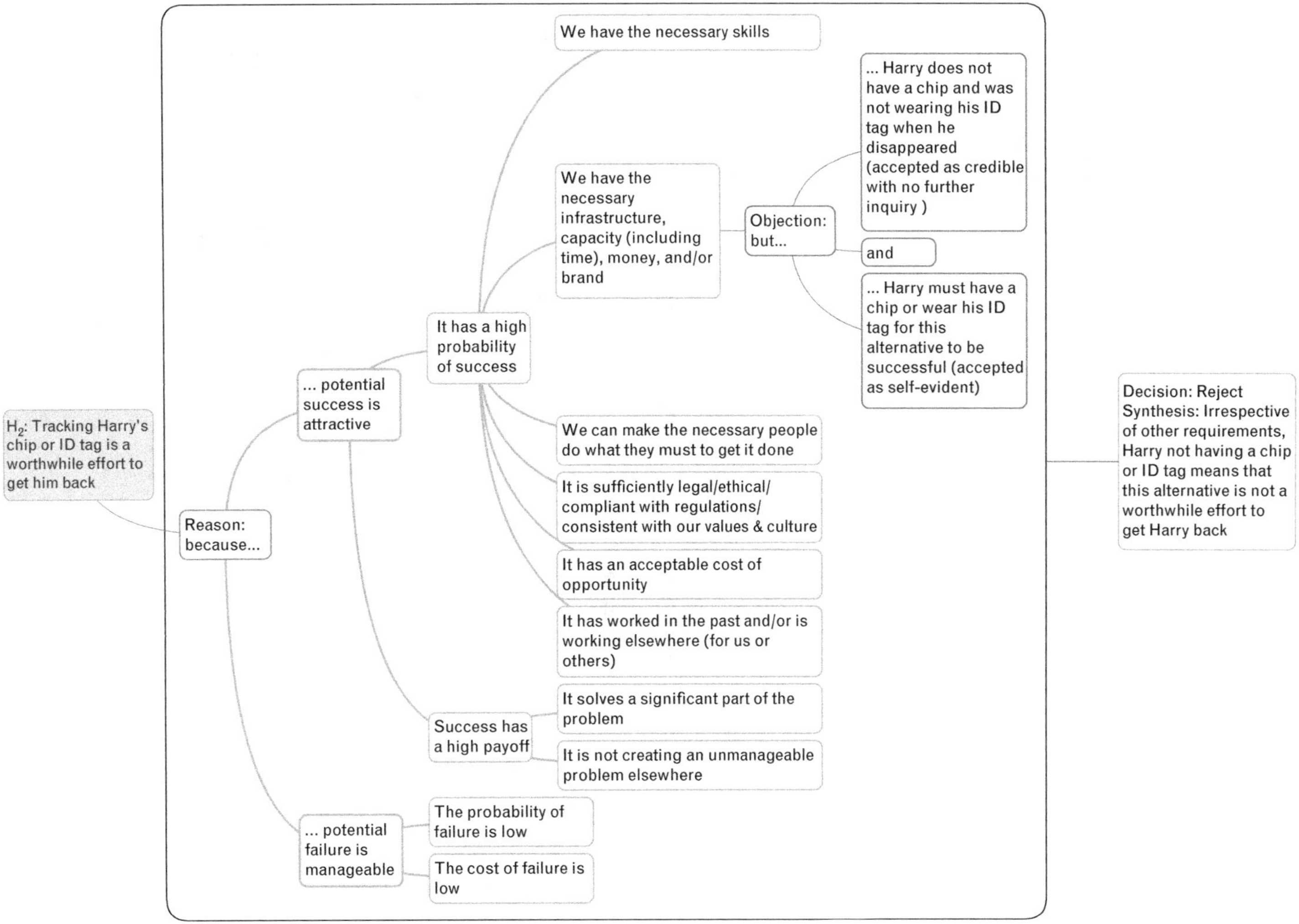

**FIGURE 6.4:** Screening can be useful to discard unfeasible alternatives.

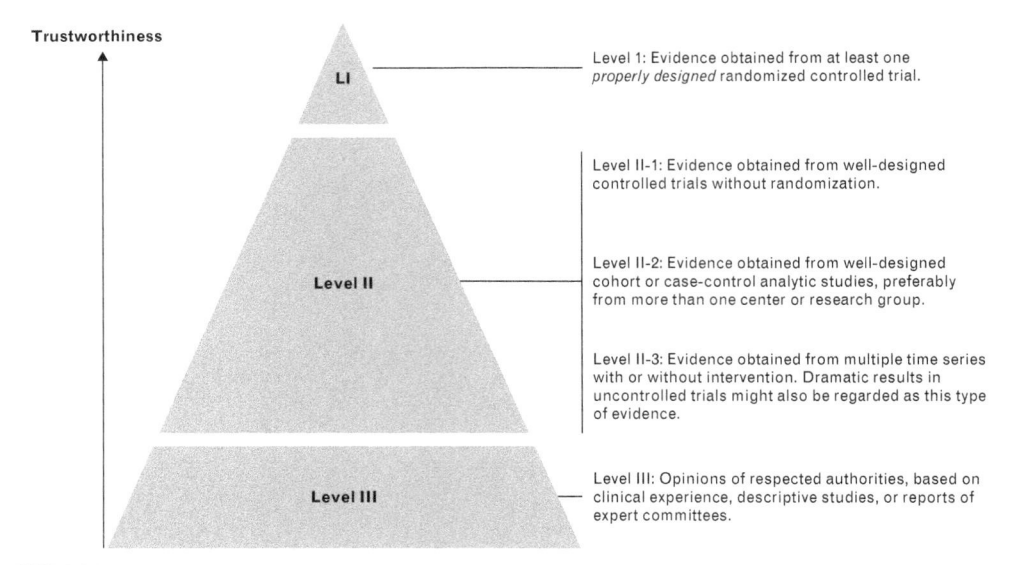

**FIGURE 6.5:** Not all evidence is equally trustworthy.
After (U.S. Preventive Services Task Force, 1989).

Level 1: Evidence obtained from at least one *properly designed* randomized controlled trial.

Level II-1: Evidence obtained from well-designed controlled trials without randomization.

Level II-2: Evidence obtained from well-designed cohort or case-control analytic studies, preferably from more than one center or research group.

Level II-3: Evidence obtained from multiple time series with or without intervention. Dramatic results in uncontrolled trials might also be regarded as this type of evidence.

Level III: Opinions of respected authorities, based on clinical experience, descriptive studies, or reports of expert committees.

and critically appraise its strength.[17] Develop a willingness to put aside conventional wisdom and unsupported beliefs and substitute them, in the words of Pfeffer and Sutton, "with an unrelenting commitment to gather the necessary facts to make more informed and intelligent decisions."[18]

**Grade the strength of evidence.** The strength of evidence ranges from weak to strong, where the latter should trump the former, irrespective of the source's charisma.[19] Putting this into practice may not be as obvious as it sounds, and organizations in some disciplines and industries have issued guidelines to help people grade the strength of evidence. For instance, in medicine, results from randomized controlled trials are the "gold standard," to be trusted more than results from trials conducted without randomization (see Figure 6.5). "Randomized controlled" means that the participants are assigned randomly to the group receiving the treatment or to the control group, which may receive a placebo. At the next level is evidence obtained from well-designed controlled trials without randomization. Next is the evidence obtained from individual cases. And so continues the decrease in strength, until it reaches the bottom of the pyramid: expert opinions.[20]

Thompson reminds young researchers that the Royal Society's motto is *nullius in verba*—which approximately translates to *take nobody's word for it*—and he advises them to not believe all they read, even in journals and books.[21] Given that many findings, even those

---

17. (Axelsson, 1998).
18. (Pfeffer & Sutton, 2006a).
19. (Sherman, 2002) [pp. 221–222].
20. (U.S. Preventive Services Task Force, 1989), (Grimes & Schulz, 2002). See also (Schünemann et al., 2006), (Schünemann et al., 2008), (Barends, ten Have, & Huisman, 2012) [pp. 35–37].
21. (Thompson, 2013).

published in prestigious peer-reviewed journals, cannot be reproduced,[22] Thompson's advice seems wise. And yet it is at odds with the practice in some industries where the opinions of so-called gurus are readily followed without any further evidence than their own assertions.[23]

## 1.2. DO NOT BOIL THE OCEAN

Screening hypotheses requires gathering appropriate evidence. For some problems, the principal challenge will be to find relevant data. In other situations, you might have so much information readily available that your primary challenge will be to stay afloat above it all.

When looking for data, you may use a brute-force approach—gather all the information available about the subject and then analyze it to see what is useful. Or, you may adopt a targeted approach, first thinking about the information you need, then thinking about where to find it, then gathering it, and finally stepping back to see what it means for your problem.

The brute force/ground-up/boiling-the-ocean/there's-a-pony–in–here–somewhere (I'm throwing in a few images, in case you want to enter a metaphor contest) approach seems acceptable if you have a lot of time; it requires digging around, analyzing great volumes of data, and going through the inductive process of identifying what it all means as a body of evidence. This approach, however, is usually not advisable. One problem is that, in the end, you will probably use only a fraction of the information you have gathered, so the signal-to-noise ratio is low, and you are spending a lot of resources gathering and ordering all that useless data; that is to say, the process is inefficient. It is also ineffective, given that this gathering of peripheral data may facilitate pseudodiagnosticity.[24]

Rather, it is usually preferable to adopt a more focused approach. Identify the data you need to get, get it, go back up to see how that changes the picture, and decide what your next action should be. This requires not getting sucked into a part of the analysis so much that you lose track of what is more important; that is to say, always keep the big picture in mind. In cases where you have identified the required information, but it is not yet available, consider integrating it into your analysis/report with a "not yet available" tag as a placeholder.[25]

## 1.3. TRIANGULATE ON ANSWERS

As we have discussed in Chapter 4, an item of evidence is usually compatible with more than one hypothesis. Indeed, Taleb's turkey, based on observations that the farmer fed him every morning, incorrectly concluded that he was in a safe place, a costly mistake on the eve of Thanksgiving. It is also common to gather incorrect evidence about a hypothesis as a result of error or deception. To sidestep this issue, you should corroborate findings from

---

22. (Open Science Collaboration, 2015). See also (Ioannidis, 2005).
23. See (Pfeffer & Sutton, 2006b) [pp. 45–46].
24. See (Arkes & Kajdasz, 2011) [pp. 157–161], Chapter 4.
25. (Pfeffer & Sutton, 2006b) [pp. 18–21].

Receiver 2
•

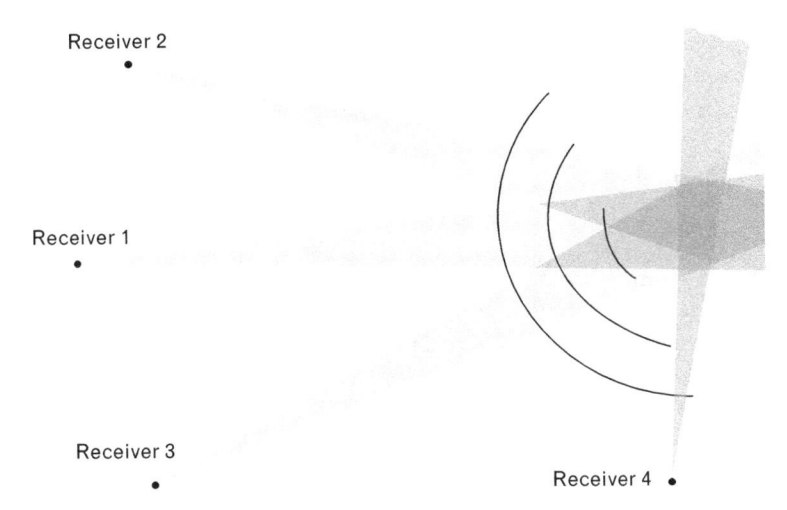

Receiver 1
•

Receiver 3
•                          Receiver 4 •

**FIGURE 6.6:** Triangulate on answers—that is, get evidence from independent sources—to improve the reliability of your analysis.

*independent* sources before concluding—the key word being independent, otherwise the repeated information will be overweighted.[26]

In telecommunication, the source of a radio signal can be worked out through the use of a goniometer.[27] Two or more receivers can be used to each identify the bearing of a signal at each receiving station and, knowing where these are located, an analyst can triangulate the directions to find the sources (see Figure 6.6).

There are a couple of lessons to learn from this analogy:

- Everything else held equal, the more sources the better (in Figure 6.6 the intersection of all 4 rays is darker than any of 3, 2, or 1), and
- Different perspectives are better than similar ones (the overlap from receivers 1 and 4 in Figure 6.6—which have almost perpendicular positions with respect to the source—is much smaller than that of receivers 1 and 2, which have close to identical perspectives, thereby zeroing-in much more efficiently on the source.[28]

So if at all possible, when testing hypotheses approach them from various angles and rely on independent sources. This is especially valid when you encounter contradictory evidence; there, triangulating evidence from independent sources may be especially useful because it reduces errors and increases innovation and the robustness of estimates.[29]

26. (National Research Council, 2011) [p. 130]. See also (Armstrong, 2001) and (Schum, 1994) [pp. 124–126] for corroborative and converging evidence.

27. See, for instance, (Tsuruda & Hayashi, 1975).

28. The Allies relied on a large number of widely spaced listening posts to pinpoint the location of German U-boats during World War II, see (Blair, 2000) [p. 76].

29. (National Research Council, 2011) [p.177]. See also (Cottrell, 2011) [pp. 142–144], (Institute of Medicine, 2014) [pp. 69–77].

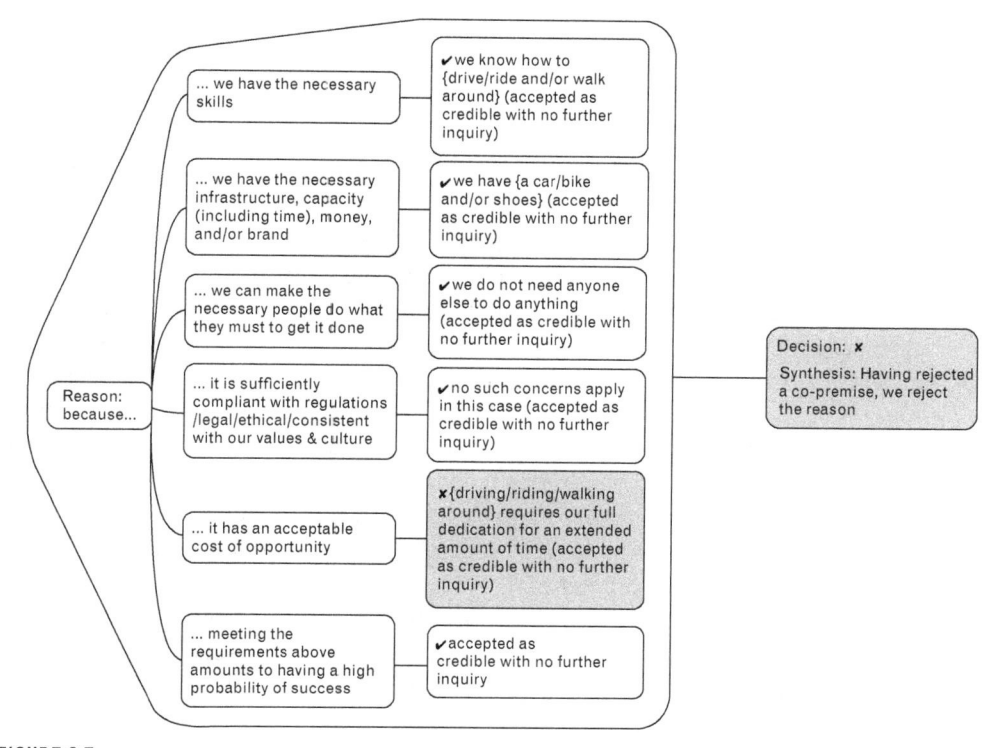

FIGURE 6.7: Maps are useful to capture your analysis, the evidence supporting it, and your conclusions.

### 1.4. CAPTURE THE RESULTS OF YOUR ANALYSIS IN THE MAP

In Gauch's words, "at most, a scientific argument may be correct; at least, it should be fully disclosed. Full disclosure is the first and minimal requirement for clear scientific reasoning."[30]

Maps are useful to identify what analysis you need to do and capture the evidence supporting your conclusions. But they also are useful to follow Gauch's precepts by allowing you to capture your conclusions (see Figure 6.7). Someone reviewing your analysis may disagree with your conclusions, but at least there will be no ambiguity as to how you reached them.

# 2. COMPARE THE PERFORMANCE OF THE REMAINING ALTERNATIVES AND DECIDE

Having screened all the alternatives and created the subset of those that are acceptable, you still need to decide which one(s) to implement. Sometimes, choosing one precludes

---

30. (Gauch, 2003) [p. 131].

you from choosing another; for example, to go from New York to London once, taking a plane precludes you from taking a boat or swimming. In other situations, you may be able to implement several alternatives: To increase the profitability of your company you may decide to reduce costs *and* increase revenues. But even then, your limited resources—or other constraints—may prevent you from implementing both alternatives simultaneously. So the question remains, in which order should you implement your alternatives?

In complex problems, one frequently aims at deciding among various options while considering multiple objectives. For instance, in deciding how to search for Harry, you may want to select the alternative that gives you the best chance of success. But a quick result may also be attractive; after all, you would rather find him within hours than within days. Similarly, the cost associated with retrieving him might be a consideration.

We all make countless decisions every day, and for many of those—choosing what clothes to wear, deciding on biking or driving to work, etc.—approaching the decision process informally is perfectly appropriate. There is, however, considerable evidence showing that we suffer from a number of biases that seriously impede our ability to consider the multiple dimensions of complex problems.[31]

For such problems, therefore, it usually is wiser to use a multiattribute utility decision tool rather than an intuitive approach.[32] One of these tools is the simple multiattribute rating technique exploiting ranks (SMARTER). The idea is to break down the problem into small parts and look at each part separately. As Table 6.1 shows, applying SMARTER is an eight-stage process:[33]

Let's look at these steps in detail and apply them in Harry's case.

1. **Identify the decision maker(s).** John will be the decision maker. (In those situations where you have several decision makers, it is advisable to try to persuade them all to cooperate.[34])

---

TABLE 6.1: Applying SMARTER to a decision problem can be achieved following an eight-step process[a]

1  Identify the decision maker(s)
2  Identify the alternative courses of action
3  Identify the attributes of the decision
4  Evaluate the performance of each alternative on each attribute
5  Assign a weight to each attribute
6  Compute a weighted average score for each alternative
7  Make a provisional decision
8  Perform sensitivity analysis

[a]after (Goodwin & Wright, 2009) (p. 34).

---

31. (Kahneman, Slovic, & Tversky, 1982), (Bazerman & Moore, 2008) [p. 179], (Makridakis & Gaba, 1998) [pp. 12–13].
32. See, for instance (Dawes & Corrigan, 1974), (Dawes, 1979).
33. See, for instance (Goodwin & Wright, 2009) [p. 34].
34. (Edwards, 1977).

2. **Identify the alternative courses of action.** We have already done this: In Chapter 5 we considered all possible alternatives and in the previous sections we weeded out those that were unsuitable. In the end, we are left with five alternatives from which to choose (see Table 6.2).
3. **Identify the attributes of the decision.** Attributes are those criteria, those properties of the alternatives that matter to us when making our decision. Keeney & Raiffa describe a good set of attributes as:
    - **Complete**, that is, the set covers all the important aspects of the problem;
    - **Operational**, that is, the set can be meaningfully used in the analysis;
    - **Decomposable**, that is, aspects of the evaluation process can be simplified by breaking it down into parts;
    - **Nonredundant**, that is, there is no double counting of impacts; and
    - **Minimal**, that is, the problem is kept as small as possible.[35]

Although you want to find a set of attributes that appropriately captures what is important to the decision maker, you do not want to include too many attributes, because this can complicate operations unnecessarily. To accomplish this, you may simply omit less important attributes.[36]

In Harry's case, identifying attributes may look like this: the individual likelihood of success of each alternative is obviously important and, therefore, should be considered. So should the timeliness of each course of action: Although it is possible to call pet associations now (at 5 PM), it will not be possible to do so at 10 PM. Posting signs in the neighborhood, however, is something we could do at night. Therefore, choosing to implement alternatives in the right order may enable us to implement more by a given deadline. (So an alternative with a high score in timeliness would be one that does not have to be implemented right away and that allows us to pursue other alternatives simultaneously. An alternative with a low score in timeliness would require immediate and undivided attention.) Other attributes may be the anticipated speed of success and the lack of cost of implementing the alternative (see Table 6.3).

---

TABLE 6.2: **After an initial screening, we are left with five alternatives for Harry's case**

| |
|---|
| $H_1$: Search the neighborhood |
| $H_2$: Track Harry's chip or ID tag |
| $H_3$: Inform people likely to know about missing animals |
| $H_4$: Post virtual announcements |
| $H_5$: Check announcements |
| $H_6$: Enable Harry to come back by himself |

---

35. (Ralph L. Keeney & Raiffa, 1993) [p. 50]. See also (Ralph L Keeney, 2007) [pp. 117–118].
36. (Edwards, 1977) [p. 328].

TABLE 6.3: The Third Step in Applying SMARTER is to Identify the Attributes of the Decision

Attributes that we select to rank the various alternatives in Harry's case:

| Individual likelihood of success | Timeliness | Speed of success | Low cost |

4. **Evaluate the performance of each alternative on each attribute.** One way to do this is to rank alternatives by giving them each a score between 0 and 100, 0 going to the least preferred option and 100 to the most.[37]

Although evaluating performance may be done subjectively, for instance by asking relevant experts and stakeholders for their opinions, research can make your decision more evidence-based. For instance, to evaluate the individual likelihood of success of each alternative for finding Harry, we can adapt the results of a study that identified the effectiveness of various courses of action for finding lost dogs (see Table 6.4).[38]

The study does not map perfectly to our approach: a hypothesis is not included, others do not map one-to-one, and it is unclear whether the analysis, performed several years ago in a different part of the country, is applicable to Harry's case. So judgment is required to evaluate its relevance. Upon reflection, however, we feel more comfortable using this data than going with our own guess, so we use it as a basis to evaluate the individual likelihood of success of the alternatives, transferring the original percentages to values on a 0–100 scale where we assign 100 to the best alternative and 0 to the worst (see Table 6.5).

TABLE 6.4: To Help Us Evaluate the Likelihood of Success of Each Search Strategy, We Use Data Published in Similar Settings[a]

|  | Individual likelihood of success |
| --- | --- |
| $H_1$: Searching the neighborhood | 15% |
| $H_2$: Tracking Harry's chip or ID tag | 28% |
| $H_3$: Informing people likely to know about missing animals | 35% |
| $H_4$: Posting virtual announcements | 5% |
| $H_5$: Checking announcements | N/A |
| $H_6$: Enabling Harry to come back by himself | 8% |

[a] Adapted from Lord, Wittum, Ferketich, Funk, & Rajala-Schultz, 2007.

37. (Goodwin & Wright, 2009) [p. 38], (Edwards, 1977). This is a direct-rating method. For alternatives, see (Eisenführ et al., 2010) [pp. 113–122].
38. (Lord et al., 2007). See also (Weiss, Slater, & Lord, 2012).

TABLE 6.5: We Translate the Performance of Each Alternative to a Score between 0 (Worst) and 100 (Best)

|  | Individual likelihood of success | Value |
|---|---|---|
| $H_1$: Searching the neighborhood | 15% | 50 |
| ~~$H_2$: Tracking Harry's chip or ID tag~~ | ~~28%~~ | N/A |
| $H_3$: Informing people likely to know about missing animals | 35% | 100 |
| $H_4$: Posting virtual announcements | 5% | 15 |
| $H_5$: Checking announcements | N/A | 0 |
| $H_6$: Enabling Harry to come back on his own | 8% | 30 |

We then assign values to the other alternatives using the space between their scores to indicate the strength of our preference for them. Note that precision in the values is not necessary because it usually requires significant changes to alter rankings.[39]

Table 6.6 shows the performance of the alternatives in all four attributes. (Lord et al.'s study also listed the time dogs were lost in each case, thereby helping us evaluate the "quickness of success.")

5. **Assign a weight to each attribute.** Next, we assign weights to the attributes to reflect how comparatively important each is to the decision maker. One way to do this is to use the centroid method, which is a two-step process. The first step is to ask the decision maker to rank the attributes.[40] To do so, ask the decision maker: "Imagine a new alternative, the worst possible alternative, one that has the worst possible performance on all attributes. Now imagine that you can improve its performance in just one attribute,

TABLE 6.6: We then Evaluate the Performance of all Alternatives on the Three Other Attributes

|  | Individual likelihood of success | Timeliness | Speed of success | Low cost |
|---|---|---|---|---|
| $H_1$: Searching the neighborhood | 50 | 100 | 100 | 90 |
| $H_3$: Informing people likely to know about missing animals | 100 | 100 | 80 | 100 |
| $H_4$: Posting virtual announcements | 15 | 20 | 20 | 0 |
| $H_5$: Checking announcements | 0 | 0 | 0 | 100 |
| $H_6$: Enabling Harry to come back on his own | 30 | 90 | 100 | 100 |

39. (Goodwin & Wright, 2009) [pp. 38–39].
40. (Edwards & Barron, 1994) [p. 316].

TABLE 6.7: Rank Order Centroid Weights

| Rank of attribute | Number of attributes (k) | | | | | |
|---|---|---|---|---|---|---|
| | 2 | 3 | 4 | 5 | 6 | 7 |
| 1 | 0.750 | 0.611 | 0.521 | 0.457 | 0.408 | 0.370 |
| 2 | 0.250 | 0.278 | 0.271 | 0.257 | 0.242 | 0.228 |
| 3 | | 0.111 | 0.146 | 0.157 | 0.158 | 0.156 |
| 4 | | | 0.063 | 0.090 | 0.103 | 0.109 |
| 5 | | | | 0.040 | 0.061 | 0.073 |
| 6 | | | | | 0.028 | 0.044 |
| 7 | | | | | | 0.020 |

enabling it to go from the worst performance to the best possible performance. Which attribute would you improve?" Once the decision maker has selected one of the attributes, repeat the question, asking him to exclude the attribute he has just selected. Repeat the operation until all attributes have been selected. You now have a ranking of attributes from the most important (selected first) to the least important (selected last).

The second step in the process is to assign weights using the rank order centroid weights (ROC).[41] The value of the weights depends on the number of attributes. For $k$ attributes,

The weight of the first attribute, $w_1$, is: $w_1 = (1 + 1/2 + 1/3 + \cdots + 1/k)/k$,
the weight of the second attribute, $w_2$, is: $w_2 = (0 + 1/2 + 1/3 + \cdots + 1/k)/k$,
the weight of the third attribute, $w_3$, is: $w_3 = (0 + 0 + 1/3 + \cdots + 1/k)/k$, and so forth.[42]

Table 6.7 provides rank order centroid weights for analyses, including up to seven attributes.[43]

In Harry's case, we ask John to imagine a terrible alternative, one that has almost no chance of succeeding, requires immediate and full attention, will take several weeks to succeed, and will cost $1,000 to implement. If he could improve just one of these attributes, we ask, which would it be? He selects *individual likelihood of success*. We then ask him this question again, barring *individual likelihood of success* as an option. Because he wants to implement as many alternatives as possible in a matter of hours, he selects *timeliness*. He then has to choose between *speed of success* and *low cost*, and goes for the former, yielding the ranking of attributes shown in Table 6.8.

TABLE 6.8: John's Ranking of the Attributes' Importance in Finding Harry

| Individual likelihood of success | > | Timeliness | > | Speed of success | > | Low cost |

41. See, for instance (Goodwin & Wright, 2009) [p. 64–65].
42. (Olson, 1996) [p. 46].
43. See (Edwards & Barron, 1994) for ROCs in analyses with up to 16 attributes.

TABLE 6.9: Weights of the Attributes in Finding Harry

| Individual likelihood of success | Timeliness | Speed of success | Low cost |
|---|---|---|---|
| 0.521 | 0.271 | 0.146 | 0.063 |

Next, we assign a weight to each attribute. Referring to Table 6.7 and choosing the column referring to four attributes yields the weights (see Table 6.9).

6. **Compute a weighted average score for each alternative.** Next, we look at the overall performance of each alternative by multiplying its value with the respective weight of the attribute and adding those. (Note: This assumes that the additive model is appropriate, which requires that attributes be independent from one another.[44]) Table 6.10 shows the weighted scores of each alternative.
7. **Make a provisional decision.** The last column of Table 6.10 shows the ranking of the courses of action as defined by our technique. We can use it to review the model with the decision maker and discuss its appropriateness.
8. **Perform a sensitivity analysis.** Before committing to the decision, we should evaluate how sensitive our results are with respect to changes in the model, which will help us assess the robustness of our current ranking. Changing the values in Table 6.10 shows that comparatively large changes in the performance of each alternative on the attributes are needed to generate a change in our ranking.[45]

TABLE 6.10: Evaluating the Performance of Alternatives and Weighting Attributes Allows Us to Rank the Attractiveness of Each Alternative to Get Harry Back

|  | Individual likelihood of success | Timeliness | Speed of success | Low cost | Weighted score | Ranking |
|---|---|---|---|---|---|---|
| Weight | 0.52 | 0.27 | 0.15 | 0.06 |  |  |
| $H_1$: Searching the neighborhood | 50 | 100 | 100 | 90 | 73 | 2 |
| $H_3$: Informing people likely to know about missing animals | 100 | 100 | 80 | 100 | 97 | 1 |
| $H_4$: Posting virtual announcements | 15 | 20 | 20 | 0 | 16 | 4 |
| $H_5$: Checking announcements | 0 | 0 | 0 | 100 | 6 | 5 |
| $H_6$: Enabling Harry to come back on his own | 30 | 90 | 100 | 100 | 61 | 3 |

44. (Goodwin & Wright, 2009) [p. 46].
45. This is called a flat maxima, see (Goodwin & Wright, 2009) [p. 50].

Although we presented the approach as a succession of stages, remember that the process is not necessarily linear: it is perfectly acceptable to move backward as new insight appears.[46]

## 3. MODIFY YOUR MAP AS YOU GO

Think of developing your solution map as charting an unknown territory between your current position (your key question) and your destination (the solution[s] that you will end up choosing). In that sense, your map is a dynamic document that evolves as you gather evidence about your problem and form your conclusions. This means that you should capture your progress in your map. For instance, as you rule out some hypotheses, you should cross them out in the map; that is, keep them in the map for future reference, but signal that they are no longer under consideration and explain why. Similarly, you can restructure branches as you uncover new information and realize that your original layout is not appropriately MECE or insightful.

Also, remember that once you have started your analysis, one of your map's important contributions is to allow you to see where each item of information fits in the big picture, thus helping ensure that you do not waste time on tangential or irrelevant issues. But this works only if you consult the map. So, sticking with the road-map analogy, keep your map visible and refer to it periodically.

## 4. CAPTURE QUICK AND SMALL WINS

In a study, psychologists Simons and Chabris had students watch a short video of a few people passing around a basketball, instructing them to count the number of passes. During the segment, an actor wearing a gorilla suit enters the picture, walks slowly, stops in the middle of the screen, turns to face the camera, thumps his chest, and resumes his walk to exit the picture. Although this whole episode is clearly visible to anyone watching the video casually, a majority of the subjects in the study fail to see the gorilla![47] This study illustrates how, while one is focused on one aspect of a problem, it is easy to miss something that, under different circumstances, would be obvious.

Even the best analysis is just that, an analysis, and those do not solve problems. Implemented solutions do. A benefit of being methodical in your approach is that you investigate all the dimensions of your problem. Doing so, you look at parts of your operation that you may not have really thought enough about, which may help you identify partial victories along the way.

---

46. (Goodwin & Wright, 2009) [pp. 54–55].
47. (Simons & Chabris, 1999), (Simons, 2000). The study is based on one by Becklen and Cervone (Becklen & Cervone, 1983).

Quick wins—or the proverbial low-hanging fruit—are improvements that can be pursued easily and quickly and that, if you seize them, do not preclude you from pursuing an overarching solution later on. They do not necessarily solve your entire problem but may take you incrementally closer to where you want to be. Leadership consultant Michael Watkins argues that quick wins, or wins secured early in one's tenure, build your credibility and create momentum.[48] Nobel laureate Medawar agrees: "It is psychologically most important to *get results*, even if they are not original."[49]

In Chapter 4, we saw how serendipity required not just stumbling upon an unexpected result but also recognizing its value. Capturing quick wins along your solution process is similar in that it requires you to keep a soft focus.[50]

One way to secure quick wins is to target easy problems: some professional sport teams, for instance, acquire a reputation of excellence not doing any better than others against stronger opponents but by consistently beating below-average teams.[51]

Quick wins can be very positive: Van Buren and Safferstone, analyzing the performance of newly promoted leaders, found that most top performers had managed to secure a quick win early in their tenure.[52] Indeed, in a setting where analysis can go on for weeks or longer, being able to secure a victory, even a small one, can go a long way toward reassuring your boss that putting you in charge was the right decision. It can also reassure your team that you are not stuck in analysis paralysis, thereby helping to build much needed support and momentum.

Van Buren and Safferstone also note, however, that the relentless pursuit of quick wins may be counterproductive. Implementing quick wins is valuable as long as it does not significantly distract resources from your main target and does not close off any of the alternatives that you may want to pursue once you finish your analysis. Going from New York to London, you probably should not buy a boat ticket before you have analyzed whether flying serves your purpose better (that is, unless the consequences of buying a ticket that you will end up not using are minimal; for instance, the ticket is easy to buy and fully refundable). But you can, for instance, renew an out-of-date passport; that will not take much of your time, and it will be useful in all cases.

So, when solving complex problems, it can be useful to visualize your actions as a part of a portfolio: early in the resolution process, dedicate most of your effort to analysis but consider keeping some bandwidth to pursue actions that might get you closer to a solution without closing doors in the future. As you move forward in the resolution, gradually decrease the attention you give to analysis to free up more resources to pursue actions.

**Consider adding small wins**. Sometimes, the solution to your problem is a collection of partial solutions. For instance, in some settings, serving a large number of clients each buying a small quantity may be attractive. Indeed, Amazon has a competitive advantage

---

48. (Watkins, 2004).
49. (Medawar, 1979) [p. 17].
50. See, for instance (Pfeffer & Sutton, 2006b) [p. 149–150].
51. (Weick, 1984).
52. (Van Buren & Safferstone, 2009).

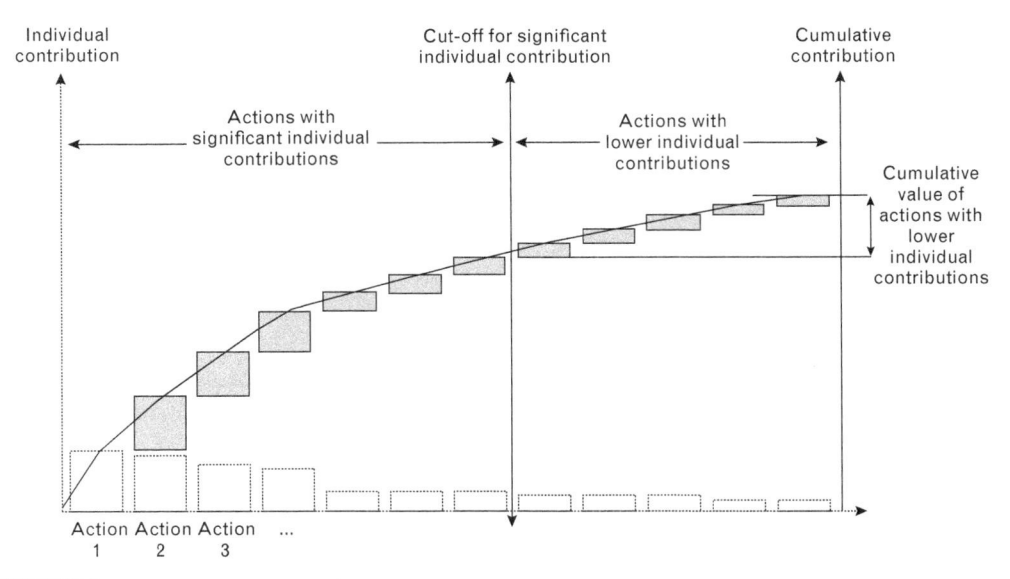

**FIGURE 6.8:** The cumulative value of solutions with lower individual contributions may be significant.

over brick-and-mortar booksellers in its ability to carry in its stock books that are low in demand but that, in their ensemble, compound to a significant sales volume.[53] You may want to check whether the same dynamic might apply to your problem: perhaps there, too, implementing a collection of partial solutions can result in a sizable cumulative effect (see Figure 6.8).

## 5. WHAT ABOUT HARRY?

Having ranked the attractiveness of the various courses of action (Table 6.6), we performed a sensitivity analysis to test the robustness of the results and reflect on their implications. Our decision model recommended first informing people likely to know about missing animals before -2- searching the neighborhood, and -3- enabling Harry to come back on his own. When our sensitivity analysis revealed that the results were robust—that is, it took comparatively large changes in our assumptions to modify the ranking—we accepted these results as a prioritization of our search activities.

So far, we have gone through the analysis part of our problem-resolution process: we identified *what* problem we wanted to solve (Chapter 1), *why* we were facing that problem in the first place (Chapters 2 to 4), and *how* we should resolve it (Chapters 5 and 6). But knowing how we can solve our problem is not enough. So, next, we need to implement the solution(s) we have selected. This usually starts with convincing key stakeholders that our conclusions are sound. That is the object of Chapter 7.

---

53. (Anderson, 2004).

# NOTES

**Phantom alternatives.** The fifth option, checking announcements, although appearing to be an actual option is not or, at least, is not until Harry's finder posts an announcement. These illusory choices are called phantom alternatives.[54]

**Making better decisions.** Bazerman and Moore propose six concrete ways for making better decisions: "use decision-analysis tools, acquire expertise, debias your judgment, reason analogically, take an outsider's view, and understand biases in others."[55]

**More on decision tools.** A number of tools can help you make decisions with multiattributes. See, for instance (Olson, 1996) and (Goodwin & Wright, 2009) for a description of alternatives. Our motivation for presenting only SMARTER is to keep things simple, which is critical for adoption by practitioners.[56]

**Evaluating performance of alternatives.** Sometimes an attribute ranks naturally against the convention of the larger number being preferred—such as cost: intuitively an alternative with a lower cost should be better than one with a larger one, everything else being constant. Therefore, it makes sense to have the scores vary in that direction; that is, low score is low cost, high score is high cost. To do so, one way is to reverse the attribute, replacing "cost" by "cheapness" or "lack of cost." This may help reduce cognitive load when reviewing scores.

---

54. (Pratkanis & Farquhar, 1992).
55. (Bazerman & Moore, 2008) [pp. 179–199].
56. (Rousseau, 2012) [p. 68]; see also (Edwards & Barron, 1994) [p. 310].

CHAPTER 7

# SELL THE SOLUTION—COMMUNICATE EFFECTIVELY

*General Stanley A. McChrystal, the leader of American and NATO forces in Afghanistan, was shown a PowerPoint slide in Kabul last summer that was meant to portray the complexity of American military strategy, but looked more like a bowl of spaghetti.*

*"When we understand that slide, we'll have won the war," General McChrystal dryly remarked, one of his advisers recalled, as the room erupted in laughter. [. . .]*

*Senior [military officers say a PowerPoint presentation] does come in handy when the goal is not imparting information, as in briefings for reporters.*

*The news media sessions often last 25 minutes, with 5 minutes left at the end for questions from anyone still awake. Those types of PowerPoint presentations, Dr. Hammes said, are known as "hypnotizing chickens."*[1]

Effective problem resolution requires convincing key stakeholders that your analysis and your conclusions are valid so that you can transition from your analysis to implementation. As such, you must be able to summarize your findings in a message that makes a persuasive argument.

Therefore, communicating your results is an integral part of your effort, one that is worthy of careful consideration.[2] You may communicate your conclusions in any one of several types of media, but because presentations have become omnipresent in the workplace, this chapter focuses on those. Note, however, that many of the themes discussed below are equally relevant for other forms of media.

Assembling a persuasive message—that is, creating a compelling story and delivering it effectively—requires using effective rhetoric and slide design. In general, the difficulty in assembling such a message is not so much in our inability to use language as it is in identifying what we want to say. This process starts with determining our objectives.

---

1. (Bumiller, 2010).
2. (Keisler & Noonan, 2012).

TABLE 7.1: A *From–To/Think–Do Matrix* Helps Clarify the Change We Want to Induce in Our Audience's Thinking and Behavior with Our Presentation

|  | From | To |
|---|---|---|
| Think | **What they think now:** To recover Harry, we should search the neighborhood right way. | **What they should think after the presentation:** First, we should inform people likely to know about missing animals that Harry is missing. |
| Do | **What they do (or do not do) now:** They are printing announcements to distribute and post in the neighborhood. | **What they should do (or stop doing) after the presentation:** Speak with people likely to know about missing animals. |

# 1. DETERMINE YOUR OBJECTIVES

The first step in preparing your presentation should be to answer one question: How do you want your presentation to change your audience's thinking and behavior? Indeed, if your audience is walking out of your presentation thinking and behaving as they did before, then what is the point of having the presentation in the first place? Some argue that certain presentations are merely informational and are not aimed at promoting change. Although mere information may be the primary objective of some presentations, even those are usually also prescriptive, aiming at promoting some change.[3] For instance, a prototypical example of an informational presentation in a managerial setting is a progress report on a project, but even those aim at some change, such as strengthening the audience's confidence in the management of the project.

Identifying the change we want in an audience is hard work, which may explain why we default to thinking that some presentations are merely informational, when, in fact, they are not. To help you identify the change you want in your audience, consider using Abela's From–To/Think–Do matrix, which spells out where your audience currently is (in both their thinking and behavior) and where you want your presentation to take them.[4] Table 7.1 shows such a matrix for Harry's case.

# 2. TELL A COMPELLING STORY

Stories are powerful tools to drive people to take action. Harvard psychologist Howard Gardner believes that one's ability to tell a story is a crucial component of successful leadership.[5] Using stories can greatly enhance your presentation for several reasons: Stories create anticipation, thereby helping an audience maintain attention;[6] they link the various

---

3. See, for instance, (Alley, 2003) [p. 28].
4. (Abela, 2008) [p. 31].
5. (Burke, 2014) [pp. 293–294].
6. (Alley, 2013) [pp. 35–39].

elements of even complex wholes, which creates a frame that enhances recollection;[7] and they introduce emotions, which also helps recollection.[8]

When it comes to crafting and delivering compelling stories, turning to the movie industry can be inspirational. Robert McKee, a screenwriting lecturer, points out that storytelling helps a presenter transcend merely intellectual arguments: "Stories fulfill a profound human need to grasp the patterns of living—not merely as an intellectual exercise, but within a very personal, emotional experience."[9]

## 2.1. PREPARING YOUR SLIDE DECK, IN A NUTSHELL

Before we dive into details, here is an overview of our approach to creating slide decks. Start preparing your presentation by summarizing your story at a high level, as in Figure 7.1.

Next, distribute this summary in taglines of slides, by placing one idea per slide, as in Figure 7.2. This will probably be an iterative process and you might find that some units of thought do not belong to your main message. Rather than deleting those, just place them in an appendix.

Then populate the slides with the evidence that supports each of these taglines, as in Figure 7.3. Ideally, this evidence comes in visuals—photos, drawings, graphs, etc.—rather than in written form.

In that sense, each slide becomes a self-contained capsule with an idea in its tagline and the evidence supporting it in the body of the slide. That way, your slide deck becomes a central repository of the information that you have collected. In addition, it is modular: You can move the slides around to create a message crafted for a specific presentation and store in the appendix whichever slides that are not necessary for that particular instance (see Figure 7.4).

Because your taglines amount to your storyline, someone reading only those should understand your story completely. It is important to check periodically that this remains the case as you assemble your slides and edit their taglines.

---

My friend's dog, Harry, is missing and we need your help to find him.

Specifically, we have identified 6 major ways to get him back. Unfortunately, we don't have enough resources to pursue all, therefore we need to prioritize. Our analysis shows that we should start with enlisting others, so that's what we'll do.

Our analysis also suggests that taking action in the neighborhood is a very good mid-term approach. Finally, we'll take some actions to enable him to come back on his own.

To implement successfully, we need your assistance; will you help?

FIGURE 7.1: First, craft your storyline—the summary of your message—in a succinct story.

---

7. (Shaw, Brown, & Bromiley, 1998), (McKee & Fryer, 2003).

8. (Abela, 2008) [p. 65].

9. (McKee & Fryer, 2003). For more on storytelling, also see (Woodside, Sood, & Miller, 2008), (Barry & Elmes, 1997), (Lounsbury & Glynn, 2001), (Kosara & Mackinlay, 2013).

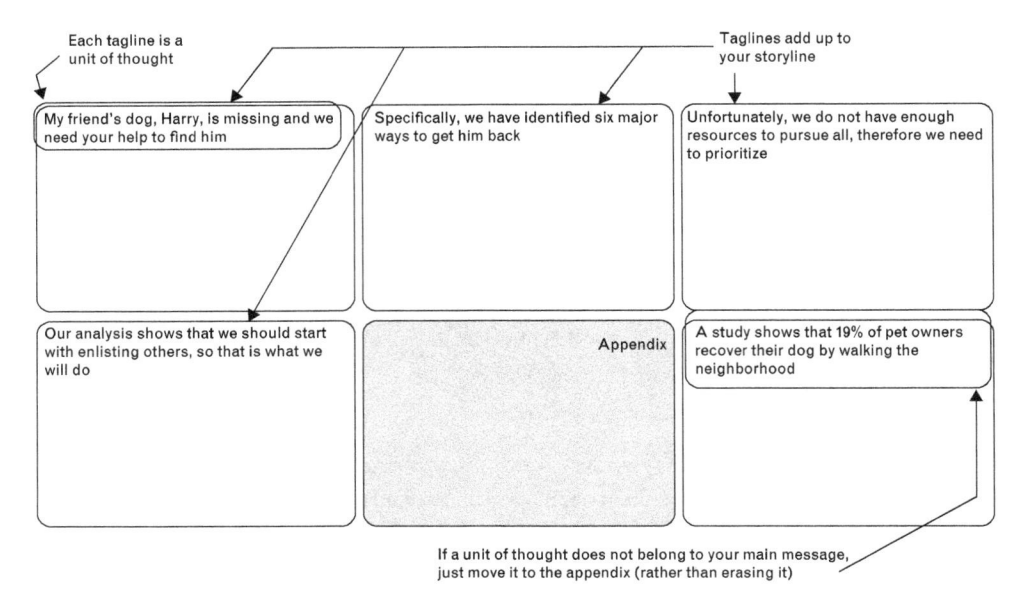

**FIGURE 7.2**: Distribute your story onto taglines.

An important implication is that preparing an effective presentation takes time, in part, because assembling the reasons supporting your conclusions might help you identify gaps in your logic. Given this, leave yourself ample time; ideally starting early in your project and capturing your findings in slides as you go along.

The rest of the chapter explains how to do this and gives some guidelines for the delivery of the presentation.

## 2.2. USE THE RIGHT KINDS OF ARGUMENTS

*The Western Australian government's shark-attack policy is heavily influenced by "Jaws," the classic Hollywood thriller that's terrorized audiences since 1975 — and that's a terrible, terrible thing, according to Christopher Neff, a public policy lecturer at the University of Sydney's Department of Government and International Relations.*

*In the movie, a great white with a taste for human flesh and a desire for revenge slaughters residents of a New England beach town before it's eventually hunted down and killed.*

*In real life, Neff argues, the government's "imminent threat policy," which was designed to catch and kill sharks in the wake of an attack, "is predicated on Hollywood fiction"—the idea that once a shark has bitten someone, it will strike again and again.*

*Neff examined shark policies between 2000 and 2014 and found "striking similarities" to the film. He has a name for the influence cinematic fiction plays on real-life policy: The "Jaws" Effect.*

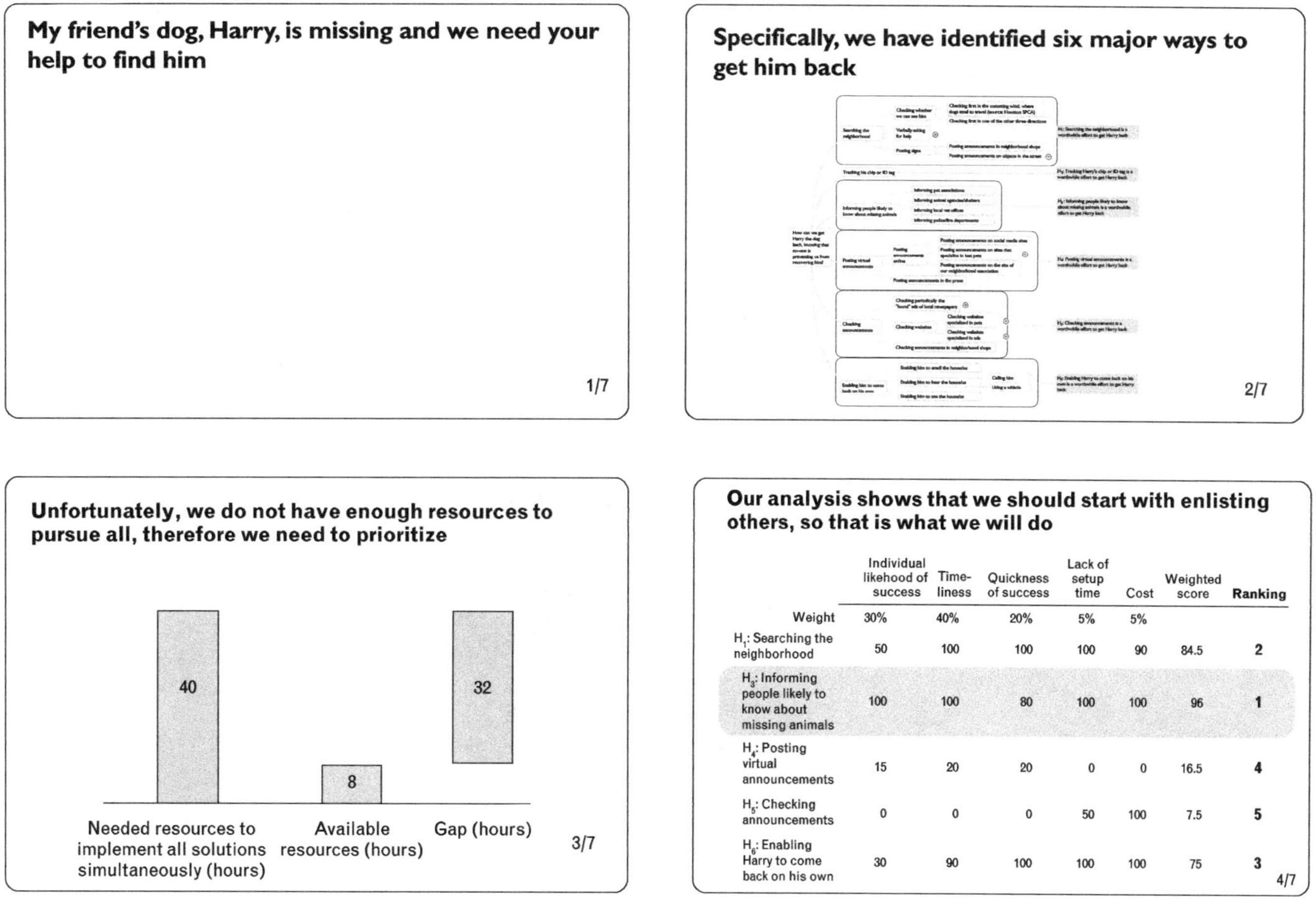

FIGURE 7.3: Then populate the body of the slides with the evidence that supports each tagline.

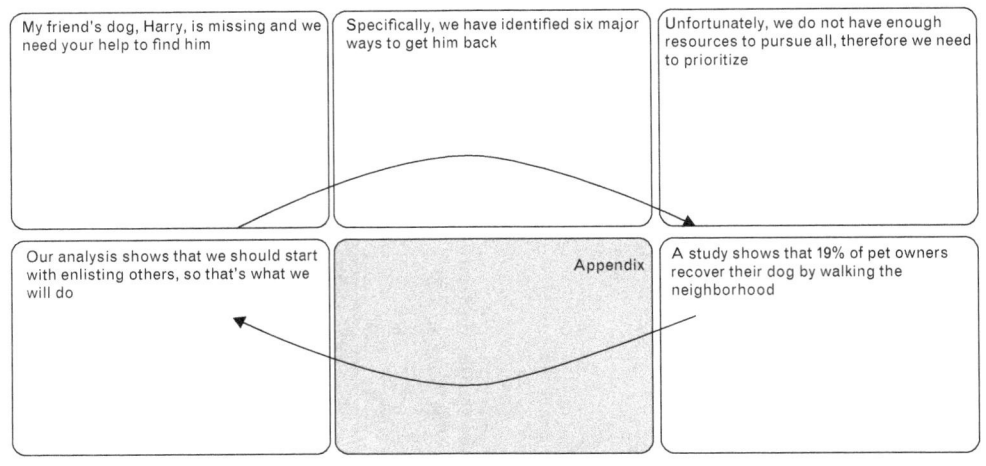

[Figure 7.4 diagram with boxes:
- "My friend's dog, Harry, is missing and we need your help to find him"
- "Specifically, we have identified six major ways to get him back"
- "Unfortunately, we do not have enough resources to pursue all, therefore we need to prioritize"
- "Our analysis shows that we should start with enlisting others, so that's what we will do"
- "Appendix"
- "A study shows that 19% of pet owners recover their dog by walking the neighborhood"]

Move slides in and out of the appendix and modify their order in the main deck to create the message that you want

**FIGURE 7.4:** Use your slide deck as a central repository for your analysis, relegating to the appendix whichever ideas are not needed for your presentation.

> "This policy is using myths as the basis for killing sharks that are protected by law and which provides no real beach safety," Neff said in a statement. "This fiction serves an important political purpose because films allow politicians to rely on familiar narratives following shark bites to blame individual sharks in order to make the events governable and to trump evidence-based science."
>
> The evidence, according to Neff, says that shark bites are rarely fatal and that there is no such thing as a "rogue shark" that hunts humans. Since 1580, Neff said, there have been a reported 2,569 shark-bite incidents off six of the seven continents (some of the statistics are based on oral history), according to the International Shark Attack File.[10]

Countless examples in our everyday life, and in our management of national affairs, show that we often elect a course of action that is not the one we ought to adopt, if we were basing our actions on an impartial look at the evidence and a logic-driven process.[11] So appealing solely to an audience's logic may not be enough to persuade them to follow your recommendation, irrespective of its foundational robustness.

Although logic has driven our actions in the resolution process up to here, effective persuasion is arguably best achieved by appealing to more than your audience's rationality: Aristotelian persuasion relies on three pillars—*ethos* (character/reputation/credibility), *pathos* (emotions), and *logos* (logic) (see Figure 7.5)—in addition to *kairos* (timing).[12]

---

10. (Holley, 2014).

11. For instance, proposing to rely on evidence to guide policymaking is so unusual that it is newsworthy (see [Dionne, 2014]).

12. See, for instance (Giluk & Rynes-Weller, 2012) [p. 146–148, 151], (McCroskey & Teven, 1999), (Alley, 2013) [pp. 95–101].

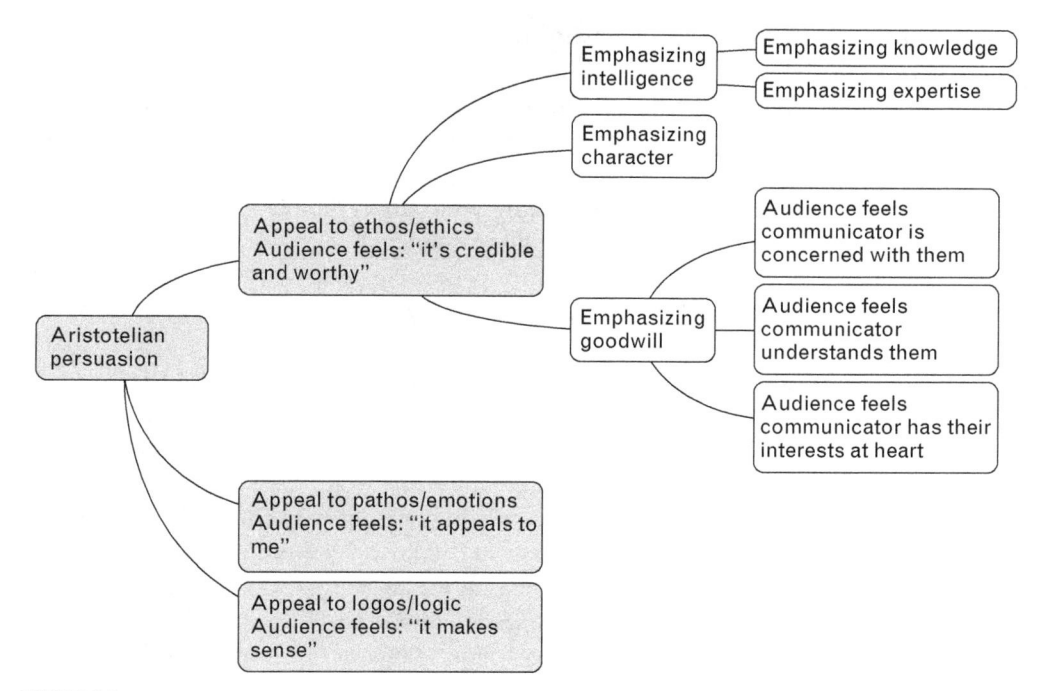

**FIGURE 7.5:** Aristotelian persuasion has three pillars: ethos, pathos, and logos.

Ethics, emotions, and logic; to persuade audiences, the Aristotelian way, they should feel "it's credible and worthy, it appeals to me, and it makes sense."[13]

**Emphasize your ethics/credibility/character—ethos.** Ethical appeal encompasses putting forth your authority and credibility, including intelligence, character, and goodwill. It is conveyed by your tone, the style of your message, and your reputation.[14] Ethos can be powerful: sometimes, people accept a message based on who delivers it without questioning the substance in depth.[15] In an evidence-based setting, however, ethos-driven persuasion should be the weakest: One should not trust a message only because of who delivers it. In reality, this happens frequently, at least in some settings: For instance, the popularity of management gurus who profess theories with little data to support their message indicates a lack of questioning by executives.[16] The takeaway is that, as a speaker, you should use your ethos but not abuse it. Symmetrically, as an audience member, you should question the arguments put in front of you, irrespective of the source.[17]

Although intuition would suggest that higher credibility results in higher persuasion, it is not always so. Yalch and Elmore-Yalch found that greater expertise leads to greater persuasion only if the message includes quantitative information; they also warn that the use

---

13. (Konnikova, 2014).
14. (Bartunek, 2007).
15. This is an instance of persuasion through the peripheral route; see (Petty & Cacioppo, 1984).
16. (Pfeffer & Sutton, 2006) [pp. 45–47].
17. (Sherman, 2002) [p. 221]. See also Chapter 2.

of quantitative information by people who are perceived as nonexperts undermines their persuasion.[18]

One way to help build credibility is to not only present data that supports your claim but present opposing claims and refute them convincingly. Paraphrasing McKee, it is the dark side of a story that makes it interesting.[19] By putting forth that not all is rosy, you expose your own shortcomings—thereby highlighting your strong points—which makes your story more compelling. Lawyers call this "stealing thunder."[20]

Another way is to look your best: Attractive people are perceived to be more talented, kind, able, and honest than unattractive people.[21] So pay attention to your overall appearance, including your clothes and grooming.

**Appeal to your audience's rationality—logos.** Present your logic and the evidence that led you to your conclusions. Your issue maps and analyses support *logos*. This is the nucleus of our approach, so it is a necessary part of our report, but it is not sufficient, because logic's power to change people's minds is limited. Indeed, as we have discussed, we suffer from a number of biases, including giving unduly high credence to the evidence that supports our own position while discounting opposing evidence.[22] Appealing to logic relates to using the *central route*, which relies on direct, mindful, and information-based arguments.[23]

**Appeal to your audience's emotions—pathos.** Emotions are a potent driver of actions in human beings, so understand your audience's motivations and generate the emotions that will sway them your way. The identified-victim effect, for instance, that leverages the increased willingness of people to help to save a real person, rather than a statistical one, is a documented instance of appealing to an audience's emotions. Goodwin and Wright note how "the simple addition of a picture and name of the child to a description of the child's illness elicits more donations."[24] McKee points out that uniting ideas with an emotion is a lot more effective than just using logic: "The best way to do that is by telling a compelling story. In a story, you not only weave a lot of information into the telling but you also arouse your listener's emotions and energy. Persuading with a story is hard. Any intelligent person can sit down and make lists. It takes rationality but little creativity to design an argument using conventional rhetoric. But it demands vivid insight and storytelling skill to present an idea that packs enough emotional power to be memorable. If you can harness imagination and the principles of a well-told story, then you get people rising to their feet amid thunderous applause instead of yawning and ignoring you."[25]

To be clear, I am not advising that you use the three pillars of persuasion to induce your audience into acting unethically or against their best interest. Indeed, our entire approach

---

18. (Yalch & Elmore-Yalch, 1984) [p. 526], (Artz & Tybout, 1999) [p. 52].

19. (McKee & Fryer, 2003).

20. (Allen, 1991), (Williams, Bourgeois, & Croyle, 1993), (Arpan & Roskos-Ewoldsen, 2005). See also (Pechmann, 1992), (Pfeffer & Sutton, 2006) [pp.47–48].

21. (Mobius & Rosenblat, 2006), (Eagly, Ashmore, Makhijani, & Longo, 1991), (Langlois et al., 2000), (L. L. Thompson, 2012) [pp. 163–164]. See also (Brooks, Huang, Kearney, & Murray, 2014), (Zuckerman & Driver, 1989).

22. (Nickerson, 1998).

23. (L. L. Thompson, 2012) [p. 156].

24. (Goodwin & Wright, 2009) [p.244].

25. (McKee & Fryer, 2003).

assumes that you, the analyst, act ethically along the entire resolution process. However, given that logic alone is sometimes insufficient to convince even rational people, I am advising that you should use multidimensional arguments to help bring about the needed change.[26]

**Use a strong introduction.** McKinsey's director of visual communications, Gene Zelazny, strongly advocates against dull introductions. Instead, he advises that introductions should "light a fire under the audience, to arouse enthusiasm for being there, to build anticipation for what's going to follow."[27] Harvard's Stephen Kosslyn agrees: "if [during the first five minutes of your presentation] you don't convince the audience that you have something of value to say, you will be likely to lose them."[28]

To do so, Zelazny proposes that introductions include three elements: purpose, importance, and preview. *Purpose* explains why the audience is there, *importance* spells out why resolving the issue today is critical, and *preview* gives the audience a summary of the structure of the presentation.[29]

**Skillfully advise the decisionmakers.** In those situations where you are reporting to decisionmakers, keeping a few concepts in mind may help you. When presenting alternatives, it appears to be better simply to provide information about the alternatives as opposed to recommending for or against them directly.[30] Similarly, people may follow your advice more readily if it costs them something as opposed to if they received it for free.[31] So it may be worthwhile reminding your audience of the cost associated with your analysis.

## 2.3. FIND THE RIGHT LENGTH

The length of your presentation is a function of the breadth of the material that you are presenting and the level of detail at which you are presenting it.

**Include all and only what is needed.** Decide first which themes must be included and which can be omitted. All noncritical slides can go to the appendix, where they will be ready to help you answer potential questions.

Having spent days, weeks, or months analyzing an issue, it is easy to want to include many details, but this comes at a price. Because your audience has limited processing capabilities, including superfluous information is detrimental.[32] Indeed, Alley observes that, in technical settings, many presentations fail because the presenter aims at covering too much material.[33]

So, in a way, your choice may not be whether you want to use your presentation to solve multiple issues but whether you want your overriding recommendation to go through or

---

26. A persuasive argument is not necessarily valid and vice versa. For a discussion, see (Schum, 1994) [pp. 22–23].
27. (Zelazny, 2006) [pp. 53–55].
28. (Kosslyn, 2007) [p. 25].
29. (Zelazny, 2006) [pp. 53–55].
30. (Dalal & Bonaccio, 2010).
31. (Gino, 2008).
32. This is known as the *coherence principle* in multimedia learning (Mayer & Fiorella, 2014). See further down in this chapter.
33. (Alley, 2013) [pp. 59–67].

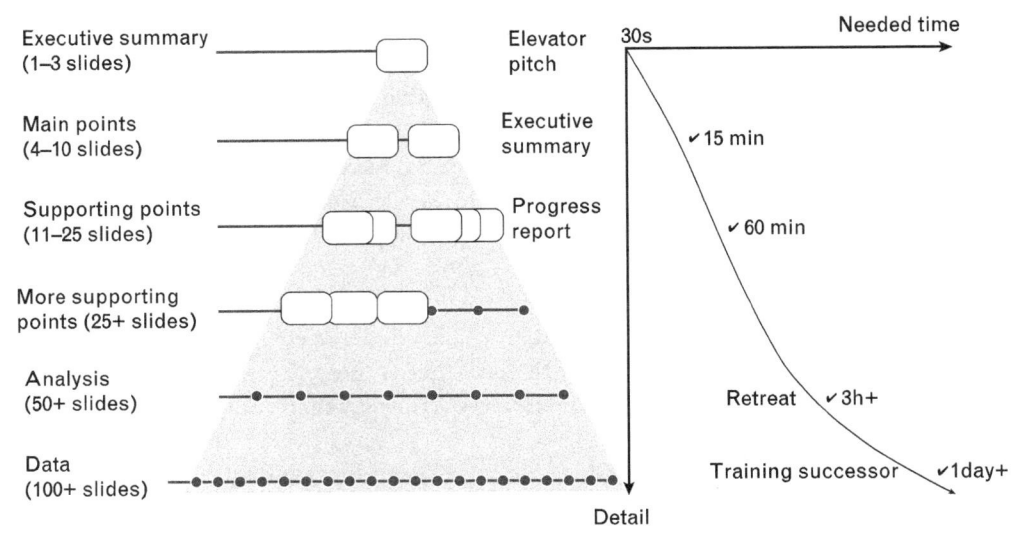

**FIGURE 7.6:** Identify the right level of detail for the specific presentation that you are preparing.

not. Side points tax your audience's working memory and may lead them to not understand critical parts or remember what you want them to remember.

**Select the right level of detail.** Former McKinsey consultant and communication specialist Barbara Minto recommends that you organize your communication in pyramids, placing your main idea at the top.[34] That main idea is your executive summary, the essence of your communication.

Right below your executive summary are your main points, and right below those are supporting points, which may come at various levels, until you get to your hypotheses and analysis. The more you drill down, the more details. Whereas communicating your main point might only take a few seconds and might be suitable for an elevator pitch, showing the details of your analysis might require hours or even days (see Figure 7.6).

So, crafting your message, you should think about the right level of detail for each part of your communication. This is a function of the time it will take to deliver as well as your perception of how much evidence will be needed to convince your audience on each point. It is perfectly acceptable to cover different subjects at different levels of detail, as long as this is the result of a conscious decision, and not because, for instance, you grossly overestimated your ability to cover material swiftly and end up spending 80% of your allotted time talking about the first of your five subjects. Thinking of your communication as a pyramid can help you keep an eye on the big picture of your message, thereby helping you identify where all pieces fit.

## 2.4. FIND A GOOD SEQUENCE

Zelazny recommends starting your communication with your conclusion and only then explaining how you reached it.[35] In an analysis we start from data to reach a conclusion.

---

34. (Minto, 2009).
35. (Zelazny, 2006) [pp. 45–46].

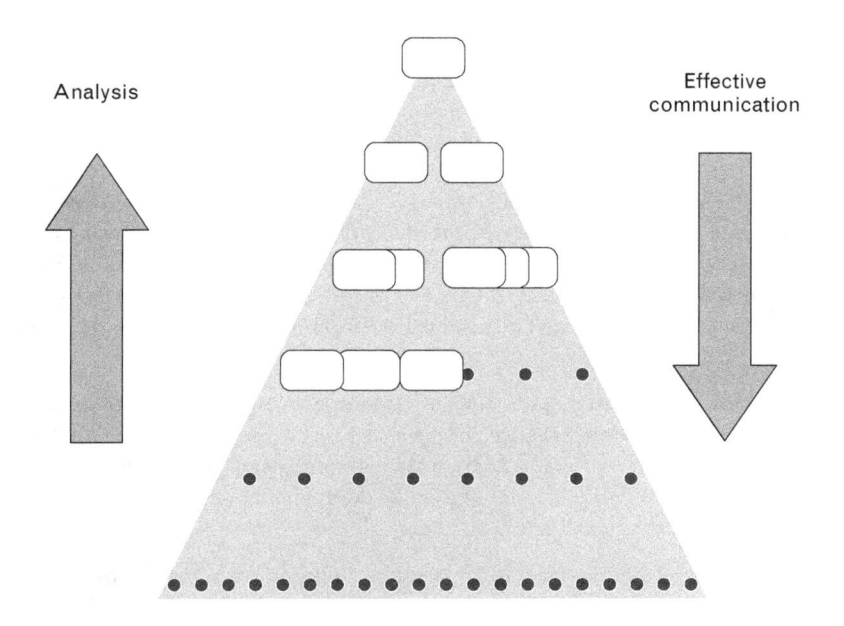

FIGURE 7.7: Resist the temptation to report your analysis process in your communication.

However, if you start with the conclusion, you are going the other way around (see Figure 7.7). This requires foregoing a chronological account of how you solved the problem.

This is to say, your communication should emphasize how your logic and evidence led you to your conclusions. For instance, in Harry's case, you may start your presentation with "Today, I'd like to explain why we should look for Harry by, first, contacting people likely to know about missing animals and gain your assistance in doing so. Here is why..." rather than "To identify how to best search for Harry, first I looked for published articles on effective ways to find lost dogs, then I searched for means that are specific to Harry's neighborhood, etc."

As an illustration of the benefit of starting with your conclusion, consider Figure 7.8, a memo written by Tom, a midlevel manager, to his boss Jim.[36]

Tom is recreating his analysis in chronological order. He is walking Jim through all the steps that led him to take his decision. The problem is that Jim does not know where Tom is going until he reads the last paragraph. So he is getting a download of information but does not know how to react to it—each bit produces the reaction "okay, so what?"—that he needs to store in his working memory. Finally, when he gets to the conclusion, he can understand how the various parts articulate and decide whether that makes sense . . . but by then he may have forgotten the details of each argument. So, having finally understood what the conclusion is, Jim may very well have to reread the message to understand how the various pieces fit together to support it.

---

36. This example is an adaptation of Zelazny's (Zelazny, 2006) [pp. 46–47].

Sell the Solution • 171

**From**: Tom

**To**: Jim

**Subject**: Update on hiring assistant

Jim,

As you know, I have been looking for an assistant that can help me with managing projects for our Latin American clients. I have been thinking about what you and I discussed and, since we need to interact frequently with Spanish speakers, I think that the person should be fluent in Spanish. Also, I am getting overflowed with projects and I need some help organizing our human and technological resources. Plus I just can't go to all the sites where we are, so I need that person to be able to travel.

Anyway, I've been looking for the right person for some time, and I have interviewed quite a few candidates. I was getting desperate because, for the salary we are ready to pay, I couldn't find someone that matched my criteria. Finally, Ed from Marketing, advised me to speak with Emma, a friend of his who he was working with before he joined the company. After resolving some time conflict, Emma and I finally got a chance to talk.

And, when we did, I realized that she meets all my requirements, so I'm going to hire her. I just wanted to let you know.

FIGURE 7.8: Putting your conclusion at the end of your message can be confusing for your audience because they must keep in mind all the items presented without knowing how they work together.

As an alternative, consider an alternative construction (Figure 7.9), where the conclusion comes before the justification.

Jim might not agree with Tom's logic: maybe he disagrees that these three criteria are the ones that Tom should consider. Or maybe he thinks that Tom should check Emma's references. Or perhaps he thinks that some of these criteria are incomplete: Emma is willing to travel. Great! But is she able? So he might have problems with Tom's reasoning, but he will

**From:** Tom
**To:** Jim
**Subject:** FYI only: I'm hiring Emma as my assistant ← The subject line summarizes the message.

Dear Jim,
I am hiring Emma as my assistant because she meets all my criteria: ← The conclusion comes before the justification.
- She speaks Spanish,
- She can manage projects,
- She is willing to travel.

No action is needed from you, I just wanted to let you know.

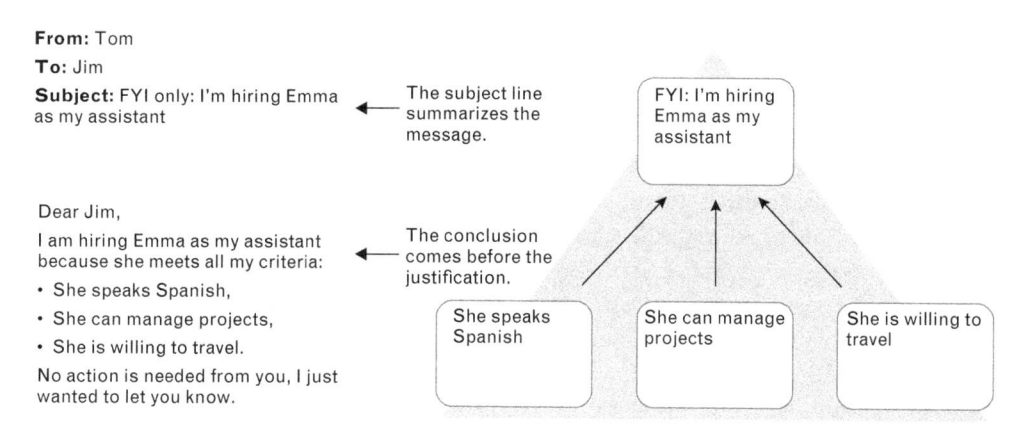

FYI: I'm hiring Emma as my assistant
↑
She speaks Spanish | She can manage projects | She is willing to travel

FIGURE 7.9: The message can be clarified by starting with the conclusion and then presenting the support for it.

not have problems understanding what it is. Now that he knows where Tom is coming from, he can react constructively.

By putting your conclusion first, and getting rid of unnecessary information, you make the message's pyramid apparent, thereby simplifying the audience's job. Knowing what your conclusion is, they can interpret each new element that appears and decide whether it supports your argument.

Although describing your analysis process may be advisable in some specific instances—say, describing a scientific experiment whose conclusions are unconvincing to the audience—information analysis specialists Keisler and Noonan advise that it "should be resisted in almost all situations."[37] Zelazny agrees: He recommends using the conclusion-first approach even if you know you will face significant pushback from the audience.[38] There, you may start off by acknowledging the disagreement: "The point of my talk today is to convince you to look for Harry by first contacting people who may know where he is. I know this goes against the general consensus and that you think that we should first post flyers and search the neighborhood, but we reached this conclusion after carefully analyzing all options. Let me show you how we got there."

# 3. USE EFFECTIVE SLIDE DESIGN

Slide presentations have been heavily criticized and, in many instances, rightfully so.[39] However, in the right setting and with appropriate design, presentations can be a highly effective tool to support your communication. Keisler and Noonan argue that the key factor for success is to ensure that you, the presenter, rather than the software, drives the communication through "a clear storyline and good slide design."[40]

### 3.1. DEFINE THE PRIMARY PURPOSE OF YOUR SLIDE DECK

Presentations answer a continuum of needs, from a visual support for your message during the presentation to a stand-alone record of the information for future reference. What constitutes an optimal slide design depends on this primary objective, so there is no one single good slide design (see Figure 7.10). If you are looking for a visual support only, you may decide to show fewer details, leaving these for you to present orally. On the other hand, if your slide deck's primary intent is a stand-alone record, you may need to specify these details.

---

37. (Keisler & Noonan, 2012).
38. (Zelazny, 2006) [p. 51].
39. See, for instance (Edward R Tufte, 2003).
40. (Keisler & Noonan, 2012).

|  | Visual support for presentation |  | Postpresentation record |
| --- | --- | --- | --- |
|  | Presents main ideas only, not details |  | Presents main ideas and supporting details |
|  | Has few words on slides (<~40) | Differences | May have more words on slides |
|  | Uses large fonts |  | Uses various font sizes to show the pyramid on the slide |
|  | May use more photos |  |  |
|  | Is self-sufficient |  | Is self-sufficient |
|  | Uses assertion-evidence structure | Similarities | Uses assertion-evidence structure |

FIGURE 7.10: Presentations answer a continuum of needs, which should impact slide design.

Of course, in many cases, a slide deck serves both purposes and you end up somewhere between these extremes. So it is important that you identify the primary goal of your slide deck and ensure it leans toward the appropriate extreme.

In both cases, my personal experience agrees with the results of studies by Alley, Garner, and others,[41] who find that summarizing each slide in a full-sentence tagline is more effective than using titles or topics. In turn, ensuring that the taglines work together to tell the story you aim to convey ensures that people will be able to understand the main ideas of the slide deck without a presenter.

**Understand the two extremes and decide where you need to be.** Figure 7.11 shows two extremes of slide design. The slide on the left, from Garr Reynolds, follows a minimalist design often seen in TED Talks. These slides often have a large image and very few, if any, words.[42] TED slides are effective to communicate to the general public.[43] In these slides, the photo and the text indicate to the audience the general idea of the slide, but the presenter is indispensable to extract the "so what?" The implication is that this approach restricts your slide presentation to being only a visual support, and there is a risk that your audience misses your message if they happen to not pay attention for a while during the presentation, or if they miss the presentation altogether and refer to the slide later on. Furthermore the visual message must remain at a high level, with few details and nuances communicated.

On the other hand, management consultants have mastered the use of slide presentations for establishing a postpresentation record in addition to providing visual support for their presentation. The slide on the right, from the Boston Consulting Group, has a much more analytic appearance than Reynolds'. Also, compared with TED slides, the message is more complex and oriented, no doubt, to an audience with a much better understanding of the subject matter. This design enables you to capture many more details and nuances.

The TED and the consultant-structure slides represent two extreme ends of a spectrum. They just happen to use one common medium, slides, to do two very different things. So,

---

41. See, for instance (Alley, 2013) [pp. 105–128], (J. Garner & Alley, 2013), (Alley & Neeley, 2005).
42. (Duarte, 2008, 2010; Reynolds, 2011), (Alley, 2013) [p. 184].
43. (Alley, 2013) [p. 172].

**Visual support for presentation**

**Postpresentation record**

Source: presentationzen.com

From Garr Reynolds. The abundant use of images promotes an emotional response.

Source: http://nyc.gov/html/nycha/downloads/pdf/BCG-report-NYCHA-Key-Findings-and-Recommendations-8-15-12vFinal.pdf

From BCG. Logic, rather than emotions, drives the communication. Also, the message is much more complex.

FIGURE 7.11: Slide decks can have various purposes; their primary objective, rather than personal preferences, should dictate the slide design.

rather than letting your personal preference guide your choice of slide design, you should optimize your slide deck for the specific use you want from it. And, irrespective of its use, your presentation should comply with the six critical principles of designing instructional slides.

## 3.2. ADHERE TO THE SIX CRITICAL PRINCIPLES OF DESIGNING INSTRUCTIONAL SLIDES

Adhering to six multimedia principles of instructional slide design can improve comprehension, reduce misconceptions, and reduce the perceived cognitive load of your audience.[44] These principles are:

1. The *multimedia principle* states that people learn better from words and pictures than from words alone.[45]
2. The *contiguity principle* states that you should minimize spacial and temporal separation between various forms of information because this makes it easier for the audience to see connections.[46]
3. The *redundancy principle* states that individuals benefit from complementary, but not identical, information presented visually and aurally.[47]
4. The *modality principle* states that people learn better when the words are spoken rather than printed.[48]
5. The *coherence principle* states that you should remove all nonessential information to help the audience integrate critical relationships and concepts.[49]
6. Finally, the *signaling principle* states that you should provide your audience with cues to help them understand the structure of your presentation and how the concepts interrelate.[50]

## 3.3. USE AN ASSERTION–EVIDENCE STRUCTURE

Originally developed for scientific, engineering, and business communication, the *assertion–evidence slide structure* consists of using a declarative sentence, as opposed to a title, in the tagline of a slide and presenting evidence in the body of the slide that supports the assertion.[51] Here is how to make it work.

---

44. (J. Garner & Alley, 2013); see also (Mayer & Fiorella, 2014).
45. (Butcher, 2014).
46. (Mayer & Fiorella, 2014).
47. (Mayer & Fiorella, 2014).
48. (Mayer & Pilegard, 2014).
49. (Mayer & Fiorella, 2014).
50. (van Gog, 2014).
51. (J. Garner & Alley, 2013).

The tagline is the main idea of the slide in the form of a full assertion —not just a title.

**Our sales are growing**

Sales (M$)

17  19  23  32
2007  2008  2009  2010

The slide's body shows (preferably with visuals, rather than text) evidence that supports its tagline.

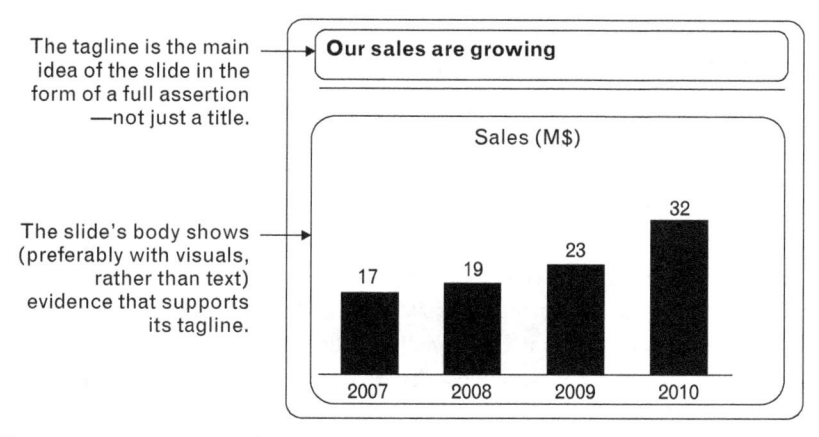

**FIGURE 7.12:** Use an assertion–evidence structure in which the tagline is a full declarative sentence and the body of the slide presents evidence that supports it.

**Present one idea per slide.** Think of each slide as a unit of thought and present just one idea per slide. If it is a complex idea, you can break it down over two or three slides if that makes it simpler for your audience.

**Use the tagline to spell out the slide's main idea in a declarative sentence.** An effective slide should enable the audience to quickly identify the point of the slide. One way to do this is to put the main point of the slide—the *assertion*—in the tagline and use the body of the slide to provide supporting evidence, primarily using visual evidence—photos, drawings, graphs, etc. (see Figure 7.12)—as opposed to text.[52] With this structure, the tagline expresses what the data means for the audience—its "so what?"—rather than what the data is—its "what."[53] It also helps the slide presentation comply with the principles of redundancy, coherence, and signaling.[54] Compared with other slide designs, this approach has been shown to enable audiences to better understand and remember the content of complex presentations.[55] Penn State professor of engineering communications Michael Alley advises that the tagline should be no more than two lines, left-justified, and capitalized as a sentence (with periods being optional).[56]

PowerPoint and other presentation packages do not make it easy to have a sentence tagline: In their templates, the slide's top element is called a title, and accommodating in that space a sentence that might be 10 or 20 words long takes some formatting effort. Perhaps as a result, a majority of presenters do not use sentences in taglines but instead use a top-phrase headline or title supported by bullet points.[57] This is problematical because such a title does not convey sufficient information: it might give some indication as to the content

---

52. (Alley, 2003, 2013; Alley & Neeley, 2005), (Doumont, 2005; Keisler & Noonan, 2012).
53. (Doumont, 2009) [p. 99].
54. (J. Garner & Alley, 2013). This is related to the concept of unity in rhetoric; see, for instance (Roche, 1979) [pp. 2–4].
55. (Alley, 2013) [pp. 119–120], (J. K. Garner, Alley, Wolfe, & Zappe, 2011), (J. Garner & Alley, 2013).
56. (Alley, 2013) [p. 131].
57. (J. K. Garner et al., 2011), (J. Garner & Alley, 2013).

Sell the Solution • 177

of the slide, but it does not make a significant contribution of its own. As such, this approach has been criticized by academics and practitioners alike.[58]

When writing your taglines, strive to make your message as clear as possible for your audience. This may prove difficult, but it is necessary. In the words of venture capitalist Guy Kawasaki—a person who spends a fair share of his life sitting in presentations: "The significance of what you're saying is not always self-evident, let alone shocking and awe-inspiring."[59] Cambridge mathematician Michael Thompson agrees: "A good rule of thumb, for most of us, is to be about twice as explicit as seems necessary."[60] The observation also applies in movies: Truffaut wrote that clarity "is *the* most important quality in the making of a film" (italics his).[61] Director Alexander Mackendrick observes that "clarity is the communication of essential and the exclusion of the non-essential, no simple matter at all, since it can be tricky to decide what is not really essential and then find a way to reduce emphasis on such things. It can take great ingenuity and considerable insight to isolate what is important (and, therefore, must be retained, even accentuated) in material that is confused or overcomplicated by irrelevancies and banalities."[62]

When choosing a tagline, recognize that several ideas can summarize the same data and choose an insightful one. Avoid *static assertions* (also called *blank assertions*): sentences that do summarize the content of the slide but that do not open links to at least one other idea in your message (see Figure 7.13).[63]

Using taglines as full declarative sentences has several major advantages:

*Sentence taglines foster recall.* Empirical evidence shows that using sentences in taglines improved the audience's recollection of details after technical presentations.[64]

*Sentence taglines help your audience orient itself during the presentation.* Confronted with a new slide, your audience immediately tries to understand why it is there; capturing the point of the slide in its tagline helps them do so.[65]

*Sentence taglines help you improve your logic.* By having to interpret your data and summarize it in a short statement, you are forced to think in depth about what you are presenting.[66] Does the data make sense? Is this conclusion really what the data is showing? Is this really what I should be showing?

*Sentence taglines help you build a compelling story.* Because your taglines as a whole amount to your storyline, you can easily identify mismatches between your overall story and the evidence that you present. This also helps you eliminate irrelevant information and pinpoint any that is missing.[67]

---

58. In technical communication, see (Doumont, 2005), (Alley & Neeley, 2005); in multimedia learning theory, see (J. Garner & Alley, 2013).
59. (Kawasaki, 2004) [p. 46].
60. (J. M. T. Thompson, 2013).
61. (Truffaut & Scott, 1983) [p. 17].
62. (Mackendrick, 2004) [p. 32].
63. See (Roche, 1979).
64. (Alley, Schreiber, Ramsdell, & Muffo, 2006), (J. K. Garner et al., 2011).
65. (Alley, 2003) [p. 126].
66. (Alley, 2013) [pp. 132–133].
67. (Alley, 2013) [pp. 133–137].

(a) We can increase profits in two ways

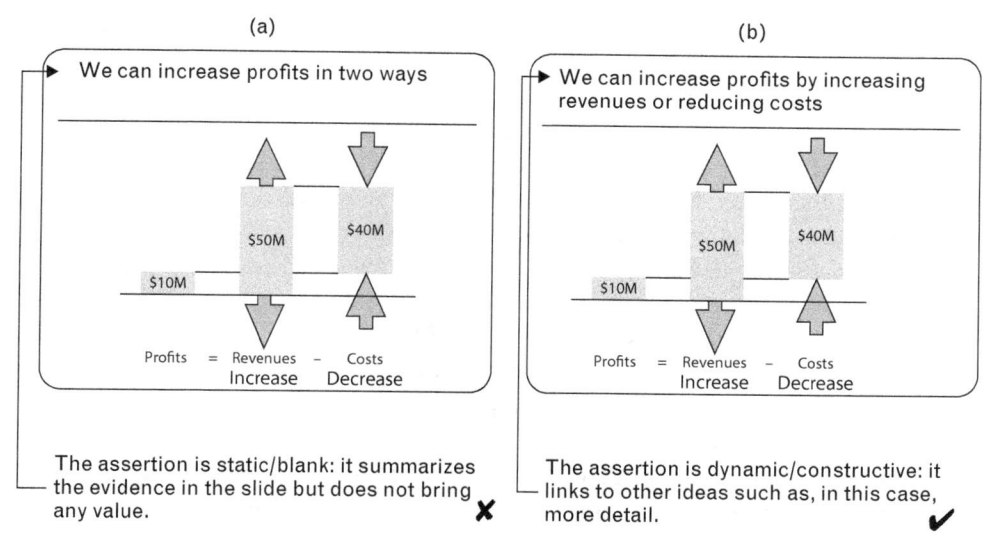

(b) We can increase profits by increasing revenues or reducing costs

The assertion is static/blank: it summarizes the evidence in the slide but does not bring any value. ✗

The assertion is dynamic/constructive: it links to other ideas such as, in this case, more detail. ✓

**FIGURE 7.13:** In taglines, avoid static assertions—those statements that are correct but add little value; instead, favor assertions that link to other ideas.

*Sentence taglines enable you to deliver your presentation in a fraction of the time.* If you have ever been in a situation where you were told to prepare a slide deck for a 60-minute presentation only to be told a few minutes before the presentation that, because a crisis arose, you now only had 15 minutes, you know the value of being able to present your message at various levels of detail. Effective taglines enable you to accommodate these situations. Presenting only taglines—that is, presenting your

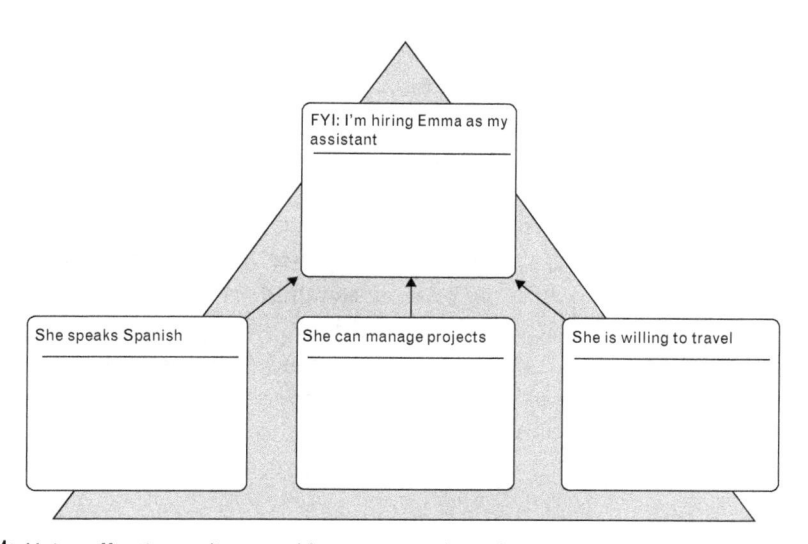

**FIGURE 7.14:** Using effective taglines enables you to go through your presentation at a more conceptual level, should you need to.

Sell the Solution • 179

message at a higher level in the pyramid (see Figure 7.14)—enables you to retain the integrity of your story while going through the slide deck much more quickly.

*Sentence taglines lay out the groundwork for a better discussion.* The tagline enables your audience to understand your interpretation of the slide's evidence by reading one sentence. They may disagree with that interpretation, but at least they understand it. The discussion can then focus on the essence of your message; for instance, finding a shared interpretation of the evidence, rather than on clarifying misunderstandings.

*Sentence taglines help you build a powerful reference deck.* A key decisionmaker may not be in the room when you present. Or someone—including you!—may want to get back to the presentation after a few weeks. Having captured the "so what?" of each slide in its tagline, it is easier to understand the essence of the message without the presenter. To be clear, using an assertion–evidence structure in your presentation does not remove the need for the presenter. Although the essence of the message is understandable just by looking at the slides, the presenter still plays an important role through emphasizing key aspects, providing more details, answering questions, making the content livelier, and so on.

## 3.4. USE AN EFFECTIVE DESIGN FOR THE BODY OF THE SLIDE

Slide design may be thought of by differentiating two aspects: the overall design of the slide and the characteristics of the visuals that you use.

### 3.4.1. DESIGN YOUR SLIDES TO FACILITATE COMPREHENSION

The primary driver for the design of your slides should be to help your audience understand your story. Following are some guidelines to help you do so.

Doumont proposes that an effective slide is one that meets three goals: it adapts to the audience, maximizes signal-to-noise ratio, and uses effective redundancy.[68] Table 7.2 explains what that means for slide design.

He summarizes the challenge of creating effective slides as expressing "a message unambiguously with as little text as possible."

**Use a consistent template.** Keeping with the notion that slide design should promote the audience's understanding, use a consistent set of overall layouts, backgrounds and text colors, font size, font type, etc. all along your presentation.[69] Use the same—or, if not possible because of space constraints, similar—font size for all taglines. Use the same placement for slide numbers on each slide. Physicist Michael McIntyre makes a strong argument that needless variation is akin to bad road signposting, which would use different names for the same place. He goes on to say that gratuitous variation "is like the original control room displays of the Three Mile Island nuclear reactor [where] the colour coding

---

68. (Doumont, 2005) [p. 68].

69. (Doumont, 2005) [pp. 99–102].

TABLE 7.2: Characteristics of Effective Slides and Implications[a]

| Effective slide design should... | To do so, slides should... |
|---|---|
| Adapt to the audience | Focus on what the information means to *that* audience (the "so what?") rather than just presenting information. |
| Maximize signal-to-noise ratio | Have as little text as possible to avoid competing with the audience's attention (which relates to the multimedia, modality, and coherence principles). |
| Use effective redundancy | Be stand-alone (as the presenter's spoken text): "deaf" audience members should understand the message by only looking at the slides and "blind" members should also be able to understand it by listening only. |

[a] After (Doumont, 2005).

to distinguish normal from abnormal functioning was varied, as in a traffic system whose red lights sometimes mean stop and sometimes go."[70]

**Use colors effectively.** Colors may help people extract information from a display, but their use must be judicious.[71] In particular, their use should be driven by functionality, rather than cosmetics.[72] In communication expert Nancy Duarte's words, "practice design, not decoration."[73] Use colors sparingly and ensure that there is sufficient contrast between the forefront elements (text, graphics, table, etc.) and the slide background.[74] Also, leverage conventions: To anyone with a driver's license, green means go/good and red means stop/bad. Also blue is cold, yellow is warmer, red is warmest, white is pure, etc. And keep in mind that using irrelevant colors is harmful.[75]

**Use large-enough fonts.** Make sure you use large font or be prepared to lose your audience. Alley recommends using type size of 28 point type for the tagline and 18 to 24 points for the body of the slide (assuming a bolded font),[76] while Kawasaki recommends using no font less than 30 points in size ... or less than the age of the oldest audience member divided by two.[77] This is easy for a presentation designed to be primarily a visual support, but it may be challenging for ones that are designed to be a detailed record. In either case, do not project anything that your audience cannot read.

**Use proper font types.** Serif typefaces—those with small lines attached to the end of letters—are argued by some to work better for documents with lots of text because they help the eye see letters as groups.[78] Some studies, however, have shown that sans serif

---

70. (McIntyre, 1997).
71. (Hoadley, 1990) [p. 125], (Abela, 2008) [p. 103].
72. (Zelazny, 1996).
73. (Duarte, 2008) [p. 259].
74. (Alley, 2013) [pp. 159–161], (Doumont, 2005).
75. (Abela, 2008) [pp. 103–104].
76. (Alley & Neeley, 2005), (Alley, 2013) [pp. 132, 138]. See also (Berk, 2011).
77. (Kawasaki, 2008).
78. (Mackiewicz, 2007a).

typefaces (Arial, Gill Sans, Tahoma, Verdana, Calibri, etc.) perform better than serif ones on four dimensions: comfortable to read, professional, interesting, and attractive. In one study, Gill Sans scored well in all categories, and Jo Mackiewicz, a professor of professional communication at Iowa State University, recommends it for use on slides.[79]

**Draw attention with bold characters.** Stay away from italic and underlined text; italics can be difficult to read and underlined text adds noise, which complicates recognition.[80] Also, avoid exclusive use of capital letters, which slow reading and take more space than traditional typeset.[81] You also may decide to write numbers with digits, as opposed to spelling them out, given that this reduces the number of characters on the slide and offers a visual anchor.

**Use a clear and concise style.** Novelist George Orwell offered advice on writing:

"(i) Never use a metaphor, simile or other figure of speech which you are used to seeing in print.
(ii) Never use a long word where a short one will do.
(iii) If it is possible to cut a word out, always cut it out.
(iv) Never use the passive where you can use the active.
(v) Never use a foreign phrase, a scientific word or a jargon word if you can think of an everyday English equivalent.
(vi) Break any of these rules sooner than say anything outright barbarous."[82]

Orwell's directives align with Cornell English professor William Strunk's own recommendations—including his beautifully efficient "omit needless words."[83] To help you do so, Table 7.3 shows some common instances of bloating and alternatives for them.

**Avoid redundancy of written and oral text.** Simultaneous presentation of identical written and oral material interferes with, rather than helps, the presentation and is less efficient than auditory-only text.[84] This is because such redundancy of information requires coordination, which is highly taxing on the audience's working memory.[85] Therefore, except for your taglines, you should have as little text as possible on your slides—use visuals instead of bullet points, for instance.[86]

**Do not write sideways.** Unless you want your audience to stretch their neck muscles, do not force them to tilt their heads to read your visuals.

---

79. (Mackiewicz, 2007a). See also (Alley, 2013) [pp. 132, 154–155]. However, the superiority of sans serif fonts is disputed; see (Abela, 2008) [p. 102] for a discussion.
80. (Alley & Neeley, 2005), (Alley, 2013) [pp. 132, 155].
81. (Alley & Neeley, 2005).
82. (Orwell, 1970) [p. 139].
83. (Strunk, 2015) [p. 27].
84. (Kalyuga, Chandler, & Sweller, 2004), (Jamet & Le Bohec, 2007), (Mayer, Heiser, & Lonn, 2001), (Mayer & Fiorella, 2014) [p. 279].
85. (Kalyuga & Sweller, 2014). See also (Kalyuga, Chandler, & Sweller, 2000): "the most advantageous format when instructing inexperienced learners in a domain was a visually presented diagram combined with simultaneously presented auditory explanations."
86. (Doumont, 2005).

TABLE 7.3: Avoid Bloating

| Do not use... | Use... |
|---|---|
| in order to | to |
| in the event of | if |
| each and every | each |
| forward progress | progress |
| merge together | merge |
| goals and objectives | goals (or objectives) |
| prior to | before |
| utilize | use |
| personal opinion | opinion |
| in reference to | about |
| the reason for | because |

**Keep slides simple.** During the presentation, your slides should support your message visually and facilitate its memorization. As such, they should not compete with you, the presenter, who remains the primary conveyor of information. Simple slides are more effective because visual complexity reduces people's ability to pass on information to long-term memory.[87]

**Remove everything unnecessary.** Adhering with the principle of coherence, and in line with the previous point, remove all unnecessary information so as to help improve understanding and recall.[88] This includes removing all information that can distract from the main point of the slide, including references, the logo of the organization if it is an internal presentation, animations that only serve a cosmetic purpose, etc. Applying the principle of coherence to numbers, use decimals only when absolutely necessary. In fact, use the unit that allows you to have the smallest number of digits to represent the quantity.

**Format tables.** Pie charts and bar charts have been found superior to tables in many instances.[89] In some cases, however, such as when trying to transmit precise numerical values, tables can be a good medium to present quantitative data. To leverage them, eliminate unnecessary lines, such as vertical lines between columns, round off numbers, and use proper units (see Figure 7.15).[90]

**Consider using analogies.** Using appropriate analogies can enhance understanding and retention, because they can relate new ideas to ones with which that your audience is familiar.[91]

For instance, imagine having to report the financial results of a division to a nonspecialist audience. Instead of using a dull table, one could opt for an image, such as that of Figure 7.16.

---

87. See (Bergen, Grimes, & Potter, 2005) [p. 333] and (Kalyuga & Sweller, 2014) [p. 259].
88. (Mayer & Fiorella, 2014), (Alley, 2013) [pp. 112–113], (Bartsch & Cobern, 2003).
89. (Spence & Lewandowsky, 1991).
90. (Booth, Colomb, & Williams, 2003) [p. 220], (Koomey, 2008) [pp. 177–185].
91. (Alley, 2013) [pp. 39–41].

| Average sale price of all farms ($) | | | | | |
|---|---|---|---|---|---|
| Region | 2004 | 2005 | 2006 | 2007 | % Increase '04 - '07 |
| Northland | 974737 | 1060886 | 1312429 | 1576769 | 61,7600% |
| Auckland | 1227622 | 1284568 | 1366692 | 1854543 | 51,0700% |
| Waikato | 1542653 | 1874722 | 2240908 | 2397778 | 55,4300% |
| Bay of Plenty | 1140639 | 1477036 | 1464838 | 1523178 | 33,5400% |
| Taranald | 1083793 | 1338477 | 1538502 | 1697586 | 56,6300% |
| Gisborne | 1104912 | 1405198 | 1430701 | 1317944 | 19,2800% |
| Hawkes Bay | 1319135 | 1308447 | 1836502 | 1875094 | 42,1500% |
| Wanganui | 1112509 | 1488938 | 1547594 | 1506120 | 35,3800% |
| Nelson | 885656 | 1292944 | 1281988 | 1656201 | 87,00% |

✗

Removing unnecessary decimals enhances legibility.

Switching units reduces the size of the numbers.

Removing vertical lines brings space to the table.

✓

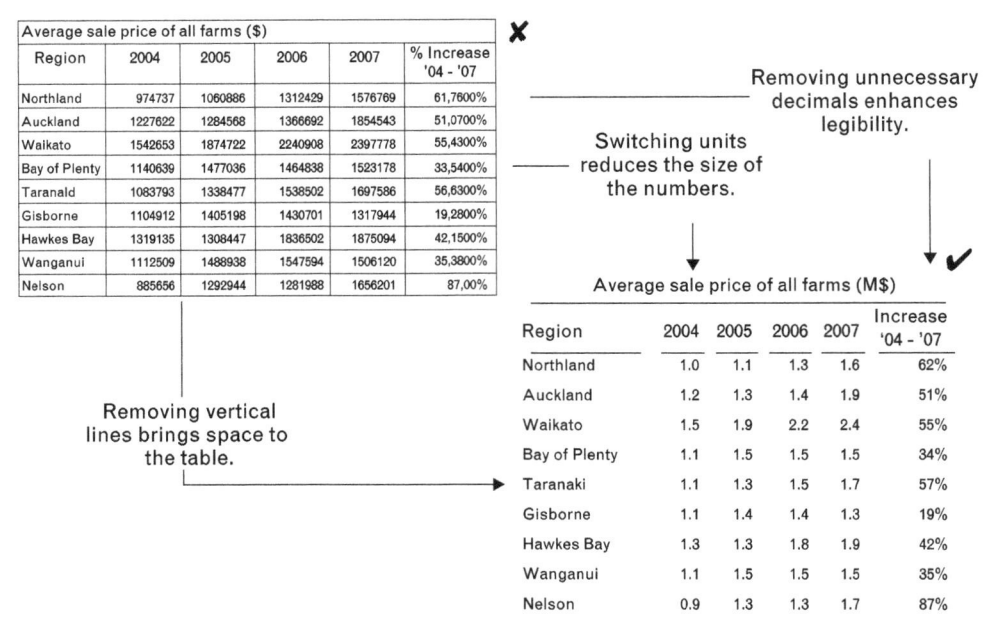

Average sale price of all farms (M$)

| Region | 2004 | 2005 | 2006 | 2007 | Increase '04 - '07 |
|---|---|---|---|---|---|
| Northland | 1.0 | 1.1 | 1.3 | 1.6 | 62% |
| Auckland | 1.2 | 1.3 | 1.4 | 1.9 | 51% |
| Waikato | 1.5 | 1.9 | 2.2 | 2.4 | 55% |
| Bay of Plenty | 1.1 | 1.5 | 1.5 | 1.5 | 34% |
| Taranaki | 1.1 | 1.3 | 1.5 | 1.7 | 57% |
| Gisborne | 1.1 | 1.4 | 1.4 | 1.3 | 19% |
| Hawkes Bay | 1.3 | 1.3 | 1.8 | 1.9 | 42% |
| Wanganui | 1.1 | 1.5 | 1.5 | 1.5 | 35% |
| Nelson | 0.9 | 1.3 | 1.3 | 1.7 | 87% |

FIGURE 7.15: Using appropriate borders and number format can significantly enhance the legibility of tables.

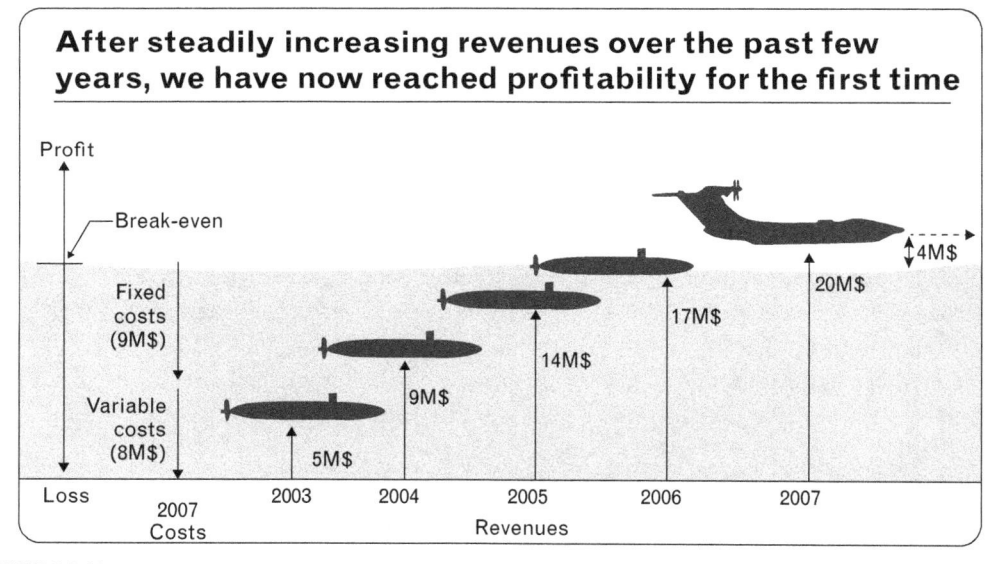

**After steadily increasing revenues over the past few years, we have now reached profitability for the first time**

FIGURE 7.16: Using images may help your audience remember your message.

Using a submarine to represent the division and the water level to show cost, the depth of the submarine becomes its position with respect to breaking even (the surface). The goal is then for the submarine to surface to take air, or generate profits. We used this analogy to provide quarterly reports over several presentations about a division that had never generated a profit over its 30-year existence. Even though there were months between successive presentations, the image helped the audience instantly recall the topic and how the new position fit with respect to historical ones. At the end of 2006, the division made its first profit, so the submarine became a seaplane: From that day on, everyone in the audience understood and remembered that the division was profitable.

**Close on a high.** The final slide is usually the one that remains projected during the ensuing conversation; as such, it is premium real estate. Therefore, avoid the common practice of just writing "thank you" or "questions?" Instead, use the final slide to summarize your main points.[92]

## 3.4.2. USE THE RIGHT VISUAL SUPPORT

Several options are available to display evidence, including quantitative charts, concept visuals, tables, photos, text, or a combination of these. Each option has its strengths and limitations.

Using text in the body of a slide goes against the modality principle,[93] so avoid it if possible. At times, however, a text support may be necessary; for instance, it can be useful to guide your audience through a logic flow.

**Use good quantitative charts.** Quantitative charts can be an excellent way to present data. You should choose the format of your quantitative chart based on your communication goal.[94]

Various resources can help you choose when to use charts and how to select appropriate ones.[95] Figure 7.17 provides some guidance adapted from these sources.

**Avoid pseudo-3D graphics.** Use 3D graphics only when they are necessary; that is, when presenting three variables at once. The 3D rendering of bar charts (or pseudo-3D effect), for instance, which comes standard in presentation packages, only presents two dimensions. Although these have been found at times to be visually appealing, they add complexity, which slows down comprehension. As such, they should generally be avoided (see Figure 7.18).[96]

**Format bar charts to improve their legibility.** Columns and line charts are useful to represent time series. Columns are best to represent series with few data points and when data is discrete, such as per period of time. When the number of data points increase or when the data is continuous, consider a line chart.[97]

Proper formatting of bar charts enhances legibility, as Figure 7.19 shows. In particular, resorting to a horizontal bar chart—instead of a vertical (column) chart—whenever the labels are long leaves you more space to write on the slide.[98]

---

92. (Alley, 2013) [pp. 181–183].
93. (Mayer et al., 2001), (Mayer, 2014) [p. 8], (Kalyuga & Sweller, 2014) [p. 255], (J. Garner & Alley, 2013).
94. (Shah & Hoeffner, 2002).
95. See (Zelazny, 1996), (Abela, 2008) [p. 99], (Visual-literacy.org), (Analytics), (Jarvenpaa & Dickson, 1988).
96. (Forsyth & Waller, 1995; Shah & Hoeffner, 2002), (Fischer, 2000) [p. 161], (Mackiewicz, 2007b), (Duarte, 2008) [pp. 76–77].
97. See (Abela, 2008) [p. 99].
98. (Zelazny, 1996) [p. 35].

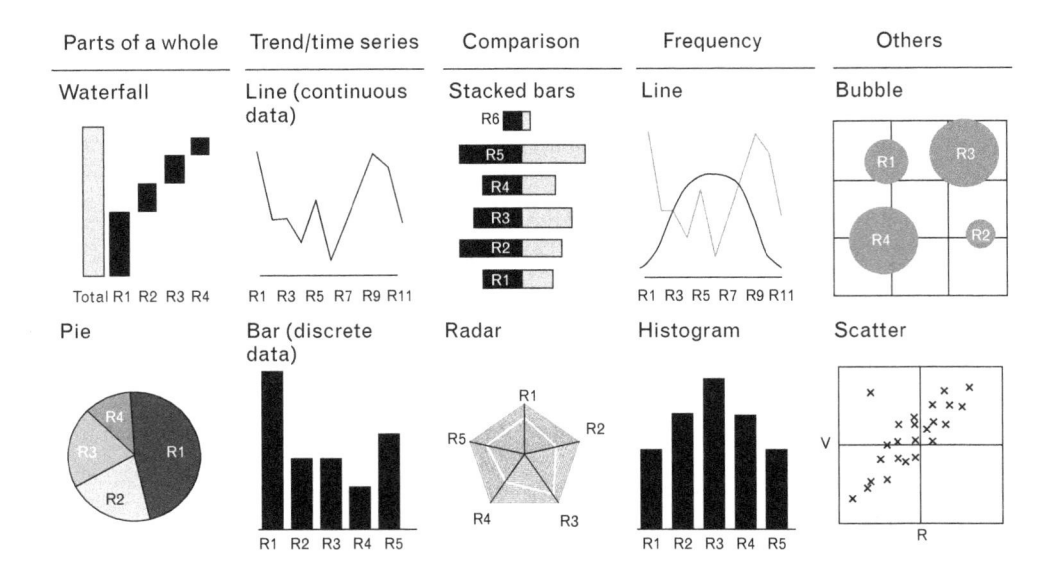

FIGURE 7.17: Choose appropriate quantitative charts for the data you are presenting.

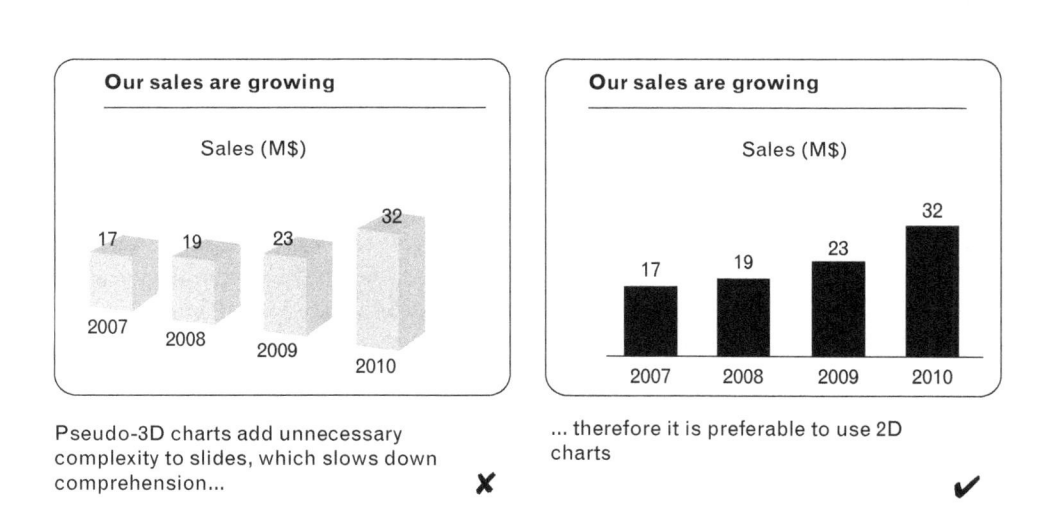

FIGURE 7.18: Because they add unnecessary complexity, avoid pseudo-3D charts.

Pseudo-3D charts add unnecessary complexity to slides, which slows down comprehension...

... therefore it is preferable to use 2D charts

The space in between bars is also important. For instance, Yau warns that setting it close to the bar width can result in confusion.[99] Removing all unnecessary lines may also further reduce clutter. Finally, including the value label of the data set in each column may help data reading and memorization.

99. (Yau, 2011).

186 • STRATEGIC THINKING IN COMPLEX PROBLEM SOLVING

**Headcount by area**

- 60
- 45
- 30
- 15
- 0

Marketing  Manufacturing  Accounting  Legal

✗

Removing unnecessary lines enhances legibility.

Removing unnecessary values labels reduces clutter.

Using a horizontal format leaves more space for long labels. →

Including the value of the data helps data retention.

**Headcount by area (FTEs)**

| Marketing | 17 |
| Manufacturing | 26 |
| Accounting | 53 |
| Legal | 25 |

✓

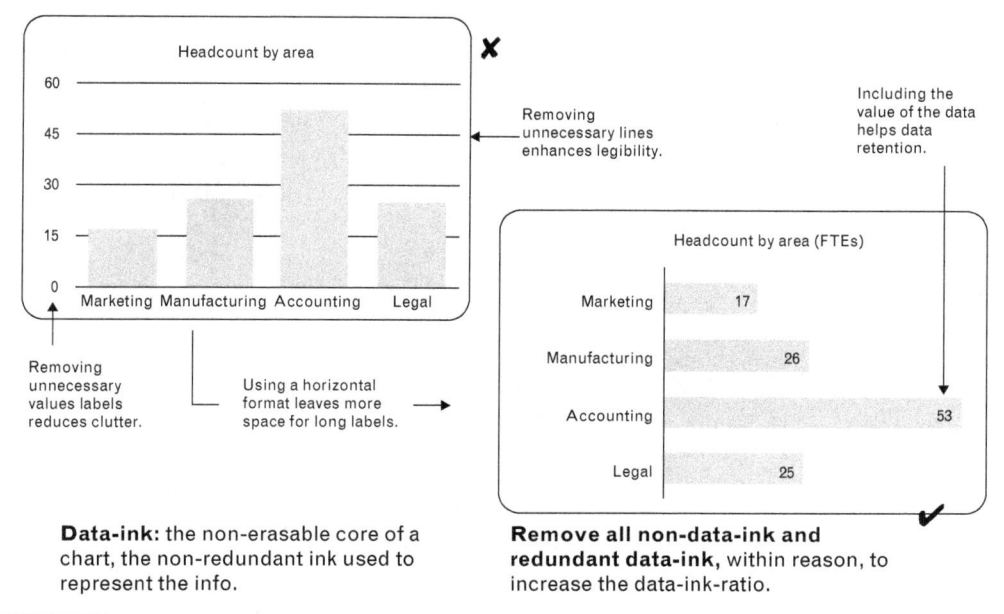

**Data-ink:** the non-erasable core of a chart, the non-redundant ink used to represent the info.

**Remove all non-data-ink and redundant data-ink,** within reason, to increase the data-ink-ratio.

FIGURE 7.19: Proper formatting of bar charts enhances legibility.

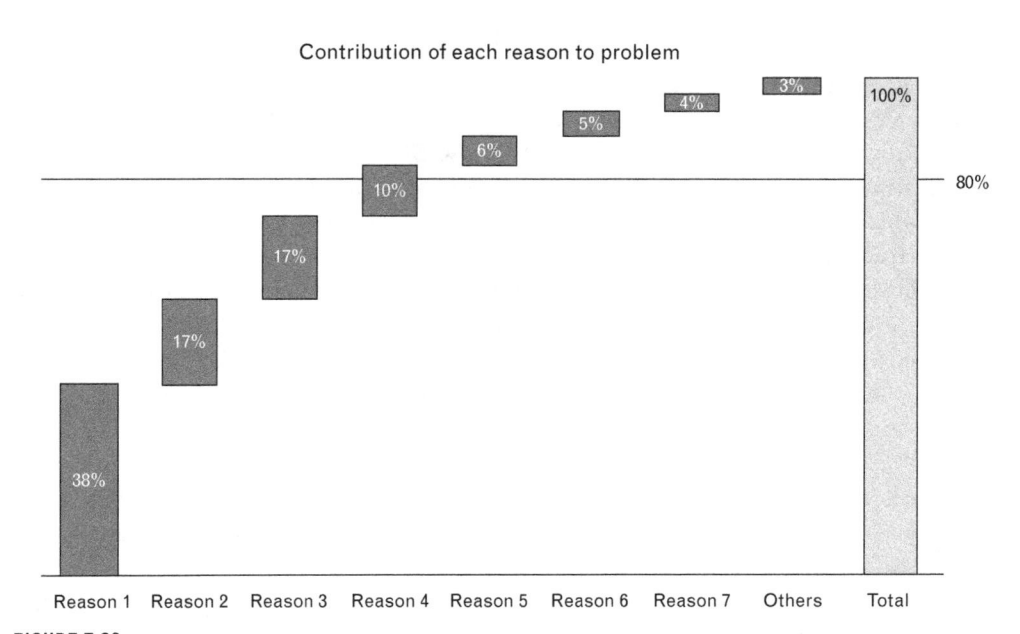

**Contribution of each reason to problem**

- Reason 1: 38%
- Reason 2: 17%
- Reason 3: 17%
- Reason 4: 10%
- Reason 5: 6%
- Reason 6: 5%
- Reason 7: 4%
- Others: 3%
- Total: 100%

80%

FIGURE 7.20: Waterfall charts can show the parts of a whole and how they accumulate.

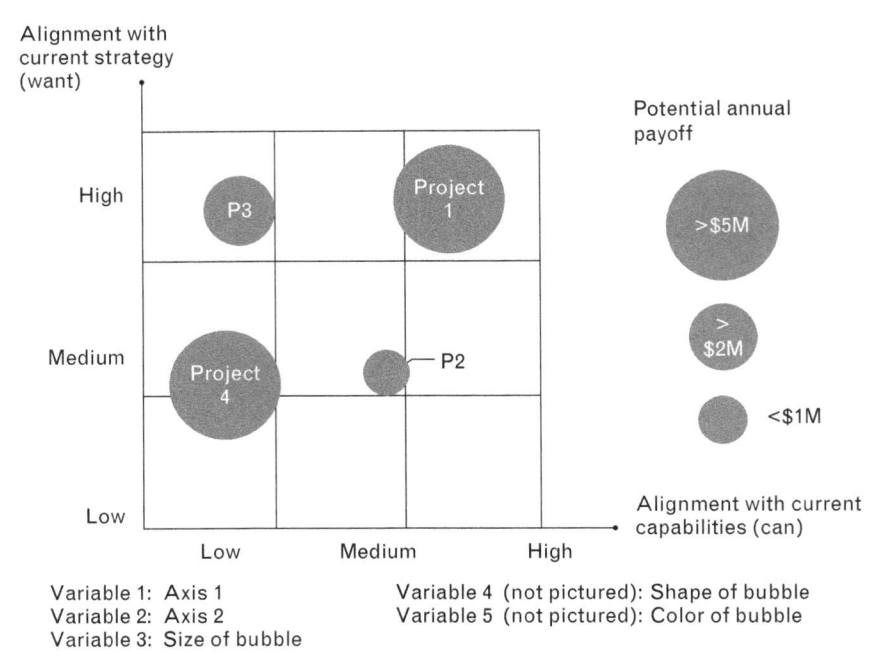

**FIGURE 7.21:** Bubble charts can show up to five variables.

**Use a waterfall chart to represent parts of a whole.** The *waterfall chart* (sometimes called *progressive chart*) is a bar chart that is useful to represent the parts of a whole. Although pie charts are traditionally used in these situations, waterfall charts may be a good substitute because they can signal thresholds, such as when you reach a given percentage, which is useful to illustrate the Pareto principle (see Figure 7.20).

**Use a bubble chart to represent data that depends on more than two variables.** When representing a data set that depends on several variables, consider using a bubble chart (see Figure 7.21). Start with a Cartesian coordinate system that uses one variable for each axis. Separate each axis in two (or three) to construct a 2x2 matrix (3x3); "high" and "low" are standard denominations. Represent the third variable by the size of the circle but make sure that the circle *area*—not its diameter—is proportional to the value pictured.[100]

It is customary for the top right quadrant to be the most desirable one, so define your dimensions accordingly. For instance, you might substitute "cost," which progresses from bad to worse as the quantity increases with "cheapness."

Note that bubble charts can accommodate up to five variables: On top of the three pictured in Figure 7.21, the color and the shape of the bubbles also may be added. Furthermore, using arrows to indicate how bubbles move over time is possible. Depicting so many variables, however, may create working memory overload. So use these charts sparingly and aim at minimizing the amount of information contained in each chart.[101]

---

100. (Viegas, Wattenberg, Van Ham, Kriss, & McKeon, 2007).
101. (Shah & Hoeffner, 2002).

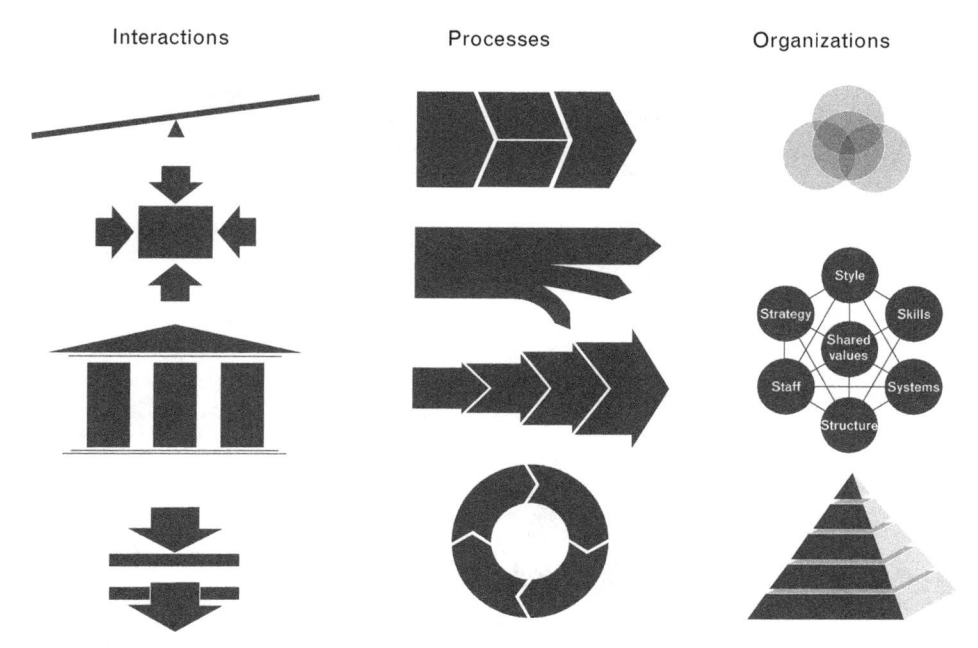

**FIGURE 7.22:** Concept visuals can be useful to represent nonquantitative data.

A drawback of bubble charts is that they do not represent overlapping data well, given that one "big" datapoint may obscure several small ones. In this case, consider using semi-transparent datapoints or log scales.

**Use good concept visuals.** Concept visuals can be useful to represent nonquantitative data, such as interactions, processes, or organizations. Figure 7.22 shows some typical examples.[102]

Concept visuals also can be immensely useful for illustrating quantitative data. Perhaps the best-known example is that of engineer Charles Joseph Minard's *Carte figurative des pertes successives en hommes de l'Armée Française dans la campagne de Russie 1812–1813* shown in Figure 7.23.[103] The map shows six variables: the army's location (including splits), the direction of movement, the size, and the temperature on specific dates. Although it may be challenging to understand the first time out and has been criticized for being too complicated,[104] it remains a beautiful example of ingenuity.

**Use spacial-flow opportunities.** In western cultures, people read left to right and from top to bottom. So people are conditioned to start at the top left of the slide.[105] This can be useful to support your point, for instance, by illustrating temporal transitions.

**Use images that explain.** The most useful images explain rather than simply decorate the written information on the slide.[106]

---

102. For more examples of concept visuals, see (Duarte, 2008) [pp. 44–61].
103. (Edward R. Tufte, 2001) [pp. 40–41].
104. (Kosslyn, 1989).
105. (Duarte, 2008) [pp. 96–97].
106. (J. Garner & Alley, 2013), (Markel, 2009).

Sell the Solution • 189

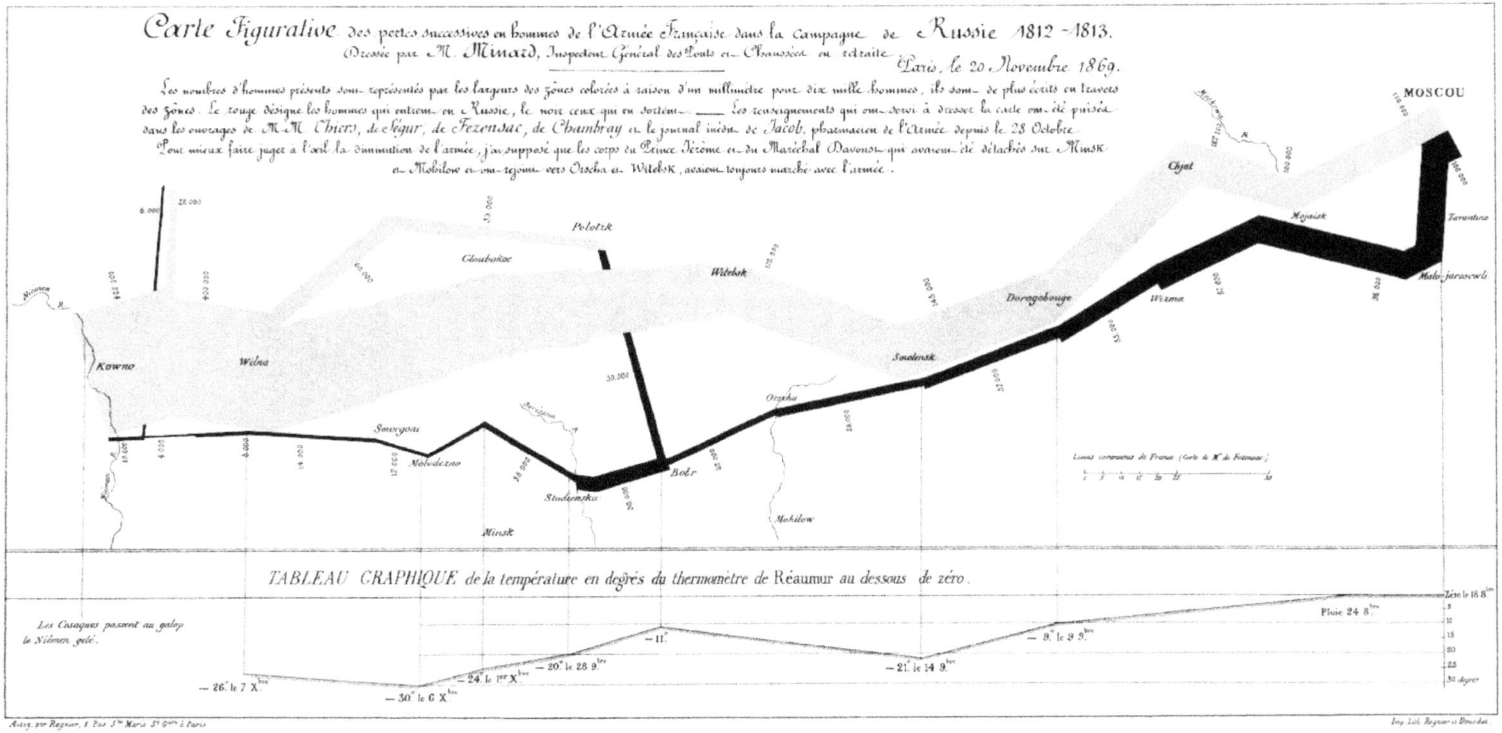

FIGURE 7.23: Minard's map links Napoléon's army's size, position, and direction with dates and temperatures during the Russian campaign.

## 3.5. FINALIZE YOUR MESSAGE

Before you call your presentation ready, review your message from your audience's point of view: Is it compatible with their communication style? Does it flow? How can you strengthen the weakest points? What are the implications of your message on your audience? Do your taglines add up to your story?

Similarly, you should check each slide one last time: Does the slide contribute in the right way to the overall story? Does the tagline summarize the content well (and, similarly, does the evidence support the assertion)? Is the point of the slide clear? Is the slide showing the information using the best medium? Does your audience need to see everything that is on the slide? Is it easy to read? Is it clear of typos?

For important presentations, rehearsing is crucial.[107] Indeed, one study showed that the number of rehearsals was a significant predictor of the quality of speech performance.[108] Also, ask others to give you feedback: Another study showed that practicing in front of an audience is correlated with better performance and that the larger the practice audience, the better the performance.[109]

# 4. DELIVER

Although success depends significantly on your setup, a great delivery is also critical. Here are some guidelines to make your delivery memorable, in a positive way.

## 4.1. BEFORE: PREPARE YOUR AUDIENCE AND YOUR SUPPORT

**Aim at the presentation being an anticlimax.** Ideally, by the time you present, the key members of your audience will know your premises, pieces of evidence, and broad conclusions. They will agree with you or, at least, you will have found some common ground with them. This may require meeting with the members of your audience individually before your presentation to understand their perspective, make them feel that they have been heard, and identify how you can convince each. In that sense, it may be helpful to think of the final presentation as a milestone where, as a group, you formalize agreements that you have obtained beforehand with each key stakeholder.

**Leverage reciprocity.** Think back to the last time you stopped at a red light and turned down the offer of a homeless person who wanted to wash your windscreen. What happened when they proceeded anyway? Did you find it hard to not give them anything? Then you know how hard it is to say no when you feel you are in someone's debt. This is called

---

107. (Alley, 2013) [pp. 207, 224], (Collins, 2004).
108. (Menzel & Carrell, 1994).
109. (Smith & Frymier, 2006).

*reciprocity*, and it promotes long-term cooperation:[110] If you do me a favor, I feel compelled to do what you asked of me. It is not rational—you did not ask them to wash your windscreen, in fact, you refused—but it works.

**Bring a backup of your presentation on a different medium.** Come early to set up the room—including the projector, lights, and microphone—and troubleshoot. If you are planning to project from a laptop, you may want to also bring a backup of your presentation on a memory stick or another device.

## 4.2. WATCH YOUR LANGUAGE

Effective presenters are skilled at both expressing themselves and listening well. You express yourself orally and with the rest of your body. Here are some guidelines to make both more effective.

**Use pitch to highlight your message.** Using different pitch can help you avoid having a monotone voice that would bore your audience. Also, be careful how you stress phrases, as their meaning can change based on pitch only. Here is an illustration taken from Stephen Allen, a communication consultant. Consider telling someone: "Marketing gave me these numbers." Now, say it out loud, stressing a different word each time, and observe how the meaning changes:

"*Marketing* gave me these numbers." They did not, Finance did.
"Marketing *gave* me these numbers." They did not, I stole them from them.
"Marketing gave *me* these numbers." They did not. They gave them to Jim.
"Marketing gave me *these* numbers." They did not. They gave me others.
"Marketing gave me these *numbers*." They did not. They gave me charts.

**Use volume to signal transitions.** Speak loudly enough so that everyone can hear you, but modulate the volume of your voice to attract attention to important ideas and to signal transition between ideas.

**Modulate your pace for emphasis.** Slowing down to signal important points can help you maintain the audience's interest. You may also pause for effect; for example, to signal an important point, to let some information sink in, to transition between ideas, or to give the audience time to read your slides and formulate questions.

**Appreciate silence.** Just as projecting a blank slide is effective when a slide would not promote understanding or retention of a point,[111] you should not feel obliged to talk all the time. Avoid filler words and use pauses to your advantage: let the data sink in, gain thinking time, and assess the audience's reaction.[112]

In addition to voice, a strong body language conveys credibility. Components of body language are stance, movement, gestures, and eye contact.

**Make eye contact to engage your audience.** Establishing eye contact helps you connect with the audience and monitor their reaction. Education expert Jannette Collins

---

110. (Flynn, 2003), (Parks & Komorita, 1998), (Cialdini, 2001b) [p. 20].
111. See, for instance (Alley, 2013) [pp. 106–107].
112. (Gelula, 1997).

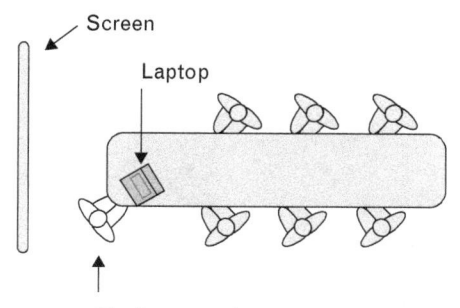

**FIGURE 7.24:** Ensure that your audience can see both you and your slides and talk to them, rather than to your slides.

[Diagram caption: Sit closest to the projection screen with your back to it so that your audience can see both you and your slides.]

suggests that you maintain eye contact with someone for three to five seconds or until you have finished expressing your idea.[113]

**Find a relaxed default position that works for you.** Stand up straight, distribute your weight on both feet, and ensure that you do not shift your weight periodically from one side to the other. Use gesture to emphasize specific words or ideas and to describe shapes, size, numbers, directions . . . .[114] When answering questions, move toward the questioner without being intimidating. Move away from the podium and walk around. Do not walk too fast or always in the same pattern and avoid repeatedly crossing the projection if you use a front projector. Also, avoid "tattooing" your face with the slide. For audio, a hand-free microphone, such as a clip-on, gives you more freedom of gesture.

On which side of the projector do you prefer to stand? Give some thought to this; if you are on the left, you have easier access to the axes and to the beginning of bullet points, but you will be pointing mainly with your left hand, which can be awkward for right-handed speakers.

When projecting, having a feedback screen in presenter mode allows you to see your current slide and the next, which is useful for transitions. Good transition phrases include "so far we have been talking about . . ., next let's talk about . . .," "so we have established that . . .; now let's look at . . .," or "therefore. . . ."

If you are presenting from a laptop at a conference table, sit closest to the screen with your back to it. That way you will project behind you, enabling your audience to see both you and your slides at the same time (see Figure 7.24).

**Work in harmony with your slides.** Keisler and Noonan propose a technique for working with your visuals: Display a slide then pause; look at an audience member and explain the slide to that person, paraphrasing it; and discuss the main insights.[115]

---

113. (Collins, 2004).
114. See (Alley, 2013) [pp. 248–250], (Collins, 2004), (Gelula, 1997) for further thoughts on movements.
115. (Keisler & Noonan, 2012).

**Use short sentences in the active voice.** Maintain a one-on-one conversation: Communicate one idea at a time and talk to one person, maintaining eye contact. Talk to people, not equipment.

Remember: Practice spontaneity.

### 4.3. LISTEN WELL

Engage your audience and ask them to participate. One way to do this is by carefully listening to how they react to your material.[116] Whenever you receive feedback, stop talking and reflect on your audience's opinions and feelings; treat questions as an opportunity to connect. Let your audience ask you questions and ask them questions.

Listen to the oral message but also pay attention to the nonverbal clues. Treat listening as an opportunity to gain insight into their position. Part of your listening should also be through monitoring your audience and picking up clues: you can respond to puzzled looks by slowing down and clarifying your arguments while restlessness and boredom are a cue that you should move on.[117]

### 4.4. ANSWER WELL

Doumont suggests using a four-step approach to answering questions: "1. *listen* to the whole question, to ensure you understand it; 2. *repeat/rephrase* as needed, so others understand it, too; 3. *think* to construct an answer that is brief and to the point; and 4. *answer* the whole audience, keeping eye contact with all."[118]

**Anticipate questions** and prepare your answer beforehand. Ensure that your presentation discusses the key questions and have backup slides at the ready for answering secondary questions.

**Decide when to argue and when not to:** Choose the hills you are ready to fight for. Think before you speak and before you respond.

**Use your answer to connect.** Engage through eye contact and check that your answer satisfies the questioner. Consider repeating the question before answering it, especially if it is a large audience and the questioner does not have a microphone, there is a potential ambiguity in the question, or you need a little extra time to formulate your answer.

If you do not know the answer to a question, say so: you will not risk saying something wrong and you will bring more credibility to the things that you do know. You also may offer to check on a piece of information and get back to the person who asked you. If you do offer to check, make sure that you follow through.

---

116. (Lussier & Achua, 2007) [p. 202].
117. (Kosslyn, 1989) [p. 53].
118. (Doumont, 2009) [p. 117]. See also (Alley, 2013) [pp. 264–268].

## 4.5. CLOSE ON A HIGH

Summarize often in your presentation, including in your closing statement, which should have an overall summary. Also, agree on the next steps: define the next tasks, deadlines, and owners. In particular, commit to answering the questions for which you did not have an answer.

### 4.5.1. CONSIDER STARTING YOUR REPORT ON THE FIRST WEEK

In academia, people tend to leave the communication for the end of a project: most PhD students I see do not start writing their dissertation until they are in their final year. In contrast, as a management consultant, I was encouraged to start writing my report very early—as early as the first week of an engagement—*before* I had gathered the evidence to support my conclusions.[119] Then, as I conducted my analysis, when I found that my initial guesses were not supported by the evidence, I changed my original story.

Writing early helps you organize your thinking in a storyline. During your first week or so, create the storyline of your final report, capturing the introduction of your problem and what you expect the solution to be. Naturally, at this stage, most of this will be speculative.

To account for the mix of established facts and speculations in your storyline, signal explicitly which elements are guesses; for instance, write "tentative" on the corresponding slide (see Figure 7.25 below). These early slides are only placeholders and you should not hesitate to change them should the evidence warrant it.

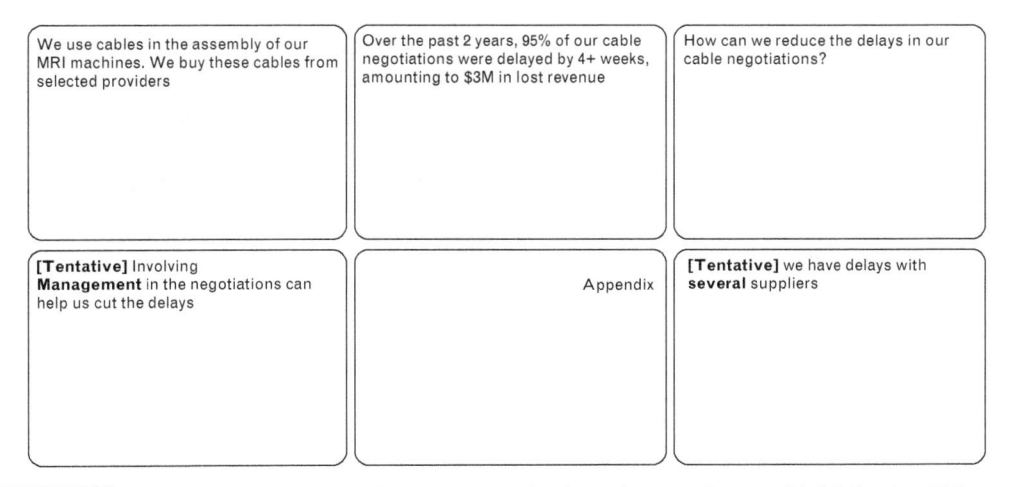

| We use cables in the assembly of our MRI machines. We buy these cables from selected providers | Over the past 2 years, 95% of our cable negotiations were delayed by 4+ weeks, amounting to $3M in lost revenue | How can we reduce the delays in our cable negotiations? |
|---|---|---|
| **[Tentative]** Involving **Management** in the negotiations can help us cut the delays | Appendix | **[Tentative]** we have delays with **several** suppliers |

**FIGURE 7.25:** An early storyline shows how your story develops. Assumptions are highlighted until they are checked and either validated or changed.

---

119. See also (Davis, Keeling, Schreier, & Williams, 2007).

Starting early also will help guide your research. With your storyline in hand, you must now populate your slides with the evidence that supports your taglines. As we have discussed in previous chapters, this does not mean that you should look only for supporting evidence, but having a clear storyline will help you identify which data you need to gather. By building your story from the top down, you will see where the gaps are and identify the evidence you need to fill them in. This helps you focus your thinking, avoid noncritical details, and keep on target. This focus is important because, as we have seen, peripheral data can dilute important but weak signals.[120]

In your analysis process, you may come across countless reports, technical papers, articles, and so on. To keep track of these, consider summarizing each in a slide and placing the slide in the appendix of your presentation, which then serves as a central repository. It is difficult at the beginning of a project to see how all the pieces of the puzzle will fit, but having a quick summary of evidence on a slide makes it easier to see, as a whole, what your body of evidence amounts to. This central repository helps you retrieve evidence easily, providing a written analog to your working memory, which is valuable because our working memory is known to limit our ability to solve complex problems, in particular our ability to consider more than one hypothesis.[121]

Starting to prepare your presentation early also helps you avoid the penultimate-day syndrome. If you ever pulled an all-nighter before an exam or a presentation, you will remember that you were hardly at your best for the big event. By starting to work on your presentation at the beginning of your project, you can see your story evolve and can keep track of how far it is from completion. This way you minimize the risk of finding large gaps hours before handing in your report. You also can improve the persuasiveness of your message by having time to think about how you want to structure it and by integrating key elements as you uncover them. An added benefit is that giving a progress report is as simple as deciding which slides go in the main slide deck and in which order. Therefore, you are always ready to report your progress at any moment with little preparation.

Finally, starting early can help you coordinate your team because it enables you to see the proverbial forest and how the work of each team member fits into that big picture. It also gives the team a sense of direction and clarifies roles and goals—team members also can see where their contributions fit into the big picture and how indispensable they are—which may help bring higher team performance.[122]

Therefore, starting to prepare your presentation early has many advantages. However, these advantages come with a significant drawback: Starting your writing early requires you to take a posture early, before you have had a chance to look at evidence. This may reinforce confirmation bias, which as we have seen, is already so prevalent that it certainly needs no reinforcement.[123] Therefore, you must demonstrate a steadfast commitment to adapting your views in light of new evidence.

---

120. See (Nisbett, Zukier, & Lemley, 1981), (Arkes & Kajdasz, 2011) [p. 157], and Chapter 4.
121. (Dunbar & Klahr, 2012) [p. 706].
122. (Castka, Bamber, Sharp, & Belohoubek, 2001; Kerr & Bruun, 1983) (Levi, 2011) [p. 60].
123. See, for instance (National Research Council, 2011) [p. 164].

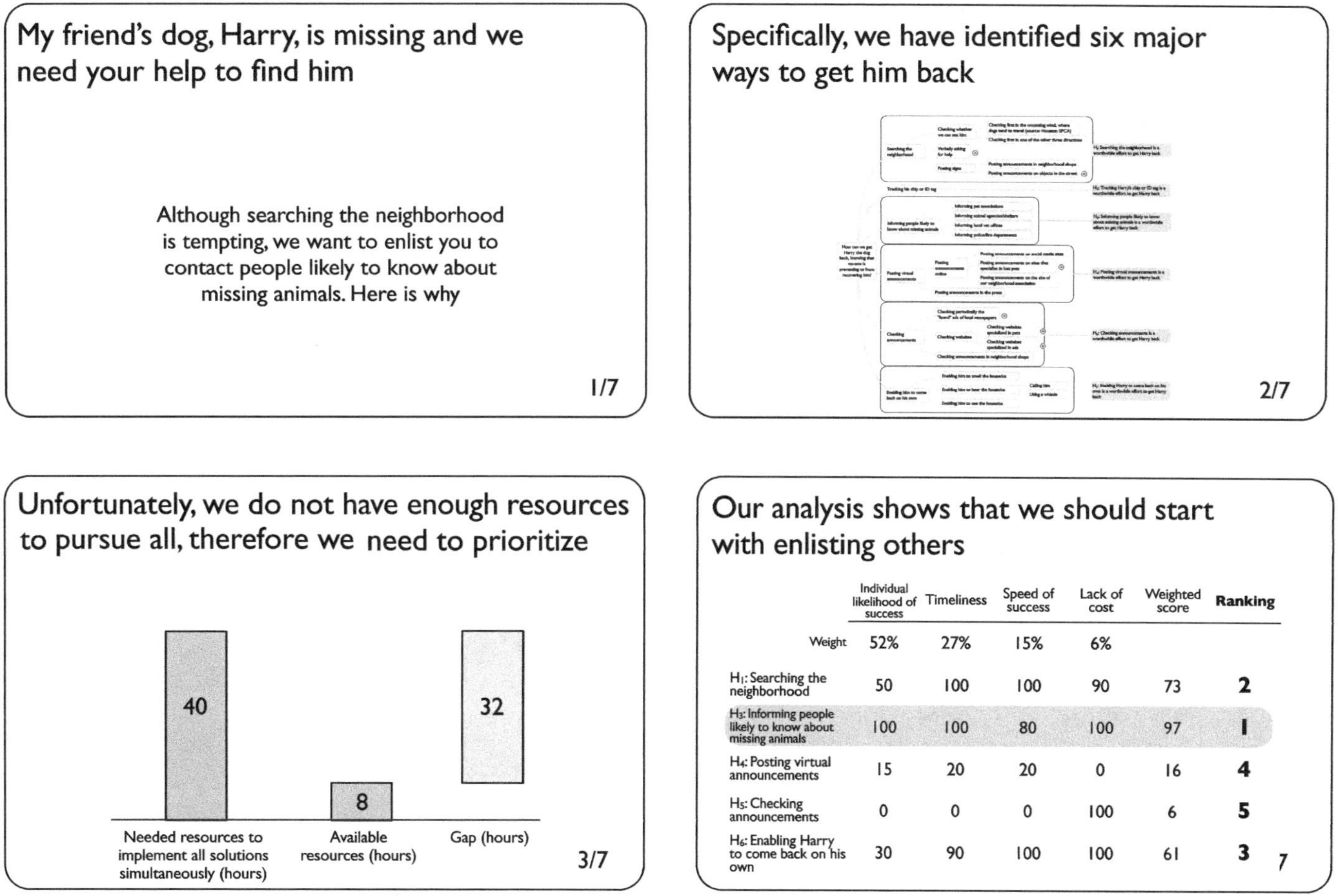

## 1/7

**My friend's dog, Harry, is missing and we need your help to find him**

Although searching the neighborhood is tempting, we want to enlist you to contact people likely to know about missing animals. Here is why

## 2/7

**Specifically, we have identified six major ways to get him back**

## 3/7

**Unfortunately, we do not have enough resources to pursue all, therefore we need to prioritize**

| | Needed resources to implement all solutions simultaneously (hours) | Available resources (hours) | Gap (hours) |
|---|---|---|---|
| | 40 | 8 | 32 |

## 

**Our analysis shows that we should start with enlisting others**

| | Individual likelihood of success | Timeliness | Speed of success | Lack of cost | Weighted score | Ranking |
|---|---|---|---|---|---|---|
| Weight | 52% | 27% | 15% | 6% | | |
| H₁: Searching the neighborhood | 50 | 100 | 100 | 90 | 73 | 2 |
| H₃: Informing people likely to know about missing animals | 100 | 100 | 80 | 100 | 97 | 1 |
| H₄: Posting virtual announcements | 15 | 20 | 20 | 0 | 16 | 4 |
| H₅: Checking announcements | 0 | 0 | 0 | 100 | 6 | 5 |
| H₆: Enabling Harry to come back on his own | 30 | 90 | 100 | 100 | 61 | 3 |
| | | | | | | 7 |

FIGURE 7.26: In Harry's case, we choose a logic-driven approach for communicating our results.

### Then, we should take action in the neighborhood

| | Individual likelihood of success | Timeliness | Quickness of success | Lack of setup time | Cost | Weighted score | Ranking |
|---|---|---|---|---|---|---|---|
| Weight | 30% | 40% | 20% | 5% | 5% | | |
| $H_1$: Searching the neighborhood | 50 | 100 | 100 | 100 | 90 | 84.5 | 2 |
| $H_3$: Informing people likely to know about missing animals | 100 | 100 | 60 | 100 | 100 | 95 | 1 |
| $H_4$: Posting virtual announcements | 15 | 20 | 20 | 0 | 0 | 16.5 | 4 |
| $H_5$: Checking announcements | 0 | 0 | 0 | 50 | 100 | 7.5 | 5 |
| $H_6$: Enabling Harry to come back on his own | 30 | 90 | 100 | 100 | 100 | 75 | 3 |

5/7

### Only then we will take active steps to enable him to come back on his own

| | Individual likelihood of success | Timeliness | Quickness of success | Lack of setup time | Cost | Weighted score | Ranking |
|---|---|---|---|---|---|---|---|
| Weight | 30% | 40% | 20% | 5% | 5% | | |
| $H_1$: Searching the neighborhood | 50 | 100 | 100 | 100 | 90 | 84.5 | 2 |
| $H_3$: Informing people likely to know about missing animals | 100 | 100 | 80 | 100 | 100 | 96 | 1 |
| $H_4$: Posting virtual announcements | 15 | 20 | 20 | 0 | 0 | 16.5 | 4 |
| $H_5$: Checking announcements | 0 | 0 | 0 | 50 | 100 | 7.5 | 5 |
| $H_6$: Enabling Harry to come back on his own | 30 | 90 | 100 | 100 | 100 | 75 | 3 |

6/7

### To implement successfully, we need your assistance. Will you help?

| | # | Owner | Due date |
|---|---|---|---|
| Animal shelter | 713-555-1234 | Me | Today, 18h |
| Pet assoc. #1 | 713-555-1235 | Me | Today, 18h45 |
| Pet assoc. #2 | 713-555-1236 | Me | Today, 19h |
| Police dept. | 713-555-1237 | You | Today, 18h |
| Fire dept. | 713-555-1238 | You | Today, 18h45 |
| Veterinarian #1 | 713-555-1239 | You | Today, 19h |
| Etc. | | | |

7/7

**FIGURE 7.27:** In Harry's case, we choose a logic-driven approach for communicating our results (continued).

# 5. WHAT ABOUT HARRY?

As highlighted at the beginning of the chapter, our first step is to identify what we want to achieve with our presentation. Preparing a think/do—from/to matrix, shown in Table 7.1, helps us do that. Next, we craft a tentative storyline (see Figure 7.2) before distributing each idea in the tagline of slides. We then populate the slides with evidence supporting the taglines (see Figures 7.26 and 7.27).

In Harry's case, we choose an approach almost entirely based on logic. This is acceptable, but remember that this is only one of several options. Also note that in Figures 7.26 and 7.27, the taglines differ slightly from our original storyline in Figure 7.2. This is common because distributing our thinking across various slides, and seeing it related to supporting evidence, introduces a new perspective that may trigger changes in our thinking and require some iterations to maintain the intra- and interslide coherence of the taglines.

Chapter 7 explained how to communicate effectively and convince the key stakeholders of your project that the solution approach you have selected is appropriate. If you were a strategy consultant a few years ago, this is where you would call it a day, celebrate copiously, celebrate some more, and move on to your next project. For the rest of us, though, the problem is not solved yet and it will not be until you implement the solution approach, monitor its effectiveness, and take corrective action as needed. Chapter 8 gives some pointers on how to do this.

# NOTES

**Promoting change.** Harvard's Howard Gardner has identified seven levers to facilitate change: *Reason*—making rational arguments (using logic, analogies, etc.); *Research*—presenting relevant data; *Resonance*—ensuring the audience feels right about it; *Redescription*—presenting the same idea in different formats; *Resources and rewards*—offering positive and negative reinforcement; *Real-world events*—leveraging happenings beyond our control; and *Resistances*—overcoming longstanding contrary beliefs.[124]

**Making informational presentations effective.** Alley recommends aiming at maximizing the logic and straightforwardness of such presentations. He also suggests following the adage: *Tell them what you're going to tell them, tell them, and tell them what you told them.*[125]

**Storytelling is an important aspect of getting funded.** Martens et al. confirmed that it is true that successful entrepreneurs often are effective storytellers.[126]

**Suiting the story to the desired effect.** Stephen Denning proposed elements that a story should include to generate a specific effect (Denning, 2006).

---

124. (Gardner, 2006) [pp. 15–18].
125. (Alley, 2003) [p. 27].
126. (Martens, Jennings, & Jennings, 2007).

**Pyramids are old.** Management consultants routinely refer to using pyramids in communication as "thinking Minto" or "being Minto," in reference to Barbara Minto. However, the technique of placing one's main idea on top—or foremost in the report—is at least 150 years old; Edwin Stanton, President Lincoln's secretary of war, already used pyramids. The approach has been widely used in journalism for the past 120 years.[127]

**Telling your conclusions first.** Some disagree with Zelazny that it is always better to tell your conclusion first and then support it. The argument goes that when there is unexpected or bad news, it is better to let the audience connect the dots on their own.[128]

**Principled multimedia presentation.** There are additional principles to multimedia learning aside from the six we discussed, including segmenting and pretraining principles.[129]

**Assertion–evidence is needed.** *The New Yorker* magazine's last page is a cartoon without a caption. The magazine invites readers to submit captions and publishes three finalists a few weeks after. It only takes one look at these to realize that, based on the same data—a cartoon—interpretations can go in all directions. So assume that your conclusion *is not* obvious and place it at the top of your slides.

**Assertion–evidence structure and other slide designs.** The assertion–evidence technique originated at Hughes Aircraft in the 1970s and is best suited for presenting technical material.[130] For other types of communications, other slide designs have been proposed.[131]

**Taglines and overloading working memory.** Although Kalyuga et al. identified that the simultaneous presentation of identical written and oral messages is detrimental to learning, they note that this applies only for large portions of text.[132] Specifically, "When text is presented in small, easily managed sequential portions with sufficient temporal breaks between them, a concurrent presentation of identical written and auditory material might not cause deleterious effects on learning."

**The various names of taglines.** Taglines are also known as "action leads"[133] and "headlines,"[134] among other names.

**Less is more, yet again.** There is strong evidence supporting the *coherence principle*, which states that people learn better when extraneous material is omitted rather than included.[135]

**Creating waterfall charts.** Waterfall charts can be challenging to prepare the first time, in part because they do not come standard in most spreadsheet and presentation packages. However, you can easily create one using a stacked bar chart, with two series. Set the bottom series as transparent (with a stroke and filling of the same color as the background of the slide), and make its value equal to the cumulative sum of the previous quantities of the

---

127. (Lidwell, Holden, & Butler, 2010) [pp. 140–141], (Mindich, 1998) [pp. 64–94].
128. (Keisler & Noonan, 2012).
129. (Mayer, 2014).
130. (Alley, 2013) [p. 116].
131. (Duarte, 2008, 2010; Reynolds, 2011).
132. (Kalyuga et al., 2004) [p. 579].
133. (Keisler & Noonan, 2012).
134. (Alley, 2013).
135. (Mayer & Fiorella, 2014).

top series (e.g., in Figure 7.20, the value of the bottom series for "reason 3" is set to 38% + 17% = 55%).

**Improving your persuasion.** Cialdini offers six ideas to improve how you persuade: "Uncover real similarities and offer genuine praise; give what you want to receive; use peer power whenever it is available; make their commitments active, public and voluntary; expose your expertise—do not assume it is self-evident; and highlight unique benefits and exclusive information."[136] Hoy and Smith add four more: acquire their trust; treat people fairly; demonstrate that you can succeed; and show optimism.[137]

**Removing animations.** Animated visuals appear to be superior to static ones only when they convey extra information.[138]

**"Implementation? We don't really do that."** Just a few years ago, if you were a strategy consultant, you could call it a day after producing your report on what your client should do. So you might find some solace in knowing that, in today's era of tight budgets, even the elite strategy consultancies have to worry about implementation.[139]

---

136. (Cialdini, 2001a).
137. (Hoy & Smith, 2007).
138. (Tversky, Morrison, & Betrancourt, 2002), (Abela, 2008) [p. 105].
139. (The Economist, 2013).

CHAPTER 8

# IMPLEMENT AND MONITOR THE SOLUTION

You have convinced your project's key stakeholders that your proposed solution is the right one; next you need to implement it. This chapter provides guidelines and basic concepts of project management and team leadership to help you do so.[1]

Complex problems may require the analysis to span weeks or months and involve many team members. So, although the ideas in this chapter come at the end of the book and are geared toward implementing a specific solution, they apply equally well to conducting a complex analysis.

## 1. ORGANIZE THE PROJECT

In many settings, skillfully managing the expectations of stakeholders goes a long way toward keeping them satisfied with the outcome of a project.[2] A critical component of managing expectations is to ensure that these people understand the project: They should know what the project will deliver and what it will *not* deliver, how long it will take, how much it will cost, how it will be completed, and what the benefits will be.

### 1.1. DEVELOP THE PROJECT PLAN

To help you build shared understanding about the project, you may want to capture the critical information in a project plan or charter. The project plan helps you validate with

---

1. Because project and team management are expansive subjects, we are merely introducing them here. For more, see, for instance (Thompson, 2011), (Kerzner, 2003), (Söderlund, 2004).

2. See, for instance (Pellegrinelli, Partington, Hemingway, Mohdzain, & Shah, 2007), (Appleton-Knapp & Krentler, 2006), (Kappelman, McKeeman, & Zhang, 2006), (Schmidt, Lyytinen, & Mark Keil, 2001), (Hartman & Ashrafi, 2002), (Wright, 1997).

your client the key aspect of the project: its scope, objectives, deliverables, risks, deadlines, roles, etc. Figure 8.1 shows a possible outline for such a document.

When preparing the plan, be proactive: Think about the internal and external issues that might arise and identify your project's key success factors.

It is possible or even likely that you will have difficulty agreeing with the stakeholders on all aspects of the project. Indeed, various people, each with his or her own perspective on the situation, might have different goals. This is one of the primary motivations behind developing a plan; if there are differences, better they arise early on than later.

To build your plan, you will have to think about how you will reach your deliverables. So defining the key characteristics of the project and planning the work (next section) will

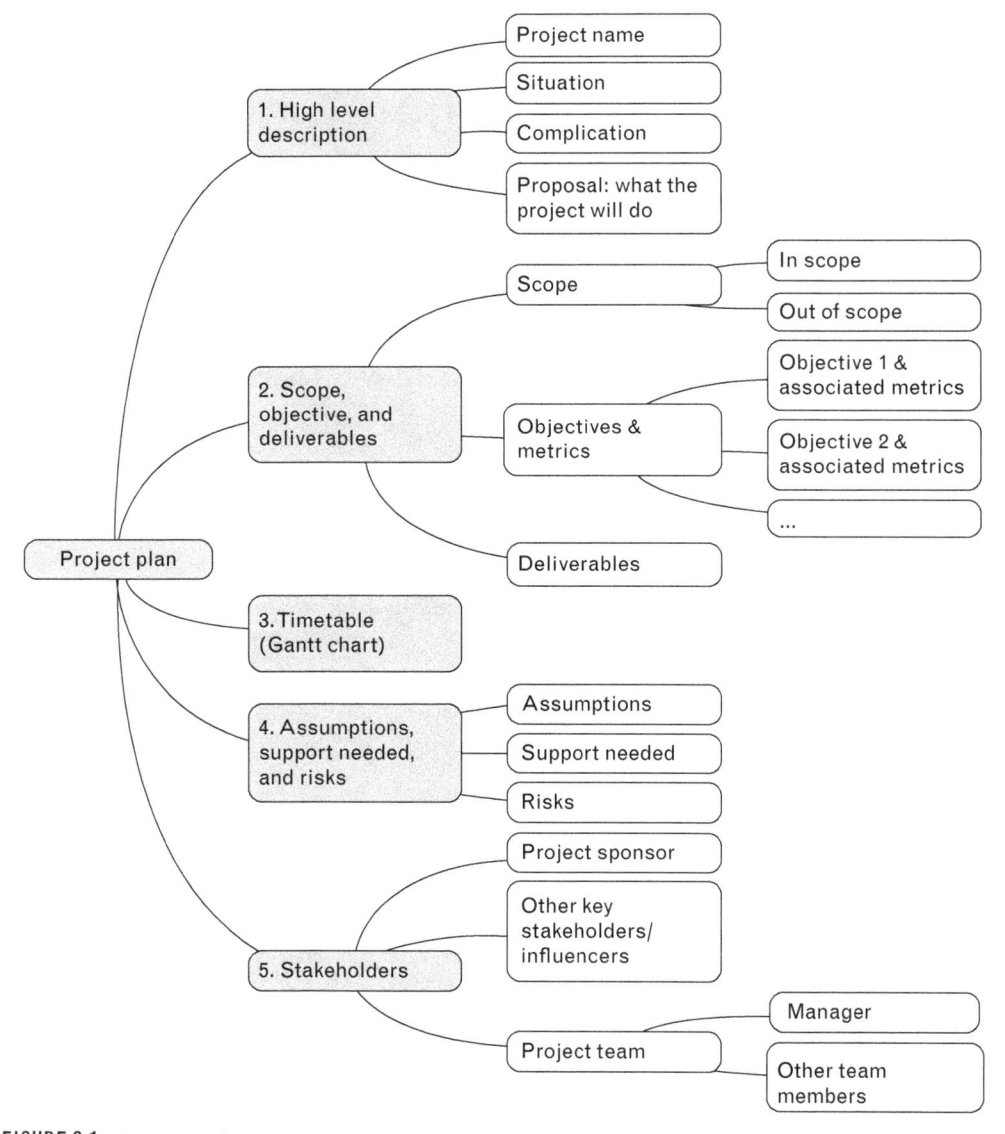

FIGURE 8.1: A project charter summarizes a project's critical information.

204 • STRATEGIC THINKING IN COMPLEX PROBLEM SOLVING

likely be iterative activities. Once you have agreed on a project plan, you may want to ask your client to write a project charter—a one- or two-page document that summarizes the key characteristics of the project—and sign it. This will be useful to formalize your mandate as the project leader and crystalize the project scope, which might be helpful in preventing scope creep (see further in this chapter).

### 1.2. DEVELOP THE WORK PLAN

Taking a top-down approach, break down the project into pieces. Define goals and deadlines for each activity, identifying potential dependencies, and assign resources—people and equipment. You may want to use a Gantt chart to document your original work plan against a horizontal timeline, as Figure 8.2 shows.[3]

Although this process seems trivial, keep in mind that it is notoriously hard to estimate accurately the time needed for executing complex projects, as cognitive scientist Douglas Hofstadter humorously pointed out in his recursive law: "Hofstadter's Law: it always takes longer than you expect, even when you take into account Hofstadter's Law."

### 1.3. DEFINE SUCCESS

The traditional measures of success for project management are cost, time, and quality/specifications—the iron triangle or the triple constraint.[4] However, you will probably want to have a more precise picture of your progress and results. To help you evaluate how successful your project is, identify appropriate metrics, or key performance indicators (KPIs).[5]

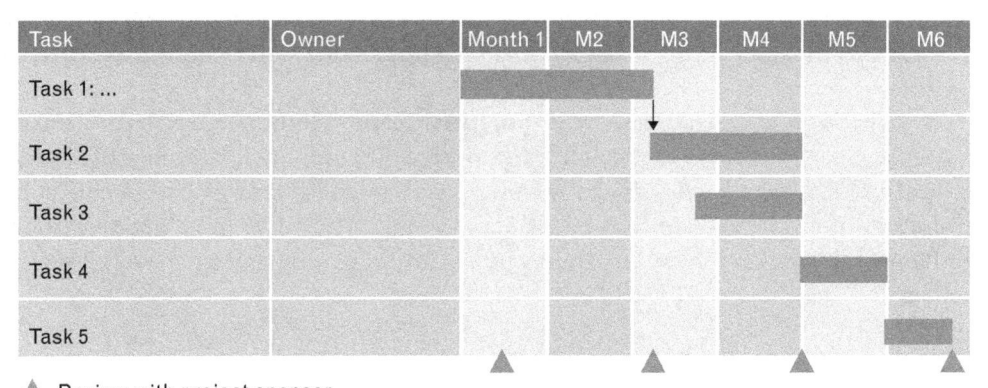

| Task | Owner | Month 1 | M2 | M3 | M4 | M5 | M6 |
|---|---|---|---|---|---|---|---|
| Task 1: ... | | | | | | | |
| Task 2 | | | | | | | |
| Task 3 | | | | | | | |
| Task 4 | | | | | | | |
| Task 5 | | | | | | | |

▲ Review with project sponsor

**FIGURE 8.2:** A Gantt chart summarizes the timetable of your project.

---

3. See, for instance (Meredith & Mantel Jr, 2009) [pp. 342–344].
4. (Atkinson, 1999), (Frame, 2003) [p. 6]. See also (White & Fortune, 2002).
5. See, for instance (Parmenter, 2007) [pp. 1–17].

# 2. MANAGE THE PROJECT

In the old days, many strategy consultants used to leave it to their clients to implement the decisions they had recommended; after all, the thinking went, the analysis is the hard part. Except that it is not: In many settings where implementation requires that people change how they do things, implementation is harder.[6] As management expert Peter Drucker puts it, culture eats strategy for breakfast. And a look at the over 40% failure rate of mergers and acquisitions seems to confirm this view.[7] "Successful integration depends upon the shared perception of both partnering organizations that aspects of the other culture are attractive and worth preserving."[8]

So a significant part of managing strategic change projects is managing people and the social, political, cultural, and cognitive dimensions of the changes that the projects bring. The following are guidelines to help you do so.

## 2.1. LEAD YOUR TEAM

A large part of your success depends on how you manage the people on your team (assuming you have one). As the team leader, you may have a scope of responsibility that exceeds that of your formal authority, which requires you to be a skilled coordinator and influencer.[9] Using "temporary" teams to solve complex, ill-defined problems is the norm in various high-reliability settings such as airline cockpits and emergency room operations. In these, there is empirical evidence that non-technical skills training results in improved team work.[10]

**Consider forming a more homogeneous team.** If you have control over assembling your team, you may consider forming one with people who have a *homogeneous* expertise. Indeed, although diversity helps creativity, it can impede implementation because it gets in the way of optimal teamwork.[11] That is, you may be better served by using a heterogeneous team in the early stages of problem solving but relying on a homogeneous one for implementation.

**Look for high social skills in your potential team members.** Group performance does not seem to be strongly correlated to the average or maximum intelligence of its members. Instead, it is correlated with the members' average social sensitivity, the equality of distribution of conversational turn-taking (i.e., no one is dominating the conversation), and the proportion of women.[12] In other words, look for people who are good at working together.

---

6. (Bryant, 2010).
7. (Cartwright & Schoenberg, 2006).
8. (Cartwright & Cooper, 1993).
9. (Frame, 2003) [pp. 18–19, 29–36].
10. See, for instance (Fletcher et al., 2003; R. Flin & Maran, 2004; R. Flin, O'Connor, & Mearns, 2002; Helmreich, 2000; Yule, Flin, Paterson-Brown, & Maran, 2006)
11. (D. G. Ancona & Caldwell, 1992). See also (Cronin & Weingart, 2007).
12. (Woolley, Chabris, Pentland, Hashmi, & Malone, 2010).

TABLE 8.1: **Emotional Intelligence Has Four Components**[a]

| | |
|---|---|
| Self awareness | Ability to understand your emotions and how they affect your life. This includes having realistic self-confidence: understanding your strengths and limitations, operating with competence, and knowing when to rely on teammates. It also includes managing your feelings: understanding what triggers them and how you can control them. |
| Self management | Ability to control disruptive emotions, including negative ones—for example, anger, anxiety, worry. This involves staying calm under pressure and developing resilience, that is, recovering quickly from adversity. It also includes showing emotional balance: instead of blowing up at people, being able to let them know what is wrong and what the solution is. |
| Social awareness | Ability to understand others. This includes showing empathy and listening well: paying full attention to the speaker, understanding what she or he is saying without taking over. It also includes putting things in a way that others can understand, accurately reading others' feelings, and welcoming questions. |
| Relationship management | Ability to work well with others. This includes communicating compellingly: putting your arguments in persuasive ways so as to clarify expectations and motivate people. It also includes creating an environment where people feel relaxed working with you. |

[a]After R. Lussier & C. Achua. (2007) and D. Goleman. (2015, April 7).

**Value and use emotional intelligence.** There is evidence supporting that emotional intelligence is positively linked with team performance.[13] Actively managing emotions is an important component of team leadership effectiveness;[14] as such, you will benefit from developing your emotional quotient or emotional intelligence (EQ or EI). EQ has four components: self awareness, social awareness, self management, and relationship management (see Table 8.1).[15]

Improving your EQ starts with recognizing its value and how well you are faring. Lawrence Turman is the Chair of the Peter Stark Producing Program at the University of Southern California, and the producer of various movies including *The Graduate*. As a movie producer he knows a few things about managing a team of people with large egos to reach a common goal. For Turman, being an effective producer requires one to be a psychologist and a therapist: "Some people are blessed with that sensitivity and some are not, but being aware how important it is, and training yourself to be a really good listener, will give you a big leg up."[16]

**Use structured interviews to select team members.** Structured interviews are more predictive of job performance than unstructured ones, because they reduce the discretion

---

13. (Jordan & Troth, 2004), (Thompson, 2011) [pp. 105–106].
14. (Prati, Douglas, Ferris, Ammeter, & Buckley, 2003).
15. (Lussier & Achua, 2007) [pp. 39–40]. See also (Goleman, 2015).
16. (Turman, 2005) [p. 147].

of the interviewer in the decision-making process, which has been shown to lead to more reliable and acceptable hiring practices.[17] Ideas to structure an interview include: basing all content on a job analysis; standardizing all questions (asking the same questions in the same order to the various candidates); limiting prompting, follow-up, and elaboration on questions; asking the candidate to relate actual work experiences to prompted situations (i.e., behavioral interview); and asking the candidate for a course of action in a hypothetical scenario (i.e., situational interview).[18]

## 1. AGREE ON EXPECTATIONS

Many problems arise in organizations as a result of a mismatch between expectations and actions, so managing expectations is valuable. Brown and Swartz propose that the various parties examine their expectations to identify potential gaps.[19] Once common ground has been identified, summarizing it in an expectations memo that can be periodically reviewed helps ensure an appropriate deployment of efforts and resources. The memo serves to ensure that roles and responsibilities are clear; it establishes a basis to set development objectives and is useful for evaluating the performance of the team members.

The project manager and team members are jointly responsible for writing the expectations memo at the beginning of the project and for reviewing it at appropriate times; for instance, when reaching a milestone. If you are the manager, you should explain that all team members have mutual accountability: individuals do not succeed or fail; the entire team does.

**Set challenging yet attainable goals.** "We choose to go to the moon. We choose to go to the moon in this decade and do the other things, not because they are easy, but because they are hard, because that goal will serve to organize and measure the best of our energies and skills, because that challenge is one that we are willing to accept, one we are unwilling to postpone, and one which we intend to win, and the others, too."[20] President Kennedy's famous 1962 speech at Rice University played a critical role in helping to secure public support for the Apollo program.[21] In a similar way, identifying specific goals may help you inspire your team and manage expectations; these goals should be challenging yet attainable.[22]

**Demonstrate and demand a can-do attitude.** Explain that "I have no idea" does not work. If you do not have the answer, find the answer. If there is no data, find proxy data. There are always ways to get closer to an answer: focus—and make sure that your team focuses—on finding these and not on whatever they do not have.

---

17. (Bragger, Kutcher, Morgan, & Firth, 2002), (Macan, 2009).
18. See (Levashina, Hartwell, Morgeson, & Campion, 2014), (Bragger et al., 2002) for reviews.
19. (Brown & Swartz, 1989).
20. (Kennedy, 1962).
21. See (Emanuel, 2013).
22. (Barling, Weber, & Kelloway, 1996).

**Expect people to help others be successful.** Stanford's Pfeffer and Sutton note that helping others is a critical component of wisdom, an essential talent.[23] My personal experience illustrates this: one of the ideas that I greatly appreciated at Accenture was that our performance evaluation formally included an item that recorded how good we were at helping others be successful. When evaluation time came, this was not measured by my ability to tell my evaluator how much I had helped others but, rather, by how much my evaluator had heard my peers say how good I was at making them successful.

**Motivate your people to seek help.** Asking for and accepting help is also a component of Pfeffer and Sutton's wisdom.[24] As a new consultant, I once admitted to my boss that I had asked the help of another team member on an assignment. Fresh from academia, I expected a scolding: after all, was this not cheating? Instead, he congratulated me! For him, what mattered was the overall performance of the team. The ability of one of his team members to recognize his limitations and seek the efficient way to overcome them—by seeking help rather than searching alone or, worse, pretending that they did not exist—was the right way to go.[25]

**Develop and communicate your high expectations.** The *Pygmalion effect*—the fact that your expectation of an employee's performance can become self fulfilling—has been verified in various settings.[26] Observing the effect's impact on people's creativity, management professors Tierney and Farmer advise that as a manager you should clearly communicate high expectations to the members of your team and bolster their confidence that they can get the job done.[27]

**Ensure that errors have a low cost.** Making errors is an inherent part of the learning process, so it should be encouraged, as long as their impact is manageable. You should create an environment where people feel safe to make mistakes and report them.[28]

**Promote speaking up.** Team members speaking up about their observations, questions, and concerns brings high value to teams. Studying operating room teams, Harvard University's Amy Edmondson found that team leaders encouraging team members to speak up promoted the successful use of a new technology. The encouragement came in the form of explaining the value of speaking up, creating psychological safety through recognizing their own fallibilities, and emphasizing teamwork through minimizing the concerns about power and status differences.[29]

---

23. (Pfeffer & Sutton, 2006b) [p. 104]. For tips on how to give and receive help, see (Schein, 2010) [pp.144–157].

24. (Pfeffer & Sutton, 2006b) [p. 104].

25. Management professors Hansen and Nohria have proposed that interunit collaboration is a way for organizations to improve their competitiveness. Through a survey of executives, they identified four major barriers to collaboration. The first is the unwillingness to seek input and learn from others. (The other three are: inability to seek and find expertise, unwillingness to help, and inability to work together and transfer knowledge.) See (Hansen & Nohria, 2004).

26. See, for instance (McNatt, 2000). For the value of setting specific and challenging goals on performance, see also (Rousseau, 2012) [p. 69].

27. (Tierney & Farmer, 2004).

28. See (Pfeffer & Sutton, 2006b) [pp. 105–106]. See also Edmondson [p. 87] whose study supports that organizations should encourage discussing and correcting mistakes (Edmondson, 1996).

29. (Edmondson, 2003) [p. 1446]. See also (Nembhard & Edmondson, 2006).

## 2. ADAPT YOUR LEADERSHIP STYLE TO THE SITUATION

Just as a single golf club is not optimal for all shots, there is no one leadership style that is most effective in all situations. Instead, effective leaders adapt their style to the situation, choosing to engage with others in some settings and making decisions alone in others.

Goleman identified six leadership styles, summarized in Table 8.2, and his research indicates that leaders who can use at least four of these styles are most effective. Although this may look daunting, Goleman observes that leadership relies heavily on emotional intelligence, which can be improved. Therefore, one can acquire new styles. Furthermore, he

TABLE 8.2: Goleman's Six Leadership Styles[a]

|  | Authoritative | Affiliative | Democratic |
|---|---|---|---|
| Leader's modus operandi | Mobilizes people toward a vision | Creates harmony and builds emotional bonds | Forges consensus through participation |
| The style in a phrase | "Come with me." | "People come first." | "What do you think?" |
| Underlying emotional intelligence competencies | Self-confidence, empathy, change catalyst | Empathy, building relationships, communication | Collaboration, team leadership, communication |
| When the style works best | When changes require a new vision, or when a clear direction is needed | To heal rifts in a team or to motivate people during stressful circumstances | To build buy-in or consensus, or to get input from valuable employees |
| Overall impact on climate | ++ | + | + |

|  | Coaching | Coercive | Pacesetting |
|---|---|---|---|
| Leader's modus operandi | Develops people for the future | Demands immediate compliance | Sets high standards for performance |
| The style in a phrase | "Try this." | "Do what I tell you." | "Do as I do, now." |
| Underlying emotional intelligence competencies | Developing others, empathy, self-awareness | Drive to achieve, initiative, self-control | Conscientiousness, drive to achieve, initiative |
| When the style works best | To help an employee improve performance or develop long-term strengths | In a crisis, to kick start a turnaround, or with problem employees | To get quick results from a highly motivated and competent team |
| Overall impact on climate | + | − | − |

[a](Goleman, 2000), (R. Tannenbaum & Schmidt, 1973), (Vroom & Jago, 1978).

notes that mastering these styles is not always needed if one can build a team with people who can use the styles that one does not have.[30]

Analyzing the performance of airline crews, leadership specialist Robert Ginnett identified that highly effective captains, when they meet their crew for the first time during the preflight briefing session, demonstrate their adaptive leadership styles through three activities.[31] First, they *establish their competence* as the captain; for instance, by demonstrating rationality using a judicious organization for the meeting. Second, they *acknowledge their own imperfection*; for instance, by addressing some of their vulnerabilities or shortcomings. And third, they *engage the crew* by modifying the meeting to incorporate some of the elements that emerge during it. This allows them to communicate an expectation of flexible authority depending on the situation.

## 3. DELEGATE

Skillful delegation is beneficial to you, the leader, not just because it allows you to focus your efforts elsewhere, but also because it can improve team performance and employee happiness.[32]

You may want to use your issue maps to foster that sense of ownership within the team. Indeed, your map makes the various parts of the problem come to the fore. By assigning ownership of the workstream associated with various branches to specific team members, you can help them see how their contribution impacts the overall effort. This also can be used to clarify your expectations from them.

Delegation should also be your go-to technique in areas where you are not competent; there, you should not make decisions or take action but rely on the people who are qualified to do so.[33]

## 4. USE THE RIGHT PEOPLE IN THE RIGHT PLACES

Perhaps one of the most insightful questions I have heard as a consultant was from a senior manager on a large project when I started out. He said, "Arnaud, are we using you as we should?" If I have an important unique skill but am being tied up doing something else that could be easily done by someone else, then I am not used optimally.[34]

If you are a team leader, you should assign your people where they can provide the best value; that is, ideally, each person does first what they can do better than anyone else.

---

30. (Goleman, 2000).
31. (Ginnett, 2010) [pp. 100–102]. See also (Orasanu, 2010) [p. 171]. For an example of application of all three activities, see (Rogers, 2010) [p. 307].
32. See, for instance, (Özaralli, 2003), (Cohen, Ledford, & Spreitzer, 1996), (Carson, Tesluk, & Marrone, 2007), (Pfeffer & Veiga, 1999), (Mathieu, Maynard, Rapp, & Gilson, 2008) [p. 427].
33. (Drucker, 2004).
34. This is related to the concept of comparative advantage; see (Einhorn & Hogarth, 1981) [p. 26].

**Use the Pareto principle to decide how to deploy your resources.** Not all aspects of your project deserve the same amount of your (and your team's) attention. We introduced the Pareto Principle in Chapter 4 and it is useful here, too: by deploying more resources where they are most needed, you can increase your effectiveness. In psychologist Howard Garnder's words, "It is important to be judicious about where one places one's efforts, and to be alert to 'tipping points' that abruptly bring a goal within (or beyond) reach."[35]

## 5. COACH YOUR TEAM EFFECTIVELY

Coaching includes providing motivational feedback to improve performance.[36] Effective feedback is necessary for learning[37] and may result in markedly improved performances.[38]

You should provide both positive and negative feedback, even if giving the latter makes you feel uncomfortable. Negative feedback is usually best given privately and should be given in a timely fashion, usually immediately after the matter.[39] Additional recommended techniques to make feedback effective include: creating an unthreatening environment; eliciting thoughts and feelings before giving feedback; being nonjudgmental; focusing on behaviors; basing feedback on observed and specific facts; and proposing ideas for improvement.[40]

You also may coach your team through developing a charismatic influence—articulating a vision, appealing to followers' values, and using analogies and metaphors—which enhances followers' motivation.[41] Showing enthusiasm (being upbeat, especially in the face of adversity) also may help you get your team on board emotionally and increase their confidence.[42]

The most inspirational leaders I have worked with were working for their teams. They kept an open environment where it was clear, expected even, for anyone to ask questions and provide feedback. Early in one of my first consulting engagements, the manager in charge—several pay grades above mine—took the time to welcome me to the team. Part of his message was, "Arnaud, we do not expect you to know everything, but we expect you to ask if you do not know." That helped establish that the environment was open.

Maintaining an open environment may start with keeping your office door open—at least some of the time. Another great boss I had, when asked a question, would invariably stop typing on his computer—or stop doing whatever else he was doing but, as management consultants it seems that all we all did all the time was type away—shut off his laptop and listen to me carefully. He looked me in the eye and engaged with what I was saying.

---

35. (H. Gardner, 2006) [p. 8].
36. (Lussier & Achua, 2007) [p. 211].
37. (National Research Council, 2011a) [p. 52]; see also (Cannon & Witherspoon, 2005).
38. (Murphy & Daan, 1984), (Rousseau, 2012) [p. 69].
39. (Moss & Sanchez, 2004).
40. (Hewson & Little, 1998). See also (Shute, 2008) for a review.
41. (Aguinis & Kraiger, 2009) [pp. 455–456].
42. (Turman, 2005) [p. 149].

I knew that, at that moment, I had his undivided attention. He also was skilled at showing that this offer was limited in time because, after two minutes, he would go back to what he was doing. But I knew that I could have his attention whenever I needed it and that I needed to prepare before soliciting it.

## 6. RUN SUCCESSFUL MEETINGS

Meetings can be a necessary evil: although needed, they often are wasteful.[43] You can take actions before, during, and after a meeting to make it more effective and efficient. Here are some ideas.

**Before the meeting**, clearly define and communicate the objective(s) through focused discussions, because doing so is positively related with team satisfaction and team effectiveness.[44] Possible reasons for having a meeting include: to provide information, without any action, decision, or conclusion (e.g., to provide a progress report); to decide what to do next; to decide how to do the next actions; or to change the organization's framework. If these objectives can be achieved in a different way—say, individually or collectively, by e-mail or phone—consider doing so.

Using an effective agenda helps speed-up and clarify the meeting.[45] When structuring the agenda, include not just a theme (e.g., "Harry") but what you want to achieve (e.g., "Decide who is doing what for finding Harry") and how long you expect it will take the group to cover the topic (e.g., "15 minutes"). Distributing the agenda ahead of time, Antony Jay recommends two or three days before, helps participants prepare.[46] Sending the agenda ahead of time is positively correlated with perceived effectiveness of meetings, perhaps because it allows participants to come prepared and, therefore, contribute more effectively.[47] You also should consider organizing the agenda so that the most important items come first; that way the group will have a chance to address them even if time becomes short.[48]

Professor of management Leigh Thompson recommends specifying ground rules for meetings and enforcing them.[49] These might include everyone arriving on time, adhering to assigned time for each item, and sticking to the agenda.

**During the meeting**, think of yourself, the chair, as the servant of the group rather than the master. Antony Jay proposes that the chair should make a limited contribution to the discussion, serving more as a facilitator than an actor. In that sense, the chair assists the group in reaching the best conclusion efficiently, which entails interpreting and clarifying, moving the discussion forward, and bringing the group to resolutions that everyone

---

43. For a review, see (Romano & Nunamaker Jr, 2001).
44. (Bang, Fuglesang, Ovesen, & Eilertsen, 2010), (Allen et al., 2012).
45. Using an agenda, as well as taking minutes, also has been shown to help meetings start and end on time (Volkema & Niederman, 1996).
46. (Jay, 1976).
47. (Leach, Rogelberg, Warr, & Burnfield, 2009).
48. (Lussier & Achua, 2007) [p. 321].
49. (Thompson, 2011) [pp. 355–356].

understands and accepts as being the group's, even if individual participants disagree.[50] As the group's facilitator, it is important for the chair to remain impartial.[51]

An effective chair deals both with the subject and the participants. Dealing with the subject includes introducing the issue (Why is it on the agenda? What is known so far?) and presenting a position: What needs to be done and what are the possible courses of action? As such, the chair keeps the meeting pointed toward the objective and closes the discussion early enough.[52]

There are various reasons for closing a discussion before reaching a decision, for instance, if more facts are required, if the meeting needs the viewpoints of people not present, if participants need more time to think about the subject, if events are changing, if there is insufficient time to cover the subject properly, or if a subset of the group can settle the matter outside the meeting.[53]

Once this is done, the final component of dealing with each agenda item is to summarize agreements.[54]

Dealing with people includes starting and finishing on time.[55] It also includes controlling the group dynamic, including limiting overly talkative participants; engaging silent participants, especially those who are quiet because of nervousness or hostility; protecting the weak, for instance, by highlighting their contributions; encouraging the contention of ideas while discouraging the contention of personalities; discouraging the squashing of suggestions; coming to the most senior members last given that junior participants may not feel comfortable speaking once someone of high authority has pronounced on a topic; and closing on an achievement.[56] It is important that you establish open communication because this supports group performance;[57] in particular, participants should feel free to speak up whenever they feel that the meeting's objectives are unclear.[58]

One way to promote progress in groups where participants are argumentative is to apply de Bono's Six Thinking Hats technique whereby, at any given moment, all participants look at one and only one specific aspect of the issue.[59] In particular, by forcing all group members to consider one specific aspect of an idea or proposal at a time—for example, "let's spend five minutes to think about how we can make this idea work and then we will spend five minutes reflecting on why it might not work." This approach might be useful to constructively engage a self-appointed devil's advocate who tends to only see what is wrong with any proposal.

End the meeting on time. Before doing so, review the commitments, ask for suggestions for future agenda items, and fix the time and place of the next meeting.

---

50. (Jay, 1976).
51. (Nixon & Littlepage, 1992).
52. (Jay, 1976).
53. (Jay, 1976).
54. See (Thompson, 2011) [p. 356].
55. Not only is starting and finishing on time good manners, there is empirical evidence supporting that it is correlated with perceived meeting effectiveness (Nixon & Littlepage, 1992), (Leach et al., 2009).
56. (Jay, 1976). See also (Whetten & Camerron, 2002) [pp. 551–552].
57. See (Nixon & Littlepage, 1992) for empirical evidence and a discussion.
58. (Bang et al., 2010).
59. (De Bono, 1999), (Schellens, Van Keer, De Wever, & Valcke, 2009).

**After the meeting,** send the minutes as soon as possible. Instead of detailing precisely who said what, minutes should focus on clearly identifying the major decisions reached, the action items (who is doing what by when), and the open issues.[60]

## 7. COMMUNICATE EFFECTIVELY IN ALL MEDIA FORMS

The previous chapter provided some ideas to communicate effectively using presentations, and many of these principles also apply when communicating with phones, e-mails, or in person. In particular, ensure that you clearly express the objective of your communication, that you make your pyramid apparent, and that you point to clear next steps. Start with your conclusion. Write clearly and concisely.[61] Write well. Use the active voice, plain English—that is, avoid jargon, buzzwords, and acronyms that might cause a problem for your audience—precise language, and correct grammar, spelling, and punctuation. Here are additional ideas:

**Make the pyramid apparent in the table of contents of a report.** Just as the structure of your presentation should be visible in its outline and its taglines, the structure of a written report should also be apparent. You can use two places to do that: in the table of contents for parts, chapters, and sections and in the actual body of the text for paragraphs. Figure 8.3 below provides two examples of tables of content. The first shows a list of objectives with no indication of what those are. In contrast, the second establishes a

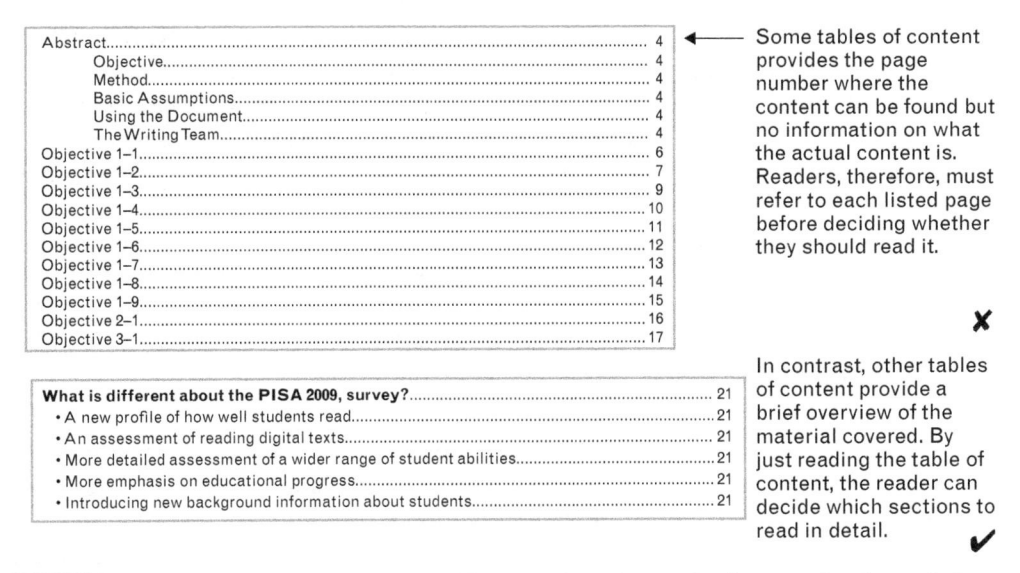

| | |
|---|---|
| Abstract............................................................................ 4 | Some tables of content provides the page number where the content can be found but no information on what the actual content is. Readers, therefore, must refer to each listed page before deciding whether they should read it. |
|     Objective...................................................................... 4 | |
|     Method......................................................................... 4 | |
|     Basic Assumptions........................................................ 4 | |
|     Using the Document..................................................... 4 | |
|     The Writing Team......................................................... 4 | |
| Objective 1–1............................................................... 6 | |
| Objective 1–2............................................................... 7 | |
| Objective 1–3............................................................... 9 | |
| Objective 1–4............................................................. 10 | |
| Objective 1–5............................................................. 11 | |
| Objective 1–6............................................................. 12 | |
| Objective 1–7............................................................. 13 | |
| Objective 1–8............................................................. 14 | |
| Objective 1–9............................................................. 15 | |
| Objective 2–1............................................................. 16 | |
| Objective 3–1............................................................. 17 | ✗ |
| **What is different about the PISA 2009, survey?**........ 21 | In contrast, other tables of content provide a brief overview of the material covered. By just reading the table of content, the reader can decide which sections to read in detail. ✓ |
| • A new profile of how well students read.................... 21 | |
| • An assessment of reading digital texts....................... 21 | |
| • More detailed assessment of a wider range of student abilities........ 21 | |
| • More emphasis on educational progress.................... 21 | |
| • Introducing new background information about students........ 21 | |

**FIGURE 8.3:** All tables of content are not equal. The second one, by succinctly answering the reader's questions, enables the reader to decide quickly whether to read each section.

---

60. (Whetten & Camerron, 2002) [pp. 549–550].
61. See (Lussier & Achua, 2007) [p. 201].

Implement and Monitor the Solution   •   215

> *PISA seeks to assess how well 15-year-olds are prepared for life's challenges.*
>
> PISA seeks to measure how well young adults, at age of 15 and therefore approaching the end of compulsory schooling, are prepared to meet the challenges of today's knowledge societies. The assessment is forward-looking, focusing on young people's ability to use their knowledge and skills to meet real-life challenges, rather than merely on the extent to which they have mastered a specific school curriculum. This orientation reflects a change in the goals and objectives of curricula themselves, which are increasingly concerned with what students can do with what they learn at school, and not merely whether they can reproduce what they have learned.

The pyramid can also be apparent in the body of the report if you summarize each paragraph in the margin. The reader can then choose the level of details she is interested in:

- Minimum – read only the table of contents,
- Medium – read the table of content and the paragraph summaries,
- Maximum – read the entire document.

**FIGURE 8.4:** One also can make the pyramid apparent in the body of the text by summarizing each section in the margin.

question-and-answer dialogue with the reader to enable her to decide quickly whether to read each section.

Figure 8.4 shows how you can also make the pyramid apparent in the body of the text. By summarizing each section in the margin, one enables the reader to quickly grasp the overall content and help her decide whether she is interested in reading the full section. Used in conjunction with a thoughtful table of contents, this technique enables the reader to choose one of three levels of details at which to read the report: reading only the table of contents provides the shortest overview of the report; reading the table of contents and the paragraph summaries provides a closer look; and reading the full report provides the most detail.

**Write effective e-mails.** E-mails and other text-based communications have the potential to make you appear less competent, thoughtful, and intelligent than oral communication.[62] But e-mail can be a more effective communication medium than face-to-face communication in some settings; for instance, when discussing tasks of low ambiguity.[63] Doumont, Kawasaki, and others offer guidelines to write more effective e-mails:[64]

- Address the e-mail to those who must act, copy those who must know but not act.
- Include in the subject line a reason why the addressee should read the message. One way to do so is to phrase the subject line in two parts: the general topic and the objective of the message (e.g., Finding Harry—Are you OK with engaging others in the search?). If the topic changes over an exchange, update the subject line.

---

62. (Schroeder & Epley, 2015).
63. (Valacich, Paranka, George, & Nunamaker, 1993). See also (Frohlich & Oppenheimer, 1998).
64. See (Doumont, 2009) [p. 157], (Kawasaki, 2008) [pp. 205–208].

- Address only one topic per e-mail because this makes it easier to keep track of conversations.[65]
- Introduce your topic with a situation, complication, and the key question: the one question you want to resolve with the e-mail.
- Keep e-mails concise, ideally no more than three paragraphs.[66] In addition to being concise, write clearly and courteously considering purpose, clarity, consistency, and tone.[67]
- If you fail to keep your e-mail short, you may consider using boldface type for the important parts. Also, for longer e-mails, you may want to start with your conclusion and then provide details (e.g., "Would you be okay with starting to look for Harry by engaging others in the search? Here is why...").
- Include your signature if it is useful.
- If applicable, specify who does what when—that is, the owners, actions, and dates—aiming at conciseness and clarity. If the addressee needs to take action, indicate so explicitly but politely.

**Listen actively.** Active listening includes physically hearing, interpreting, evaluating, and responding or asking for clarification if the communicator was unclear. Effective listeners also are able to suspend premature judgment during a conversation; that is, they do not assume that what they expect is what they are going to hear. Effective listeners also are able to pick up on nonverbal cues such as body language and facial expressions. Mastering these skills requires ongoing practice.[68]

## 8. KEEP YOUR TEAM INFORMED

Good communication can have a strong impact on your team's motivation.[69] For airline crews, effective team leadership involves encouraging participation in task planning and completion, stating the plan clearly, consulting the team on whether a change should be made, and so forth.[70]

Managing your team is a continuous process. In summary:

- Ensure that they know how the project is going, especially if there are complications.
- Have clear expectations for each team member and ensure these are clear to each of them, too.
- Make your project an opportunity for your team to grow. Paraphrasing Napoléon, people are like digits, they only acquire value through their position.

---

65. (Ashley, 2005) [p.22].
66. Kawasaki asks for no more than five sentences (Bryant, 2010).
67. (Ashley, 2005) [p.22]. See also (Crainer & Dearlove, 2004).
68. (Department of the Air Force, 1998). See also (Archer & Stuart-Cox, 2013) [pp. 19–20].
69. (Clarke, 1999).
70. (Rhona Flin et al., 2003).

- Provide positive and negative feedback quickly.
- Talk with everyone often and on an informal basis.
- Coach continuously.
- Ensure that everyone provides feedback on how the project is going and on how it could go better.

## 9. MANAGE PROGRESS

Periodically, perhaps every week, review your progress against your original plan. If progress is too slow or too expensive, take corrective action.

Managing progress also includes managing your boss. If you disagree with your boss, this means deciding when to push back and when to give in. For instance, should you find that your boss has made a mistake, how you report it can go a long way toward having it fixed. In airline crews, junior team members are trained to use specific communication tactics to be more effective in signaling errors made by their superiors. These tactics include describing clearly the nature of the problem, suggesting solutions while leaving the final decision to the boss, and explaining why your suggestions are good ideas.[71]

## 10. DEMONSTRATE HIGH ETHICAL STANDARDS

If not for ideological purposes, maintaining high ethical standards will help you stay away from being caught in lies, a difficult situation to get out of.[72]

## 11. NETWORK

Networking—defined as building, maintaining, and using relationships—provides access to knowledge, resources, and power.[73] In addition, you should use your team's network toward three ends: conduct ambassadorial activities (such as marketing the project to management, managing its reputation, lobbying for resources, and keeping track of advocates and detractors), scout for information across your organization, and coordinate tasks with other units.[74]

This is valid not just for project management but for your career in general, because better networking is related to career success.[75]

---

71. (Orasanu, 2010) [p. 168], (Fischer & Orasanu, 2000).
72. (Lussier & Achua, 2007) [p. 134].
73. (Brass, Galaskiewicz, Greve, & Tsai, 2004), (Inkpen & Tsang, 2005).
74. (D. Ancona, Bresman, & Kaeufer, 2002).
75. (Wolff & Moser, 2009).

Effective networking includes acquiring and managing a group of mentors who can be your trusted advisors.[76] As a mentee, you should be an active participant in the relationship as opposed to a passive receptor. One way to do this is to "manage up": take ownership of the relationship by planning the meetings, setting up the agenda, asking questions, listening, completing assignments, and requesting feedback.[77]

## 12. NEGOTIATE

Whenever achieving your goals requires you to cooperate with others, you need to negotiate.[78] Therefore, whether we realize it—and whether we like it—we all negotiate every day. As such, being able to negotiate well is critical to our success,[79] and yet there is overwhelming evidence that we are for the most part ineffective negotiators.[80]

Negotiation can serve at least three purposes: creating value, claiming value, and building trust.[81] Negotiation is an expansive subject and is far too broad for this chapter, so the following are only a few basic ideas.[82]

**Distinguish the people from the problem to focus on interests.** It is often valuable to differentiate the parties' interests from the positions they take on the various issues being negotiated.[83] Emotions and egos can get entangled in the problem, resulting in people taking things personally. To avoid this, Fisher et al. and others recommend that you manage:

- **Perceptions**—putting yourself in their shoes, discussing their perceptions and yours, involving them in the process
- **Emotions**—understanding emotions (yours and theirs), allowing them to vent, without reacting to emotional outbursts—and
- **Communication**—listening actively, speaking to be understood, and not speaking more than necessary.[84]

Having done so, you should aim at reconciling interests, rather than focusing on positions.

**Identify your BATNA.** Your best alternative to a negotiated agreement (BATNA) is the course of action that you would choose if you failed to reach an agreement with the

---

76. (De Janasz, Sullivan, & Whiting, 2003).
77. (Zerzan, Hess, Schur, Phillips, & Rigotti, 2009).
78. (Thompson, 2012) [p. 2].
79. (Spector, 2004).
80. (Van Boven & Thompson, 2003), (Thompson, 2012) [p. 5].
81. (Thompson, 2012) [p. 2].
82. For more on negotiation, see, for instance (Bazerman & Neale, 1992), (Thompson, 2012), (Raiffa, Richardson, & Metcalfe, 2002), and (Fisher, Ury, & Patton, 1991).
83. (Sebenius, 1992).
84. (Ramsey & Sohi, 1997), (Fisher et al., 1991) [p. 23–36].

other parties.[85] Knowing your BATNA puts a floor on what you should be ready to accept; indeed, you are negotiating to produce a better outcome than you could get without negotiating, therefore you should refuse any deal that is worse than your BATNA.[86] Having an alternative increases outcomes (both yours and the joint outcome) and the better your alternative is against the other parties', the larger your benefit.[87] Note that your BATNA is not fixed but, rather, fluctuates. At any time, it is either improving or deteriorating. So, should it be appropriate, you can invest effort in creating alternatives.[88] Indeed, good BATNAs do not usually exist but, rather, must be created.[89] One way of doing so is to follow Bazerman and Neale's falling-in-love rule: When house hunting (or being engaged in similar high-stakes efforts), "fall in love with three, not one."[90] This amounts to delaying satisficing, that is, not stopping your search as soon as you have found one satisfactory solution but, instead, continuing to generate options (see Chapter 3).

**Create value.** Although a negotiation between parties is easily thought of as an exercise in getting the larger portion of a fixed-size pie, it also can be an exercise in creating value, that is, in making the pie bigger.[91] Therefore, you may want to think about alternatives that are beneficial for all parties. To create value, Fisher and his colleagues propose that you drop the assumption that the pie has a fixed size, let go of searching for a single answer, and stop thinking that "solving their problem is their problem." In that sense, the process of creating value mimics how we identified alternative solutions (see Chapter 5).

**First be nice, then mirror.** When negotiating with someone as part of a wider relationship, should you aim at cooperating (being nice) or being selfish (attempting to secure as much as you can for yourself)? Being selfish may give you the highest short-term payoff, but cooperating has the biggest reward in the long run. After organizing computer tournaments where game theorists pitched various negotiation strategies against one another, political scientist Robert Axelrod concluded that you should first cooperate and then imitate the other party's last action.[92] The key is to realize that you and the other party are communicating through your actions. Cooperating (i.e., starting nice) sends the message that you are willing to make some accommodations. If the other party adopts a dominating strategy, then you should reciprocate that aggression. Likewise, if they are nice, then be nice. Continue imitating their last move in each subsequent instance. This creates a cooperative environment where the parties learn to search for an integrative agreement.[93]

---

85. (Fisher et al., 1991) [pp. 97–106].
86. (Thompson, 2012) [p. 15].
87. (Pinkley, Neale, & Bennett, 1994).
88. (Brett, 2000).
89. (Ury, 2007) [p. 23].
90. (Bazerman & Neale, 1992) [p. 69].
91. (Fisher et al., 1991) [p. 56].
92. (R. Axelrod, 1980a, 1980b), (R. Axelrod & Hamilton, 1981).
93. (M. A. Nowak & Sigmund, 1992).

Axelrod offers four prescriptions for this strategy to work: (1) do not be envious (if they are the first to defect, they will have it their way one more time than you—accept this and move on[94]); (2) be nice, that is, do not be the first to defect; (3) reciprocate cooperation and defection; and (4) be clear: communicate unambiguously that you will reciprocate their actions.[95]

## 2.2. MANAGE YOUR CLIENTS

Often you will have several clients: at least one decisionmaker plus one or several key stakeholders. Managing your relationships with them and managing their expectations is critical because ineffective stakeholder management is one of the biggest causes of project failure.[96]

Managing expectations includes focusing fuzzy expectations, making implicit expectations more explicit, and calibrating unrealistic expectations.[97]

Build credibility early and reinforce it frequently. Engage your project's clients early so they get a chance to have the team address their issues. Report frequently, perhaps weekly, and keep them informed of problems and potential problems.[98]

### 1. UNDERPROMISE AND OVERDELIVER

Establishing and maintaining high credibility requires demonstrating that you are trustworthy. At the very least, this means meeting deadlines,[99] but in general you might be well served to constantly underpromise and overdeliver. Stanford's Tom Byers advises entrepreneurs to follow five rules: (1) Show up on time; (2) Be nice to people; (3) Do what you say you will do; (4) Deliver more than you promise; and (5) Work with enthusiasm and passion.[100]

### 2. BE PROACTIVE

Understand your client's needs and management style and quickly build credibility (by underpromising and overdelivering, being reliable, demonstrating strong ethical standards, and showing respect for all).

**Come prepared.** If you are invited to a meeting but have not received an agenda, come with one of your own, especially if you are the junior person in the room. You may not need

---

94. This is related to the concept that, to establish a stable cooperative solution, you may have to strive for a satisfactory payoff rather than an optimal one; see (Simon, 1996) [pp.37–38].
95. (R. M. Axelrod, 1984), (Bazerman & Neale, 1992) [p. 163–165], (Parks & Komorita, 1998).
96. (Nelson, 2007).
97. (Ojasalo, 2001).
98. (Wright, 1997).
99. (Lussier & Achua, 2007) [p. 133].
100. (Madson, 2005) [p. 135].

to use it, but if the senior person in the meeting looks at you asking, "So, why are we here?," you will be prepared.

**Understand the political landscape.** Although it is natural to think that organizations make decisions rationally, managerial decision-making is often not rational, with politics and power both playing key roles.[101] Understanding these dynamics—such as identifying the power yielders and their motivations—may be critical to the success of your efforts.

## 3. AVOID SCOPE CREEP

One of your clients is the one paying for the project, for instance, your boss. But once the project gets underway, you usually interact more with other people—such as end users—who may have a different agenda. They may ask you to include additional considerations that are important to them in your projects, resulting in scope creep. Therefore, it may be advisable to develop a scope management plan that involves your client(s).[102] Having a clear project plan can help you avoid scope creep from the onset of your project.

By the way, this is valid for anyone on your team: It is usually not a good idea to let any of your team members do significant extra work at the request of stakeholders without this being mandated by the decisionmakers.

## 4. COMMUNICATE

Communicate frequently, updating your client(s) and other stakeholders on the progress of your project. This is also valid for bad news: better that they learn such things from you than from another source.[103]

## 2.3. MANAGE RISKS

You should manage risks not just in the preparation phase, as we discussed, but also along the course of the project. Risks can be of many kinds, including inappropriate leadership support, changes in the buy-in of stakeholders, or scope creep.[104] Risks have two primary components: the probability of their occurrence and the impact of occurrence. These two components must be considered along with your own tolerance toward risk.[105] You can handle a risk in one of four ways, shown here from most risk-adverse to least:[106]

---

101. (Lussier & Achua, 2007) [pp. 132–133].
102. (Dey, Kinch, & Ogunlana, 2007). See also (Papke-Shields, Beise, & Quan, 2010).
103. For more on delivering bad news and the impact on projects, see (Sussman & Sproull, 1999), (Smith & Keil, 2003).
104. (Nelson, 2007). See also (Bradley, 2008).
105. (Kerzner, 2003) [pp. 653–654].
106. (Kerzner, 2003) [pp. 682–686], (zur Muehlen & Ho, 2006).

- **Transfer the risk.** Pass on the risk to someone else, for instance, by purchasing an insurance policy;
- **Control/mitigate the risk.** Continuously re-evaluate the risk, both the likelihood and impact of occurrence, and develop contingency plans;
- **Avoid the risk.** Before a specific risk occurs, elect an alternative that does not include the risk; and
- **Assume the risk.** Accept the risk and proceed.

Managing risks requires you to identify and prioritize the risks, plan how you will manage them, and monitor as you go. To help you do so, consider maintaining a top-five risk list and conduct interim reviews.[107]

## 2.4. CLOSE

**Debrief.** Proper debriefs can improve individual and team performance significantly.[108] Pilots and astronauts routinely debrief after their flights, which allows them to identify mistakes and ways to avoid them in the future. The debriefing process also increases their bonding. This is challenging because significant learning requires admitting that one makes mistakes, which can generate a perception of incompetence.[109]

To mitigate this, acknowledge the value of each member's participation, reinforce the importance of self-reflection, ask open-ended questions, and build an open and safe environment. Build an environment in which it is accepted that everybody makes mistakes, where members accept and respect one another, and where it is clear that the debriefing will remain confidential.[110] It should be clear that holding a debriefing session does not signal that something went wrong but, rather, generates an opportunity for groups to discuss what they have learned.[111]

**Share the glory.** In an information economy, employers strive to attract and retain talented employees. Therefore, being credited for contributions is important for your career.[112]

This does not mean, however, that you should attribute others' contributions to yourself or even that you should take all the credit that you deserve. Indeed, generously attributing credit to coworkers is a way to engage them, and employee satisfaction and engagement are related to business outcomes.[113] Therefore, generously attributing credit to your team members may support the success of your team.

---

107. (Nelson, 2007).
108. (S. I. Tannenbaum & Cerasoli, 2013).
109. (Ron, Lipshitz, & Popper, 2006).
110. (R. Gardner, 2013; Rall, Manser, & Howard, 2000; Ron et al., 2006).
111. (National Research Council, 2011a) [p. 27], (Rogers, 2010) [pp. 311–312].
112. (Fisk, 2006).
113. (Harter, Schmidt, & Hayes, 2002).

## 3. SELECT AND MONITOR KEY METRICS

Variances—discrepancies between your original plans and progress to date—are an integral part of project management. As such, your goal is not so much to try to avoid them as it is to keep them acceptably small.[114] To help you do so, you should identify and continuously monitor a set of metrics that helps you recognize discrepancies early and enables you to take corrective action quickly.

## 4. DOCUMENT EVERYTHING THAT YOU THINK CAN BE USEFUL IN THE FUTURE

Every problem-solving process is a learning opportunity. Make sure that you take advantage of it.

## 5. UPDATE YOUR MAPS AS NEW INFORMATION APPEARS

Even this late in the problem-resolution process, your maps remain a guide and a central repository. If new evidence surfaces, you should include it in your map. You should also crossout branches, add new ones, and change your conclusions as warranted.

## 6. WHAT ABOUT HARRY?

Having decided that it was best to first enlist others in looking for Harry, we reached out to a neighbor who has seven dogs and who we, therefore, appointed "the dog expert." He gave us the phone number of the president of the local pet association. When we called, we went straight to his voicemail, so we left a message and prepared to search the neighborhood. Within minutes, however, he returned our call. Although he was on a business trip thousands of miles away, he had already been contacted by someone living a few blocks away from Harry's house, who had found Harry and was keeping him until we could retrieve him. All told, we were reunited with Harry a couple of hours after noticing his disappearance. Talk about the value of having a network!

---

114. (Frame, 2003) [p. 11].

Chapter 8 completed our in-depth description of a problem-resolution process. In the last chapter, we will discuss some final thoughts on being an effective problem solver, including attitudes that you should adopt in the process and skills that you should nurture.

# NOTES

**Another one bites the dust.** Some estimates show over 70% of mergers "fail to deliver their intended benefits and destroy economic value in the process."[115]

**Evidence-based management, or lack thereof.** Although medicine is leading the way in using evidence-based research to guide the practice, some argue that management is not there yet[116] and neither is intelligence analysis.[117]

**Get some feedback (and do not blame the weatherman).** Compared with numerous professionals, including clinicians, most professional weather forecasters appear to not be as prone to overconfidence, at least for their weather predictions. This has been attributed to their receiving constant and timely feedback on the accuracy of their predictions, which greatly facilitates learning.[118]

**"Teamwork? That's not what I trained for."** Robert Ginnett at the U.S. Air Force Academy notes how our current educational system, which encourages and rewards individual performance, is at odds with how graduates are expected to work for the rest of their lives: as part of teams.[119] If even fighter pilots—arguably highly individualistic professionals, at least in the general public's belief—see themselves as working in teams, perhaps our educational system should start training and rewarding students not just for individual tasks but also for collective ones.

**No consensus on optimal team size.** There is no widespread agreement in the literature as far as an optimal team size. Some studies note that having more members is better. Others find a sweet spot between too few and too many (fewer than 10 is desirable; so is having the smallest number of people who can get the job done[120]). Still others find no correlation between the number of members and performance.[121]

**Transformational leadership.** Transformational leadership may be defined as "the ability of a leader to influence the values, attitudes, beliefs, and behaviors of others by working with and through them in order to accomplish the organization's mission and purpose."[122]

---

115. (Pfeffer & Sutton, 2006b) [pp. 3–4].
116. (Barends, ten Have, & Huisman, 2012; Pfeffer & Sutton, 2006a, 2007; Rousseau, 2006; Rynes, Giluk, & Brown, 2007), (National Research Council, 2011b) [pp. 324–325]. For an entertaining insight into consulting and further evidence supporting this claim, see (Stewart, 2009).
117. (National Research Council, 2011b) [pp. 96–97].
118. (Nickerson, 1998) [p. 189].
119. (Ginnett, 2010).
120. (Thompson, 2011) [p. 82].
121. See (Kozlowski & Bell, 2003) [p. 12] for a review.
122. (Özaralli, 2003).

TABLE 8.3: You Can Think of a Team as Being One of Five Kinds[a]

| Team | Key Characteristic | Indication |
| --- | --- | --- |
| Face-to-face team | Our common idea of what a team is. Members sit together and rely heavily on their interactions with one another. | When output requires contributions from diverse members with complementary expertise. |
| Virtual team | As face-to-face but members are not co-located | When interdependent tasks are needed but members live in different places. |
| Surgical team | Members work together but one individual is ultimately responsible. The focus is on ensuring that the lead has all the assistance that members can provide. | When extremely high individual insight, expertise, and/or creativity is needed. It is the writing of a play, rather than its performance. |
| Co-acting team | Members have their own tasks in the group. | When tasks require parallel efforts with little interactions. |
| Sand dune team | Have fluid composition and boundaries: people become members and leave as needed. They may have a more solid core. | When resources are scare. |

[a]After J. R. Hackman & M. O'Connor. (2004). What makes for a great analytic team? Individual vs. team approaches to intelligence analysis. *Intelligence Science Board, Office of the Director of Central Intelligence, Washington, DC*.

**No one likes a dictator.** Although using an autocratic leadership style may be the most efficient in some situations, a participatory approach is preferred by most team members.[123]

**On negotiation.** There are two primary schools of negotiation: the primarily cooperative—which is more problem-solving oriented, aiming at ensuring that all parties benefit—and the primarily competitive one, which is more adversarial.[124] Empirical data suggests that it is more difficult to be an effective competitive negotiator than an effective cooperative one.[125]

**Five kinds of teams.** Hackman and O'Connor identified five kinds of teams, each with their own peculiarities[126] (see Table 8.3).

**Growing the pie.** Revising an agreement in such a way that it makes at least one party better off without making anyone worse off is known as a Pareto improvement.[127]

**Tit-for-tat, Pavlov, and other negotiation strategies.** An alternative to Axelrod's tit-for-tat (i.e., "first be nice, then mirror") is a Pavlov strategy: cooperate if, and only if, both players used the same alternative in the previous round. Compared to tit-for-tat, Pavlov

---

123. See (Heilman, Hornstein, Cage, & Herschlag, 1984), (Thompson, 2011) [p. 284].

124. See (Schneider, 2002) [pp. 148–150].

125. (Schneider, 2002) [p. 167, 190]. See also (Bazerman & Neale, 1992), (Fisher et al., 1991), (Ury, 2007), (Malhotra & Bazerman, 2007).

126. (Hackman & O'Connor, 2004).

127. (Malhotra & Bazerman, 2007) [p. 65].

corrects inadvertent mistakes and exploits unconditional cooperators.[128] Pavlov is ineffective in noisy environments[129] and tit-for-tat has limitations of its own in noisy environments or when cooperation may be mistaken for deception.[130] Offering additional (but not unconditional) generosity may improve tit-for-tat's results in noisy environments.[131]

**"Welcome to the meeting, please remain standing."** A study at the University of Missouri found that, for making decisions, sit-down meetings were 34% longer than stand-up ones but did not produce better decisions.[132]

**Gain perspective through asking yourself some questions.** The Space Flight Resource Management program trains astronauts in nontechnical skills that are essential for mission success. Among its resources is a list of questions to help them ensure whether they are on the right track. Examples include: "Do we all agree on what we will be doing next?" "Is there a climate for openness?" and "Are conflicts resolved with mutual respect intact?"[133]

**More debrief best practices.** Salas et al. propose 12 evidence-based best practices for debriefing medical teams: 1. Make it diagnostic; 2. Create a supportive learning environment; 3. Encourage leaders and members to be attentive to teamwork processes; 4. Teach how to conduct good debriefs; 5. Ensure members are comfortable during debriefs; 6. Focus on a few critical issues; 7. Describe specific interactions that were involved; 8. Use objective performance indicators to support feedback; 9. Provide outcome feedback later and less frequently than process feedback; 10. Provide feedback for individuals and teams as appropriate; 11. Provide feedback quickly; 12. Keep track for future sessions.[134]

---

128. (M. Nowak & Sigmund, 1993).
129. (Wu & Axelrod, 1995).
130. For a review, see (Parks & Komorita, 1998).
131. (Bendor, Kramer, & Stout, 1991).
132. (Bluedorn, Turban, & Love, 1999).
133. (Pruyn & Sterling, 2006).
134. (Salas et al., 2008).

CHAPTER 9

# DEALING WITH COMPLICATIONS AND WRAP UP

As closure, this chapter takes a step back to look at the entire problem-solving process and give some final guidelines. These apply to managing the process and managing yourself, the problem solver.

## 1. MANAGE THE PROCESS

Taking a look at the previous eight chapters, our approach to problem solving can appear daunting. In fact, for many problems, applying the methodology fully is counterproductive. The observations of decision specialists von Winterfeldt and Edwards on how they use decision tools seem directly relevant to this setting, too: "We ourselves use elements of decision analysis (e.g., probability estimates) daily but perform full analyses to facilitate or to check on personal decisions only once or twice per year. The cost of systematic, careful thought using formally appropriate tools is high enough that even experts do not routinely or casually incur it."[1]

Our definition of strategic thinking—a process that includes design, analysis, and synthesis; design to identify the key activities needed, analysis to assemble and process the necessary data, and synthesis to produce a solution that results from a choice between alternative courses of action—indeed starts with design to identify the key activities needed. Some situations call for the application of the entire methodology, others might be better served with a partial application. As such, rather than seeing this approach as a rigid framework that must be applied in its entirety or left entirely alone, I would encourage you to see

---

1. See (von Winterfeldt & Edwards, 1986) [p. 3].

it as a series of independent modules, each of which you may decide to use or not use based on your best judgment applied to your specific situation.

## 1.1. UNDER PRESSURE, RETAIN CRITICAL ELEMENTS

Our technique is not well-suited to problems that require a resolution in a matter of seconds, minutes, or even hours, because such problems do not typically give one the luxury of developing two issue maps and the rest of the analysis that we discussed. In fact, even when dealing with nonimmediate problems, you may come under time constraints. And other constraints may apply as well; for instance, you may not have the budget available to conduct the entire analysis as you would wish.

If at all possible, you should resist these time pressures because additional stress seldom promotes effective problem solving. For instance, the 21-day Congressional deadline imposed in 2002 on the analysis of whether Iraq had weapons of mass destruction is believed to have been an important factor in why analysts reached the wrong conclusions.[2]

Rejecting deadlines is seldom an option, however, and meeting them requires us to make some assumptions and "cut corners" in other ways.[3] In these cases, bypassing some steps altogether to concentrate on finding and implementing solutions is a possibility (see Figure 9.1 [c]). But this is risky, because incorrectly framing or diagnosing your problem could lead you to consider inappropriate solutions. Instead, you may prefer to retain all four steps, allocating a shorter time to each as shown in Figure 9.1 (d).

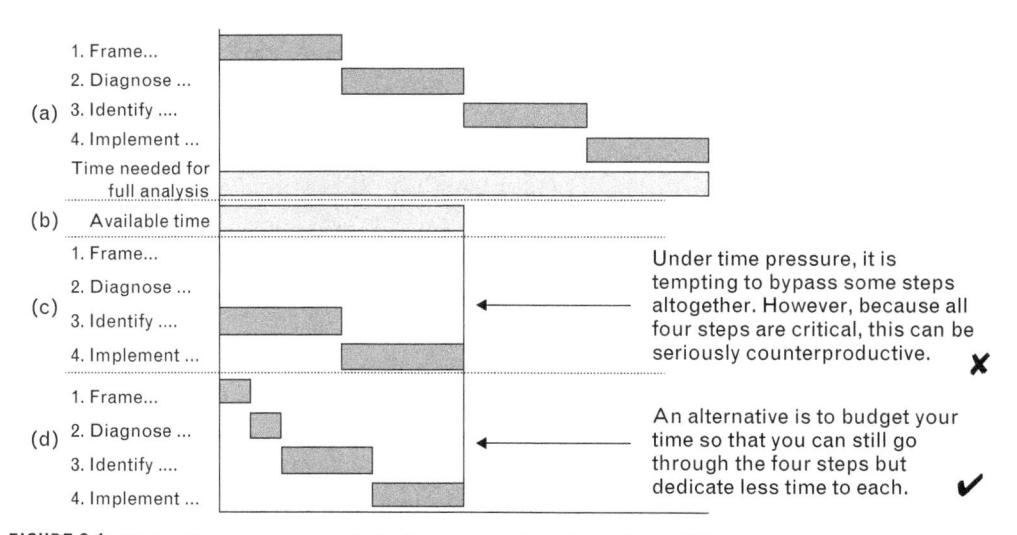

**FIGURE 9.1:** Under time pressure, refrain from bypassing steps, if possible.

2. (George & Bruce, 2008) [p. 180].
3. (Boicu, Tecuci, & Schum, 2008).

230 • STRATEGIC THINKING IN COMPLEX PROBLEM SOLVING

The key is to find the time to accommodate all critical parts of the process by sacrificing the not-critical-but-nice-to-have parts. Basadur proposes that, under time pressure, you consider sacrificing some divergence.[4] This seems sensible: If you remove the framing step altogether, you risk solving the wrong problem. Whatever you do after that will build on a shaky foundation. In contrast, if you retain that framing step and make time for it by cutting the time you allocate to developing your solution map, you may not identify the great solutions that full divergence would provide but, instead, only discover good-enough solutions. This is certainly not ideal, but a good-enough solution to the right problem trumps a great one to the wrong problem.

In some instances where there is not sufficient time to diagnose the problem properly and where time is extremely short, pilots are encouraged to resort to *procedural management*, whereby they treat the situation as an emergency and manage it without clearly defining the problem.[5] A successful application of the technique is Captain Sullenberger's landing of USAir 1549 in the Hudson River after losing both engines on take-off after experiencing bird strikes. Sullenberger's initial plan after the impact was to land at Teterboro Airport but, realizing he did not have sufficient altitude, he opted for the water landing instead.[6]

## 1.2. JUMP BACK AND FORTH BETWEEN STEPS IF NEEDED

Although the problem-solving process we introduced is sequential, it might be useful to think of it as a collection of spaces rather than formal steps given that, on some projects, it is necessary to move back and forth.[7] Indeed, complex, ill-defined, nonimmediate problems (CIDNI) usually are so messy that, despite your best efforts, you may not fully understand the problem well into the diagnosis or the search for solutions. Borrowing from Rittel and Webber's description of wicked problems, "problem understanding and problem resolution are concomitant to each other."[8] Uncovering evidence may trigger you to revise your thinking, thereby warranting iterating between steps. This is another characteristic shared with decision problems where the process is recursive in nature and analysts are warned that not iterating among steps might be an indication of looking at the problem too superficially.[9]

Note that revising your thinking in light of new evidence is challenging, because you have to let go of previous progress, which appears to be wasteful.[10]

---

4. See (Basadur, 1995) [p.66] for a discussion.

5. (Orasanu, 2010) [pp. 156–157].

6. See (Hersman, Hart, & Sumwalt, 2010).

7. Speaking of spaces rather than steps is common in design thinking; see, for instance, (Brown, 2008), (Brown & Wyatt, 2010).

8. (Rittel & Webber, 1973).

9. (von Winterfeldt & Edwards, 1986) [p. 27].

10. This is the sunk cost fallacy. See Chapter 2, (Arkes & Blumer, 1985), (Arkes & Ayton, 1999).

## 1.3. DECIDE WHETHER TO SHARE YOUR MAPS

Involving stakeholders in the resolution process can promote success because providing people with a sense of ownership over an idea is linked to enhancing the commitment and effort they devote to the success of the idea.[11] So involving stakeholders early and often is beneficial not just as a source of additional ideas but also as a way to facilitate their implementation.

To involve stakeholders, you may choose to expose them to your issue map(s) or you may not. In my experience, the best approach depends primarily on the personality of the stakeholder and the ability of your map to foster a constructive conversation with that person. Certain people will feel overwhelmed by an issue map and see this tool as one that does not resonate with them, while others will get caught in the game of divergent thinking that a map can promote. So if there is a guideline here, it is not so much whether you should expose your stakeholders to your maps as a matter of standard practice, but, rather, that you remain sufficiently observant to identify whether exposure would be productive in your particular instance.

# 2. MANAGE YOURSELF

Good leaders know their strengths and limitations and identify ways to compensate the latter.[12] You need to understand yourself, your expertise, *and* your limitations. This section provides guidelines on what skills you should develop and ideas to help you develop them.

## 2.1. DEVELOP THE RIGHT SKILL SET AND ATTITUDE

**Beware of natural tendencies with a negative impact.** Negotiation specialist Leigh Thompson identifies four traits that limit our abilities to negotiate effectively that also may limit our ability to think strategically.[13] In previous chapters, we already have covered the first three: *being overconfident* (see Chapters 1, 3, 8), *falling prey to confirmation bias* (Chapters 3, 4), and *satisficing* (Chapter 3). Thompson's fourth trait, *suffering from self-reinforcing incompetence,* prevents us from experimenting with new courses of action because of the risks associated with experimentation.

Aside from keeping in check these negative tendencies, from which we all seem to suffer, you may want to actively develop beneficial skills.

**Hone your designer skills.** Engineer Clive Dym and his colleagues note that good designers share key skills, including tolerating ambiguity; keeping the big picture in sight;

---

11. For example, (Baer & Brown, 2012), (Avey, Avolio, Crossley, & Luthans, 2009) and Chapter 2.
12. (Toegel & Barsoux, 2012).
13. (L. L. Thompson, 2012) [pp. 6–7]

handling uncertainty; making decisions; being a good team member; and thinking and communicating effectively.[14] Good design skills also require mixing rational and emotional approaches.

**Hone your researcher skills.** As we discussed in Chapter 1, the UK Research Councils has identified a number of skills that aspiring researchers should develop (see Table 1.2), all of which are traits of an effective problem solver.[15]

**Embrace failing, if appropriate. Part 1: Ensure the cost of failure is manageable.** In some settings, failure is not an option, which rules out a trial-and-error approach. For instance, think about the Project Gemini and the Apollo Program, which consisted of building on successes in progressively more complex missions—first, go into earth orbit, then dock, then go to lunar orbit, etc., as opposed to aiming at landing on the moon with their first mission, failing, and trying again. In such unforgiving settings, one has to rely on successes only, a constraint that Cambridge fluid dynamicist Michael Thompson conveys to young researchers: "Like a surgeon, you have to strive to be right all of the time."[16] But in other settings, making failures low-cost occurrences with a high learning potential can be extremely beneficial. For instance, a low cost of failure is sometimes credited to be a key enabler of Silicon Valley's entrepreneurial success.[17]

**Embrace failing, if appropriate. Part 2: Ensure failing provides a valuable learning opportunity.** So, although failing can be desirable, it must be in a setting where failures are learning opportunities. Organizational theorist Russell Ackoff separates *errors of commission* (doing something that you should not have done) from *errors of omission* (failing to do something you should have done). He notes that the latter usually have the bigger impact and yet typical accounting only catches the former. He also suggests that managers should reward the best mistakes in their organizations, "best" defined as the ones that generated the highest level of learning.[18] Making mistakes is an inherent part of learning something new and, as such, it should be encouraged, so long as you learn from your mistakes.

**Keep a learning mentality.** Carol Dweck, a development psychologist at Stanford, has looked extensively at people's mindsets and has come to realize that an ability can be seen in one of two ways: In the first outlook, an ability is fixed and must be proven. In the second, it is developable through learning. If one adopts the learning philosophy, failure is not about making mistakes or being fired from a job. It is about not growing, not fulfilling one's potential.[19] To adopt a learning mentality requires being able to admit one's weaknesses and shortcomings, which takes courage and integrity as well as a safe environment. Given this, establishing such a culture and environment is an essential part of NASA's debriefing process.[20]

---

14. (Dym, Agogino, Eris, Frey, & Leifer, 2005).
15. (Research Councils UK, 2001). For additional skills, see also (Siddique et al., 2012).
16. (J. M. T. Thompson, 2013).
17. See (Seelig, 2009) [pp. 71–98].
18. (Ackoff, 2006).
19. (Dweck, 2006) [pp. 15–16].
20. (Rogers, 2010) [p. 311].

**Keep a soft focus.** Psychologist Barbara Spellman notes that having a question in mind is necessary to be able to process a large mass of information. But she also points out that being too focused on one question may induce people to miss information that is right in front of them.[21] (Recall the gorilla of Chapter 6.) So, if at all possible, you should keep some bandwidth to retain some situational awareness and to pursue targets of opportunity that may appear during your resolution process (see section on serendipitous findings in Chapter 4).

**Trust carefully.** If done well, deception is likely difficult to detect.[22] People can barely discriminate lies from truths. In fact, a meta-analysis concluded that we are only slightly better at detecting deception than what we could achieve by flipping a coin (54%).[23]

Deception detection seems to improve significantly, in specific conditions, when assisted by technology, such as a polygraph.[24] New technology, such as the Preliminary Credibility Assessment Screening System, that rely on sensors to measure the electrical conductivity of the skin and changes in blood-flow also seem to provide improved results.[25]

If you do not have access to these types of technologies, however, the outlook is not very promising. Indeed, research indicates that training or prior experience do not improve one's ability to detect deception.[26]

Spellman notes that detecting deception starts with having the motivation to look for patterns of deception in a source or having the belief that such patterns may exist.[27] Also, it appears that there are cues to deception. In a study, social psychologist DePaulo and her colleagues found that liars seem less forthcoming, tell less compelling tales, make a more negative impression, and are tenser than truth tellers.[28] They warn, however, that the association of such cues with deceit is only probabilistic and, therefore, additional evidence is needed. In this context, practical guidelines are limited. So you may be best served following the Russian saying: trust, but verify.

## 2.2. BECOME WISER

If we think of wisdom as an ability to judiciously balance opposites, then being wise goes a considerable way toward making you an effective problem solver. Indeed, balancing opposites permeates all aspects of the problem-solving process: One has to balance thinking creatively with thinking critically; acting with humility with showing decisiveness; being

---

21. See (National Research Council, 2011b) [pp. 128–129]. See also (Pfeffer & Sutton, 2006) [p. 149–150].

22. For example, (Jung & Reidenberg, 2007), (Simmons, Nides, Rand, Wise, & Tashkin, 2000). For a review, see (Williams, 2012).

23. (Bond & DePaulo, 2006).

24. (National Research Council Committee on National Statistics, 2003) [p. 4].

25. See (Senter, Waller, & Krapohl, 2006), (National Research Council, 2010) [pp. 13–16].

26. (Meissner & Kassin, 2002), (Garrido, Masip, & Herrero, 2004).

27. (Fischhoff & Chauvin, 2011) [pp. 126–127].

28. (DePaulo et al., 2003). A widely held stereotype of the behavior of liars, gaze aversion, bears negligible relationships to lying (Global Deception Research Team, 2006).

analytical with following one's intuition;[29] speaking up—even when not in a position of authority—and letting go;[30] and so on.[31]

**Adapt as you go.** It may be useful to think of solving CIDNI problems as a project in itself; and, in project management, things go wrong.[32] When they do, you need to judiciously balance your original plans with your reaction to the new set of circumstances.

**Balance humility and decisiveness.** Using a Platonic definition of wisdom—knowing what you know and knowing what you do not know—management professors Pfeffer and Sutton advise that people should adopt beliefs that enable them "to keep acting with knowledge while doubting what they know, and to openly acknowledge the imperfections in even their best ideas along the way."[33] They further note that knowing what you know and knowing what you do not know "enables people to act on their (present) knowledge while doubting what they know, so they can do things *now*, but can keep learning along the way."[34] Michael Thompson agrees, observing that "knowing what you *do not know* is perhaps even more important than knowing what you do know" (italics his).[35]

Balancing self confidence and insecurity can be particularly challenging because, as Cornell psychologists Justin Kruger and David Dunning observed, people with limited knowledge in a specific domain not only reach erroneous conclusions, but their incompetence prevents them from realizing it.[36]

**Seek feedback.** Similar to intelligence analysis, complex problem solving is an exercise in judgment under uncertainty, a task where we face many shortcomings.[37] In particular, we easily experience higher confidence than evidence warrants. One debiasing technique to reduce overconfidence is to question why we may be particularly confident in an outcome.[38] Another technique is the timely use of high-quality feedback, which can help us better calibrate our judgments.[39] Therefore, you should seek feedback often.

**Use your intuition judiciously.** Although this book has focused primarily on the rational side of problem solving, intuition and instincts are an integral part of the process. Indeed, they help in deciding, for instance, which hypotheses to test first, which aspects of your analysis to push further, or which style of communication will be most effective for a given audience.

---

29. Or risk one of two ailments, "paralysis by analysis" and "extinction by instinct"; see (Langley, 1995). See also (Makridakis & Gaba, 1998) [p. 21].

30. For an example in airline crews, see (Ginnett, 2010) [pp. 98–99].

31. Management professors Bazerman and Moore introduce another definition of wisdom as the ability to recognize that we (you!) are biased and to account for it (Bazerman & Moore, 2008) [p. 180].

32. (Frame, 2003) [p. 17].

33. (Pfeffer & Sutton, 2006) [pp. 52–53].

34. (Pfeffer & Sutton, 2006) [p. 103].

35. (J. M. T. Thompson, 2013).

36. This is called the Dunning-Kruger effect; see (Kruger & Dunning, 1999).

37. (Kahneman, Slovic, & Tversky, 1982).

38. (L. L. Thompson, 2012) [pp. 199–200].

39. (Arkes, 2001), (National Research Council, 2011a) [p. 25], (National Research Council, 2011b) [p. 150].

Zoologist and Nobel laureate Peter Medawar advises young researchers to see science as imaginative guesswork that "involves the exercise of common sense supported by a strong understanding."[40] British mathematician John Littlewood notes that "most of the best work starts in hopeless muddle and floundering, sustained on the 'smell' that something is there."[41] Following your intuition and being impartially analytical are both necessary conditions for success. Neither one can compensate for the other, and over-reliance on either one can be detrimental. So, rather than attempting to ignore your intuition and instincts, it seems that the better approach is to use them, albeit reflectively.[42] As my mentor and good friend, Pol Spanos, says: "intuition is a great servant but a terrible master."

**Learn to operate with less-than-ideal evidence.** We have advocated for an evidence-based approach. As discussed in Chapter 6, at least in medicine, the highest-quality evidence is that derived from randomized trials. In some settings, however, such evidence is not available nor is it necessary. This was illustrated in an article published in the 2003 Christmas issue of the *British Medical Journal*—which features spoofs. Gordon Smith and Jill Pell, the authors, looked at the effectiveness of parachutes in preventing death or major trauma on people jumping out of airplanes. Noting that the effectiveness of parachutes had not been subject to rigorous evaluation by using randomized controlled trials, they concluded that, "everyone might benefit if the most radical protagonists of evidence-based medicine organized and participated in a double blind, randomized, placebo-controlled, crossover trial of the parachute."[43] In such a study, two groups would be formed at random. Participants in one group would receive parachutes and, since it would be placebo-controlled, participants in the other group would receive backpacks (control group). Neither the participants nor the organizers would know which group is which (double blind). The "crossover" part means that, after some time, participants would switch groups. That is, no matter how they were randomly assigned initially, participants at one point or another would be assigned to the control group, jumping out of an airplane without a parachute. The article makes a good point that using only highest-quality evidence is not always possible. Sometimes, observations from less rigorous analyses are sufficient. Here, as at many other points in the resolution process, you must judiciously balance the peculiarities of your situation with quality standards to decide what makes sense *for the case at hand*.

## 2.3. PRACTICE

In many instances, the only difference between the stellar and the good is the hours of practice.[44] Many ideas in this book look simple. But the process of applying these ideas and getting to the answers is not. It is like tennis: experienced players may make it look easy,

---

40. (Medawar, 1979) [p. 93].
41. (McIntyre, 1997).
42. See also (Greenhalgh, 2002) and (Sheppard, Macatangay, Colby, & Sullivan, 2009) [pp. 36–37].
43. (Smith & Pell, 2003).
44. See (Ness, 2012) [p. 7].

but you cannot become a good player just by reading about it. You have to practice.[45] Since Simon and Chase's 1973 paper about chess ("How does one become a master in the first place? The answer is *practice*—thousands of hours of practice."),[46] the value of deliberate practice in acquiring expertise has been established in a number of activities, including music[47] and sports.[48] It stands to reason that developing expertise in solving complex problems is no different.

**Develop resilience.** Practicing means that you will face some setbacks, some of which you will be able to avoid and some that will be outside of your influence. These setbacks are not as important as how you confront them. Positively adjusting to adversity—that is, having *resilience*—is therefore critical. The good news is that you can increase your resilience, for instance, by promoting positive emotions (through demonstrating optimism and appreciating and using humor), increasing your cognitive flexibility, having spirituality, developing strong social supports, and developing an active coping style (including exercising).[49]

## 3. WHAT ABOUT HARRY?

Harry is not my friend John's dog. It is my dog. Apart from that and changing his name, his story is entirely true. He went missing one Wednesday afternoon while I was teaching, and initially my wife Justyna and I were pretty confident that the housekeeper had, if not kidnapped him, at least opened the gate for him to escape. After all, what is the probability that the dog should go missing—when he had not for a long time—on the very day that we fired our unstable and threatening housekeeper?

So, in my mind, kidnapping it was, and I was torn between calling the police and calling the housekeeper. Needless to say, if I had chosen the latter, I would have used a few French expletives. But luckily, we—and by "we" I mean Justyna—decided to first ask the neighbors if they had seen anything. When one of them told us that he had seen Harry by himself in front of the house after the yard crew had been there, my entire outlook changed.

The picture still was not clear: Because Harry barks loudly when the yard crew comes, because he was seen in front of the house after they had arrived, and yet the crew reported not having seen or heard him that day, something did not add up. Maybe the neighbor was mistaken (or lied) or maybe the crew had realized that they had screwed up and tried to cover it up. We decided to trust our neighbor's testimony, which turned out to be the right call, and went to look for Harry as a missing dog and found him in less than an hour. All that without insulting the housekeeper.

---

45. (Polya, 1945) [p. 4]. For the superiority of experience-based training over didactic lecturing in acquiring negotiation skills, see (L. L. Thompson, 2012) [p. 185].
46. (Simon & Chase, 1973).
47. (Ericsson, Krampe, & Tesch-Römer, 1993).
48. See (Baker & Côté, 2003), (Ericsson, 2004) for reviews.
49. (Southwick, Vythilingam, & Charney, 2005). See also (Jackson, Firtko, & Edenborough, 2007).

I would be lying if I reported that while looking for Harry I wrote a *what* card, a *why* card, and a *how* card; developed a diagnostic issue map and a solution map; looked for peer-reviewed evidence on the likelihood of various causes for the disappearance of pets; used a multiattribute utility decision tool; and captured my conclusions in a carefully crafted message that I delivered to Justyna to convince her that Harry probably had not been kidnapped and that we should look for him as such. Indeed, as we touched on in Chapter 1, Harry going missing is one of those types of problems where one does not need to apply the full methodology. I did, however, run through these steps mentally, and I credit this mental process for helping me switch from a intuitive/System 1 thinking mode (call the housekeeper to accuse her and, since I am being honest, most likely insult her, too) to a reflective/System 2 mode. So, not only did the methodology help us find our dog faster, it also saved me the embarrassment of having to apologize to that poor housekeeper.

As for the yard crew, we gave them the benefit of the doubt, and we left it at that.

Then, a few weeks later, Harry disappeared again. We had not fired our housekeeper that day, but the disappearance again happened on the day of the week that the lawn crew had come. It took us only a superficial Bayesian analysis to decide that this was no coincidence. So we had a conversation with the crew. To their credit, Harry has not gone missing since.

Well, not because of them, that is.

# NOTES

**Too much of a good thing?** Some argue that even an excess of excellence is not desirable because it can undermine success (Coman & Ronen, 2009).

# REFERENCES

CHAPTER 1

Adams, J. L. (2001). *Conceptual blockbusting: A guide to better ideas*. Cambridge, MA: Basic Books.

Allen, D. G., Bryant, P. C., & Vardaman, J. M. (2010). Retaining talent: Replacing misconceptions with evidence-based strategies. *The Academy of Management Perspectives, 24*(2), 48–64.

Arkes, H. R., & Kajdasz, J. (2011). Intuitive theories of behavior. In B. Fischhoff & C. Chauvin (Eds.), *Intelligence analysis: Behavioral and social scientific foundations* (pp. 143–168). Washington, DC: National Academies Press.

Arkes, H. R., Wortmann, R. L., Saville, P. D., & Harkness, A. R. (1981). Hindsight bias among physicians weighing the likelihood of diagnoses. *Journal of Applied Psychology, 66*(2), 252.

Assink, M. (2006). Inhibitors of disruptive innovation capability: a conceptual model. *European Journal of Innovation Management, 9*(2), 215–233.

Bardwell, L. V. (1991). Problem-framing: A perspective on environmental problem-solving. *Environmental Management, 15*(5), 603–612.

Basadur, M. (1995). Optimal ideation-evaluation ratios. *Creativity Research Journal, 8*(1), 63–75.

Basadur, M., Graen, G. B., & Scandura, T. A. (1986). Training effects on attitudes toward divergent thinking among manufacturing engineers. *Journal of Applied Psychology, 71*(4), 612.

Basadur, M., Runco, M. A., & Vega, L. A. (2000). Understanding how creative thinking skills, attitudes and behaviors work together: A causal process model. *The Journal of Creative Behavior, 34*(2), 77–100.

Bassok, M., & Novick, L. R. (2012). Problem solving. In K. J. Holyoak & R. G. Morrison (Eds.), *The Oxford handbook of thinking and reasoning* (pp. 413–432). New York: Oxford University Press.

Bazerman, M. H., & Moore, D. A. (2008). *Judgment in managerial decision making*. Hoboken, NJ: John Wiley & Sons.

Beaufre, A. (1963). *Introduction à la stratégie* (Vol. 6): Centre d'études de politique étrangère.

Blair, C. (2000). *Hitler's U-boat war: The hunters 1939–1942* (Vol. 1). New York: Modern Library.

Brightman, H. J. (1978). Differences in ill-structured problem solving along the organizational hierarchy. *Decision Sciences, 9*(1), 1–18.

Brown, T., & Wyatt, J. (2010). Design thinking for social innovation. *Development Outreach, 12*(1), 29–43.

Careers Research and Advisory Centre. (2010). Researcher Development Statement. Retrieved from https://www.vitae.ac.uk/vitae-publications/rdf-related/researcher-development-statement-rds-vitae.pdf

Chi, M. T., Bassok, M., Lewis, M. W., Reimann, P., & Glaser, R. (1989). Self-explanations: How students study and use examples in learning to solve problems. *Cognitive Science, 13*(2), 145–182.

Dawson, N. V., Connors, A. F., Speroff, T., Kemka, A., Shaw, P., & Arkes, H. R. (1993). Hemodynamic assessment in managing the critically ill: Is physician confidence warranted? *Medical Decision Making, 13*(3), 258–266.

Feynman, R. P. (1997). *Surely you're joking, Mr. Feynman!: Adventures of a curious character*: WW Norton & Company.

Feynman, R. P. (1998). Cargo cult science. *Engineering and Science, 37*(7), 10–13.

Fischhoff, B. (1982). Debiasing. In D. Kahneman, P. Slovic, & A. Tversky (Eds.), *Judgment under uncertainty: Heuristics and biases* (pp. 422–444). New York: Cambridge University Press.

Gauch, H. G. (2003). *Scientific method in practice*. Cambridge, UK: Cambridge University Press.

Gawande, A. (2009). *The Checklist Manifesto*. New York: Picador.

Golec, L. (2009). The art of inconsistency: Evidence-based practice my way. *Journal of Perinatology, 29*(9), 600–602.

Graetz, F. (2002). Strategic thinking versus strategic planning: towards understanding the complementarities. *Management Decision, 40*(5), 456–462.

Grasso, D., & Burkins, M. B. (2010). Beyond technology: The holistic advantage. In D. Grasso & M. B. Burkins (Eds.), *Holistic engineering education* (pp. 1–10). New York: Springer.

Grint, K. (2005). Problems, problems, problems: The social construction of "leadership." *Human Relations, 58*(11), 1467–1494.

Grol, R. (2001). Successes and failures in the implementation of evidence-based guidelines for clinical practice. *Medical Care, 39*(8), II-46–II-54.

Hammond, J. S., Keeney, R. L., & Raiffa, H. (2002). *Smart choices: A practical guide to making better decisions*. New York: Random House.

Hayes, J. R. (1989). *The complete problem solver* (2nd ed.). New York: Routledge.

Heracleous, L. (1998). Strategic thinking or strategic planning? *Long Range Planning, 31*(3), 481–487.

Heyland, D. K., Dhaliwal, R., Day, A., Jain, M., & Drover, J. (2004). Validation of the Canadian clinical practice guidelines for nutrition support in mechanically ventilated, critically ill adult patients: Results of a prospective observational study.* *Critical Care Medicine, 32*(11), 2260–2266.

Holley, S. (1997). Handsome Dan takes a bite out of Yale history. *Yale Herald*, (23), Summer.

Holyoak, K. J. (2012). Analogy and relational reasoning. In K. J. Holyoak & R. G. Morrison (Eds.), *The Oxford handbook of thinking and reasoning* (pp. 234–259). New York: Oxford University Press.

Holyoak, K. J., & Koh, K. (1987). Surface and structural similarity in analogical transfer. *Memory & Cognition, 15*(4), 332–340.

Jonassen, D. H. (1997). Instructional design models for well-structured and ill-structured problem-solving learning outcomes. *Educational Technology Research and Development, 45*(1), 65–94.

Jonassen, D. H. (2000). Toward a design theory of problem solving. *Educational Technology Research and Development, 48*(4), 63–85.

Jonassen, D. H. (2011). *Learning to solve problems: A handbook for designing problem-solving learning environments*. New York: Routledge

Kahneman, D. (2011). *Thinking, fast and slow*. New York: Farrar, Straus and Giroux.

Karvonen, K. (2000). *The beauty of simplicity*. Paper presented at the 2000 conference on Universal Usability.

Katzenbach, J. R. (1993). *The wisdom of teams: Creating the high-performance organization*. New York: HarperCollins.

Klayman, J., & Ha, Y.-W. (1987). Confirmation, disconfirmation, and information in hypothesis testing. *Psychological Review, 94*(2), 211.

Klayman, J., & Ha, Y.-w. (1989). Hypothesis testing in rule discovery: Strategy, structure, and content. *Journal of Experimental Psychology: Learning, Memory, and Cognition, 15*(4), 596.

Kotovsky, K. (2003). Problem solving—Large/small, hard/easy, conscious/nonconscious, problem-space/problem-solver—The issue of dichotomization. In J. E. Davidson & R. J. Sternberg (Eds.), *The psychology of problem solving* (pp. 373–383), Cambridge, UK: Cambridge University Press.

Kulkarni, D., & Simon, H. A. (1988). The processes of scientific discovery: The strategy of experimentation. *Cognitive Science, 12*(2), 139–175.

Leach, B. (2013, January 13). Dognappings: organised gangs behind a surge of dog thefts across the country. *The Telegraph*. Retrieved from http://www.telegraph.co.uk/lifestyle/pets/9797749/Dognappings-organised-gangs-behind-a-surge-of-dog-thefts-across-the-country.html.

Leung, O., & Bartunek, J. M. (2012). Enabling evidence-based management: Bridging the gap between academics and practitioners. In D. M. Rousseau (Ed.), *The Oxford handbook of evidence-based management* (pp. 165–180). New York: Oxford University Press.

Liedtka, J. M. (1998). Strategic thinking: Can it be taught? *Long Range Planning, 31*(1), 120–129.

Makridakis, S., & Gaba, A. (1998). *Judgment: its role and value for strategy*. Fontainebleau, France: INSEAD.

Manathunga, C., Lant, P., & Mellick, G. (2006). Imagining an interdisciplinary doctoral pedagogy. *Teaching in Higher Education, 11*(3), 365–379.

Manathunga, C., Lant, P., & Mellick, G. (2007). Developing professional researchers: research students' graduate attributes. *Studies in Continuing Education, 29*(1), 19–36.

Mason, R. O., & Mitroff, I. I. (1981). *Challenging strategic planning assumptions: Theory, cases, and techniques*. New York: Wiley.

McIntyre, M. E. (1998). Lucidity and science III: Hypercredulity, quantum mechanics, and scientific truth. *Interdisciplinary Science Reviews, 23*(1), 29–70.

Mintzberg, H. (1994). The fall and rise of strategic planning. *Harvard Business Review, 72*(1), 107–114.

National Association of Colleges and Employers. (2014). The job outlook for the class of 2014.

National Research Council. (2011a). *Intelligence analysis for tomorrow: Advances from the behavioral and social sciences*. Washington, DC: National Academies Press.

National Research Council. (2011b). *Intelligence analysis: Behavioral and social scientific foundations*. Washington, DC: National Academies Press.

National Research Council. (2012). *Discipline-based education research: Understanding and improving learning in undergraduate science and engineering*. Washington, DC: National Academies Press.

National Research Council. (2014). *Convergence: Facilitating transdisciplinary integration of life sciences, physical sciences, engineering, and beyond*. Washington, DC: National Academies Press.

Ness, R. B. (2012). Tools for innovative thinking in epidemiology. *American Journal of Epidemiology, 175*(8), 733–738.

Nickerson, R. S. (1998). Confirmation bias: A ubiquitous phenomenon in many guises. *Review of General Psychology, 2*(2), 175.

Perkins, D. N., & Salomon, G. (1989). Are cognitive skills context-bound? *Educational Researcher, 18*(1), 16–25.

Pfeffer, J., & Sutton, R. I. (2006a). Evidence-based management. *Harvard Business Review, 84*(1), 62.

Pfeffer, J., & Sutton, R. I. (2006b). *Hard facts, dangerous half-truths, and total nonsense: Profiting from evidence-based management*: Harvard Business Press.

Pfeffer, J., & Sutton, R. I. (2007). Suppose we took evidence-based management seriously: Implications for reading and writing management. *Academy of Management Learning & Education, 6*(1), 153–155.

Pretz, J. E., Naples, A. J., & Sternberg, R. J. (2003). Recognizing, defining, and representing problems. In J. E. Davidson & R. J. Sternberg (Eds.), *The psychology of problem solving* (pp. 3–30). New York: Cambridge University Press.

Rauen, C. A., Chulay, M., Bridges, E., Vollman, K. M., & Arbour, R. (2008). Seven evidence-based practice habits: Putting some sacred cows out to pasture. *Critical Care Nurse, 28*(2), 98–123.

Reeves, J., Denicolo, P., Metcalfe, J., & Roberts, J. (2012). The vitae researcher development framework and researcher development statement: Methodology and validation report. *Cambridge: The Careers Research and Advisory Centre (CRAC) Ltd.* Retrieved from https://www.vitae.ac.uk/vitae-publications/rdf-related/researcher-development-framework-rdf-vitae-methodology-report-2012.pdf.

Reiter-Palmon, R., & Illies, J. J. (2004). Leadership and creativity: Understanding leadership from a creative problem-solving perspective. *The Leadership Quarterly, 15*(1), 55–77.

Research Councils UK. (2001). *Joint statement of the Research Councils'/AHRB's skills training requirements for research students.* London: Research Councils UK.

Rittel, H. W. (1972). *On the planning crisis: Systems analysis of the "first and second generations."* Institute of Urban and Regional Development.

Rousseau, D. M. (2006). Is there such a thing as "evidence-based management?" *Academy of Management Review, 31*(2), 256–269.

Rousseau, D. M. (2012). *The Oxford handbook of evidence-based management.* New York: Oxford University Press.

Rousseau, D. M., & McCarthy, S. (2007). Educating managers from an evidence-based perspective. *Academy of Management Learning & Education, 6*(1), 84–101.

Sackett, D. L., Rosenberg, W. M., Gray, J. A., Haynes, R. B., & Richardson, W. S. (1996). Evidence based medicine: What it is and what it isn't. *BMJ: British Medical Journal, 312*(7023), 71.

Sanbonmatsu, D. M., Posavac, S. S., Kardes, F. R., & Mantel, S. P. (1998). Selective hypothesis testing. *Psychonomic Bulletin & Review, 5*(2), 197–220.

Savransky, S. D. (2002). *Engineering of creativity: Introduction to TRIZ methodology of inventive problem solving.* Boca Raton, FL: CRC Press.

Sheldon, T. A., Cullum, N., Dawson, D., Lankshear, A., Lowson, K., Watt, I., . . . Wright, J. (2004). What's the evidence that NICE guidance has been implemented? Results from a national evaluation using time series analysis, audit of patients' notes, and interviews. *BMJ, 329*(7473), 999.

Sheppard, S., Macatangay, K., Colby, A., & Sullivan, W. M. (2009). *Educating engineers: Designing for the future of the field.* San Francisco, CA: Jossey-Bass.

Silver, N. (2012). *The signal and the noise: Why so many predictions fail—but some don't.* New York: Penguin.

Simon, H. A. (1974). The structure of ill structured problems. *Artificial Intelligence, 4*(3), 181–201.

Smith, G. F. (1988). Towards a heuristic theory of problem structuring. *Management Science, 34*(12), 1489–1506.

Smith, M. U. (1991). A view from biology. In M. U. Smith (Ed.), *Toward a unified theory of problem solving: Views from the content domains* (pp. 1–21). New York: Routledge.

Smith, S. M., & Ward, T. B. (2012). Cognition and the creation of ideas. In K. J. Holyoak & R. G. Morrison (Eds.), *Oxford handbook of thinking and reasoning* (pp. 456–474). New York: Oxford University Press.

Straus, S. E., Glasziou, P., Richardson, W. S., & Haynes, R. B. (2011). *Evidence-based medicine: How to practice and teach it* (4th ed.). Toronto, Canada: Elsevier.

Straus, S. E., & Jones, G. (2004). What has evidence based medicine done for us? *BMJ, 329*(7473), 987–988.

Strobel, J., & van Barneveld, A. (2009). When is PBL more effective? A meta-synthesis of meta-analyses comparing PBL to conventional classrooms. *Interdisciplinary Journal of Problem-based Learning, 3*(1), 4.

Tetlock, P. (2005). *Expert political judgment: How good is it? How can we know?* Princeton University Press.

Theocharis, T., & Psimopoulos, M. (1987). Where science has gone wrong. *Nature, 329*(6140), 595–598.

Thomke, S., & Feinberg, B. (2009). Design thinking and innovation at Apple. *Harvard Business School*, 1–12.

Tversky, A., & Kahneman, D. (1981). The framing of decisions and the psychology of choice. *Science*, 211(4481), 453–458.

Twardy, C. (2010). Argument maps improve critical thinking. *Teaching Philosophy*, 27(2), 95–116.

United Nations. Millennium Development Goals. Retrieved May 9, 2013 from http://www.un.org/millenniumgoals/

VanGundy, A. B. (1988). *Techniques of structured problem solving*. New York: Van Nostrand Reinhold.

Weiner, J. (2014, September, 26). The STEM paradoxes: Graduates' lack of non-technical skills, and not enough women. *The Washington Post*.

Welch, H. G. (2015). *Less medicine more health: 7 assumptions that drive too much medical care*. Boston, MA: Beacon Press.

Wenke, D., & Frensch, P. A. (2003). Is success or failure at solving complex problems related to intellectual ability? In J. E. Davidson & R. J. Sternberg (Eds.), *The psychology of problem solving* (pp. 87–126). New York: Cambridge University Press.

Woods, D. R. (2000). An Evidence-Based Strategy for Problem Solving. *Journal of Engineering Education*, 89(4), 443–459.

Wuchty, S., Jones, B. F., & Uzzi, B. (2007). The increasing dominance of teams in production of knowledge. *Science*, 316(5827), 1036–1039.

## CHAPTER 2

Adams, J. L. (2001). *Conceptual blockbusting: A guide to better ideas*. Cambridge, MA: Basic Books.

Arkes, H. R., & Ayton, P. (1999). The sunk cost and Concorde effects: are humans less rational than lower animals? *Psychological Bulletin*, 125(5), 591.

Arkes, H. R., & Blumer, C. (1985). The psychology of sunk cost. *Organizational Behavior and Human Decision Processes*, 35(1), 124–140.

Austhink. (2006). Argument Mapping Tutorials. Retrieved January 14, 2014, from http://austhink.com/reason/tutorials/

Bardwell, L. V. (1991). Problem-framing: A perspective on environmental problem-solving. *Environmental Management*, 15(5), 603–612.

Bassok, M., & Novick, L. R. (2012). Problem solving. In K. J. Holyoak & R. G. Morrison (Eds.), *The Oxford handbook of thinking and reasoning* (pp. 413–432). New York: Oxford University Press.

Berger, W. (2010). *CAD Monkeys, Dinosaur Babies, and T-Shaped People: Inside the World of Design Thinking and How It Can Spark Creativity and Innovation*. New York: Penguin.

Brownell, K. D., Farley, T., Willett, W. C., Popkin, B. M., Chaloupka, F. J., Thompson, J. W., & Ludwig, D. S. (2009). The public health and economic benefits of taxing sugar-sweetened beverages. *New England Journal of Medicine*, 361(16), 1599–1605.

Burke, W. W. (2014). *Organization change: Theory and practice* (4th ed.). Thousand Oaks: CA. Sage.

Conklin, J. (2005). *Dialogue mapping: Building shared understanding of wicked problems*. Chichester, UK: John Wiley & Sons.

Cousins, R. D. (1995). Why isn't every physicist a Bayesian? *American Journal of Physics*, 63(5), 398–410.

Davis, I., Keeling, D., Schreier, P., & Williams, A. (2007). The McKinsey approach to problem solving. *McKinsey Staff Paper* (66), 27.

de La Fontaine, J. (1882). *The Fables of La Fontaine* (E. Wright & J. Gibbs, Trans.). Project Gutenberg's The Fables of La Fontaine.

DeHaan, R. L. (2011). Teaching creative science thinking. *Science*, 334(6062), 1499–1500.

Dougherty, D., & Heller, T. (1994). The illegitimacy of successful product innovation in established firms. *Organization Science, 5*(2), 200–218.

Efron, B. (1986). Why isn't everyone a Bayesian? *The American Statistician, 40*(1), 1–5.

Eisner, H. (2002). *Essentials of project and systems engineering management* (2nd ed.): New York: John Wiley & Sons.

Eliasson, J. (2009). A cost–benefit analysis of the Stockholm congestion charging system. *Transportation Research Part A: Policy and Practice, 43*(4), 468–480.

Eliasson, J., Hultkrantz, L., Nerhagen, L., & Rosqvist, L. S. (2009). The Stockholm congestion–charging trial 2006: Overview of effects. *Transportation Research Part A: Policy and Practice, 43*(3), 240–250.

Evans, J. S. B. (2012). Dual-process theories of deductive reasoning: facts and fallacies. In K. J. Holyoak & R. G. Morrison (Eds.), *The Oxford handbook of thinking and reasoning* (pp. 115). New York: Oxford University Press.

Frame, J. D. (2003). *Managing projects in organizations: how to make the best use of time, techniques, and people.* San Francisco, CA: John Wiley & Sons.

Gawande, A. (2009). *The Checklist Manifesto.* New York: Picador.

Gershon, N., & Page, W. (2001). What storytelling can do for information visualization. *Communications of the ACM, 44*(8), 31–37.

Glöckner, A., & Witteman, C. (2010). Beyond dual-process models: A categorisation of processes underlying intuitive judgement and decision making. *Thinking & Reasoning, 16*(1), 1–25.

Grasso, D., & Martinelli, D. (2010). Holistic engineering. In D. Grasso & M. Brown Burkins (Eds.), *Holistic engineering education* (pp. 11–15). New York: Springer.

Hammond, J. S., Keeney, R. L., & Raiffa, H. (2002). *Smart choices: A practical guide to making better decisions.* New York: Random House.

Heuer, R. J., & Pherson, R. H. (2011). *Structured analytic techniques for intelligence analysis.* Washington, DC: CQ Press.

Institute of Medicine. (2014). *The current state of obesity solutions in the United States: Workshop summary.* Washington, DC: The National Academies Press.

Jonassen, D. H. (2000). Toward a design theory of problem solving. *Educational Technology Research and Development, 48*(4), 63–85.

Kahneman, D. (2002). Maps of bounded rationality: A perspective on intuitive judgment and choice. *Nobel Prize Lecture, 8*, 351–401.

Kahneman, D. (2003). Maps of bounded rationality: Psychology for behavioral economics. *The American Economic Review, 93*(5), 1449–1475.

Kahneman, D. (2011). *Thinking, fast and slow.* New York: Farrar, Straus and Giroux.

Kahneman, D., & Frederick, S. (2002). Representativeness revisited: Attribute substitution in intuitive judgment. In T. Gilovich, D. Griffin, & D. Kahneman (Eds.), *Heuristics and biases: The psychology of intuitive judgment* (pp. 49–81). New York: Cambridge University Press.

Kahneman, D., & Klein, G. (2009). Conditions for intuitive expertise: a failure to disagree. *American Psychologist, 64*(6), 515.

Kahneman, D., Lovallo, D., & Sibony, O. (2011). Before you make that big decision. *Harvard Business Review, 89*(6), 50–60.

Kaplan, E. H. (2011). Operations research and intelligence analysis. In B. Fischhoff & C. Chauvin (Eds.), *Intelligence analysis: Behavioral and social scientific foundations* (pp. 31–56). Washington, DC: National Academies Press.

Kerzner, H. R. (2003). *Project management: A systems approach to planning, scheduling, and controlling* (8th ed.). Hoboken, NJ: John Wiley & Sons.

Levin, I. P., Schneider, S. L., & Gaeth, G. J. (1998). All frames are not created equal: A typology and critical analysis of framing effects. *Organizational Behavior and Human Decision Processes, 76*(2), 149–188.

MacDonald, N., & Picard, A. (2009). A plea for clear language on vaccine safety. *Canadian Medical Association Journal, 180*(7), 697–698.

Mackendrick, A. (2004). *On film-making: An introduction to the craft of the director.* New York: Faber and Faber, Inc.

Markman, A. B., Wood, K. L., Linsey, J. S., Murphy, J. T., & Laux, J. P. (2009). Supporting innovation by promoting analogical reasoning. In A. B. Markman & K. L. Wood (Eds.), *Tools for innovation: The science behind the practical methods that drive new ideas* (pp. 85–103). New York: Oxford University Press.

McKee, R. (1997). *Story: Substance, structure, style, and the principles of screenwriting.* New York: HarperCollins.

McKee, R., & Fryer, B. (2003). Storytelling that moves people. *Harvard Business Review, 81*(6), 51–55.

Minto, B. (2009). *The pyramid principle: Logic in writing and thinking.* Harlow, UK: Pearson Education.

Moulton, C.-a., Regehr, G., Lingard, L., Merritt, C., & MacRae, H. (2010). 'Slowing down when you should': Initiators and influences of the transition from the routine to the effortful. *Journal of Gastrointestinal Surgery, 14*(6), 1019–1026.

National Research Council. (2011). *Intelligence analysis: Behavioral and social scientific foundations.* Washington, DC: National Academies Press.

Ness, R. B. (2012a). *Innovation generation: How to produce creative and useful scientific ideas.* New York: Oxford University Press.

Ness, R. B. (2012b). Tools for innovative thinking in epidemiology. *American Journal of Epidemiology, 175*(8), 733–738.

PADI. (2009). *Rescue Diver Course.* Professional Association of Diving Instructors.

Pretz, J. E., Naples, A. J., & Sternberg, R. J. (2003). Recognizing, defining, and representing problems. In J. E. Davidson & R. J. Sternberg (Eds.), *The psychology of problem solving* (pp. 3–30). New York: Cambridge University Press.

Ramanujam, R., & Rousseau, D. M. (2006). The challenges are organizational not just clinical. *Journal of Organizational Behavior, 27*(7), 811–827.

Rider, Y., & Thomason, N. (2010). Cognitive and pedagogical benefits of argument mapping: LAMP guides the way to better thinking. In A. Okada, S. J. Buckingham Shum, & T. Sherborne (Eds.), *Knowledge Cartography: Software tools and mapping techniques* (pp. 113–130). London: Springer.

Rittel, H. W. (1972). On the planning crisis: Systems analysis of the "First and Second Generations." *Bedriftsokonomen, 8*, 390–396.

Rozenblit, L., & Keil, F. (2002). The misunderstood limits of folk science: An illusion of explanatory depth. *Cognitive Science, 26*(5), 521–562.

Scapens, R. W. (2006). Understanding management accounting practices: A personal journey. *The British Accounting Review, 38*(1), 1–30.

Schauer, F. (2009). *Thinking like a lawyer: A new introduction to legal reasoning.* Cambridge, MA: Harvard University Press.

Shaw, M. E. (1958). Some effects of irrelevant information upon problem-solving by small groups. *The Journal of Social Psychology, 47*(1), 33–37.

Sherman, L. W. (2002). Evidence-based policing: Social organization of information for social control. In E. Waring & D. Weisburd (Eds.), *Crime and social organization* (pp. 217–248). New Brunswick, NJ: Transactions Publishers.

Singer, S. R., Nielsen, N. R., & Schweingruber, H. A. (2012). *Discipline-based education research: Understanding and improving learning in undergraduate science and engineering.* Washington, DC: National Academies Press.

Smith, G. F. (1988). Towards a heuristic theory of problem structuring. *Management Science, 34*(12), 1489–1506.

Stanovich, K. E., & West, R. F. (2000). Individual differences in reasoning: Implications for the rationality debate? *Behavioral and Brain Sciences, 23*(5), 645–665.

Steingraber, S. (2010). *Living downstream: An ecologist's personal investigation of cancer and the environment.* Cambridge, MA: Da Capo Press.

Straus, S. E., Glasziou, P., Richardson, W. S., & Haynes, R. B. (2011). *Evidence-based medicine: How to practice and teach it* (4th ed.). Toronto, CA: Elsevier.

Thibodeau, P. H., & Boroditsky, L. (2011). Metaphors we think with: The role of metaphor in reasoning. *PLoS One, 6*(2), e16782.

Thompson, J. M. T. (2013). Advice to a young researcher: with reminiscences of a life in science. *Philosophical Transactions of the Royal Society of London A: Mathematical, Physical and Engineering Sciences, 371*(1993), 20120425.

Thompson, L. (2003). Improving the creativity of organizational work groups. *The Academy of Management Executive, 17*(1), 96–109.

Thompson, L. L. (2012). *The mind and heart of the negotiator* (5th ed.). Upper Saddle River, NJ: Prentice Hall.

Tversky, A., & Kahneman, D. (1981). The framing of decisions and the psychology of choice. *Science, 211*(4481), 453–458.

Twardy, C. (2010). Argument maps improve critical thinking. *Teaching Philosophy, 27*(2), 95–116.

von Winterfeldt, D., & Edwards, W. (1986). *Decision analysis and behavioral research*: Cambridge, UK: Cambridge University Press.

## CHAPTER 3

Adams, J. L. (2001). *Conceptual blockbusting: A guide to better ideas.* Cambridge, MA: Basic Books.

Ainsworth, S., Prain, V., & Tytler, R. (2011). Drawing to learn in science. *Science, 333*, 2.

Andersen, B., & Fagerhaug, T. (2006). *Root cause analysis: simplified tools and techniques.* Milwaukee, WI: ASQ Quality Press.

Anderson, C. (2004). The long tail. *Wired, 12*(10), 170–177.

Anderson, T., Schum, D., & Twining, W. (2005). *Analysis of evidence.* New York: Cambridge University Press.

Arkes, H. R., Christensen, C., Lai, C., & Blumer, C. (1987). Two methods of reducing overconfidence. *Organizational Behavior and Human Decision Processes, 39*(1), 133–144.

Arnheiter, E. D., & Maleyeff, J. (2005). The integration of lean management and Six Sigma. *The TQM Magazine, 17*(1), 5–18.

Assink, M. (2006). Inhibitors of disruptive innovation capability: a conceptual model. *European Journal of Innovation Management, 9*(2), 215–233.

Austhink. (2006, December 7, 2006). Argument Mapping Tutorials. Retrieved January 14, 2014.

Baddeley, A. (1992). Working memory. *Science, 255*(5044), 556–559.

Baddeley, A. (2003). Working memory: Looking back and looking forward. *Nature Reviews Neuroscience, 4*(10), 829–839.

Baker, W. E., & Sinkula, J. M. (2002). Market orientation, learning orientation and product innovation: delving into the organization's black box. *Journal of Market-Focused Management, 5*(1), 5–23.

Barrier, P. A., Li, J. T.-C., & Jensen, N. M. (2003, February). *Two words to improve physician-patient communication: what else?* In Mayo Clinic Proceedings. 78(2), 211–214, Elsevier.

Bassok, M., & Novick, L. R. (2012). Problem solving. In K. J. Holyoak & R. G. Morrison (Eds.), *The Oxford handbook of thinking and reasoning* (pp. 413–432). New York: Oxford University Press.

Berger, W. (2010). *CAD monkeys, dinosaur babies, and T-shaped people: Inside the world of design thinking and how it can spark creativity and innovation.* New York: Penguin.

Berner, E. S., & Graber, M. L. (2008). Overconfidence as a cause of diagnostic error in medicine. *The American Journal of Medicine, 121*(5), S2–S23.

Bettman, J. R., Johnson, E. J., & Payne, J. W. (1991). Consumer decision making. *Handbook of consumer behavior, 44*(2), 50–84.

Blessing, S. B., & Ross, B. H. (1996). Content effects in problem categorization and problem solving. *Journal of Experimental Psychology: Learning, Memory, and Cognition, 22*(3), 792.

Bommer, J. J., & Scherbaum, F. (2008). The use and misuse of logic trees in probabilistic seismic hazard analysis. *Earthquake Spectra, 24*(4), 997–1009.

Breyfogle F. W.III, (2003). *Implementing Six Sigma: smarter solutions using statistical methods*. Hoboken, NJ: Wiley.

Brinkmann, A. (2003). Graphical knowledge display–Mind mapping and concept mapping as efficient tools in mathematics education. *Mathematics Education Review, 16*, 35–48.

Browne, G. J., & Pitts, M. G. (2004). Stopping rule use during information search in design problems. *Organizational Behavior and Human Decision Processes, 95*(2), 208–224.

Browne, G. J., Pitts, M. G., & Wetherbe, J. C. (2007). Cognitive stopping rules for terminating information search in online tasks. *MIS Quarterly, 31*(1), 89–104.

Brownlow, S., & Watson, S. (1987). Structuring multi-attribute value hierarchies. *Journal of the Operational Research Society, 38*(4), 309–317.

Brynjolfsson, E., Hu, Y., & Simester, D. (2011). Goodbye pareto principle, hello long tail: The effect of search costs on the concentration of product sales. *Management Science, 57*(8), 1373–1386.

Brynjolfsson, E., Hu, Y. J., & Smith, M. D. (2006). From niches to riches: The anatomy of the long tail. *Sloan Management Review, 47*(4), 67–71.

Buckingham Shum, S. J., MacLean, A., Bellotti, V. M. E., & Hammond, N. V. (1997). Graphical argumentation and design cognition. *Human-Computer Interaction, 12*(3), 267–300.

Buzan, T. (1976). *Use both sides of your brain*. New York: Dutton.

Cavallucci, D., Lutz, P., & Kucharavy, D. (September 29–October 2, 2002). *Converging in problem formulation: a different path in design*. Paper presented at the Proceedings of the Design Engineering Technical Conferences and Computer and Information in Engineering Conference, Montréal, Canada.

Chamberlin, T. C. (1965). The method of multiple working hypotheses. *Science, 148*(3671), 754–759.

Christensen, B. T., & Schunn, C. D. (2007). The relationship of analogical distance to analogical function and preinventive structure: The case of engineering design. *Memory & Cognition, 35*(1), 29–38.

Christensen, B. T., & Schunn, C. D. (2009). Putting blinkers on a blind man. Providing cognitive support for creative processes with environmental cues. In A. B. Markman & K. L. Wood (Eds.), *Tools for innovation: The science behind the practical methods that drive new ideas* (pp. 48–74). New York: Oxford University Press.

Clark, R. M. (2010). *Intelligence analysis: a target-centric approach*. Washington, DC: CQ press.

Collins, J. C., & Porras, J. I. (1996). Building your company's vision. *Harvard Business Review, 74*(5), 65–77.

Conklin, J. (2005). *Dialogue mapping: Building shared understanding of wicked problems*. Chichester, UK: John Wiley & Sons.

Cox, M., Irby, D. M., & Bowen, J. L. (2006). Educational strategies to promote clinical diagnostic reasoning. *New England Journal of Medicine, 355*(21), 2217–2225.

Croskerry, P. (2002). Achieving quality in clinical decision making: cognitive strategies and detection of bias. *Academic Emergency Medicine, 9*(11), 1184–1204.

Davies, M. (2010). Concept mapping, mind mapping and argument mapping: what are the differences and do they matter? *Higher Education, 62*(3), 279–301. doi: 10.1007/s10734-010-9387-6

De Bono, E. (1970). *Lateral thinking: Creativity step by step*. New York: Harper Perennial.

Diffenbach, J. (1982). Influence diagrams for complex strategic issues. *Strategic Management Journal, 3*(2), 133–146.

Ditto, P. H., & Lopez, D. F. (1992). Motivated skepticism: Use of differential decision criteria for preferred and nonpreferred conclusions. *Journal of Personality and Social Psychology*, 63(4), 568.

Dubé-Rioux, L., & Russo, J. E. (1988). An availability bias in professional judgment. *Journal of Behavioral Decision Making*, 1(4), 223–237.

Dufresne, R. J., Gerace, W. J., Hardiman, P. T., & Mestre, J. P. (1992). Constraining novices to perform expert-like problem analyses: Effects on schema acquisition. *The Journal of the Learning Sciences*, 2(3), 307–331.

Dunbar, K. N., & Klahr, D. (2012a). Scientific thinking and reasoning. In K. J. Holyoak & R. G. Morrison (Eds.), *The Oxford handbook of thinking and reasoning* (pp. 701–718). New York: Oxford University Press.

Dunbar, K. N., & Klahr, D. (2012b). Scientific thinking and reasoning. In K. J. Holyoak & R. G. Morrison (Eds.), *The Oxford handbook of thinking and reasoning* (p. 17). New York: Oxford University Press.

Duncker, K., & Lees, L. S. (1945). On problem-solving. *Psychological Monographs*, 58(5).

Dwyer, C. P., Hogan, M. J., & Stewart, I. (2010). The evaluation of argument mapping as a learning tool: Comparing the effects of map reading versus text reading on comprehension and recall of arguments. *Thinking Skills and Creativity*, 5(1), 16–22.

Eden, C. (1992). On the nature of cognitive maps. *Journal of Management Studies*, 29(3), 261–265.

Eden, C. (2004). Analyzing cognitive maps to help structure issues or problems. *European Journal of Operational Research*, 159(3), 673–686.

Eisenführ, F., Weber, M., & Langer, T. (2010). *Rational decision making*. Heidelberg, Germany: Springer.

Elstein, A. S. (2009). Thinking about diagnostic thinking: a 30-year perspective. *Advances in Health Sciences Education*, 14(1), 7–18.

Elstein, A. S., & Schwarz, A. (2002). Evidence base of clinical diagnosis: Clinical problem solving and diagnostic decision making: selective review of the cognitive literature. *BMJ: British Medical Journal*, 324(7339), 729.

Enkel, E., & Gassmann, O. (2010). Creative imitation: exploring the case of cross-industry innovation. *R&D Management*, 40(3), 256–270.

Eppler, M. J. (2006). A comparison between concept maps, mind maps, conceptual diagrams, and visual metaphors as complementary tools for knowledge construction and sharing. *Information Visualization*, 5(3), 202–210.

Estrada, C. A., Isen, A. M., & Young, M. J. (1997). Positive affect facilitates integration of information and decreases anchoring in reasoning among physicians. *Organizational Behavior and Human Decision Processes*, 72(1), 117–135.

Fenton, N., Neil, M., & Lagnado, D. A. (2012). A general structure for legal arguments about evidence using Bayesian networks. *Cognitive Science*, 37(1), 61–102.

Fiol, C. M., & Huff, A. S. (1992). Maps for managers: where are we? Where do we go from here? *Journal of Management Studies*, 29(3), 267–285.

First, M. B. (2005). Mutually exclusive versus co-occurring diagnostic categories: the challenge of diagnostic comorbidity. *Psychopathology*, 38(4), 206–210. doi: 10.1159/000086093

Fischhoff, B. (1982). Debiasing. In D. Kahneman, P. Slovic, & A. Tversky (Eds.), *Judgment under uncertainty: Heuristics and biases* (pp. 422–444). New York: Cambridge University Press.

Fischhoff, B., Slovic, P., & Lichtenstein, S. (1978). Fault trees: Sensitivity of estimated failure probabilities to problem representation. *Journal of Experimental Psychology: Human Perception and Performance*, 4(2), 330.

Gavetti, G., & Rivkin, J. W. (2005). How strategists really think. *Harvard Business Review*, 83(4), 54–63.

Gentner, D. (1983). Structure-mapping: A theoretical framework for analogy. *Cognitive Science*, 7(2), 155–170.

Gentner, D., & Toupin, C. (1986). Systematicity and surface similarity in the development of analogy. *Cognitive Science*, 10(3), 277–300.

Gick, M. L., & Holyoak, K. J. (1980). Analogical problem solving. *Cognitive Psychology*, 12(3), 306–355.

Goodwin, P., & Wright, G. (2009). *Decision analysis for management judgment* (4th ed.). Chichester, UK: John Wiley & Sons.

Green, A. E., & Dunbar, K. N. (2012). Mental function as genetic expression: Emerging insights from cognitive neurogenetics. In K. J. Holyoak & R. G. Morrison (Eds.), *The Oxford handbook of thinking and reasoning* (p. 90). New York: Oxford University Press.

Grönroos, C. (1997). From marketing mix to relationship marketing: towards a paradigm shift in marketing. *Management Decision, 35*(4), 322–339.

Hackman, J. R., & Wageman, R. (1995). Total quality management: empirical, conceptual, and practical issues. *Administrative Science Quarterly*, 309–342.

Hafner, C. D. (1987). Conceptual organization of case law knowledge bases. Paper presented at the Proceedings of the 1st international conference on Artificial Intelligence and Law. Boston, MA.

Halford, G. S., Baker, R., McCredden, J. E., & Bain, J. D. (2005). How many variables can humans process? *Psychological Science, 16*(1), 70–76.

Hammond, J. S., Keeney, R. L., & Raiffa, H. (1998). The hidden traps in decision making. *Harvard Business Review, 76*(5), 47–58.

Hammond, J. S., Keeney, R. L., & Raiffa, H. (2002). *Smart choices: A practical guide to making better decisions.* New York: Random House.

Hepler, A. B., Dawid, A. P., & Leucari, V. (2007). Object-oriented graphical representations of complex patterns of evidence. *Law, Probability and Risk, 6*(1–4), 275–293.

Heuer, R. J., & Pherson, R. H. (2011). *Structured analytic techniques for intelligence analysis.* Washington, DC: CQ Press.

Higgins, J. M. (1994). *101 creative problem solving techniques: The handbook of new ideas for business.* Winter Park: FL: New Management Publishing Company.

Holyoak, K. J. (2012). Analogy and relational reasoning. In K. J. Holyoak & R. G. Morrison (Eds.), *The Oxford handbook of thinking and reasoning* (pp. 234–259). New York: Oxford University Press.

Holyoak, K. J., & Koh, K. (1987). Surface and structural similarity in analogical transfer. *Memory & Cognition, 15*(4), 332–340.

Holyoak, K. J., & Thagard, P. (1989). Analogical mapping by constraint satisfaction. *Cognitive Science, 13*(3), 295–355.

Holyoak, K. J., & Thagard, P. (1997). The analogical mind. *American Psychologist, 52*(1), 35.

Hora, S. C. (2007). Eliciting probabilities from experts. In W. Edwards, R. F. Miles, & D. von Winterfeldt (Eds.), *Advances in decision analysis: From foundations to applications* (pp. 129–153). New York: Cambridge University Press.

Howard, R. A. (1989). Knowledge maps. *Management Science, 35*(8), 903–922.

Howard, R. A., & Matheson, J. E. (2005). Influence diagrams. *Decision Analysis, 2*(3), 127–143.

Hurson, T. (2007). *Think better.* New York: McGraw-Hill.

Isen, A. M., Daubman, K. A., & Nowicki, G. P. (1987). Positive affect facilitates creative problem solving. *Journal of Personality and Social Psychology, 52*(6), 1122.

Ishikawa, K. (1982). *Guide to quality control* (2nd ed.). New York: Asian Productivity Organization.

Jansson, D. G., & Smith, S. M. (1991). Design fixation. *Design Studies, 12*(1), 3–11.

Joseph, G.-M., & Patel, V. L. (1990). Domain knowledge and hypothesis generation in diagnostic reasoning. *Medical Decision Making, 10*(1), 31–44.

Kahneman, D. (2011). *Thinking, fast and slow.* New York: Farrar, Straus and Giroux.

Kaplan, R. S., & Norton, D. P. (2000). *Having trouble with your strategy?: Then map it.* Harvard Business School Publishing Corporation.

Kazancioglu, E., Platts, K., & Caldwell, P. (6–8 July, 2005). *Visualization and visual modelling for strategic analysis and problem-solving*. Paper presented at the Proceedings of the Ninth International Conference on Information Visualisation. London, UK.

Keeney, R. L. (1992). *Value-focused thinking: A path to creative decision making*. Cambridge, MA: Harvard University Press.

Keinan, G. (1987). Decision making under stress: scanning of alternatives under controllable and uncontrollable threats. *Journal of Personality and Social Psychology, 52*(3), 639.

Klayman, J., Soll, J. B., González-Vallejo, C., & Barlas, S. (1999). Overconfidence: It depends on how, what, and whom you ask. *Organizational Behavior and Human Decision Processes, 79*(3), 216–247.

Kulpa, Z. (1994). Diagrammatic representation and reasoning. *Machine Graphics & Vision, 3*, 77–103.

Larkin, J. H., & Simon, H. A. (1987). Why a diagram is (sometimes) worth ten thousand words. *Cognitive Science, 11*(1), 65–100.

Lee, W.-S., Grosh, D. L., Tillman, F. A., & Lie, C. H. (1985). Fault tree analysis, methods, and applications—a review. *Reliability, IEEE Transactions on, 34*(3), 194–203.

Leonhardt, D. (2005, October 13). Flexible as FedEx. *San Diego Union Tribune*.

Linsey, J., Tseng, I., Fu, K., Cagan, J., Wood, K., & Schunn, C. (2010). A study of design fixation, its mitigation and perception in engineering design faculty. *Journal of Mechanical Design, 132*(4), 041003.

Macpherson, R., & Stanovich, K. E. (2007). Cognitive ability, thinking dispositions, and instructional set as predictors of critical thinking. *Learning and Individual Differences, 17*(2), 115–127. doi: 10.1016/j.lindif.2007.05.003

Mahoney, M. J., & DeMonbreun, B. G. (1977). Psychology of the scientist: An analysis of problem-solving bias. *Cognitive Therapy and Research, 1*(3), 229–238.

Maier, N. R. F. (1963). *Problem-solving discussions and conferences: Leadership methods and skills*. New York: McGraw-Hill.

Martins, E., & Terblanche, F. (2003). Building organisational culture that stimulates creativity and innovation. *European Journal of Innovation Management, 6*(1), 64–74.

McIntyre, M. E. (1997). Lucidity and science I: Writing skills and the pattern perception hypothesis. *Interdisciplinary Science Reviews, 22*(3), 199–216.

McKenzie, C. R. (1997). Underweighting alternatives and overconfidence. *Organizational Behavior and Human Decision Processes, 71*(2), 141–160.

Miller, G. A. (1956). The magical number seven, plus or minus two: some limits on our capacity for processing information. *Psychological Review, 63*(2), 81.

Mingers, J. (1989). An empirical comparison of pruning methods for decision tree induction. *Machine Learning, 4*(2), 227–243.

Minto, B. (2009). *The pyramid principle: logic in writing and thinking*. Harlow, UK: Pearson Education.

Mitchell, G. (2003). Mapping evidence law. *FSU College of Law, Public Law Research Paper* (75).

National Research Council. (2011). *Intelligence analysis: Behavioral and social scientific foundations*. Washington, DC: National Academies Press.

Ness, R. B. (2012). *Innovation generation: How to produce creative and useful scientific ideas*. New York: Oxford University Press.

Nickerson, R. S. (1998). Confirmation bias: a ubiquitous phenomenon in many guises. *Review of General Psychology, 2*(2), 175.

Nixon, C. T., & Littlepage, G. E. (1992). Impact of meeting procedures on meeting effectiveness. *Journal of Business and Psychology, 6*(3), 361–369.

Novak, J. D. (1990). Concept maps and Vee diagrams: Two metacognitive tools to facilitate meaningful learning. *Instructional Science, 19*(1), 29–52.

Novak, J. D., & Cañas, A. J. (2006). The theory underlying concept maps and how to construct them. *Florida Institute for Human and Machine Cognition, 1.*

Ohmae, K. (1982). *The mind of the strategist.* New York: McGraw-Hill.

Okada, A., Shum, S. J. B., & Sherborne, T. (2010). *Knowledge cartography: software tools and mapping techniques.* London, UK: Springer.

Oldham, G. R., & Cummings, A. (1996). Employee creativity: Personal and contextual factors at work. *Academy of Management Journal, 39*(3), 607–634.

Olson, D. L. (1996). *Decision aids for selection problems.* New York: Springer.

Orasanu, J. (2010). Flight crew decision-making. In B. G. Kanki, R. L. Helmreich, & J. Anca (Eds.), *Crew resource management* (pp. 147–180). San Diego, CA: Elsevier.

Osborn, A. F. (1953). *Applied imagination—Principles and procedures of creative writing.* New York: Charles Scribner's Sons.

Parnes, S. J. (1961). Effects of extended effort in creative problem solving. *Journal of Educational Psychology, 52*(3), 117.

Pfister, J. (2010). Is there a need for a maxim of politeness? *Journal of Pragmatics, 42*(5), 1266–1282. doi: 10.1016/j.pragma.2009.09.001

Pinar, A., Meza, J., Donde, V., & Lesieutre, B. (2010). Optimization strategies for the vulnerability analysis of the electric power grid. *SIAM Journal on Optimization, 20*(4), 1786–1810.

Platt, J. R. (1964). Strong inference. *Science, 146*(3642), 347–353.

Pretz, J. E., Naples, A. J., & Sternberg, R. J. (2003). Recognizing, defining, and representing problems. In J. E. Davidson & R. J. Sternberg (Eds.), *The psychology of problem solving* (pp. 3–30). New York: Cambridge University Press.

Prime Minister's Strategy Unit. (2004). Strategy survival guide. *Cabinet Office, Admiralty Arch, The Mall, London SW1A 2WH.*

Quinlan, J. R. (1986). Induction of decision trees. *Machine Learning, 1*(1), 81–106.

Quinlan, J. R. (1987). Simplifying decision trees. *International Journal of Man-Machine Studies, 27*(3), 221–234.

Reed, C., Walton, D., & Macagno, F. (2007). Argument diagramming in logic, law and artificial intelligence. *The Knowledge Engineering Review, 22*(01), 87. doi: 10.1017/s0269888907001051

Reiter-Palmon, R., & Illies, J. J. (2004). Leadership and creativity: Understanding leadership from a creative problem-solving perspective. *The Leadership Quarterly, 15*(1), 55–77.

Ribaux, O., & Margot, P. (1999). Inference structures for crime analysis and intelligence: the example of burglary using forensic science data. *Forensic Science International, 100*(3), 193–210.

Rider, Y., & Thomason, N. (2010). Cognitive and pedagogical benefits of argument mapping: LAMP guides the way to better thinking. In A. Okada, S. J. Buckingham Shum, & T. Sherborne (Eds.), *Knowledge cartography: Software tools and mapping techniques* (pp. 113–130). London: Springer.

Rooney, J. J., & Heuvel, L. N. V. (2004). Root cause analysis for beginners. *Quality Progress, 37*(7), 45–56.

Russo, J. E., & Kolzow, K. J. (1994). Where is the fault in fault trees? *Journal of Experimental Psychology: Human Perception and Performance, 20*(1), 17.

Russo, J. E., & Schoemaker, P. J. (1992). Managing overconfidence. *Sloan Management Review, 33*(2), 7–17.

Sample, S. B., & Bennis, W. (2002). *The contrarian's guide to leadership.* San Francisco, CA: Jossey-Bass.

Schoemaker, P. J. (1995). Scenario planning: a tool for strategic thinking. *Sloan Management Review, 36,* 25.

Schum, D. A. (1994). *The evidential foundations of probabilistic reasoning.* Evanston: IL: Northwestern University Press.

Shachter, R. D. (1986). Evaluating influence diagrams. *Operations Research, 34*(6), 871–882.

Shalley, C. E. (1995). Effects of coaction, expected evaluation, and goal setting on creativity and productivity. *Academy of Management Journal, 38*(2), 483–503.

Shalley, C. E., Zhou, J., & Oldham, G. R. (2004). The effects of personal and contextual characteristics on creativity: Where should we go from here? *Journal of Management, 30*(6), 933–958.

Shum, S. B. (2003). The roots of computer supported argument visualization. In P. A. Kirschner, S. J. Buckingham Shum, & C. S. Carr (Eds.), *Visualizing argumentation: Software tools for collaborative and educational sense making* (pp. 3–24). London: Springer.

Simon, H. A. (1972). Theories of bounded rationality. In C. B. McGuire & R. Radner (Eds.), *Decision and organization* (Vol. 1, pp. 161–176). Amsterdam: North-Holland Publishing Company.

Simon, H. A. (1990). Invariants of human behavior. *Annual Review of Psychology, 41*(1), 1–20.

Simon, H. A. (1996). *The sciences of the artificial*. Cambridge, MA: MIT press.

Smith, S. M., & Blankenship, S. E. (1991). Incubation and the persistence of fixation in problem solving. *The American Journal of Psychology*, 61–87.

Smith, S. M., & Ward, T. B. (2012). Cognition and the creation of ideas. In K. J. Holyoak & R. G. Morrison (Eds.), *Oxford handbook of thinking and reasoning* (pp. 456–474). New York: Oxford University Press.

Smith, S. M., Ward, T. B., & Schumacher, J. S. (1993). Constraining effects of examples in a creative generation task. *Memory & Cognition, 21*(6), 837–845.

Spellman, B. A., & Holyoak, K. J. (1996). Pragmatics in analogical mapping. *Cognitive Psychology, 31*(3), 307–346.

Spellman, B. A., & Schnall, S. (2009). Embodied rationality. *Queen's LJ, 35*, 117.

Taleb, N. N. (2007). *The Black Swan: The impact of the highly improbable*. New York: Random House.

Thompson, L. L. (2011). *Making the team: A guide for managers* (4th ed.). Upper Saddle River, New Jersey: Pearson.

Tversky, A., & Kahneman, D. (1974). Judgment under uncertainty: Heuristics and biases. *Science, 185*(4157), 1124–1131.

Twardy, C. (2010). Argument maps improve critical thinking. *Teaching Philosophy, 27*(2), 95–116.

Tweney, R. D., Doherty, M. E., & Mynatt, C. R. (1981). *On scientific thinking*. New York: Columbia University Press.

van Gelder, T. (2001, December). *How to improve critical thinking using educational technology*. Paper presented at the meeting at the crossroads: Proceedings of the 18th Annual Conference of the Australasian Society for Computers in Learning in Tertiary Education (pp. 539–548). Melbourne: Biomedical Multimedia Unit, The University of Melbourne.

van Gelder, T. (2003). Enhancing deliberation through computer supported argument visualization *Visualizing argumentation* (pp. 97–115): Springer.

van Gelder, T. (2005). Enhancing and augmenting human reasoning. *Evolution, Rationality and Cognition: A Cognitive Science for the Twenty-First Century*, 162–181.

van Gelder, T. (2005). Teaching critical thinking: Some lessons from cognitive science. *College Teaching, 53*(1), 41–48.

van Gelder, T. and P. Monk (2016). "Improving reasoning project." Retrieved March 4, 2016, from http://www.vangeldermonk.com/improvingreasoning.html.

van Steenburgh, J. J., Fleck, J. I., Beeman, M., & Kounios, J. (2012). Insight. In K. J. Holyoak & R. G. Morrison (Eds.), *The Oxford handbook of thinking and reasoning* (pp. 475–491). New York: Oxford University Press.

Van Waterschoot, W., & Van den Bulte, C. (1992). The 4P classification of the marketing mix revisited. *The Journal of Marketing*, 83–93.

Vesely, W. E., Goldberg, F. F., Roberts, N. H., & Haasl, D. F. (1981). *Fault tree handbook*. Washington, DC: Nuclear Regulatory Commission.

Vlek, C., Prakken, H., Renooij, S., & Verheij, B. (2013, June). *Modeling crime scenarios in a Bayesian network*. Paper presented at the Proceedings of the Fourteenth International Conference on Artificial Intelligence and Law, ACM Press, New York, pp. 150–159.

von Winterfeldt, D., & Edwards, W. (1986). *Decision analysis and behavioral research*. Cambridge, UK: Cambridge University Press.

von Winterfeldt, D., & Edwards, W. (2007). Defining a decision analytic structure. In W. Edwards, R. F. Miles, & D. von Winterfeldt (Eds.), *Advances in decision analysis: From foundations to applications* (pp. 81–103). New York: Cambridge University Press.

Weisberg, R. W., & Alba, J. W. (1981). An examination of the alleged role of "fixation" in the solution of several" insight" problems. *Journal of Experimental Psychology: General, 110*(2), 169.

Wiebes, E., Baaij, M., Keibek, B., & Witteveen, P. (2007). *The craft of strategy formation: Translating business issues into actionable strategies*. Southern Gate, UK: John Wiley & Sons.

Wojick, D. (1975). *Issue analysis—An introduction to the use of issue trees and the nature of complex reasoning* Retrieved from http://www.stemed.info/reports/Wojick_Issue_Analysis_txt.pdf

Yates, J. F., Lee, J.-W., & Shinotsuka, H. (1996). Beliefs about overconfidence, including its cross-national variation. *Organizational Behavior and Human Decision Processes, 65*(2), 138–147.

## CHAPTER 4

Anderson, T., Schum, D., & Twining, W. (2005). *Analysis of evidence*. New York: Cambridge University Press.

André, P., Teevan, J., & Dumais, S. T. (2009, 26–30 October). *Discovery is never by chance: designing for (un)serendipity*. Paper presented at the Proceedings of the Seventh Association of Computing Machinery Conference on Creativity and Cognition. Berkeley, CA.

Arkes, H. R., & Kajdasz, J. (2011). Intuitive theories of behavior. In B. Fischhoff & C. Chauvin (Eds.), *Intelligence analysis: Behavioral and social scientific foundations* (pp. 143–168). Washington, DC: The National Academies Press.

Ask, K., Rebelius, A., & Granhag, P. A. (2008). The "elasticity" of criminal evidence: a moderator of investigator bias. *Applied Cognitive Psychology, 22*(9), 1245–1259. doi: 10.1002/acp.1432

Austhink. (2006). Argument Mapping Tutorials. Retrieved January 14, 2014, from http://austhink.com/reason/tutorials/

Barends, E., ten Have, S., & Huisman, F. (2012). Learning from other evidence-based practices: the case of medicine. In D. M. Rousseau (Ed.), *The Oxford handbook of evidence-based management* (pp. 25–42). New York: Oxford University Press.

Bastardi, A., & Shafir, E. (1998). On the pursuit and misuse of useless information. *Journal of Personality and Social Psychology, 75*(1), 19.

Bazerman, M. H., & Moore, D. A. (2008). *Judgment in managerial decision making*. Hoboken, NJ: John Wiley & Sons.

Bex, F., & Verheij, B. (2012). Solving a murder case by asking critical questions: An approach to fact-finding in terms of argumentation and story schemes. *Argumentation, 26*(3), 325–353.

Beyth-Marom, R., & Fischhoff, B. (1983). Diagnosticity and pseudodiagnosticity. *Journal of Personality and Social Psychology, 45*(6), 1185.

Blumer, A., Ehrenfeucht, A., Haussler, D., & Warmuth, M. K. (1987). Occam's razor. *Information Processing Letters, 24*(6), 377–380.

Boicu, M., Tecuci, G., & Schum, D. (2008, 3–4 December). Intelligence Analysis Ontology for Cognitive Assistants. Proceedings of the Conference *Ontology for the Intelligence Community*. Fairfax, VA.

Brynjolfsson, E., Hu, Y., & Simester, D. (2011). Goodbye pareto principle, hello long tail: The effect of search costs on the concentration of product sales. *Management Science, 57*(8), 1373–1386.

Cannon, W. B. (1940). The role of chance in discovery. *The Scientific Monthly, 50*, 204–209.

Chamberlin, T. C. (1965). The method of multiple working hypotheses. *Science, 148*(3671), 754–759.

Church, B. K. (1991). An examination of the effect that commitment to a hypothesis has on auditors' evaluations of confirming and disconfirming evidence. *Contemporary Accounting Research, 7*(2), 513–534.

Clarke, R. V., & Eck, J. E. (2005). Crime analysis for problem solvers. Washington, DC: Center for Problem Oriented Policing.

Cornell University Law School. Rule 401. Test for Relevant Evidence. Retrieved April 7, 2014, from http://www.law.cornell.edu/rules/fre/rule_401

Cousins, R. D. (1995). Why isn't every physicist a Bayesian? *American Journal of Physics, 63*(5), 398–410.

Cowan, N. (2000). The magical number 4 in short-term memory: A reconsideration of mental storage capacity. *Behavioral and Brain Sciences, 24*(1), 87–114.

Cowley, M., & Byrne, R. M. (2004, February). *Chess masters' hypothesis testing.* Paper presented at the Proceedings of 26th Annual Conference of the Cognitive Science Society. Mahwah, NJ.

Cowley, M., & Byrne, R. M. (2005, February). *When falsification is the only path to truth.* Paper presented at the 27th Annual Conference of the Cognitive Science Society. Stresa, Italy.

Davis, R. H. (2006). Strong inference: rationale or inspiration? *Perspectives in Biology and Medicine, 49*(2), 238–250.

Dawson, E., Gilovich, T., & Regan, D. T. (2002). Motivated Reasoning and Performance on the Wason Selection Task. *Personality and Social Psychology Bulletin, 28*(10), 1379–1387.

Dawson, N. V., Connors, A. F., Speroff, T., Kemka, A., Shaw, P., & Arkes, H. R. (1993). Hemodynamic assessment in managing the critically ill: Is physician confidence warranted? *Medical Decision Making, 13*(3), 258–266.

Doherty, M. E., Mynatt, C. R., Tweney, R. D., & Schiavo, M. D. (1979). Pseudodiagnosticity. *Acta Psychologica, 43*(2), 111–121.

Dunbar, K. N., & Klahr, D. (2012). Scientific thinking and reasoning. In K. J. Holyoak & R. G. Morrison (Eds.), *The Oxford handbook of thinking and reasoning* (pp. 701–718). New York: Oxford University Press.

Dunbar, M. (1980). The blunting of Occam's Razor, or to hell with parsimony. *Canadian Journal of Zoology, 58*(2), 123–128.

Edwards, K., & Smith, E. E. (1996). A disconfirmation bias in the evaluation of arguments. *Journal of Personality and Social Psychology, 71*(1), 5.

Fenton, N., & Neil, M. (2010). Comparing risks of alternative medical diagnosis using Bayesian arguments. *Journal of Biomedical Informatics, 43*(4), 485–495.

Fenton, N., Neil, M., & Lagnado, D. A. (2012). A general structure for legal arguments about evidence using Bayesian networks. *Cognitive Science, 37*(1), 61–102.

Fine, G. A., & Deegan, J. G. (1996). Three principles of Serendip: insight, chance, and discovery in qualitative research. *International Journal of Qualitative Studies in Education, 9*(4), 434–447.

Fischhoff, B., & Chauvin, C. (2011). *Intelligence analysis: Behavioral and social scientific foundations.* Washington, DC: National Academies Press.

Fisk, C. E. (1972). The Sino-Soviet border dispute: A comparison of the conventional and Bayesian methods for intelligence warning. *Studies in Intelligence, 16*(2), 53–62.

Gabbay, D., & Woods, J. (2006). Advice on abductive logic. *Logic Journal of IGPL, 14*(2), 189–219.

Gauch, H. G. (2003). *Scientific method in practice.* Cambridge, UK: Cambridge University Press.

Gawande, A. (2011, January 24). The hot spotters. *The New Yorker.*

Gawande, A. (2015, May 11). Overkill: An avalanche of unnecessary medical care is harming patients physically and financially. What can we do about it? *The New Yorker.*

George, R. Z., & Bruce, J. B. (2008). *Analyzing intelligence: Origins, obstacles, and innovations.* Washington, DC: Georgetown University Press.

Giluk, T. L., & Rynes-Weller, S. (2012). Research findings practitioners resist: Lessons for management academics from evidence-based medicine. In D. M. Rousseau (Ed.), *The Oxford handbook of evidence-based management* (pp. 130–164). New York: Oxford University Press.

Gorman, M. E., & Gorman, M. E. (1984). A comparison of disconfirmatory, confirmatory and control strategies on Wason's 2–4–6 task. *The Quarterly Journal of Experimental Psychology, 36*(4), 629–648.

Gorman, M. E., Gorman, M. E., Latta, R. M., & Cunningham, G. (1984). How disconfirmatory, confirmatory and combined strategies affect group problem solving. *British Journal of Psychology, 75*(1), 65–79.

Gustafson, D. H., Edwards, W., Phillips, L. D., & Slack, W. V. (1969). Subjective probabilities in medical diagnosis. *IEEE Transactions on Man-Machine Systems, 10*(3), 61–65.

Hepler, A. B., Dawid, A. P., & Leucari, V. (2007). Object-oriented graphical representations of complex patterns of evidence. *Law, Probability and Risk, 6*(1–4), 275–293.

Heuer, R. J. (1999). *Psychology of intelligence analysis*: Center for the Study of Intelligence. Washington, DC: Central Intelligence Agency.

Heuer, R. J., & Pherson, R. H. (2011). *Structured analytic techniques for intelligence analysis*. Washington, DC: CQ Press.

Hill, A. B. (1965). The environment and disease: association or causation? *Proceedings of the Royal Society of Medicine, 58*(5), 295.

Hoffman, R. R., Shadbolt, N. R., Burton, A. M., & Klein, G. (1995). Eliciting knowledge from experts: A methodological analysis. *Organizational Behavior and Human Decision Processes, 62*(2), 129–158.

Juran, J. M. (1975). The non-Pareto principle; mea culpa. *Quality Progress, 8*(5), 8–9.

Kakas, A. C., Kowalski, R. A., & Toni, F. (1992). Abductive logic programming. *Journal of Logic and Computation, 2*(6), 719–770.

Kell, D. B., & Oliver, S. G. (2004). Here is the evidence, now what is the hypothesis? The complementary roles of inductive and hypothesis-driven science in the post-genomic era. *Bioessays, 26*(1), 99–105. doi: 10.1002/bies.10385

Kent, S. (1964). Words of estimative probability. *Studies in Intelligence, 8*(4), 49–65.

King, R. D. (2010). Rise of the robo scientists. *Scientific American, 304*(1), 72–77.

Klahr, D., Fay, A. L., & Dunbar, K. (1993). Heuristics for scientific experimentation: A developmental study. *Cognitive Psychology, 25*(1), 111–146.

Klayman, J., & Ha, Y.-W. (1987). Confirmation, disconfirmation, and information in hypothesis testing. *Psychological Review, 94*(2), 211.

Klayman, J., & Ha, Y.-w. (1989). Hypothesis testing in rule discovery: Strategy, structure, and content. *Journal of Experimental Psychology: Learning, Memory, and Cognition, 15*(4), 596.

Koriat, A., Lichtenstein, S., & Fischhoff, B. (1980). Reasons for confidence. *Journal of Experimental Psychology: Human Learning and Memory, 6*(2), 107.

Lemann, N. (2015, October 12). The network man—Reid Hoffman's big idea. *The New Yorker*.

Lord, C. G., Ross, L., & Lepper, M. R. (1979). Biased assimilation and attitude polarization: the effects of prior theories on subsequently considered evidence. *Journal of Personality and Social Psychology, 37*(11), 2098.

Macpherson, R., & Stanovich, K. E. (2007). Cognitive ability, thinking dispositions, and instructional set as predictors of critical thinking. *Learning and Individual Differences, 17*(2), 115–127.

Mahoney, M. J., & DeMonbreun, B. G. (1977). Psychology of the scientist: An analysis of problem-solving bias. *Cognitive Therapy and Research, 1*(3), 229–238.

Maxfield, M. G., & Babbie, E. R. (2012). *Research methods for criminal justice and criminology* (3rd ed.). Belmont, CA: Wadsworth.

McIntyre, M. E. (1998). Lucidity and science III: Hypercredulity, quantum mechanics, and scientific truth. *Interdisciplinary Science Reviews, 23*(1), 29–70.

Miller, G. A. (1956). The magical number seven, plus or minus two: some limits on our capacity for processing information. *Psychological Review, 63*(2), 81.

Mitchell, M. L., & Jolley, J. M. (2009). *Research design explained*. Belmond, CA: Wadsworth.

Mynatt, C. R., Doherty, M. E., & Tweney, R. D. (1978). Consequences of confirmation and disconfirmation in a simulated research environment. *The Quarterly Journal of Experimental Psychology, 30*(3), 395–406.

National Research Council. (2010). *Field evaluation in the intelligence and counterintelligence context: Workshop summary.* Washington, DC: National Academies Press.

National Research Council. (2011a). *Intelligence analysis for tomorrow: Advances from the behavioral and social sciences.* Washington DC: National Academies Press.

National Research Council. (2011b). *Intelligence analysis: Behavioral and social scientific foundations.* Washington, DC: National Academies Press.

Ness, R. (2013). *Genius unmasked.* New York: Oxford University Press.

Ness, R. B. (2012a). *Innovation generation: How to produce creative and useful scientific ideas.* New York: Oxford University Press.

Ness, R. B. (2012b). Tools for innovative thinking in epidemiology. *American Journal of Epidemiology, 175*(8), 733–738.

Neustadt, R. E., & May, E. R. (1986). *Thinking in time: The uses of history for decision makers.* New York: Simon & Schuster.

Nickerson, R. S. (1998). Confirmation bias: a ubiquitous phenomenon in many guises. *Review of General Psychology, 2*(2), 175.

Nisbett, R. E., Zukier, H., & Lemley, R. E. (1981). The dilution effect: Nondiagnostic information weakens the implications of diagnostic information. *Cognitive Psychology, 13*(2), 248–277.

Oliver, R., Bjoertomt, O., Greenwood, R., & Rothwell, J. (2008). "Noisy patients"—can signal detection theory help? *Nature Clinical Practice Neurology, 4*(6), 306–316.

Oreskes, N. (2004). The scientific consensus on climate change. *Science, 306*(5702), 1686.

Oreskes, N., Shrader-Frechette, K., & Belitz, K. (1994). Verification, validation, and confirmation of numerical models in the earth sciences. *Science, 263*(5147), 641–646.

Oskamp, S. (1965). Overconfidence in case-study judgments. *Journal of Consulting Psychology, 29*(3), 261.

Page, S. E. (2008). *The difference: How the power of diversity creates better groups, firms, schools, and societies.* Princeton, NJ: Princeton University Press.

Pardo, M. S., & Allen, R. J. (2008). Juridical proof and the best explanation. *Law and Philosophy, 27*(3), 223–268.

Patel, V. L., Arocha, J. F., & Zhang, J. (2012). Medical reasoning and thinking. In K. J. Holyoak & R. G. Morrison (Eds.), *The Oxford handbook of thinking and reasoning* (pp. 736–754). New York: Oxford University Press.

Pfeffer, J., & Sutton, R. I. (2006). *Hard facts, dangerous half-truths, and total nonsense: Profiting from evidence-based management.* Boston, MA: Harvard Business Press.

Philips, B., Ball, C., Sackett, D. L., Badenoch, D., Straus, S. E., Haynes, R. B., & Dawes, R. M. (March 2008). *Levels of evidence.* Retrieved January 20, 2015.

Phillips, L. D., & Edwards, W. (1966). Conservatism in a simple probability inference task. *Journal of Experimental Psychology, 72*(3), 346.

Platt, J. R. (1964). Strong inference. *Science, 146*(3642), 347–353.

Pope, S., & Josang, A. (2005). Analysis of competing hypotheses using subjective logic: CRC for Enterprise Distributed Technology.

Pople, H. E. (1973). *On the mechanization of abductive logic.* Paper presented at the IJCAI.

Popper, K. (2002). *The logic of scientific discovery.* London: Routledge.

Prakken, H. (2014). On direct and indirect probabilistic reasoning in legal proof. *Law, Probability and Risk,* mgu013.

Puga, J. L., Krzywinski, M., & Altman, N. (2015). Points of Significance: Bayes' theorem. *Nature Methods, 12*(4), 277–278.

Reichenbach, H. (1973). *The rise of scientific philosophy*. Berkeley, CA: University of California Press.

Ringle, K. (1990, May 6). When more is less. *Washington Post*.

Rosenberg, W., & Donald, A. (1995). Evidence based medicine: an approach to clinical problem-solving. *BMJ: British Medical Journal, 310*(6987), 1122.

Rowe, G., & Reed, C. (2010). Argument diagramming: the *Araucaria* project. In *Knowledge Cartography* (pp. 163–181). London: Springer.

Rowley, J. E. (2007). The wisdom hierarchy: representations of the DIKW hierarchy. *Journal of Information Science, 33*(2), 163–180.

Russell, S. J., Norvig, P., Canny, J. F., Malik, J. M., & Edwards, D. D. (1995). *Artificial intelligence: a modern approach* (Vol. 2). Englewood Cliffs, NJ: Prentice Hall.

Schauer, F. (2009). *Thinking like a lawyer: a new introduction to legal reasoning*. Cambridge, MA: Harvard University Press.

Schoemaker, P. J. (1995). Scenario planning: a tool for strategic thinking. *Sloan Management Review, 36*, 25.

Schum, D., Tecuci, G., Boicu, M., & Marcu, D. (2009). Substance-blind classification of evidence for intelligence analysis. In Proceedings of the Conference "Ontology for the Intelligence Community: Setting the Stage for High-level Knowledge Fusion," George Mason University, Fairfax, Virginia Campus, 20–22 October 2009.

Schum, D. A. (1994). *The evidential foundations of probabilistic reasoning*. Evanston, IL: Northwestern University Press.

Schum, D. A. (2009). A science of evidence: contributions from law and probability. *Law, Probability and Risk, 8*(3), 197–231.

Schum, D. A., & Morris, J. R. (2007). Assessing the competence and credibility of human sources of intelligence evidence: contributions from law and probability. *Law, Probability and Risk, 6*(1–4), 247–274.

Schunemann, H. J., Jaeschke, R., Cook, D. J., Bria, W. F., El-Solh, A. A., Ernst, A., . . . Krishnan, J. A. (2006). An official ATS statement: grading the quality of evidence and strength of recommendations in ATS guidelines and recommendations. *American Journal of Respiratory and Critical Care Medicine, 174*(5), 605–614.

Shekelle, P. G., Woolf, S. H., Eccles, M., & Grimshaw, J. (1999). Clinical guidelines: developing guidelines. *BMJ: British Medical Journal, 318*(7183), 593.

Snyder, M., & Swann, W. B. (1978). Hypothesis-testing processes in social interaction. *Journal of Personality and Social Psychology, 36*(11), 1202.

Son, L. K., & Kornell, N. (2010). The virtues of ignorance. *Behavioural Processes, 83*(2), 207–212.

Spellman, B. A. (2011). Individual reasoning. In C. Chauvin & B. Fischhoff (Eds.), *Intelligence analysis: Behavioral and social scientific foundations*. Washington, DC: National Academies Press.

Surowiecki, J. (2005). *The wisdom of crowds*. New York: Random House.

Taleb, N. N. (2007). *The black swan: The impact of the highly improbable*. New York: Random House.

Tecuci, G., Schum, D., Boicu, M., Marcu, D., & Russell, K. (2011). *Toward a computational theory of evidence-based reasoning*. 18th International Conference on Control Systems and Computer Science, University Politehnica of Bucharest. May 24–27.

Tecuci, G., Schum, D. A., Marcu, D., & Boicu, M. (2014). Computational approach and cognitive assistant for evidence–based reasoning in intelligence analysis. *International Journal of Intelligent Defence Support Systems, 5*(2), 146–172.

Tenenbaum, J. B., Kemp, C., Griffiths, T. L., & Goodman, N. D. (2011). How to grow a mind: Statistics, structure, and abstraction. *Science, 331*(6022), 1279–1285.

Thagard, P. (1989). Explanatory coherence. *Behavioral and Brain Sciences, 12*(3), 435–502.

Thagard, P. (2005). Testimony, credibility, and explanatory coherence. *Erkenntnis, 63*(3), 295–316.

Thagard, P. R. (1978). The best explanation: Criteria for theory choice. *The Journal of Philosophy*, 76–92.

Thompson, M. A., Mugavero, M. J., Amico, K. R., Cargill, V. A., Chang, L. W., Gross, R., Bartlett, J. G. (2012). Guidelines for improving entry into and retention in care and antiretroviral adherence for persons with HIV: evidence-based recommendations from an International Association of Physicians in AIDS Care panel. *Annals of Internal Medicine, 156*(11), 817–833.

Tversky, A., & Kahneman, D. (1973). Availability: A heuristic for judging frequency and probability. *Cognitive Psychology, 5*(2), 207–232.

Tversky, A., & Kahneman, D. (1974). Judgment under uncertainty: Heuristics and biases. *Science, 185*(4157), 1124–1131.

Twardy, C. (2010). Argument maps improve critical thinking. *Teaching Philosophy, 27*(2), 95–116.

Tweney, R. D., Doherty, M. E., & Kleiter, G. D. (2010). The pseudodiagnosticity trap: Should participants consider alternative hypotheses? *Thinking & Reasoning, 16*(4), 332–345.

Tweney, R. D., Doherty, M. E., & Mynatt, C. R. (1981). *On scientific thinking*. New York: Columbia University Press.

Tweney, R. D., Doherty, M. E., Worner, W. J., Pliske, D. B., Mynatt, C. R., Gross, K. A., & Arkkelin, D. L. (1980). Strategies of rule discovery in an inference task. *Quarterly Journal of Experimental Psychology, 32*(1), 109–123.

U.S. Senate Select Committee on Intelligence. (2008). Senate Intelligence Committee Unveils Final Phase II Reports on Prewar Iraq Intelligence.

Vale, N. B. d., Delfino, J., & Vale, L. F. B. d. (2005). Serendipity in medicine and anesthesiology. *Revista Brasileira de Anestesiologia, 55*(2), 224–249.

Van Andel, P. (1994). Anatomy of the unsought finding. Serendipity: Origin, history, domains, traditions, appearances, patterns and programmability. *The British Journal for the Philosophy of Science, 45*(2), 631–648.

van Gelder, T. (2005). Teaching critical thinking: Some lessons from cognitive science. *College Teaching, 53*(1), 41–48.

van Gelder, T. (2008). Can we do better than ACH? *AIPIO News*(55).

Vlek, C., Prakken, H., Renooij, S., & Verheij, B. (2013, June). *Modeling crime scenarios in a Bayesian network.* Paper presented at the Proceedings of the Fourteenth International Conference on Artificial Intelligence and Law, ACM Press, New York, pp. 150–159.

von Winterfeldt, D., & Edwards, W. (1986). *Decision analysis and behavioral research.* Cambridge, UK: Cambridge University Press.

Wason, P. C. (1960). On the failure to eliminate hypotheses in a conceptual task. *Quarterly Journal of Experimental Psychology, 12*(3), 129–140.

Welch, H. G. (2015). *Less medicine more health: 7 assumptions that drive too much medical care.* Boston, MA: Beacon Press.

Zimmerman, C. (2000). The development of scientific reasoning skills. *Developmental Review, 20*(1), 99–149. doi: 10.1006/drev.1999.0497

Zlotnick, J. (1972). Bayes' theorem for intelligence analysis. *Studies in Intelligence, 16*(2), 43–52.

## CHAPTER 5

Ancona, D. G., & Caldwell, D. F. (1992). Demography and design: Predictors of new product team performance. *Organization Science, 3*(3), 321–341.

Basadur, M., Graen, G. B., & Scandura, T. A. (1986). Training effects on attitudes toward divergent thinking among manufacturing engineers. *Journal of Applied Psychology, 71*(4), 612.

Bassok, M., & Novick, L. R. (2012). Problem solving. In K. J. Holyoak & R. G. Morrison (Eds.), *The Oxford handbook of thinking and reasoning* (pp. 413–432). New York: Oxford University Press.

Bettenhausen, K. L. (1991). Five years of groups research: What we have learned and what needs to be addressed. *Journal of Management, 17*(2), 345–381.

Brown, T. (2008). Design thinking. *Harvard Business Review, 86*(6), 84.

Brown, V. R., & Paulus, P. B. (2002). Making group brainstorming more effective: Recommendations from an associative memory perspective. *Current Directions in Psychological Science, 11*(6), 208–212.

Clapham, M. M. (2003). The development of innovative ideas through creativity training. In L. V. Shavinina (Ed.), *The International Handbook on Innovation*, pp. 366–376. Oxford, UK: Elsevier.

Dalkey, N., & Helmer, O. (1963). An experimental application of the Delphi method to the use of experts. *Management Science, 9*(3), 458–467.

De Bono, E. (1970). *Lateral thinking: Creativity step by step.* New York: Harper Perennial.

Diehl, M., & Stroebe, W. (1987). Productivity loss in brainstorming groups: Toward the solution of a riddle. *Journal of Personality and Social Psychology, 53*(3), 497.

Duncker, K., & Lees, L. S. (1945). On problem-solving. *Psychological Monographs, 58*(5).

Dugosh, K. L., et al. (2000). Cognitive stimulation in brainstorming. *Journal of Personality and Social Psychology, 79*(5), 722.

Eesley, C. E., Hsu, D. H., & Roberts, E. B. (2014). The contingent effects of top management teams on venture performance: Aligning founding team composition with innovation strategy and commercialization environment. *Strategic Management Journal, 35*(12), 1798–1817.

Finke, R. A., Ward, T. B., & Smith, S. M. (1992). *Creative cognition: Theory, research, and applications.* Cambridge, MA: MIT Press.

Fisher, R., Ury, W. L., & Patton, B. (1991). *Getting to yes: Negotiating agreement without giving in* (2nd ed.). New York: Penguin.

Geschka, H., Schaude, G. R., & Schlicksupp, H. (1976). Modern techniques for solving problems. *International Studies of Management & Organization, 6,* 45–63.

Gick, M. L., & Holyoak, K. J. (1980). Analogical problem solving. *Cognitive Psychology, 12*(3), 306–355.

Ginnett, R. C. (2010). Crews as groups: Their formation and their leadership. In B. G. Kanki, R. L. Helmreich, & J. Anca (Eds.), *Crew resource management* (pp. 79–110). San Diego, CA: Elsevier.

Goodman, C. M. (1987). The Delphi technique: a critique. *Journal of Advanced Nursing, 12*(6), 729–734.

Gray, J. (2013). *Henri Poincaré: A scientific biography.* Princeton, NJ: Princeton University Press.

Guilford, J. P. (1956). The structure of intellect. *Psychological Bulletin, 53*(4), 267.

Hammond, J. S., Keeney, R. L., & Raiffa, H. (1998). The hidden traps in decision making. *Harvard Business Review, 76*(5), 47–58.

Hammond, J. S., Keeney, R. L., & Raiffa, H. (2002). *Smart choices: A practical guide to making better decisions.* New York: Random House.

Hargadon, A., & Sutton, R. I. (1997). Technology brokering and innovation in a product development firm. *Administrative Science Quarterly, 42,* 716–749.

Heslin, P. A. (2009). Better than brainstorming? Potential contextual boundary conditions to brainwriting for idea generation in organizations. *Journal of Occupational and Organizational Psychology, 82*(1), 129–145.

Hoffman, L. R., & Maier, N. R. (1961). Quality and acceptance of problem solutions by members of homogeneous and heterogeneous groups. *The Journal of Abnormal and Social Psychology, 62*(2), 401.

Holyoak, K. J. (2012). Analogy and relational reasoning. In K. J. Holyoak & R. G. Morrison (Eds.), *The Oxford handbook of thinking and reasoning* (pp. 234–259). New York: Oxford University Press.

Hong, L., & Page, S. E. (2001). Problem solving by heterogeneous agents. *Journal of Economic Theory, 97*(1), 123–163.

Hong, L., & Page, S. E. (2004). Groups of diverse problem solvers can outperform groups of high-ability problem solvers. *Proceedings of the National Academy of Sciences of the United States of America, 101*(46), 16385–16389.

Jehn, K. A., Northcraft, G. B., & Neale, M. A. (1999). Why differences make a difference: A field study of diversity, conflict and performance in workgroups. *Administrative Science Quarterly, 44*(4), 741–763.

Jeppesen, L. B., & Lakhani, K. R. (2010). Marginality and problem-solving effectiveness in broadcast search. *Organization Science, 21*(5), 1016–1033.

Jones, M. D. (1998). *The thinker's toolkit: 14 powerful techniques for problem solving.* New York: Three Rivers Press.

Katz, R., & Allen, T. J. (1982). Investigating the Not Invented Here (NIH) syndrome: A look at the performance, tenure, and communication patterns of 50 R & D Project Groups. *R & D Management, 12*(1), 7–20.

Kaur, R., Kumar, P., & Singh, R. P. (2014). A journey of digital storage from punch cards to cloud. *IOSR Journal of Engineering, 4*(3), 36–41.

Kavadias, S., & Sommer, S. C. (2009). The effects of problem structure and team diversity on brainstorming effectiveness. *Management Science, 55*(12), 1899–1913.

Kelley, T. (2001). *The art of innovation: lessons in creativity from IDEO, America's leading design firm.* New York: Random House.

Kohn, N. W., & Smith, S. M. (2011). Collaborative fixation: Effects of others' ideas on brainstorming. *Applied Cognitive Psychology, 25*(3), 359–371.

Kozlowski, S. W., & Bell, B. S. (2003). Work groups and teams in organizations. In W. C. Borman, D. R. Ilgen, & R. J. Klimoski (Eds.), *Handbook of psychology: Vol. 12. Industrial and organizational psychology* (pp. 333–375). New York: John Wiley & Sons.

Lehrer, J. (2012). Groupthink: The brainstorming myth. *The New Yorker, 30*, 12.

Linsey, J. S., Clauss, E., Kurtoglu, T., Murphy, J., Wood, K., & Markman, A. (2011). An experimental study of group idea generation techniques: understanding the roles of idea representation and viewing methods. *Journal of Mechanical Design, 133*(3), 031008.

Loewenstein, J. (2012). Thinking in business. In K. J. Holyoak & R. G. Morrison (Eds.), *The Oxford handbook of thinking and reasoning* (pp. 755–773). New York: Oxford University Press.

Madson, P. R. (2005). *Improv wisdom: Don't prepare, just show up.* New York: Bell Tower.

Mannix, E., & Neale, M. A. (2005). What differences make a difference? The promise and reality of diverse teams in organizations. *Psychological Science in the Public Interest, 6*(2), 31–55.

Mason, R. O., & Mitroff, I. I. (1981). *Challenging strategic planning assumptions: Theory, cases, and techniques.* New York: John Wiley & Sons.

Mathieu, J., Maynard, M. T., Rapp, T., & Gilson, L. (2008). Team effectiveness 1997–2007: A review of recent advancements and a glimpse into the future. *Journal of Management, 34*(3), 410–476.

McLeod, P. L., Lobel, S. A., & Cox, T. H. (1996). Ethnic diversity and creativity in small groups. *Small Group Research, 27*(2), 248–264.

Mullen, B., Johnson, C., & Salas, E. (1991). Productivity loss in brainstorming groups: A meta-analytic integration. *Basic and Applied Social Psychology, 12*(1), 3–23.

Mullen, P. M. (2003). Delphi: myths and reality. *Journal of Health Organization and Management, 17*(1), 37–52.

National Research Council. (2011a). *Intelligence analysis for tomorrow: Advances from the behavioral and social sciences.* Washington, DC: National Academies Press.

National Research Council. (2011b). *Intelligence analysis: Behavioral and social scientific foundations.* Washington, DC: National Academies Press.

National Research Council. (2014). *Convergence: Facilitating transdisciplinary integration of life sciences, physical sciences, engineering, and beyond.* Washington, DC: National Academies Press.

Nemeth, C. J., Personnaz, B., Personnaz, M., & Goncalo, J. A. (2004). The liberating role of conflict in group creativity: A study in two countries. *European Journal of Social Psychology, 34*(4), 365–374.

Ness, R. (2013). *Genius Unmasked.* New York: Oxford University Press.

Ness, R. B. (2012). *Innovation generation: How to produce creative and useful scientific ideas.* New York: Oxford University Press.

Orlando, A. (2015, February 4). The other guy's toolkit. *Texas Medical Center News.*

Osborn, A. F. (1948). *Your creative power.* New York: Charles Scribner's Sons.

Osborn, A. F. (1953). *Applied imagination—Principles and procedures of creative writing.* New York: Charles Scribner's Sons.

Oxley, N. L., Dzindolet, M. T., & Paulus, P. B. (1996). The effects of facilitators on the performance of brainstorming groups. *Journal of Social Behavior & Personality, 11*(4), 633.

Page, S. E. (2007). *The difference: How the power of diversity creates better groups, firms, schools, and societies.* Princeton, NJ: Princeton University Press.

Paulus, P. B., Larey, T. S., & Ortega, A. H. (1995). Performance and perceptions of brainstormers in an organizational setting. *Basic and Applied Social Psychology, 17*(1–2), 249–265.

Paulus, P. B., & Yang, H.-C. (2000). Idea generation in groups: A basis for creativity in organizations. *Organizational Behavior and Human Decision Processes, 82*(1), 76–87.

Poincaré, H. (1908). L'invention mathématique. *Revue générale des Sciences, 19,* 521–526.

Posner, M. I. (1973). *Cognition: An introduction.* Glenview, IL: Scott, Foresman and Company.

Prime Minister's Strategy Unit. (2004). Strategy survival guide. *Cabinet Office, Admiralty Arch, The Mall, London, UK.*

Rider, Y., & Thomason, N. (2010). Cognitive and pedagogical benefits of argument mapping: LAMP guides the way to better thinking. In A. Okada, S. J. Buckingham Shum, & T. Sherborne (Eds.), *Knowledge cartography: Software tools and mapping techniques* (pp. 113–130). London: Springer.

Rowe, G., & Wright, G. (2001). Expert opinions in forecasting: the role of the Delphi technique. In Armstrong, J. S. (Ed.), *Principles of forecasting: A handbook for researchers and practitioners* (pp. 125–144). Boston, MA: Kluwer Academic Publishers.

Scott, G., Leritz, L. E., & Mumford, M. D. (2004). The effectiveness of creativity training: A quantitative review. *Creativity Research Journal, 16*(4), 361–388.

Seelig, T. (2009). *What I wish I knew when I was 20: A crash course on making your place in the world.* New York: HarperCollins.

Shah, J. J., Smith, S. M., & Vargas-Hernandez, N. (2003). Metrics for measuring ideation effectiveness. *Design Studies, 24*(2), 111–134.

Smith, S. M., & Ward, T. B. (2012). Cognition and the creation of ideas. In K. J. Holyoak & R. G. Morrison (Eds.), *The Oxford handbook of thinking and reasoning* (pp. 456–474). New York: Oxford.

Snyder, A., Mitchell, J., Ellwood, S., Yates, A., & Pallier, G. (2004). Nonconscious idea generation. *Psychological Reports, 94*(3c), 1325–1330.

Sutton, R. I., & Hargadon, A. (1996). Brainstorming groups in context: Effectiveness in a product design firm. *Administrative Science Quarterly, 41,* 685–718.

Thompson, L. (2003). Improving the creativity of organizational work groups. *The Academy of Management Executive, 17*(1), 96–109.

Thompson, L. L. (2011). *Making the Team: A Guide for Managers* (4th ed.). Upper Saddle River, NJ: Pearson.

Thompson, L. L. (2012). *The mind and heart of the negotiator* (5th ed.). Upper Saddle River, NJ: Prentice Hall.

Turner, M. E., & Pratkanis, A. R. (1998). Twenty-five years of groupthink theory and research: Lessons from the evaluation of a theory. *Organizational Behavior and Human Decision Processes, 73*(2), 105–115.

Uzzi, B., & Spiro, J. (2005). Collaboration and creativity: The small world problem. *American Journal of Sociology, 111*(2), 447–504.

Van de Ven, A. H., & Delbecq, A. L. (1974). The effectiveness of nominal, Delphi, and interacting group decision making processes. *Academy of Management Journal, 17*(4), 605–621.

VanGundy, A. B. (1988). *Techniques of structured problem solving.* New York: Van Nostrand Reinhold.

Verberne, T. (1997, August 1). Creative Fitness. *Training & Development, 51*(8), 69–71.

Vroom, V. H., Grant, L. D., & Cotton, T. S. (1969). The consequences of social interaction in group problem solving. *Organizational Behavior and Human Performance, 4*(1), 77–95.

Watson, W. E., Kumar, K., & Michaelsen, L. K. (1993). Cultural diversity's impact on interaction process and performance: Comparing homogeneous and diverse task groups. *Academy of Management Journal, 36*(3), 590–602.

Welch, H. G. (2015). *Less medicine more health: 7 assumptions that drive too much medical care*. Boston, MA: Beacon Press.

Williams, K. Y., & O'Reilly, C. A. (1998). Demography and diversity in organizations: A review of 40 years of research. *Research in Organizational Behavior, 20*, 77–140.

## CHAPTER 6

Abrahamson, E. (1996). Management fashion. *Academy of Management Review, 21*(1), 254–285.

Anderson, C. (2004). The long tail. *Wired, 12*(10), 170–177.

Archer, N. P., & Ghasemzadeh, F. (1999). An integrated framework for project portfolio selection. *International Journal of Project Management, 17*(4), 207–216.

Ariely, D., & Loewenstein, G. (2006). The heat of the moment: The effect of sexual arousal on sexual decision making. *Journal of Behavioral Decision Making, 19*(2), 87–98.

Arkes, H. R., & Kajdasz, J. (2011). Intuitive theories of behavior. In B. Fischhoff & C. Chauvin (Eds.), *Intelligence analysis: Behavioral and social scientific foundations* (pp. 143–168). Washington, DC: The National Academies Press.

Armstrong, J. S. (2001). Combining forecasts. In Armstrong, J. S. (Ed.), *Principles of forecasting: A handbook for researchers and practioners* (pp. 417–439). Boston, MA: Kluwer Academic Publishers.

Axelsson, R. (1998). Towards an evidence-based health care management. *The International Journal of Health Planning and Management, 13*(4), 307–317.

Barends, E., ten Have, S., & Huisman, F. (2012). Learning from other evidence-based practices: the case of medicine. In D. M. Rousseau (Ed.), *The Oxford handbook of evidence-based management* (pp. 25–42). New York: Oxford University Press.

Bazerman, M. H., & Moore, D. A. (2008). *Judgment in managerial decision making*. Hoboken, NJ: John Wiley & Sons.

Becklen, R., & Cervone, D. (1983). Selective looking and the noticing of unexpected events. *Memory & Cognition, 11*(6), 601–608.

Blair, C. (1996). *Hitler's U-boat war: The hunters 1939–1942* (Vol. 1). New York: Modern Library.

Cottrell, S. (2011). *Critical thinking skills: Developing effective analysis and argument* (2nd ed.). London, UK: Palgrave Macmillan.

Dawes, R. M. (1979). The robust beauty of improper linear models in decision making. *American Psychologist, 34*(7), 571.

Dawes, R. M., & Corrigan, B. (1974). Linear models in decision making. *Psychological Bulletin, 81*(2), 95.

Denrell, J. (2003). Vicarious learning, undersampling of failure, and the myths of management. *Organization Science, 14*(3), 227–243.

Edwards, W. (1977). How to use multiattribute utility measurement for social decision making. *Systems, Man and Cybernetics, Institute of Electrical and Electronics Engineers Transactions on Systems, Man, and Cybernetics, 7*(5), 326–340.

Edwards, W., & Barron, F. H. (1994). SMARTS and SMARTER: Improved simple methods for multiattribute utility measurement. *Organizational Behavior and Human Decision Processes, 60*(3), 306–325.

Eisenführ, F., Weber, M., & Langer, T. (2010). *Rational decision making*. Heidelberg, Germany: Springer.

Gauch, H. G. (2003). *Scientific method in practice*. Cambridge, UK: Cambridge University Press.

Goodwin, P., & Wright, G. (2009). *Decision analysis for management judgment* (4th ed.). Chichester, UK: John Wiley & Sons.

Grimes, D. A., & Schulz, K. F. (2002). An overview of clinical research: the lay of the land. *The Lancet, 359*(9300), 57–61.

Institute of Medicine. (2014). *Evaluation design for complex global initiatives: Workshop summary*. Washington, DC: The National Academies Press.

Ioannidis, J. P. (2005). Why most published research findings are false. *PLoS Medicine, 2*(8), e124.

Kahneman, D., Slovic, P., & Tversky, A. (Eds.). (1982). *Judgment under uncertainty: Heuristics and biases*. Cambridge, UK: Cambridge University Press.

Keeney, R. L. (1982). Decision analysis: an overview. *Operations Research, 30*(5), 803–838.

Keeney, R. L. (1992). *Value-focused thinking: A path to creative decision making*. Cambridge, MA: Harvard University Press.

Keeney, R. L. (2007). Developing objectives and attributes. In W. Edwards, R. F. Miles, & D. von Winterfeldt (Eds.), *Advances in decision analysis: From foundations to applications* (pp. 104–128). New York: Cambridge University Press.

Keeney, R. L., & Raiffa, H. (1993). *Decisions with multiple objectives: preferences and value trade-offs*, Cambridge, UK: Cambridge University Press.

Leebron, D. (2015). SAILS framework. Personal communication.

Lord, L. K., Wittum, T. E., Ferketich, A. K., Funk, J. A., & Rajala-Schultz, P. J. (2007). Search and identification methods that owners use to find a lost dog. *Journal of the American Veterinary Medical Association, 230*(2), 211–216.

Luce, R. D., & Raiffa, H. (1957). *Games and decisions: Introduction and critical survey*. New York: Dover.

Makridakis, S., & Gaba, A. (1998). *Judgment: its role and value for strategy*. In G. Wight and P. Goodwin (Eds.), *Forecasting with judgment*. Chichester, UK. John Wiley & Sons.

Medawar, P. B. (1979). *Advice to a young scientist*. New York: Basic Books.

National Research Council. (2011). *Intelligence analysis: Behavioral and social scientific foundations*. Washington, DC: National Academies Press.

Olson, D. L. (1996). *Decision aids for selection problems*. New York: Springer.

Open Science Collaboration. (2015). Estimating the reproducibility of psychological science. *Science, 349*(6251), aac4716.

Pfeffer, J., & Sutton, R. I. (2006a). Evidence-based management. *Harvard Business Review, 84*(1), 62.

Pfeffer, J., & Sutton, R. I. (2006b). *Hard facts, dangerous half-truths, and total nonsense: Profiting from evidence-based management*. Boston, MA: Harvard Business Press.

Pratkanis, A. R., & Farquhar, P. H. (1992). A brief history of research on phantom alternatives: Evidence for seven empirical generalizations about phantoms. *Basic and Applied Social Psychology, 13*(1), 103–122.

Rousseau, D. M. (2006). Is there such a thing as "evidence-based management?" *Academy of Management Review, 31*(2), 256–269.

Rousseau, D. M. (2012). Organizational behavior's contributions to evidence-based management. In D. M. Rousseau (Ed.), *The Oxford handbook of evidence-based management* (pp. 61–78). New York: Oxford University Press.

Schum, D. A. (1994). *The evidential foundations of probabilistic reasoning*. Evanston, IL: Northwestern University Press.

Schünemann, H. J., Jaeschke, R., Cook, D. J., Bria, W. F., El-Solh, A. A., Ernst, A., Krishnan, J. A. (2006). An official ATS statement: grading the quality of evidence and strength of recommendations in ATS guidelines and recommendations. *American Journal of Respiratory and Critical Care Medicine, 174*(5), 605–614.

Schünemann, H. J., Oxman, A. D., Brozek, J., Glasziou, P., Jaeschke, R., Vist, G. E., Montori, V. M. (2008). Grading quality of evidence and strength of recommendations for diagnostic tests and strategies. *BMJ*, *336*(7653), 1106–1110.

Sherman, L. W. (2002). Evidence-based policing: Social organization of information for social control. In E. Waring & D. Weisburd (Eds.), *Crime and social organization* (pp. 217–248). New Brunswick, NJ: Transaction Publishers.

Simons, D. J. (2000). Attentional capture and inattentional blindness. *Trends in Cognitive Sciences*, *4*(4), 147–155.

Simons, D. J., & Chabris, C. F. (1999). Gorillas in our midst: Sustained inattentional blindness for dynamic events. *Perception–London*, *28*(9), 1059–1074.

Simonsohn, U. (2007). Clouds make nerds look good: Field evidence of the impact of incidental factors on decision making. *Journal of Behavioral Decision Making*, *20*(2), 143–152.

Thompson, J. M. T. (2013). Advice to a young researcher: with reminiscences of a life in science. *Philosophical Transactions of the Royal Society of London A: Mathematical, Physical and Engineering Sciences*, *371*(1993), 20120425.

Tsuruda, K., & Hayashi, K. (1975). Direction finding technique for elliptically polarized VLF electro-magnetic waves and its application to the low-latitude whistlers. *Journal of Atmospheric and Terrestrial Physics*, *37*(9), 1193–1202.

Tversky, A., & Kahneman, D. (1974). Judgment under uncertainty: Heuristics and biases. *Science*, *185*(4157), 1124–1131.

U.S. Preventive Services Task Force. (1989). *Guide to clinical preventive services*. Baltimore, MD: Williams and Wilkins.

Van Buren, M. E., & Safferstone, T. (2009). The quick wins paradox. *Harvard Business Review*, *87*(1), 55–61.

van Gelder, T. (2010). Elements of a major business decision. Retrieved June 8, 2015 from http://timvangelder.com/2010/12/09/elements-of-a-major-business-decision/

von Winterfeldt, D., & Edwards, W. (1986). *Decision analysis and behavioral research*. Cambridge: Cambridge University Press.

Watkins, M. (2004). Strategy for the critical first 90 days of leadership. *Strategy & Leadership*, *32*(1), 15–20.

Weick, K. E. (1984). Small wins: Redefining the scale of social problems. *American Psychologist*, *39*(1), 40.

Weiss, E., Slater, M., & Lord, L. (2012). Frequency of lost dogs and cats in the United States and the methods used to locate them. *Animals*, *2*(2), 301–315.

## CHAPTER 7

Abela, A. (2008). *Advanced presentations by design: Creating communication that drives action*: San Francisco, CA: Pfeiffer.

Allen, M. (1991). Meta-analysis comparing the persuasiveness of one-sided and two-sided messages. *Western Journal of Speech Communication*, *55*(4), 390–404.

Alley, M. (2003). *The craft of scientific presentations*. New York: Springer.

Alley, M. (2013). *The craft of scientific presentations* (2nd ed.). New York: Springer.

Alley, M., & Neeley, K. A. (2005). Rethinking the design of presentation slides: A case for sentence headlines and visual evidence. *Technical Communication*, *52*(4), 417–426.

Alley, M., Schreiber, M., Ramsdell, K., & Muffo, J. (2006). How the design of headlines in presentation slides affects audience retention. *Technical Communication*, *53*(2), 225–234.

Arkes, H. R., & Kajdasz, J. (2011). Intuitive theories of behavior. In B. Fischhoff & C. Chauvin (Eds.), *Intelligence analysis: Behavioral and social scientific foundations* (pp. 143–168). Washington, DC: National Academies Press.

Arpan, L. M., & Roskos-Ewoldsen, D. R. (2005). Stealing thunder: Analysis of the effects of proactive disclosure of crisis information. *Public Relations Review, 31*(3), 425–433.

Artz, N., & Tybout, A. M. (1999). The moderating impact of quantitative information on the relationship between source credibility and persuasion: A persuasion knowledge model interpretation. *Marketing Letters, 10*(1), 51–63.

Barry, D., & Elmes, M. (1997). Strategy retold: Toward a narrative view of strategic discourse. *Academy of Management Review, 22*(2), 429–452.

Bartsch, R. A., & Cobern, K. M. (2003). Effectiveness of PowerPoint presentations in lectures. *Computers & Education, 41*(1), 77–86.

Bartunek, J. M. (2007). Academic-practitioner collaboration need not require joint or relevant research: Toward a relational scholarship of integration. *Academy of Management Journal, 50*(6), 1323–1333.

Bergen, L., Grimes, T., & Potter, D. (2005). How attention partitions itself during simultaneous message presentations. *Human Communication Research, 31*(3), 311–336.

Berk, R. A. (2011). Research on PowerPoint®: From basic features to multimedia. *International Journal of Technology in Teaching and Learning, 7*(1), 24–35.

Booth, W. C., Colomb, G. G., & Williams, J. M. (2003). *The craft of research*: Chicago, IL: University of Chicago Press.

Brooks, A. W., Huang, L., Kearney, S. W., & Murray, F. E. (2014). Investors prefer entrepreneurial ventures pitched by attractive men. *Proceedings of the National Academy of Sciences, 111*(12), 4427–4431.

Bumiller, E. (2010, April 26). We have met the enemy and he is PowerPoint. *The New York Times*.

Burke, W. W. (2014). *Organization change: Theory and practice* (4th ed.). Thousand Oaks, CA: Sage.

Butcher, K. R. (2014). The multimedia principle. In R. E. Mayer (Ed.), *The Cambridge handbook of multimedia learning* (2nd ed., pp. 174–205). New York: Cambridge University Press.

Castka, P., Bamber, C., Sharp, J., & Belohoubek, P. (2001). Factors affecting successful implementation of high performance teams. *Team Performance Management, 7*(7/8), 123–134.

Cialdini, R. B. (2001a). Harnessing the science of persuasion. *Harvard Business Review, 79*(9), 72–81.

Cialdini, R. B. (2001b). *Influence: Science and practice* (Vol. 4). Boston, MA: Allyn and Bacon.

Collins, J. (2004). Giving a PowerPoint presentation: The art of communicating effectively. Education Techniques for Lifelong Learning. *Radiographics, 24*(4), 1185–1192.

Dalal, R. S., & Bonaccio, S. (2010). What types of advice do decision-makers prefer? *Organizational Behavior and Human Decision Processes, 112*(1), 11–23.

Davis, I., Keeling, D., Schreier, P., & Williams, A. (2007). The McKinsey approach to problem solving. *McKinsey Staff Paper* (66), 27.

Denning, S. (2006). Effective storytelling: strategic business narrative techniques. *Strategy & Leadership, 34*(1), 42–48.

Dionne, E. (2014, December 7). In politics, does evidence matter? *The Washington Post*.

Doumont, J.-L. (2005). The cognitive style of PowerPoint: Slides are not all evil. *Technical Communication, 52*(1), 64–70.

Doumont, J.-L. (2009). *Trees, maps, and theorems: effective communication for rational minds*. Kraainem, Belgium: Principiae.

Duarte, N. (2008). *Slide ology: the art and science of creating great presentations*. Toronto: O'Reilly Media.

Duarte, N. (2010). *Resonate: Present visual stories that transform audiences*. Hoboken, NJ: John Wiley & Sons.

Dunbar, K. N., & Klahr, D. (2012). Scientific thinking and reasoning. In K. J. Holyoak & R. G. Morrison (Eds.), *The Oxford handbook of thinking and reasoning* (pp. 701–718). New York: Oxford University Press.

Eagly, A. H., Ashmore, R. D., Makhijani, M. G., & Longo, L. C. (1991). What is beautiful is good, but . . .: A meta-analytic review of research on the physical attractiveness stereotype. *Psychological Bulletin, 110*(1), 109.

Fischer, M. H. (2000). Do irrelevant depth cues affect the comprehension of bar graphs? *Applied Cognitive Psychology, 14*(2), 151–162.

Flynn, F. J. (2003). How much should I give and how often? The effects of generosity and frequency of favor exchange on social status and productivity. *Academy of Management Journal, 46*(5), 539–553.

Forsyth, R., & Waller, A. (1995). Making your point: principles of visual design for computer aided slide and poster production. *Archives of Disease in Childhood, 72*(1), 80.

Gardner, H. (2006). *Changing minds: The art and science of changing our own and other people's minds.* Boston, MA: Harvard Business Press.

Garner, J., & Alley, M. (2013). How the design of presentation slides affects audience comprehension: A case for the assertion–evidence approach. *International Journal of Engineering Education, 29*(6), 1564–1579.

Garner, J. K., Alley, M., Wolfe, K. L., & Zappe, S. (2011). *Assertion–evidence slides appear to lead to better comprehension and recall of more complex concepts.* Paper presented at the 118th American Society for Engineering Education Annual Conference, Vancouver, BC.

Gelula, M. H. (1997). Effective lecture presentation skills. *Surgical Neurology, 47*(2), 201–204.

Giluk, T. L., & Rynes-Weller, S. (2012). Research findings practitioners resist: Lessons for management academics from evidence-based medicine. In D. M. Rousseau (Ed.), *The Oxford handbook of evidence-based management* (pp. 130–164). New York: Oxford University Press.

Gino, F. (2008). Do we listen to advice just because we paid for it? The impact of advice cost on its use. *Organizational Behavior and Human Decision Processes, 107*(2), 234–245.

Goodwin, P., & Wright, G. (2009). *Decision analysis for management judgment* (4th ed.). Chichester, UK: John Wiley & Sons.

Hoadley, E. (1990). Investigating the effects of color. *Communications of the Association for Computing Machinery, 33*(2), 120–125.

Holley, P. (2014, December 10). The Australian researcher who says his government's shark policy bites because it's based on 'Jaws.' *The Washington Post.*

Hoy, W. K., & Smith, P. A. (2007). Influence: a key to successful leadership. *International Journal of Educational Management, 21*(2), 158–167.

Jamet, E., & Le Bohec, O. (2007). The effect of redundant text in multimedia instruction. *Contemporary Educational Psychology, 32*(4), 588–598.

Jarvenpaa, S. L., & Dickson, G. W. (1988). Graphics and managerial decision making: Research-based guidelines. *Communications of the Association for Computing Machinery, 31*(6), 764–774.

Juice Analytics. Chart Chooser. Retrieved from http://labs.juiceanalytics.com/chartchooser/index.html. On June 1, 2014.

Kalyuga, S., Chandler, P., & Sweller, J. (2000). Incorporating learner experience into the design of multimedia instruction. *Journal of Educational Psychology, 92*(1), 126.

Kalyuga, S., Chandler, P., & Sweller, J. (2004). When redundant on-screen text in multimedia technical instruction can interfere with learning. *Human Factors: The Journal of the Human Factors and Ergonomics Society, 46*(3), 567–581.

Kalyuga, S., & Sweller, J. (2014). The redundancy principle in multimedia learning. In R. E. Mayer (Ed.), *The Cambridge handbook of multimedia learning* (2nd ed., pp. 247–262). New York: Cambridge University Press.

Kawasaki, G. (2004). *The art of the start: The time-tested, battle-hardened guide for anyone starting anything.* New York: Penguin.

Kawasaki, G. (2008). *Reality check: The irreverent guide to outsmarting, outmanaging, and outmarketing your competition.* New York: Penguin.

Keisler, J. M., & Noonan, P. S. (2012). Communicating analytic results: A tutorial for decision consultants. *Decision Analysis, 9*(3), 274–292.

Kerr, N. L., & Bruun, S. E. (1983). Dispensability of member effort and group motivation losses: Free-rider effects. *Journal of Personality and Social Psychology, 44*(1), 78.

Konnikova, M. (2014, January 21). The six things that make stories go viral will amaze, and maybe infuriate, you. *The New Yorker*.

Koomey, J. (2008). *Turning numbers into knowledge: mastering the art of problem solving*. Oakland, CA: Analytics Press.

Kosara, R., & Mackinlay, J. (2013). Storytelling: The next step for visualization. *Computer* (5), 44–50.

Kosslyn, S. M. (1989). Understanding charts and graphs. *Applied Cognitive Psychology, 3*(3), 185–225.

Kosslyn, S. M. (2007). *Clear and to the point: 8 psychological principles for compelling PowerPoint presentations*. New York: Oxford University Press.

Langlois, J. H., Kalakanis, L., Rubenstein, A. J., Larson, A., Hallam, M., & Smoot, M. (2000). Maxims or myths of beauty? A meta-analytic and theoretical review. *Psychological Bulletin, 126*(3), 390.

Levi, D. (2011). *Group dynamics for teams*. Thousand Oaks, CA: Sage.

Lidwell, W., Holden, K., & Butler, J. (2010). *Universal principles of design: 125 ways to enhance usability, influence perception, increase appeal, make better design decisions, and teach through design*. Gloucester, MA: Rockport Publishers.

Lounsbury, M., & Glynn, M. A. (2001). Cultural entrepreneurship: Stories, legitimacy, and the acquisition of resources. *Strategic Management Journal, 22*(6–7), 545–564.

Lussier, R., & Achua, C. (2007). *Leadership: Theory, application, & skill development* (3rd ed.). Mason, OH: Thomson South-Western.

Mackendrick, A. (2004). *On film-making: An introduction to the craft of the director*. New York: Faber and Faber, Inc.

Mackiewicz, J. (2007a). Audience perceptions of fonts in projected PowerPoint text slides. *Technical Communication, 54*(3), 295–307.

Mackiewicz, J. (2007b). Perceptions of clarity and attractiveness in PowerPoint graph slides. *Technical Communication, 54*(2), 145–156.

Markel, M. (2009). Exploiting verbal-visual synergy in presentation slides. *Technical Communication, 56*(2), 122–131.

Martens, M. L., Jennings, J. E., & Jennings, P. D. (2007). Do the stories they tell get them the money they need? The role of entrepreneurial narratives in resource acquisition. *Academy of Management Journal, 50*(5), 1107–1132.

Mayer, R. E. (2014). Introduction to multimedia learning. In R. E. Mayer (Ed.), *The Cambridge handbook of multimedia learning* (2nd ed., pp. 1–24). New York: Cambridge University Press.

Mayer, R. E., & Fiorella, L. (2014). Principles for reducing extraneous processing in multimedia learning: Coherence, signaling, redundancy, spatial contiguity, and temporal contiguity principles. In R. E. Mayer (Ed.), *The Cambridge handbook of multimedia learning* (2nd ed., pp. 279–315). New York: Cambridge University Press.

Mayer, R. E., Heiser, J., & Lonn, S. (2001). Cognitive constraints on multimedia learning: When presenting more material results in less understanding. *Journal of Educational Psychology, 93*(1), 187.

Mayer, R. E., & Pilegard, C. (2014). Principles for managing essential processing in multimedia learning: segmenting, pre-training, and modality principles. In R. E. Mayer (Ed.), *The Cambridge handbook of multimedia learning* (2nd ed., pp. 316–344). New York: Cambridge University Press.

McCroskey, J. C., & Teven, J. J. (1999). Goodwill: A reexamination of the construct and its measurement. *Communications Monographs, 66*(1), 90–103.

McIntyre, M. E. (1997). Lucidity and Science I: Writing skills and the pattern perception hypothesis. *Interdisciplinary Science Reviews, 22*(3), 199–216.

McKee, R., & Fryer, B. (2003). Storytelling that moves people. *Harvard Business Review, 81*(6), 51–55.

Menzel, K. E., & Carrell, L. J. (1994). The relationship between preparation and performance in public speaking. *Communication Education, 43*(1), 17–26.

Mindich, D. T. Z. (1998). *Just the facts: How "objectivity" came to define American journalism.* New York: New York University Press.

Minto, B. (2009). *The pyramid principle: logic in writing and thinking.* Harlow, UK: Pearson Education.

Mobius, M. M., & Rosenblat, T. S. (2006). Why beauty matters. *The American Economic Review, 96*(1), 222–235.

National Research Council. (2011). *Intelligence analysis: Behavioral and social scientific foundations.* Washington, DC: National Academies Press.

Nickerson, R. S. (1998). Confirmation bias: a ubiquitous phenomenon in many guises. *Review of General Psychology, 2*(2), 175.

Nisbett, R. E., Zukier, H., & Lemley, R. E. (1981). The dilution effect: Nondiagnostic information weakens the implications of diagnostic information. *Cognitive Psychology, 13*(2), 248–277.

Orwell, G. (1970). *Politics and the English language* (Vol. 4). New York: Harcourt, Brace, Javanovich.

Parks, C. D., & Komorita, S. S. (1998). Reciprocity research and its implications for the negotiation process. *International Negotiation, 3*(2), 151–169.

Pechmann, C. (1992). Predicting when two-sided ads will be more effective than one-sided ads: The role of correlational and correspondent inferences. *Journal of Marketing Research, 29*(November), 441–453.

Petty, R. E., & Cacioppo, J. T. (1984). The effects of involvement on responses to argument quantity and quality: Central and peripheral routes to persuasion. *Journal of Personality and Social Psychology, 46*(1), 69.

Pfeffer, J., & Sutton, R. I. (2006). *Hard facts, dangerous half-truths, and total nonsense: Profiting from evidence-based management.* Boston, MA: Harvard Business Press.

Reynolds, G. (2011). *Presentation Zen: Simple ideas on presentation design and delivery.* Berkeley, CA: New Riders.

Roche, S. M. (1979). The thought process in McKinsey reports and presentations.

Schum, D. A. (1994). *The evidential foundations of probabilistic reasoning.* Evanston, IL: Northwestern University Press.

Shah, P., & Hoeffner, J. (2002). Review of graph comprehension research: Implications for instruction. *Educational Psychology Review, 14*(1), 47–69.

Shaw, G., Brown, R., & Bromiley, P. (1998). Strategic stories: How 3M is rewriting business planning. *Harvard Business Review, 76*(3), 41–42, 44, 46–50.

Sherman, L. W. (2002). Evidence-based policing: Social organization of information for social control. In E. Waring & D. Weisburd (Eds.), *Crime and social organization* (pp. 217–248). New Brunswick, NJ: Transaction Publishers.

Smith, T. E., & Frymier, A. B. (2006). Get 'real': Does practicing speeches before an audience improve performance? *Communication Quarterly, 54*(1), 111–125.

Spence, I., & Lewandowsky, S. (1991). Displaying proportions and percentages. *Applied Cognitive Psychology, 5*(1), 61–77.

Strunk, W. (2015). *The elements of style.* Grammar, Inc.

Thompson, J. M. T. (2013). Advice to a young researcher: with reminiscences of a life in science. *Philosophical Transactions of the Royal Society of London A: Mathematical, Physical and Engineering Sciences, 371*(1993), 20120425.

Thompson, L. L. (2012). *The mind and heart of the negotiator* (5th ed.). Upper Saddle River, NJ: Prentice Hall.

Truffaut, F., & Scott, H. G. (1983). *Hitchcock.* New York: Simon and Schuster.

Tufte, E. R. (2001). *The visual display of quantitative information.* Cheshire, CT: Graphics Press.

Tufte, E. R. (2003). *The cognitive style of PowerPoint* (Vol. 2006). Cheshire, CT: Graphics Press.

Tversky, B., Morrison, J. B., & Betrancourt, M. (2002). Animation: can it facilitate? *International Journal of Human-Computer Studies, 57*(4), 247–262.

van Gog, T. (2014). The signaling (or cueing) principle in multimedia learning. In R. E. Mayer (Ed.), *The Cambridge handbook of multimedia learning* (Second ed., pp. 263–278) New York: Cambridge University Press.

Viegas, F. B., Wattenberg, M., Van Ham, F., Kriss, J., & McKeon, M. (2007). Many eyes: a site for visualization at Internet scale. *Visualization and Computer Graphics, Institute of Electrical and Electronics Engineers Transactions on Visualization and Computer Graphics, 13*(6), 1121–1128.

Visual-literacy.org. A periodic table of visualization methods. Retrieved from http://www.visual-literacy.org/periodic_table/periodic_table.html

Williams, K. D., Bourgeois, M. J., & Croyle, R. T. (1993). The effects of stealing thunder in criminal and civil trials. *Law and Human Behavior, 17*(6), 597.

Woodside, A. G., Sood, S., & Miller, K. E. (2008). When consumers and brands talk: Storytelling theory and research in psychology and marketing. *Psychology & Marketing, 25*(2), 97–145.

Yalch, R. F., & Elmore-Yalch, R. (1984). The effect of numbers on the route to persuasion. *Journal of Consumer Research, 11*, 522–527.

Yau, N. (2011). *Visualize this: the FlowingData guide to design, visualization, and statistics.* Indianapolis, IN: John Wiley & Sons.

Zelazny, G. (1996). *Say it with charts.* New York: McGraw-Hill.

Zelazny, G. (2006). *Say it with presentations.* New York: McGraw-Hill.

Zuckerman, M., & Driver, R. E. (1989). What sounds beautiful is good: The vocal attractiveness stereotype. *Journal of Nonverbal Behavior, 13*(2), 67–82.

## CHAPTER 8

Aguinis, H., & Kraiger, K. (2009). Benefits of training and development for individuals and teams, organizations, and society. *Annual Review of Psychology, 60*, 451–474.

Allen, J. A., Sands, S. J., Mueller, S. L., Frear, K. A., Mudd, M., & Rogelberg, S. G. (2012). Employees' feelings about more meetings: An overt analysis and recommendations for improving meetings. *Management Research Review, 35*(5), 405–418.

Ancona, D., Bresman, H., & Kaeufer, K. (2002). The Comparative Advantage of X-Teams. *Sloan Management Review* (Spring).

Ancona, D. G., & Caldwell, D. F. (1992). Demography and design: Predictors of new product team performance. *Organization Science, 3*(3), 321–341.

Appleton-Knapp, S. L., & Krentler, K. A. (2006). Measuring student expectations and their effects on satisfaction: The importance of managing student expectations. *Journal of Marketing Education, 28*(3), 254–264.

Archer, J., & Stuart-Cox, K. (2013). Skills for business analysis. In P. Pullan & J. Archer (Eds.), *Business Analysis and Leadership: Influencing Change.* London: Kogan Page Publishers.

Ashley, A. (2005). *Oxford handbook of commercial correspondence.* Oxford:Oxford University Press.

Atkinson, R. (1999). Project management: cost, time and quality, two best guesses and a phenomenon, it's time to accept other success criteria. *International Journal of Project Management, 17*(6), 337–342.

Axelrod, R. (1980a). Effective choice in the prisoner's dilemma. *Journal of Conflict Resolution, 24*(1), 3–25.

Axelrod, R. (1980b). More effective choice in the prisoner's dilemma. *Journal of Conflict Resolution, 24*(3), 379–403.

Axelrod, R., & Hamilton, W. D. (1981). The evolution of cooperation. *Science, 211*(4489), 1390–1396.

Axelrod, R. M. (1984). *The evolution of cooperation.* New York: Basic Books.

Bang, H., Fuglesang, S. L., Ovesen, M. R., & Eilertsen, D. E. (2010). Effectiveness in top management group meetings: The role of goal clarity, focused communication, and learning behavior. *Scandinavian Journal of Psychology, 51*(3), 253–261.

Barends, E., ten Have, S., & Huisman, F. (2012). Learning from other evidence-based practices: the case of medicine. In D. M. Rousseau (Ed.), *The Oxford handbook of evidence-based management* (pp. 25–42). New York: Oxford University Press.

Barling, J., Weber, T., & Kelloway, E. K. (1996). Effects of transformational leadership training on attitudinal and financial outcomes: A field experiment. *Journal of Applied Psychology, 81*(6), 827.

Bazerman, M. H., & Neale, M. A. (1992). *Negotiating rationally*. New York: The Free Press.

Bendor, J., Kramer, R. M., & Stout, S. (1991). When in doubt . . . Cooperation in a noisy prisoner's dilemma. *Journal of Conflict Resolution, 35*(4), 691–719.

Bluedorn, A. C., Turban, D. B., & Love, M. S. (1999). The effects of stand-up and sit-down meeting formats on meeting outcomes. *Journal of Applied Psychology, 84*(2), 277.

Bradley, J. (2008). Management based critical success factors in the implementation of Enterprise Resource Planning systems. *International Journal of Accounting Information Systems, 9*(3), 175–200.

Bragger, J. D., Kutcher, E., Morgan, J., & Firth, P. (2002). The effects of the structured interview on reducing biases against pregnant job applicants. *Sex Roles, 46*(7–8), 215–226.

Brass, D. J., Galaskiewicz, J., Greve, H. R., & Tsai, W. (2004). Taking stock of networks and organizations: A multilevel perspective. *Academy of Management Journal, 47*(6), 795–817.

Brett, J. M. (2000). Culture and negotiation. *International Journal of Psychology, 35*(2), 97–104.

Brown, S. W., & Swartz, T. A. (1989). A gap analysis of professional service quality. *The Journal of Marketing*, 92–98.

Bryant, A. (2010, March 20). Just give him 5 sentences, not 'War and Peace'. *International Herald Tribune*.

Cannon, M. D., & Witherspoon, R. (2005). Actionable feedback: Unlocking the power of learning and performance improvement. *The Academy of Management Executive, 19*(2), 120–134.

Carson, J. B., Tesluk, P. E., & Marrone, J. A. (2007). Shared leadership in teams: An investigation of antecedent conditions and performance. *Academy of Management Journal, 50*(5), 1217–1234.

Cartwright, S., & Cooper, C. L. (1993). The role of culture compatibility in successful organizational marriage. *The Academy of Management Executive, 7*(2), 57–70.

Cartwright, S., & Schoenberg, R. (2006). Thirty years of mergers and acquisitions research: Recent advances and future opportunities. *British Journal of Management, 17*(S1), S1–S5.

Clarke, A. (1999). A practical use of key success factors to improve the effectiveness of project management. *International Journal of Project Management, 17*(3), 139–145.

Cohen, S. G., Ledford, G. E., & Spreitzer, G. M. (1996). A predictive model of self-managing work team effectiveness. *Human Relations, 49*(5), 643–676.

Crainer, S., & Dearlove, D. (2004). The write stuff. *Business Strategy Review, 15*(4), 19–24.

Cronin, M. A., & Weingart, L. R. (2007). Representational gaps, information processing, and conflict in functionally diverse teams. *Academy of Management Review, 32*(3), 761–773.

De Bono, E. (1999). *Six Thinking Hats* (2nd ed.). Boston, MA: Back Bay Books.

De Janasz, S. C., Sullivan, S. E., & Whiting, V. (2003). Mentor networks and career success: Lessons for turbulent times. *The Academy of Management Executive, 17*(4), 78–91.

Department of the Air Force. (1998). *Crew Resource Management (CRM)—Basic Concepts*. Andrews Air Force Base, Maryland.

Dey, P. K., Kinch, J., & Ogunlana, S. O. (2007). Managing risk in software development projects: a case study. *Industrial Management & Data Systems, 107*(2), 284–303.

Doumont, J.-L. (2009). *Trees, maps, and theorems: effective communication for rational minds*. Kraainem, Belgium: Principiae.

Drucker, P. F. (2004). What makes an effective executive? *Harvard Business Review, 82*(6), 58–63.

Edmondson, A. C. (1996). Learning from mistakes is easier said than done: Group and organizational influences on the detection and correction of human error. *The Journal of Applied Behavioral Science, 32*(1), 5–28.

Edmondson, A. C. (2003). Speaking up in the operating room: How team leaders promote learning in interdisciplinary action teams. *Journal of Management Studies, 40*(6), 1419–1452.

Einhorn, H. J., & Hogarth, R. M. (1981). Behavioral decision theory: Processes of judgment and choice. *Journal of Accounting Research*, 1–31.

Emanuel, E. J. (2013). Going to the moon in health care: medicine's big hairy audacious goal (BHAG). *JAMA, 310*(18), 1925–1926.

Fischer, U., & Orasanu, J. (2000, August). *Error-challenging strategies: Their role in preventing and correcting errors*. Paper presented at the Proceedings of the Human Factors and Ergonomics Society Annual Meeting. San Diego, CA.

Fisher, R., Ury, W. L., & Patton, B. (1991). *Getting to yes: Negotiating agreement without giving in* (2nd ed.). New York: Penguin.

Fisk, C. L. (2006). Credit where it's due: The law and norms of attribution. *Georgetown Law Journal, 95*, 49.

Fletcher, G., Flin, R., McGeorge, P., Glavin, R., Maran, N., & Patey, R. (2003). Anaesthetists' Non-Technical Skills (ANTS): evaluation of a behavioural marker system†. *British Journal of Anaesthesia, 90*(5), 580–588.

Flin, R., & Maran, N. (2004). Identifying and training non-technical skills for teams in acute medicine. *Quality and Safety in Health Care, 13*(Suppl 1), i80–i84.

Flin, R., Martin, L., Goeters, K.-M., Hormann, H., Amalberti, R., Valot, C., & Nijhuis, H. (2003). Development of the NOTECHS (non-technical skills) system for assessing pilots' CRM skills. *Human Factors and Aerospace Safety, 3*, 97–120.

Flin, R., O'Connor, P., & Mearns, K. (2002). Crew resource management: improving team work in high reliability industries. *Team Performance Management, 8*(3/4), 68–78.

Frame, J. D. (2003). *Managing projects in organizations: how to make the best use of time, techniques, and people*. San Francisco, CA: John Wiley & Sons.

Frohlich, N., & Oppenheimer, J. (1998). Some consequences of e-mail vs. face-to-face communication in experiment. *Journal of Economic Behavior & Organization, 35*(3), 389–403.

Gardner, H. (2006). *Changing minds: The art and science of changing our own and other people's minds*. Boston, MA: Harvard Business Press.

Gardner, R. (2013). Introduction to debriefing. *Seminars in Perinatology, 37*, 166–174.

Ginnett, R. C. (2010). Crews as groups: Their formation and their leadership. In B. G. Kanki, R. L. Helmreich, & J. Anca (Eds.), *Crew resource management* (pp. 79–110). San Diego, CA: Elsevier.

Goleman, D. (2000). Leadership that gets results. *Harvard Business Review, 78*(2), 78–93.

Goleman, D. (2015, April 7). How to be emotionally intelligent. *International New York Times*.

Hackman, J. R., & O'Connor, M. (2004). What makes for a great analytic team? Individual vs. team approaches to intelligence analysis. *Intelligence Science Board, Office of the Director of Central Intelligence, Washington, DC*.

Hansen, M. T., & Nohria, N. (2004). How to build collaborative advantage. *MIT Sloan Management Review, 46*(1), 22–30.

Harter, J. K., Schmidt, F. L., & Hayes, T. L. (2002). Business-unit-level relationship between employee satisfaction, employee engagement, and business outcomes: a meta-analysis. *Journal of Applied Psychology, 87*(2), 268.

Hartman, F., & Ashrafi, R. (2002). Project management in the information systems and information technologies. *Project Management Journal, 33*(3), 5–15.

Heilman, M. E., Hornstein, H. A., Cage, J. H., & Herschlag, J. K. (1984). Reactions to prescribed leader behavior as a function of role perspective: The case of the Vroom-Yetton model. *Journal of Applied Psychology, 69*(1), 50.

Helmreich, R. L. (2000). On error management: lessons from aviation. *British Medical Journal, 320*(7237), 781–785.

Hewson, M. G., & Little, M. L. (1998). Giving feedback in medical education. *Journal of General Internal Medicine, 13*(2), 111–116.

Inkpen, A. C., & Tsang, E. W. (2005). Social capital, networks, and knowledge transfer. *Academy of Management Review, 30*(1), 146–165.

Jay, A. (1976). How to run a meeting. *Harvard Business Review, 54*(2), 43–57.

Jordan, P. J., & Troth, A. C. (2004). Managing emotions during team problem solving: Emotional intelligence and conflict resolution. *Human Performance, 17*(2), 195–218.

Kappelman, L. A., McKeeman, R., & Zhang, L. (2006). Early warning signs of IT project failure: The dominant dozen. *Information Systems Management, 23*(4), 31–36.

Kawasaki, G. (2008). *Reality check: The irreverent guide to outsmarting, outmanaging, and outmarketing your competition.* New York: Penguin.

Kennedy, J. F. (1962). John F. Kennedy Moon Speech–Rice Stadium. *Speech. John F. Kennedy Moon Speech–Rice Stadium. Rice Stadium, Houston, 12.*

Kerzner, H. R. (2003). *Project management: a systems approach to planning, scheduling, and controlling* (8th ed.). Hoboken, NJ: John Wiley & Sons.

Kozlowski, S. W., & Bell, B. S. (2003). Work groups and teams in organizations. In W. C. Borman, D. R. Ilgen, & R. J. Kilmoski (Eds.), *Handbook of psychology (Vol. 12): Industrial and Organizational Psychology* (pp. 333–375). New York: John Wiley & Sons.

Leach, D. J., Rogelberg, S. G., Warr, P. B., & Burnfield, J. L. (2009). Perceived meeting effectiveness: The role of design characteristics. *Journal of Business and Psychology, 24*(1), 65–76.

Levashina, J., Hartwell, C. J., Morgeson, F. P., & Campion, M. A. (2014). The structured employment interview: Narrative and quantitative review of the research literature. *Personnel Psychology, 67*(1), 241–293.

Lussier, R., & Achua, C. (2007). *Leadership: Theory, application, & skill development* (3rd ed.). Mason, OH: Thomson.

Macan, T. (2009). The employment interview: A review of current studies and directions for future research. *Human Resource Management Review, 19*(3), 203–218.

Madson, P. R. (2005). *Improv wisdom: Don't prepare, just show up.* New York: Bell Tower.

Malhotra, D., & Bazerman, M. H. (2007). *Negotiation genius: How to overcome obstacles and achieve brilliant results at the bargaining table and beyond.* New York: Bantam Books.

Mathieu, J., Maynard, M. T., Rapp, T., & Gilson, L. (2008). Team effectiveness 1997–2007: A review of recent advancements and a glimpse into the future. *Journal of Management, 34*(3), 410–476.

McNatt, D. B. (2000). Ancient Pygmalion joins contemporary management: a meta-analysis of the result. *Journal of Applied Psychology, 85*(2), 314.

Meredith, J. R., & Mantel Jr, S. J. (2009). *Project management: a managerial approach* (7th ed.). Hoboken, NJ: John Wiley & Sons.

Moss, S. E., & Sanchez, J. I. (2004). Are your employees avoiding you? Managerial strategies for closing the feedback gap. *The Academy of Management Executive, 18*(1), 32–44.

Murphy, A. H., & Daan, H. (1984). Impacts of feedback and experience on the quality of subjective probability forecasts. Comparison of results from the first and second years of the Zierikzee experiment. *Monthly Weather Review, 112*(3), 413–423.

National Research Council. (2011a). *Intelligence analysis for tomorrow: Advances from the behavioral and social sciences.* Washington, DC: National Academies Press.

National Research Council. (2011b). *Intelligence analysis: Behavioral and social scientific foundations.* Washington, DC: National Academies Press.

Nelson, R. R. (2007). IT project management: infamous failures, classic mistakes, and best practices. *MIS Quarterly Executive, 6*(2), 67–78.

Nembhard, I. M., & Edmondson, A. C. (2006). Making it safe: The effects of leader inclusiveness and professional status on psychological safety and improvement efforts in health care teams. *Journal of Organizational Behavior, 27*(7), 941–966.

Nickerson, R. S. (1998). Confirmation bias: a ubiquitous phenomenon in many guises. *Review of General Psychology, 2*(2), 175–220.

Nixon, C. T., & Littlepage, G. E. (1992). Impact of meeting procedures on meeting effectiveness. *Journal of Business and Psychology, 6*(3), 361–369.

Nowak, M., & Sigmund, K. (1993). A strategy of win-stay, lose-shift that outperforms tit-for-tat in the Prisoner's Dilemma game. *Nature, 364*(6432), 56–58.

Nowak, M. A., & Sigmund, K. (1992). Tit for tat in heterogeneous populations. *Nature, 355*(6357), 250–253.

Ojasalo, J. (2001). Managing customer expectations in professional services. *Managing Service Quality, 11*(3), 200–212.

Orasanu, J. (2010). Flight crew decision-making. In B. G. Kanki, R. L. Helmreich, & J. Anca (Eds.), *Crew resource management* (pp. 147–180). San Diego, CA: Elsevier.

Özaralli, N. (2003). Effects of transformational leadership on empowerment and team effectiveness. *Leadership & Organization Development Journal, 24*(6), 335–344.

Papke-Shields, K. E., Beise, C., & Quan, J. (2010). Do project managers practice what they preach, and does it matter to project success? *International Journal of Project Management, 28*(7), 650–662.

Parks, C. D., & Komorita, S. S. (1998). Reciprocity research and its implications for the negotiation process. *International Negotiation, 3*(2), 151–169.

Parmenter, D. (2007). *Key performance indicators: developing, implementing, and using winning KPIs.* Hoboken, NJ: John Wiley & Sons.

Pellegrinelli, S., Partington, D., Hemingway, C., Mohdzain, Z., & Shah, M. (2007). The importance of context in programme management: An empirical review of programme practices. *International Journal of Project Management, 25*(1), 41–55.

Pfeffer, J., & Sutton, R. I. (2006a). Evidence-based management. *Harvard Business Review, 84*(1), 62.

Pfeffer, J., & Sutton, R. I. (2006b). *Hard facts, dangerous half-truths, and total nonsense: Profiting from evidence-based management.* Boston, MA: Harvard Business Press.

Pfeffer, J., & Sutton, R. I. (2007). Suppose we took evidence-based management seriously: Implications for reading and writing management. *Academy of Management Learning & Education, 6*(1), 153–155.

Pfeffer, J., & Veiga, J. F. (1999). Putting people first for organizational success. *The Academy of Management Executive, 13*(2), 37–48.

Pinkley, R. L., Neale, M. A., & Bennett, R. J. (1994). The impact of alternatives to settlement in dyadic negotiation. *Organizational Behavior and Human Decision Processes, 57*(1), 97–116.

Prati, L. M., Douglas, C., Ferris, G. R., Ammeter, A. P., & Buckley, M. R. (2003). Emotional intelligence, leadership effectiveness, and team outcomes. *International Journal of Organizational Analysis, 11*(1), 21–40.

Pruyn, P. W., & Sterling, M. R. (2006). Space flight resource management: lessons learned from astronaut team learning. *Reflections: The SoL Journal, 7*(2), 45–57.

Raiffa, H., Richardson, J., & Metcalfe, D. (2002). *Negotiation analysis: the science and art of collaborative decision making.* Cambridge, MA: Harvard University Press.

Rall, M., Manser, T., & Howard, S. (2000). Key elements of debriefing for simulator training. *European Journal of Anaesthesiology, 17*(8), 516–517.

Ramsey, R. P., & Sohi, R. S. (1997). Listening to your customers: the impact of perceived salesperson listening behavior on relationship outcomes. *Journal of the Academy of Marketing Science, 25*(2), 127–137.

Rogers, D. G. (2010). Crew resource management: Spaceflight resource management. In B. G. Kanki, R. L. Helmreich, & J. Anca (Eds.), *Crew resource management* (pp. 301–316). San Diego, CA: Elsevier.

Romano, N. C., & Nunamaker Jr, J. F. (2001, January 3–6). *Meeting analysis: Findings from research and practice.* Proceedings of the 34th Annual Hawaii International Conference on system sciences., Maui, HA.

Ron, N., Lipshitz, R., & Popper, M. (2006). How organizations learn: Post-flight reviews in an F-16 fighter squadron. *Organization Studies, 27*(8), 1069–1089.

Rousseau, D. M. (2006). Is there such a thing as "evidence-based management?" *Academy of Management Review, 31*(2), 256–269.

Rousseau, D. M. (2012). Organizational behavior's contributions to evidence-based management. In D. M. Rousseau (Ed.), *The Oxford handbook of evidence-based management* (pp. 61–78). New York: Oxford University Press.

Rynes, S. L., Giluk, T. L., & Brown, K. G. (2007). The very separate worlds of academic and practitioner periodicals in human resource management: Implications for evidence-based management. *Academy of Management Journal, 50*(5), 987–1008.

Salas, E., Klein, C., King, H., Salisbury, M., Augenstein, J. S., Birnbach, D. J., Robinson, D. W., Upshaw, C. (2008). Debriefing medical teams: 12 evidence-based best practices and tips. *Joint Commission Journal on Quality and Patient Safety, 34*(9), 518–527.

Schein, E. H. (2010). *Helping: How to offer, give, and receive help.* San Francisco, CA: Berrett-Koehler Publishers, Inc.

Schellens, T., Van Keer, H., De Wever, B., & Valcke, M. (2009). Tagging thinking types in asynchronous discussion groups: Effects on critical thinking. *Interactive Learning Environments, 17*(1), 77–94.

Schmidt, R., Lyytinen, K., & Mark Keil, P. C. (2001). Identifying software project risks: an international Delphi study. *Journal of Management Information Systems, 17*(4), 5–36.

Schneider, A. K. (2002). Shattering negotiation myths: Empirical evidence on the effectiveness of negotiation style. *Harvard Negotiation Law Review, 7,* 143–233.

Schroeder, J., & Epley, N. (2015). The sound of intellect: speech reveals a thoughtful mind, increasing a job candidate's appeal. *Psychological Science,* 1–15.

Sebenius, J. K. (1992). Negotiation analysis: A characterization and review. *Management Science, 38*(1), 18–38.

Shute, V. J. (2008). Focus on formative feedback. *Review of Educational Research, 78*(1), 153–189.

Simon, H. A. (1996). *The sciences of the artificial* (Vol. 136). Cambridge, MA: MIT press.

Smith, H. J., & Keil, M. (2003). The reluctance to report bad news on troubled software projects: a theoretical model. *Information Systems Journal, 13*(1), 69–95.

Söderlund, J. (2004). On the broadening scope of the research on projects: a review and a model for analysis. *International Journal of Project Management, 22*(8), 655–667.

Spector, B. (2004). An interview with Roger Fisher and William Ury. *The Academy of Management Executive, 18*(3), 101–108.

Stewart, M. (2009). *The management myth: Debunking modern business philosophy.* New York: Norton.

Sussman, S. W., & Sproull, L. (1999). Straight talk: Delivering bad news through electronic communication. *Information Systems Research, 10*(2), 150–166.

Tannenbaum, R., & Schmidt, W. H. (1973). How to choose a leadership pattern. *Harvard Business Review, 36*(4), 95–101.

Tannenbaum, S. I., & Cerasoli, C. P. (2013). Do team and individual debriefs enhance performance? A meta-analysis. *Human Factors: The Journal of the Human Factors and Ergonomics Society, 55*(1), 231–245.

Thompson, L. L. (2011). *Making the team: A guide for managers* (4th ed.). Upper Saddle River, NJ: Pearson.

Thompson, L. L. (2012). *The mind and heart of the negotiator* (5th ed.). Upper Saddle River, NJ: Prentice Hall.

Tierney, P., & Farmer, S. M. (2004). The Pygmalion process and employee creativity. *Journal of Management, 30*(3), 413–432.

Turman, L. (2005). *So you want to be a producer.* New York: Three Rivers Press.

Ury, W. (2007). *Getting past no: negotiating in difficult situations.* New York: Bantam Books.

Valacich, J. S., Paranka, D., George, J. F., & Nunamaker, J. (1993). Communication concurrency and the new media a new dimension for media richness. *Communication Research, 20*(2), 249–276.

Van Boven, L., & Thompson, L. (2003). A look into the mind of the negotiator: Mental models in negotiation. *Group Processes & Intergroup Relations, 6*(4), 387–404.

Volkema, R. J., & Niederman, F. (1996). Planning and managing organizational meetings: An empirical analysis of written and oral communications. *Journal of Business Communication, 33*(3), 275–292.

Vroom, V. H., & Jago, A. G. (1978). On the validity of the Vroom-Yetton model. *Journal of Applied Psychology, 63*(2), 151–162.

Whetten, D. A., & Camerron, K. S. (2002). *Developing management skills* (5th ed.). Upper Saddle River, NJ: Pearson Education.

White, D., & Fortune, J. (2002). Current practice in project management—An empirical study. *International Journal of Project Management, 20*(1), 1–11.

Wolff, H.-G., & Moser, K. (2009). Effects of networking on career success: a longitudinal study. *Journal of Applied Psychology, 94*(1), 196.

Woolley, A. W., Chabris, C. F., Pentland, A., Hashmi, N., & Malone, T. W. (2010). Evidence for a collective intelligence factor in the performance of human groups. *Science, 330*(6004), 686–688.

Wright, J. N. (1997). Time and budget: the twin imperatives of a project sponsor. *International Journal of Project Management, 15*(3), 181–186.

Wu, J., & Axelrod, R. (1995). How to cope with noise in the iterated prisoner's dilemma. *Journal of Conflict Resolution, 39*(1), 183–189.

Yule, S., Flin, R., Paterson-Brown, S., & Maran, N. (2006). Non-technical skills for surgeons in the operating room: a review of the literature. *Surgery, 139*(2), 140–149.

Zerzan, J. T., Hess, R., Schur, E., Phillips, R. S., & Rigotti, N. (2009). Making the most of mentors: a guide for mentees. *Academic Medicine, 84*(1), 140–144.

zur Muehlen, M., & Ho, D. T.-Y. (2006). *Risk management in the BPM lifecycle.* Paper presented at the Business Process Management workshops in September 2005. Nancy, France.

## CHAPTER 9

Ackoff, R. L. (2006). Why few organizations adopt systems thinking. *Systems Research and Behavioral Science, 23*(5), 705–708.

Arkes, H. R. (2001). Overconfidence in judgmental forecasting. In J. S. Armstrong (Ed.) *Principles of forecasting: A handbook for researchers and practitioners* (pp. 495–515). Boston, MA: Springer.

Arkes, H. R., & Ayton, P. (1999). The sunk cost and Concorde effects: are humans less rational than lower animals? *Psychological Bulletin, 125*(5), 591–600.

Arkes, H. R., & Blumer, C. (1985). The psychology of sunk cost. *Organizational Behavior and Human Decision Processes, 35*(1), 124–140.

Avey, J. B., Avolio, B. J., Crossley, C. D., & Luthans, F. (2009). Psychological ownership: Theoretical extensions, measurement and relation to work outcomes. *Journal of Organizational Behavior, 30*(2), 173–191.

Baer, M., & Brown, G. (2012). Blind in one eye: How psychological ownership of ideas affects the types of suggestions people adopt. *Organizational Behavior and Human Decision Processes, 118*(1), 60–71.

Baker, J., & Côté, J. (2003). Sport-specific practice and the development of expert decision-making in team ball sports. *Journal of Applied Sport Psychology, 15*(1), 12–25.

Basadur, M. (1995). Optimal ideation–evaluation ratios. *Creativity Research Journal, 8*(1), 63–75.

Bazerman, M. H., & Moore, D. A. (2008). *Judgment in managerial decision making.* Hoboken, NJ: John Wiley & Sons.

Boicu, M., Tecuci, G., & Schum, D. (2008, 3–4 December). Intelligence analysis ontology for cognitive assistants. *Proceedings of the Conference "Ontology for the Intelligence Community: Towards Effective Exploitation and Integration of Intelligence Resources."* Fairfax, VA.

Bond, C. F., & DePaulo, B. M. (2006). Accuracy of deception judgments. *Personality and Social Psychology Review, 10*(3), 214–234.

Brown, T. (2008). Design thinking. *Harvard Business Review, 86*(6), 84–92.

Brown, T., & Wyatt, J. (2010). Design thinking for social innovation. *Development Outreach, 12*(1), 29–43.

Coman, A., & Ronen, B. (2009). Overdosed management: How excess of excellence begets failure. *Human Systems Management, 28*(3), 93–99.

DePaulo, B. M., Lindsay, J. J., Malone, B. E., Muhlenbruck, L., Charlton, K., & Cooper, H. (2003). Cues to deception. *Psychological Bulletin, 129*(1), 74–118.

Dweck, C. (2006). *Mindset: The new psychology of success.* Random House.

Dym, C. L., Agogino, A. M., Eris, O., Frey, D. D., & Leifer, L. J. (2005). Engineering design thinking, teaching, and learning. *Journal of Engineering Education, 94*(1), 103–120.

Ericsson, K. A. (2004). Deliberate practice and the acquisition and maintenance of expert performance in medicine and related domains. *Academic Medicine, 79*(10), S70–S81.

Ericsson, K. A., Krampe, R. T., & Tesch-Römer, C. (1993). The role of deliberate practice in the acquisition of expert performance. *Psychological Review, 100*(3), 363.

Fischhoff, B., & Chauvin, C. (2011). *Intelligence analysis: Behavioral and social scientific foundations.* Washington, DC: National Academies Press.

Frame, J. D. (2003). *Managing projects in organizations: how to make the best use of time, techniques, and people.* San Francisco, CA: John Wiley & Sons.

Garrido, E., Masip, J., & Herrero, C. (2004). Police officers' credibility judgments: Accuracy and estimated ability. *International Journal of Psychology, 39*(4), 254–275.

George, R. Z., & Bruce, J. B. (2008). *Analyzing intelligence: Origins, obstacles, and innovations.* Washington, DC: Georgetown University Press.

Global Deception Research Team. (2006). A world of lies. *Journal of Cross-Cultural Psychology, 37*(1), 60–74.

Greenhalgh, T. (2002). Intuition and evidence—uneasy bedfellows? *British Journal of General Practice, 52*(478), 395–400.

Hersman, D., Hart, C., & Sumwalt, R. (2010). Loss of thrust in both engines after encountering a flock of birds and subsequent ditching on the Hudson River: Accident Report NTSB/AAR-10/03, National Transportation Safety Board, Washington, DC.

Jackson, D., Firtko, A., & Edenborough, M. (2007). Personal resilience as a strategy for surviving and thriving in the face of workplace adversity: a literature review. *Journal of Advanced Nursing, 60*(1), 1–9.

Jung, B., & Reidenberg, M. M. (2007). Physicians being deceived. *Pain Medicine, 8*(5), 433–437.

Kahneman, D., Slovic, P., & Tversky, A. (Eds.). (1982). *Judgment under Uncertainty: Heuristics and Biases.* New York.

Kruger, J., & Dunning, D. (1999). Unskilled and unaware of it: how difficulties in recognizing one's own incompetence lead to inflated self-assessments. *Journal of Personality and Social Psychology, 77*(6), 1121.

Langley, A. (1995). Between" paralysis by analysis" and" extinction by instinct." *Sloan Management Review, 36,* 63.

Makridakis, S., & Gaba, A. (1998). *Judgment: its role and value for strategy.* INSEAD.

McIntyre, M. E. (1997). Lucidity and Science I: Writing skills and the pattern perception hypothesis. *Interdisciplinary Science Reviews, 22*(3), 199–216.

Medawar, P. B. (1979). *Advice to a young scientist.* New York: Basic Books.

Meissner, C. A., & Kassin, S. M. (2002). " He's guilty!": Investigator bias in judgments of truth and deception. *Law and Human Behavior, 26*(5), 469.

National Research Council. (2011a). *Intelligence analysis for tomorrow: Advances from the behavioral and social sciences.* Washington, DC: National Academies Press.

National Research Council. (2011b). *Intelligence analysis: Behavioral and social scientific foundations.* Washington, DC: National Academies Press.

Ness, R. B. (2012). *Innovation generation: how to produce creative and useful scientific ideas.* New York: Oxford University Press.

Orasanu, J. (2010). Flight crew decision-making. In B. G. Kanki, R. L. Helmreich, & J. Anca (Eds.), *Crew resource management* (pp. 147–180). San Diego, CA: Elsevier.

Pfeffer, J., & Sutton, R. I. (2006). *Hard facts, dangerous half-truths, and total nonsense: Profiting from evidence-based management.* Boston, MA: Harvard Business Press.

Polya, G. (1945). *How to solve it: A new aspect of mathematical method.* Princeton, NJ: Princeton University Press.

Research Councils UK. (2001). Joint statement of the Research Councils'/Arts and Humanities Research Board's skills training requirements for research students. London: Research Councils UK.

Rittel, H. W., & Webber, M. M. (1973). Dilemmas in a general theory of planning. *Policy Sciences, 4*(2), 155–169.

Rogers, D. G. (2010). Crew Resource Management: Spaceflight resource management. In B. G. Kanki, R. L. Helmreich, & J. Anca (Eds.), *Crew resource management* (pp. 301–316). San Diego, CA: Elsevier.

Sheppard, S., Macatangay, K., Colby, A., & Sullivan, W. M. (2009). *Educating engineers: Designing for the future of the field.* San Francisco, CA: Jossey-Bass.

Siddique, Z., Panchal, J., Schaefer, D., Haroon, S., Allen, J. K., & Mistree, F. (2012, August). *Competencies for Innovating in the 21st Century.* Paper presented at the American Society of Mechanical Engineers 2012 International Design Engineering Technical Conferences and Computers and Information in Engineering Conference. Chicago, IL.

Simmons, M. S., Nides, M. A., Rand, C. S., Wise, R. A., & Tashkin, D. P. (2000). Unpredictability of deception in compliance with physician-prescribed bronchodilator inhaler use in a clinical trial. *CHEST Journal, 118*(2), 290-295.

Simon, H. A., & Chase, W. G. (1973). Skill in chess: Experiments with chess-playing tasks and computer simulation of skilled performance throw light on some human perceptual and memory processes. *American Scientist, 61*, 394–403.

Smith, G. C., & Pell, J. P. (2003). Parachute use to prevent death and major trauma related to gravitational challenge: systematic review of randomised controlled trials. *BMJ: British Medical Journal, 327*(7429), 1459–1461.

Southwick, S. M., Vythilingam, M., & Charney, D. S. (2005). The psychobiology of depression and resilience to stress: implications for prevention and treatment. *Annual Review of Clinical Psychology, 1*, 255–291.

Thompson, J. M. T. (2013). Advice to a young researcher: with reminiscences of a life in science. *Philosophical Transactions of the Royal Society of London A: Mathematical, Physical and Engineering Sciences, 371*(1993), 20120425.

Thompson, L. L. (2012). *The mind and heart of the negotiator* (5th ed.). Upper Saddle River, NJ: Prentice Hall.

Toegel, G., & Barsoux, J.-L. (2012). How to become a better leader. *MIT Sloan Management Review, 53*(3), 51–60.

von Winterfeldt, D., & Edwards, W. (1986). *Decision analysis and behavioral research*: Cambridge: Cambridge University Press.

Williams, E. J. (2012). *Lies and cognition: How do we tell lies and can we detect them?* Cardiff University.

# INDEX

NOTE: Page numbers followed by t indicate a table. Italicized page numbers indicate a figure. Page numbers followed by n and another number indicate a numbered footnote.

abductive logic, 88–89, *89*
Abela, A., 162
ACH. *See* Analysis of Competing Hypotheses
actual causes, determination of, 79–116
    analysis phase, 87–103
    concentration on what matters, 81–83
    decision phase, 103–110
    drawing conclusions, 110
    in finding Harry, 110–112
    hypotheses set development, 79–84
    phrasing of hypotheses, 84–85
    prioritizing hypotheses testing, 85–87
Ainsworth, S., 77
Allen, R. J., 109
Alley, M., 174, 177
alternatives
    in building issue maps, *68*
    comparing performance of, 69, 149–156
    diagnosis aspect in choosing, 19
    feasibility determination, 142, *142*
    in finding Harry, 36–37, 37t
    generating, 9n25, 25, 67
    insightfulness in comparing, 67, 75
    MECE and, 67
    optimizing and, 62
    phantom alternatives, 159
    premature closure and, 47
    processes *vs.*, 120–121
    role of subconscious in choosing, 132
    satisficing and, 62
    screens for evaluating, selecting, 141–144, *142–144*

    SMARTER tool for evaluating, selecting, 150–156
    solution maps role in identifying, *121*, 141
    testing for, 139
    unsuitable, removal of, 141–149
    value in considering, 119
Alternative Uses test, 139
American Association for the Advancement of Science, 84
analogies, 128–129, 138, 183
Analysis of Competing Hypotheses (ACH)
    debate about effectiveness of, 94
    description, 92
    limitations of, 113
anchoring
    brainwriting and, 127–128
    definition, 47
Ancona, D. G., 126
answers
    communication of solutions, 194
    ICE answers in issue maps, 59, 60, *60*, *61*, 78
    MECE structure of issue maps and, 10, 58–60, 124
    problem framing and, 22–25
    solution maps and, *48*
    triangulating on, 147–148
argument/hypothesis maps
    as alternative to ACH, 94
    attributes of, 48
    benefits of using, 96, 97, *97*, 98
    benefits to critical thinking of, 38, 94
    choice of, in communicating, 164–169
    description, 94

argument/hypothesis maps (*Cont.*)
    element types in, *93*, 94
    in finding Harry, 94–96, *95*
    minimizing confirmation bias, 104
    origin of, 113
    shared properties of, 47
    van Gelder's coining of term, 113
arguments. *See also* argument/hypothesis maps
    choices for effective communication, 164–169
    compelling/tailoring to audiences, 12, 161
    graphical breakdowns of, 10
    length consideration, 39
    parallelism of, 134n53
    PEL model and, 87
    realizing logic gaps in, 134
Aristotelian persuasion, 166–169, *167*
Arjona, Javier, 113
assertion-evidence slide structure, 176–180, 200
attitudinal overconfidence, 48
Axelrod, R., 226

Bacon, Francis, 101
bar charts, 183, 185–186, *187*, 188, 200
Bassok, M., 44
Bates, Marston, 92
Bayesian inference, 103, 104–109
    basics of, 105–106
    benefits and limitations of, 106–108
    in finding Harry, *107*, 107–108, 108t
    usage examples, 106t, 108t, 109t
Bayesian networks, 47
Bazerman, M. H., 104
Beaufre, A., 18–19
belief preservation, 103–104, 114
Bellotti, V. M., 77
Berlin, Isaiah, 18
bias. *See also* confirmation bias
    hindsight bias, 15
    recall/retrievability bias, 144n10
Bird-and-Trains problem (Posner), 44
Boileau, Nicolas, 39
Bono, Edward de, 129
Boroditsky, L., 22–23, 23n5, 33
brainstorming
    debate in, 132
    example of using, 30
    facilitation of, 127
    four rules of, 125
    group *vs.* individual, 125–126
    limitations of effectiveness, 126
    Osborn's popularization of, 63
    role in improving idea generation, 128

team assemblage, 126–127
transcending, 139
brainwriting, 125, 127–128
Brownell, Kelly, 23
bubble charts, *188*, 188–189
Byrne, R. M., 101

Caldwell, D. F., 126
causes of problems. *See* actual causes; root causes
CE. *See* collectively exhaustive (CE) branches of issues maps
Chabris, C. F., 156
Chamberlin, T. C., 77
change, Gardner on facilitation of, 199
charts, quantitative, 185
CIDNI (nonimmediate) problems, 5
    challenges related to, 231
    characteristics/types of, 6
    evaluation of, 6–7
    generalist/specialist problem solvers, *8*
    issue maps and, 65
    problem framing, 21–44
    problem solving teams, 7–8, *8*
    solving process, 5–7, 17–18
    T-shaped problem solver, 7, *8*, 18
Clark, R. M., 77
closed problems, 19
co-acting teams, 226t
cognitive overconfidence, 48
collectively exhaustive (CE) branches of issues maps. *See also* independent and collectively exhaustive (ICE); mutually exclusive and collectively exhaustive (ME) structure of issue maps
    answers and, 60
    deciding when to stop and, 65
    description, 10–11, 58, *59*, 64, 75, 81
    finding Harry, 75
    generating answers and, 60
    listing theories and, 81
    right idea-generation macro activity choices, 125
    solution maps and, *120*
communication of solutions, 161–201. *See also* slides/slide decks; slides/slide decks, design principles; storyline
    advising decision makers, 169
    answering questions approach, 194
    argument choices, 164–169
    Aristotelean persuasion in, 166–169, *167*
    audience, engagement with, 194
    audience, preparation of, 191–192
    closing statement, 162
    delivery, 191–198

detail level determination, 170
determination of objectives, 162
effectiveness of informal presentations, 199
in finding Harry, 171, 199
From-To/Think-Do Matrix, 162, 162t, 199
language guidelines, 192–194
length of presentation determination, 169–170, *170*
preparation of audience, 191–192
sequencing, 170–173
storyline, crafting of, 163, *163*, 196
telling compelling stories, 162–173
use of effective slide design, 173–191
use of strong introduction, 169
complex problems
definition, 6
complication(s), 229–238
in finding Harry, 43, *118*
holding-hands rule and, 39, *40*
as *how* card component, 117, *118*
as inciting event, in screenwriting, 37n42
introductory flow and, 38–39, *39*, *40*
key question and, 35, 37, *37*, 40, 44
management of, 38, 217, 229–238
points/bullets in support of, *38*
as project chart component, *204*
rabbit rule and, *40*
storytelling introductions and, 44
team management and, 217
as *why* card component, 41, *42*, *43*
concept maps, 47
concept visuals, 185, 189, *189*
conditioning
Ness's observation on, 72
resistance to, in problem solving, 22, 23
confirmation bias
defined, 48
definition, 15, 48
in interpreting information, 15
Nickerson on, 77
strategies for reducing, 80, 104, 114
confirmatory evidence, 101–102
conforming, 126
Conklin, J., 77
convergent thinking. *See also* divergent thinking
individuals *vs.* groups use of, 127
key questions and, 28, 51
in problem solving, 9, 9–11, *17*, *17*
use of CE and, 10–11, *11*
Cousins, Robert, 44
Cowley, M., 101
creativity theory, 61

Davis, R. H., 104
decision making for hypotheses, 103–110
avoiding biases, 103–105
using Bayesian inference, 104–109
using Occam's razor, 109–110, 112
decision science, 63
decision theory, 44
decision trees
differences with issue maps, 77
shared properties with issue maps, 47
splitting paths/converging paths and, 138
deductive logic, 87–88, *89*
Delbecq, A. L., 139
Delphi method, 125, 128, 139
diagnostic definition card. *See why* card (diagnostic definition card)
diagnostic issue maps
actual cause determination and, 81
as analytic roadmap, 57
description, 2, 4, 49
divergent thinking supported by, 65
finding Harry, 4, 75–76, *76*, 89
key questions in, 79, 121, 124
MECE process and, 73
optimization and, 63
role in capturing evidence, *111*
root cause identification and, 4, 45, 79
solution map comparison, 121, 124, 136
use of abduction in development, 89
*why* questions and, 43, *48*, 50
diagnostic key question
complications and, 37, *38*
description of, 28–30
in finding Harry, 34t, 37t, *40*, *43*
identification of, 2
on project definition card, *3*, 22
rabbit/holding-hands rules and, *40*
as *what* card component, *3*, 22, 27
in *why* process, 4, *42*, *43*
dialogue maps, 47
Diehl, M., 127
Diffenbach, J., 77
dilution effect, 92
disconfirmatory evidence, *100*, 101–102, 104
divergent and convergent thinking
issue maps and, 47, 63–64
optimization and, 63
problem diagnosis and, 28
use of CE and, 10–11
use of in problem solving, 9, *9*, *17*, *17*, 28
divergent/convergent thinking patterns, 9, *9*

Index • 281

divergent thinking. *See also* convergent thinking
   benefits of, 119
   diagnostic maps and, 65
   individuals *vs.* groups use of, 127, 128n26
   issue maps and, 47, 64
   key questions and, 28, 63
   in problem solving, 9, 9–11, *11*, 17, *17*
   Smith/Ward on, 77
   use of CE and, 10–11, 125
the *do*
   alternative assessment and, 142, *145*
   in client management, 221
   description, 2, *2*, 5, 9, 17
   divergent/convergent thinking and, 9
   in finding Harry, *3*, 26, 27, 34, 69
   from-to/think-do matrix, 162, 162t, 199
   key questions and, *29*
   as project chart component, 204
   as *what* card component, *3*, 22
downward norm setting, 126
Dwyer, C. P., 77

Eden, C., 77
Edison, Thomas, 110
Edwards, W., 44, 229
Efron, B., 44
Eisenführ, F., 248, 262
Elmore-Yalch, R., 167–168
Enigma codes (World War II), 7
enlisting others, 13, *17*, 25, 34t
Eppler, M. J., 77
evidence, 97–102
   abduction and, 88–89
   absence of, 92
   ACH and, 94
   analysis/tracking of, 92
   assertion-evidence structure, *174*, 176–180, 200
   biases and, 103–105, 150
   collecting, *3*, 22, 27
   compatibility of, 147
   conclusions based on, 171
   confirmatory *vs.* disconfirmatory approach, 101–102
   consistency of, 115
   contradictory, 114, 115
   credibility attributes of, 99t
   definition, 87
   diagnosis maps and, *111*
   diagnostic, *3*, *15*, 22, 27
   differentiation of data from, 113
   disconfirmatory, *100*, 101–102, 104
   drawing conclusions from, 44, 57, 110

   evaluation of, 98, 99t
   in finding Harry, 94–95, 102, 108t, *112*
   gathering, 115, 144, 146–147, *148*, 156, 195
   grading credibility of, 113–114, *146*, 146–147
   graphical tools for marshaling, 94n52
   hypotheses maps and, *93*, 95
   identifying, 4, 13, 87, 91
   induction and, 88
   issue maps and, 47, 55, *56*, 224
   less-than-ideal, use of, 230
   misdiagnosis of, 91
   overconfidence regarding, 235
   in Presumption-Evidence-Logic model, 87
   relation to hypotheses, 100t
   relevance of, 115
   role in decision making, 8, 87
   scientific ideal in using, 16–17
   search for consistency in, 115
   slide decks use of, 163, *165*, 168, 170, 171, *174*, 176–180, 185, 196, 199, 200
   supporting *vs.* opposing, 81, 82, 84, 100–102, 102n84
   suspected/unsuspected, 92
   testing of, 54, *54*
   triangulating, 148, *148*
   trustworthiness of, *146*
   working with, 97–102
evidence-based management, 225
evidence maps, 47

face-to-face teams, 226t
fault trees, 47
Feynman, Richard
   advice to "not fool yourself," 14–15
   on "fragility of knowledge," 7
filters, for identifying key questions, 34t
finding Harry
   argument/hypothesis map for, 94–96, *95*
   communicating solutions in, 199
   complication in, 34t
   crafting of storyline for, 199
   decision tool for, 5t
   diagnostic definition *(why)* card, 43
   diagnostic issue map, *4*, 75–76, *76*
   *do* process in, 5
   enlisting others, 34t
   evidence in, 102
   four-step approach, 3–5
   framing the project, 21–22, 28–29, 33–37, 39, 41–44
   hypotheses set for, 82–83, *83*, 110, *111*, 112
   introductory flow in, 39

282 • Index

issue map, *51*
key question identification, 33–35, 34t
presentation in, 171
project definition card, 3
selecting solutions, 150–155, 158
the "so what?" in, 34
steps in four-step process, 3–5
the *how* process in, 4
the *what* process in, 3, 25–27, *27*
the *why* in, 3, 4, *26*, *27*, 33–34, 37, 43, *52*, 76, *107*, *112*
finite element analysis (FEA), 81, *82*, 113
Fiol, C. M., 77
Fischhoff, Baruch, 63
fixation, definition, 47, 69, 133
Fleming, Alexander, 103
fooling ourselves, approach to avoiding common ways, 15t
preventive evidence-based approach, 15–16
replacing unwarranted self-confidence, 16
respecting scientific ideal, 16–17
Frame, Davidson, 44
From-To/Think-Do Matrix (Abela), 162, 162t, 199

Gardner, Howard, 162, 199
Garner, J. K., 174
Gauch, H. G., 84, 149
Ginnett, Robert, 225
Goleman, D., 210t
Goodwin, P., 168
Gricean maxims, 74
groupthink, 125, 138

Hammond, J. S., 129
Hammond, N. V., 77
Hargadon, A., 139
Heuvel, L. N. V., 77
hindsight bias, 15
Hogan, M. J., 77
holding-hands rule, 38–39, *40*, 124
the *how*
convergent/divergent thinking and, *9*, *11*
description, 2, 4–5, *17*, 29
in finding Harry, 4, *26*, *27*, *34*, 133, 150, 158
in issue maps, 10, *10*, 48, *51*
key questions and, 29, *31*, *32*, *120*, *121*, 129–132
measuring creativity and, 138
parallelism and, *135*
storyline development and, *195*
as *what* card component, 3, *27*, 41
*why's* relation to, 4, 29

*how* card (solution definition card), 4, 117, *118*, 120–121, 238
how-how diagrams, 47
Huff, A. S., 77
Hurson, Tim, 61
hypotheses. *See also* argument/hypothesis maps; decision making for hypotheses; hypotheses set; issue maps, progression from question to conclusions
abductive/deductive/inductive analysis, *88*, 88–89, *89*
assigning to issue maps, 81–83
comparing, 85
convergent thinking and, 61
decision making, 103–110
diagnosis map and, 50
diagnosticity of, 116
drawing conclusions from, 57, 110
evidence in, 97–102
formal, 4, 45, *46*, 47, 51
formulation of, 2, 4
forward-/backward-driven reasoning strategies, 89, 91
*how* process and, 4
idiographic *vs.* nomothetic, 115
key questions and, 51, 84–85
linking with data, 77
mutation of, 51n36
prioritizing the testing of, 85–87
pseudo-/over-/misdiagnosis problems, 91–92
root causes and, 29
summary of main attributes, *85*
testing of, 29, 55, 65, 84, *84*, 101, 115
unequivocality of, 84, *84*
*why* process and, 4, 50
working with evidence, 97–98, 99, 99t, 100–102, 100t
hypotheses set
development of, 45, *46*, 51, 66, 79–85
for finding Harry, 82–83, *83*
issue maps and, 47, 54, 80, *80*
laying out, 51
testing, 54
hypothesis maps. *See* argument/hypothesis maps

ICE. *See* independent and collectively exhaustive (ICE)
IDEO, 125–126
idiographic hypotheses, 115
ill-defined problems, 6, 19n63, 33, 44, 206
independent and collectively exhaustive (ICE), answers in issue maps, 59, *60*, *60*, *61*, 78

individual likelihood of success, 5t, 151–154, 152t, 155t
induction by elimination, 101
inductive logic, 88, *89*
influence diagrams, 47
introductory flow, in problem framing, 35–40
    choice/use of data, 35–36
    complications, 37–38
    fine tuning, 38–40
    holding-hands rule, 38–39, *40*, 124
    intermediary steps in, *39*
    necessary/sufficient information, 35
    rabbit rule, 38–39, *40, 41*
    situation statement, concise *vs.* precise, 36–37, *37*
inventive problems, 19
Ishikawa (or cause-and-effect or fishbone) diagrams, 47
issue diagrams, 47, 77
issue maps, 45–49. *See also* collectively exhaustive (CE) branches of issues maps; diagnostic issue maps; issue maps, progression from question to conclusions; mutually exclusive (ME) branches of issues maps; solution maps
    analogical approach to unfamiliar problems, 70–72
    analytic properties of, 47
    attributes, 47–48
    CE branches, 10–11
    CIDNI problems and, 65
    components, *46*
    decision trees' differences with, 77
    decision trees' shared properties with, 47
    description, 10, *10*, 45, 47
    development issues, 77
    diagnostic, 2, *4*
    elements of, *49*
    four basic rules of, *48*, 50
    generating alternative breakdowns, 67, *68, 69*–70
    ideas for starting, 70–75
    insightfulness of, 67–70, *69*, 78
    key questions answered by, *46*, 49–50, *51*
    MECE structure of, 58–67, 72, 73, *73, 74*, 75
    mutually exclusive branches, 10
    recycling discarded variables, 72
    root causes and, *4*, 43, 45–76
    setting choice for starting, 70
    solution, 2
    spelling out elements in, 64
    usefulness in analysis/synthesis of hypotheses, 55, *55*–56
    using existing frameworks, 72–73, *74*, 75

issue maps, progression from question to conclusions, 50–57
    analysis, prioritizing and conduction, 55, *55*, 57
    assigning of hypotheses, 81–83
    extensive expansion of, 51, *52*
    hypothesis sets, drawing conclusions on, 56, *57*
    hypothesis sets, laying out of, 51, *53, 54*
    hypothesis sets, testing of, 54–55, *55*
    key question structure determination, 50, *51*
    vertical/horizontal moves, 57
    *why* question, initial step, 50
issue trees, 47

Jones, Morgan, 126

Kahneman, D., 23n5, 24, 44, 103
Kaplan, R. S., 77
Kawasaki, Guy, 178
Keisler, J. M., 173
Kelley, Tom, 126
Keynes, John Maynard, 104
key questions, in problem framing, 28–34. *See also* diagnostic key question; "so what?"
    appropriate phrasing of, 33, 34t
    complications' contributions to, 37–38, 37t, *39*, 40
    constraints/frames, 32
    diagnostic questions, 2, 3, 4, 22, 27, 28–29, 33, 34, 37t, 38t, *40*
    filters for identifying, 34t
    finding Harry, 33–35, 34t
    in issue maps, *46*
    right scope, determination of, 32, 34t
    right topic, determination of, 30–31, *31*, 34t
    what, why, how questions, 29–30
Kosslyn, Stephen, 169

Langer, T., 77
Leebron, D., 143, *143*. *See also* SAILS screen
linearity, of problem-solving process, 44
Littlewood, J. E., 50
logic trees, 47

Mackendrick, Alexander, 44, 178
MacLean, A., 77
management of complications, 229–238
    in finding Harry, 237–238
    process management, 229–232
    self-management, 232–237
management of projects, 206–211. *See also* team leadership
    attributing credit to coworkers, 223
    client management, 221–223

debriefing, 223
goal setting/prioritizing activities, 12t
progress reports, 163
return-on-investment considerations, 143
risk management, 222–223
McChrystal, Stanley A., 161
McIntyre, Michael, 50
McKee, R., 168
ME. *See* mutually exclusive (ME) branches of issues maps
MECE. *See* mutually exclusive and collectively exhaustive (MECE) structure of issue maps
Medawar, P. B., 157
Minard, Charles Joseph, 189
mind maps, 47
Minto, Barbara, 170, 200
misdiagnosing, 91
Monk, P., 77
Moore, D. A., 104
mutation of hypotheses, 51n36
mutually exclusive and collectively exhaustive (MECE) structure of issue maps, *10–11*, 17, 58–67
   actions at crossroads, *59*
   answers and, 10, 58–60, 124
   debating/criticism and, 132
   deciding when to stop, 65–67
   deferring criticism and, 60–62
   description, 10, 58, *58*, 72, 73, *120*
   differentiating causes from consequences, 124
   finding Harry, 66–67
   holding-hands rule and, 124
   with ICE answers, *61*
   ICE *vs.*, 60, *61*, 78
   making structures more, 60–67
   with MECE answers, *61*
   optimizing and, 62–65
   parallelism in, 134
   problem-solving principles and, *17*
   rules for, *48*, *120*
   satisficing and, 62–63, *63*
   steps in creating new maps, 73, 74, 75, *75*
mutually exclusive (ME) branches of issues maps. *See also* mutually exclusive and collectively exhaustive (MECE) structure of issue maps
   debating, deferring criticism, and, 132
   definition, 10, *58*
   Delphi method and, 128
   differentiating causes from consequences, 124
   finding Harry and, 83n6
   generating answers and, 60
   serendipity, designed research, and, 115–116
   solutions and, 78

negotiation, 219–220
Ness, Roberta, 24, 72
Nickerson, R. S., 77
nomothetic hypotheses, 115
nonimmediate problems. *See* CIDNI (nonimmediate) problems
Noonan, P. S., 173
Norton, D. P., 77
"not invented here" syndrome, 8
Novick, L. R., 44

objective hierarchies, 47
Occam's razor, 16, 103, 109–110, 112
Ohmae, K., 74, 77
Okada, A., 77
organization of projects
   defining success, 205
   project plan development, 203–205
   working the plan, 205
Osborn, A. F., 63
overconfidence
   attitudinal and cognitive, 48
   strategies for reducing, 78, 235
   weather forecasters and, 225
overdiagnosing, 91
Oxley, N. L., 127

Pardo, M. S., 109
Pareto, Vilfredo, 81–82
Pareto principle, 81–82, 113
Pauling, Linus, 63
PEL. *See* Presupposition-Evidence-Logic
phantom alternatives, 159
phrasing filter, 34t
Platt, J. R., 77, 84
Popper, Karl, 84, 101
Posner, M. I., 44
potential solutions. *See* solutions, potential
PowerPoint presentation package, 177–179
Prain, V., 77
premature closure, definition, 47
Presupposition-Evidence-Logic (PEL) model, 87
probability trees, 47
problem framing, 21–44
   deferring judgment in, 25
   defined, 22
   diagnostic definition *(why)* card and, 28, 41–43
   engage system 2 thinking in, 24–25
   enlistment of others in, 25
   in finding Harry, 21–22, 25–29, 33–37, 39, 41–44
   identifying/answering questions, 22–25
   introductory flow in, 35–40

problem framing (*Cont.*)
   key questions, 28–34
   resist conditioning strategy in, 23–24
   scope creep in, 25, 27
   *what* card project description, 25–27
problem solving
   challenging assumptions in, 129–130
   conventional wisdom on, 15t
   definition, 5–6
   dissecting the problem, 131
   empirical findings about, 15t
   graphical tools related to, 77
   principles of, 9, *9*, 10–11, 12t, 13–17
   subconscious work time, 132
problem solving, principles
   divergent/convergent thinking patterns, 9, *9*
   do not fool yourself, 14–17
   right skills acquisition, 11, 12t, 13
   simplicity in underlying structures, 13–14
   use of issue maps, 10–11
procedural management, 231
production blocking, 126, 127
project definition card. *See what* card
projects. *See also* management of projects; organization of projects; team leadership
   dealing with objections, 55
   defining problems in, 6
   documenting of processes, 224
   framing, 21–27
   *how* card and, *118*
   key characteristics of, 44
   key questions and, 33
   management phase, 205–223
   return-on-investment considerations, 143
   selecting/monitoring key metrics, 224
   updating maps, 224
   visual support for, 185–189
   *what* card and, 25–27, 41
   *why* card and, 42
pseudodiagnosticity, 91, 147

quantitative charts, 185, *186*
questions. *See* key questions, in problem framing

rabbit rule, in introductory flow, 38–39, *40*, *41*
research skills (useful skills), 12t
Reynolds, Garr, 174
Rittel, H. W., 231
Rooney, J. J., 77
root causes (of problems). *See also* diagnostic issue maps
   addressing, 22–23

   analysis of, 2, 4, 29
   diagnostic map and, *4*, 49
   divergent/convergent thinking and, 9
   drawing conclusions about, 50–58
   in finding Harry, 4, 82–83, *83*
   identifying/uncovering, 9, 22–23, 28, 32, 43, 45–78
   introductory flows and, *41*
   issue maps and, *4*, 43, 45–76
   key questions and, 10, 29, 49–50
   potential, identification of, 45–78
   role of issue maps in uncovering, 43
   role of *why* analyses in uncovering, 29, 43, 66
   understanding, 28, 30
routine problems, 19

Safferstone, T., 157
SAILS screen (Leebron), 143, *143*
Sample, Steven, 62
sand dune team, 226t
satisficing, 62, 63, 220, 232
Schoemaker, Paul, 61
Schum, D. A., 92, 113
scope creep, in problem framing, 25, 27, 205, 222
scope filter, 34t
screens, 141–144, *142–144*
   Gauch/full-disclosure model, 142–143
   purpose of, 141–142, *142*
   SAILS screen, 143, *143*
selecting solutions. *See* solutions, selecting
self-management, 232–237
   learning to balance opposites, 234–236
   practicing of gained skills, 236–237
   skill set/attitude development, 232–234
Senge, Peter, 18
serendipity
   designed research *vs.*, 115–116
   role in discoveries, 103
   "so what"" aspect of, 103
   value of, 157
   Van Andel's patterns of, 103
Shachter, R. D., 77
Sherborne, T., 77
Shum, Buckingham, 77
Simon, D. J., 156
simplicity in underlying structures, 13–14
skills acquisition (the right skills), 11, 12t, 13
slides/slide decks. *See also* slides/slide decks, design principles; taglines
   as central repository for analysis, *166*
   defining purpose of, 173–174, *174*, *175*, *176*
   preparation basics, 163–164

presentation package limitations, 177
tagline support in, *165*
slides/slide decks, design principles, 173–191. *See also* taglines
   analogies, 183–185
   assertion-evidence structure, 176–180, *177, 179*
   avoidance of redundancy, 182
   bold characters, 182
   characteristics/implications, *181*
   coherence principle, 176
   colors, 181
   consistent templates, 180–181
   contiguity principle, 176
   defining purpose of, 173–174, *174, 175,* 176
   extremes of design, 174, 176
   facilitating audience comprehension, 180–185
   finalization of message, 191
   fonts size and types, 181–182
   modality principle, 176
   multimedia principle, 176
   redundancy, avoidance of, 182
   redundancy principle, 176
   removal of unnecessary information, 183
   sideways writing, avoidance of, 182
   signaling principle, 176
   simplicity, 183
   tables, 183
   understanding extremes of design, 174, 176
   visual support options, 185–190
SMARTER (simple multiattribute rating technique exploiting ranks) tool, 150–156, 159
   description/purpose, 150, 150t
   specific steps, 151–155
   use in finding Harry, 151–156, 152t, 153t, 154t, 155t
Smith, S. M., 77, 128
social loafing, 126
solution definition card (*how* card), 4, 117, *118,* 120–121, 238
solution key question, 2, 3
solution maps, 2, 4, 45. *See also* solution maps, developing
   for finding Harry, 238
   *how* key question answered by, *48*
   key questions in, *48,* 121
   modifying, 156
   potential solutions identified by, 49
   removal of unsuitable alternatives, 141
   role in identifying potential solutions, 49, 119–138
solution maps, developing, 119–138, 156, 231
   alternatives *vs.* processes, 120–121, *121*

   brainstorming of ideas, 125–127
   brainwriting, 127–128
   challenging assumptions, 129–130
   controlling the number of children, 122
   debate, 132
   Delphi method, 128
   dissection of problem, 131
   elimination of single child node, 122
   ensuring MECE classification strategies, 124–132
   finding Harry, 136, *137,* 138
   giving subconscious time to work, 132
   innovation *vs.* Innovation, 131–132
   linking elements to a formal hypothesis, 136
   making branches diverge, 121
   node value identification, 123
   progress from key question to conclusions, 121–124
   self-evaluation of creativity, 132
   stopping when sufficiently explicit, 123–124
   thinking about the opposite, 130–131
   use of analogies, 128–129
solutions. *See also* communication of solutions; solutions, potential; solutions, selecting
   competing, evaluation of, 5
   conditioning and, 23
   convergent/divergent thinking and, 9, *11*
   critical steps and, 19
   diagnosticity and, 112
   drawing conclusions and, 110
   finding, 2
   in finding Harry, 70, 76, 112
   framing/diagnosing problems and, *15*
   hypotheses and, 54
   identifying, 23, 29, 76
   ill-defined problems and, 6
   implementation, 2, 17, 29
   incremental thinking, 131
   in issue maps, *10*
   mitigation tactics, 15t
   principles, 9–17
   in problem definition card, *22, 27*
   in project definition card, *3*
   satisficer and, 63
   simplification of, 36
   specialist/generalist skills, 7–8, *8*
   topic choice and, *31*
solutions, potential, 117–139
   convergent/divergent thinking and, 9
   drawing conclusions and, 110
   finding, 2
   implementation, 3
   initial step, *119,* 121

solutions, potential (*Cont.*)
   ME and, 78
   in project identification card, 3
   solution maps' role in, 49
   solution maps' role in identifying, 49, 119–138
   understanding the problem step, 28
   as *what* card component, 3, 27
solutions, selecting, 141–159
   applying SMARTER process, 150–156, 151t, 152t, 155t, 159
   capturing quick and small wins, 156–158
   comparing performance of alternatives, 149–156
   data identification, 147
   evidence-gathering, 144, 146–147
   finding Harry, 150–155, 158
   individual likelihood of success evaluation, 5t, 151–154, 152t, 155t
   modifying solution maps as needed, 156
   quick wins in, 156
   removing unsuitable alternatives, 141–149
   screens for evaluating, selecting, 141–144, *142–144*
   small wins in, 156–157
   speed of success determination, 5t, 152, 152t, 153t, 154, 155t
   triangulating on answers, 147–148
   use of maps in analysis, 149
   use of SMARTER tool in, 150–156, 152t, 155t, 159
"so what?"
   analysis of, 69, 171
   capturing, in tagline, 177, 180
   in finding Harry, 34
   finding/understanding, 14, *17*, 69
   serendipity and, 103
   in slide presentations, *181*
   System 1 thinking and, 24
speed of succes, 5t, 152, 152t, 153t, 154, 155t
Spellman, Barbara, 44
Spiro, J., 139
Steinggraber, Sandra, 28
Stewart, I., 77
stories (storytelling). *See also* communication of solutions; hypotheses
   communicating solutions with, 162–173
   compelling, 162–173
   crafting of storyline, *163*
   introductions in, 35, 44
   McKee on, 36
   reframing of thinking and, 133
   usefulness in getting funding, 199
   use of slides/slide decks, 163–164, *165*, *166*, 173–191

storyline
   advantages of starting early, 195, *195*
   crafting of, 163, *163*, 196
   in finding Harry, 199
   presentation of, 173
   as suppoft for taglines, 178, 196
strategic thinking
   advantages of, 8
   definition, 18–19, 229
Stroebe, W., 127
surgical teams, 226t
Sutton, R. I., 139
System 1 (intuitive) thinking, 24, 24n16, 44
System 2 (reflective) thinking, 24, 44

taglines (in slides/slide deck), 176–182
   alternative names for, 200
   distribution of story onto, 163, *164*
   full declarative sentences in, 174, 176, *177*, 177–180
   overloading working memory and, 200
   as storyline, 178
   storyline as support for, 178, 196
   supportive evidence in, *165*
taxonomies of problems, 19
team leadership, 206–221
   adapting to changing situations, 210–211
   agreeing on expectations, 50, 208–209
   coaching of members, 211–212
   dealing with objections, 55
   delegation role, 211
   demonstrating ethical standards, 218
   formation of team, 206
   goal setting and, 208
   Goleman's leadership styles, 210t
   information management, 217–218
   media, effective use of, 215–217
   member selection via structured interviews, 207–208
   negotiation and, 219–221
   networking and, 218–219
   progress management, 163, *172*, 218
   qualities of members, 206
   right use of people, resources, 211–212
   running successful meetings, 213–215
   team size considerations, 225
   transformational, 225
   value/use emotional intelligence, 206, 206t
teams, five types, 226t
Tetlock, Philip, 18
Thagard, P., 102
Thibodeau, P. H., 22–23, 23n5

thinking. *See also* strategic thinking
   analogical, 8
   collectively exhaustive (CE), 10–11
   convergent (critical), *9*, 9–10, 17, 28
   divergent, *9*, 9–10, 17, 28
   evidence-based, 25
   filters for clarifying, 34t
   innovative, 32
   intuitive system, 24t
   logical, 16
   modular systems of, 1
   mutually exclusive (ME), 10
   System 1 (intuitive), 24, 24n16, 44
   System 2 (reflective), 24, 44
Thompson, Leigh, 126
Thompson, Michael, 178
topic filter, 34t
transformational leadership, 225
treating symptoms, 18
T-shaped problem solver metaphor, 7, *8*, 18
Tversky, A., 23n5, 44, 103
Twardy, Charles, 38, 77
Tweney, R. D., 102
type filter, 34t
Tytler, R., 77

unequivocal hypotheses, 84
United Nations' Millennium Development Goals, 6
Unusual Uses test, 139
Uzzi, B., 139

value trees/value hierarchies, 47
Van Andel, P., 103
Van Buren, M. E., 157
Van den Bulte, C., 73
Van de Ven, A. H., 139
Van Gelder, Tim, 38, 77, 104, 113, 143, *143*.
Van Waterschoot, W., 73
virtual teams, 226t
visual support options, for slides, 185–190
   bar charts, 183, 185–186, *187*, 188, 200
   bubble charts, *188*, 188–189
   concept visuals, 185, 189, *189*
   explanatory images, 189
   good quantitative charts, 185, *186*
   pseudo-3D charts, avoidance of, 185, *186*
   spacial-flow opportunities, 189

   waterfall charts, *187*, 188, 200–201
von Winterfeld, D., 44, 229
Vroom, V. H., 139

Ward, T. B., 77, 128
waterfall charts, *187*, 188, 200–201
Watkins, Michael, 157
Webber, M. M., 231
Weber, M., 77
Welch, Gilbert, 92
the *what*
   description, 2, *2*, 17
   divergent/convergent thinking and, *9*
   in finding Harry, 3, *34*
   in framing a project, 21–22, *22*, 27, 43, 158
   in a *From-to-/Think-Do Matrix*, 162, 162t, 199
   key questions and, 28, *29*
   in the project chart, *204*
   in team management, 213–217
*what* card (project definition card), 3, *3*, 22, 22–23, 25–27, *27*, 41
the *why*
   description, 2, *4*, 17
   as diagnostic key question, 2, 28–29, *29*, 34, 37, 38, *41*, *42*, 49
   diagnostic maps and, 49, 50, 61, 64, 65, 68, 75
   divergent/convergent thinking and, *9*
   in finding Harry, 3, 4, 26, 27, 33–34, 37, 43, 52, 76, *107*, 112
   in framing a project, 21–23, 25
   holding-hands rule and, *40*
   *how's* relation to, 4, 29
   rabbit rule and, *40*
*why* card (diagnostic definition card), 28, 41–43, 117
why-why diagrams, 47
wicked problems (ill-defined problems), 44
Wigmore charts, 47
working memory, 44
Wright, G., 168

Yalch, R. F., 167–168

Zelazny, G., 169, 170, 173, 200

CPSIA information can be obtained
at www.ICGtesting.com
Printed in the USA
BVHW05s0428270718
522600BV00001B/5/P